MW00354196

TOM STRONG BOOK 1

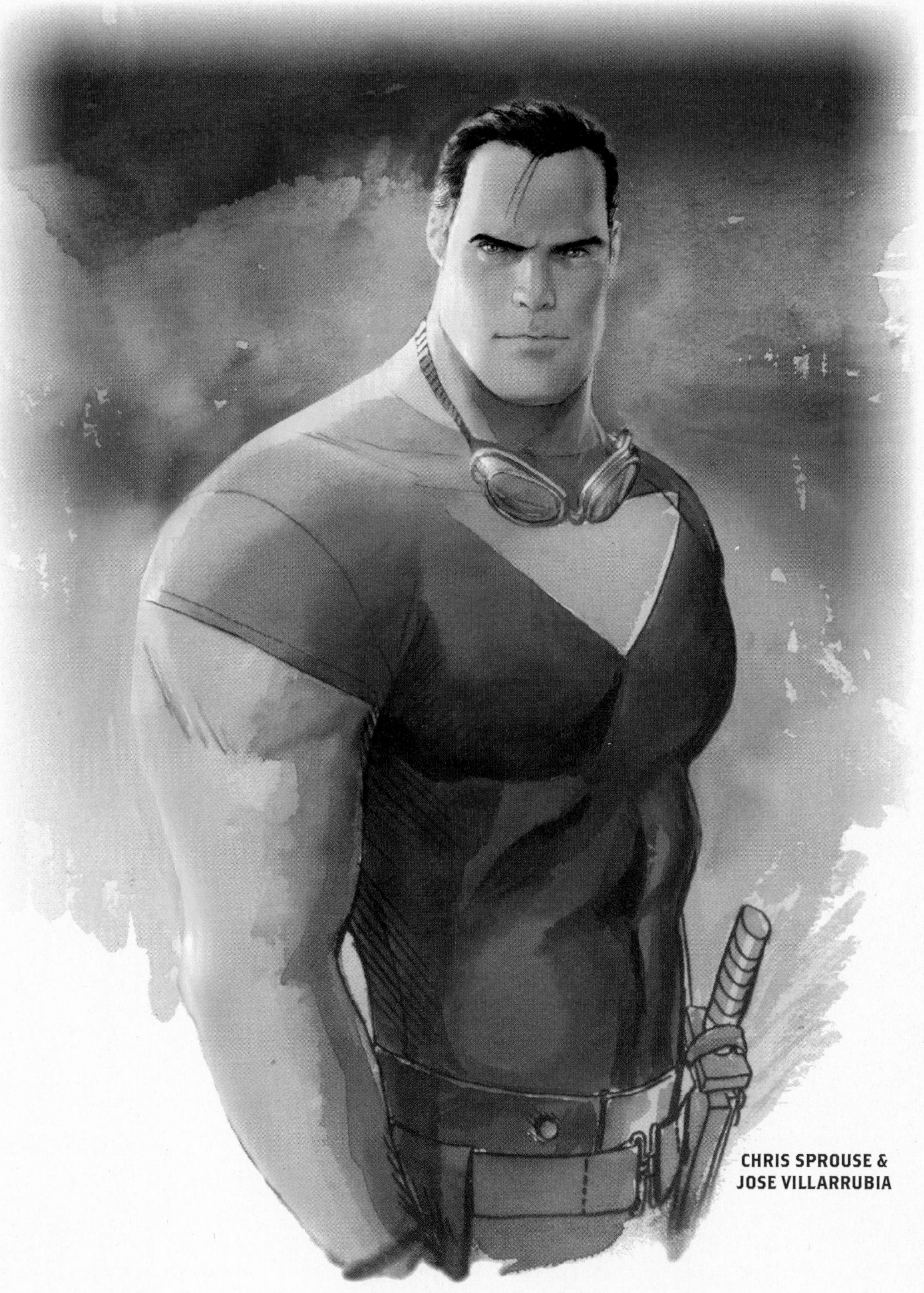

CHRIS SPROUSE &
JOSE VILLARRUBIA

JIM LEE
Editorial Director

JOHN NEE
VP and General Manager

SCOTT DUNBIER
Group Editor
Tom Strong Editor

ERIC DESANTIS
Assistant Editor

Special thanks to
Cully Hamner and Zander Cannon
for layout assistance

Front cover dustjacket art by
CHRIS SPROUSE and **JOSE VILLARRUBIA**

Back cover dustjacket art by
CHRIS SPROUSE and **ALAN GORDON**

TOM STRONG: BOOK ONE. Published by America's Best Comics, LLC. Cover, design pages and compilation © 2000 America's Best Comics, LLC. Tom Strong and all related characters and elements are trademarks of America's Best Comics. All Rights Reserved. Originally published in single magazine form as TOM STRONG, #1-7. Copyright © 1999, 2000 America's Best Comics. Editorial Offices: 7910 Ivanhoe, #438, La Jolla, CA 92037. Any similarities to persons living or dead is purely coincidental. PRINTED IN CANADA. FIRST PRINTING. ISBN 1-56389-654-0

TOM STRONG

COLLECTED EDITION
BOOK 1

ALAN MOORE
writer

CHRIS SPROUSE
penciller

ALAN GORDON
inker

ADDITIONAL ART BY

ARTHUR ADAMS **GARY FRANK & CAM SMITH** **DAVE GIBBONS** **JERRY ORDWAY**

**TAD EHRLICH
MIKE GARCIA
WILDSTORM FX**
coloring

TODD KLEIN
lettering, logos and design

TOM STRONG
created by
Alan Moore and
Chris Sprouse

**AMERICA'S
BEST COMICS**

BORN WITH THE CENTURY: TOM STRONG AND HIS CITY

It was in the "Mauve Nineties" at the end of the last century that an employee of the U.S. Patents Office, allegedly, tendered his resignation with the simple explanation that his job was obsolete because by 1899 everything had already been discovered or invented. This was by no means an unusual view. Victorian science believed that every natural phenomenon could be explained by the existence of a phantom, almost transcendental substance known as "Ether." There were some loose ends that still remained to be tied up, admittedly, but by and large the late Victorians were confident that they knew absolutely everything. They were the perfect pinnacle of human history, and, with perfection thus achieved, the science and society that followed them would be unchanging and unchanged until the end of time. Put simply, there were no surprises left. Unfortunately, during 1881, two U.S. physicists named Albert Michelson and Edward Morley proved that "Ether" did not exist; never had existed. Shortly after that, the twentieth century occurred.

Millennium City, situated not far from New York upon the eastern seaboard of America, was one of several U.S. cities built around the turning of the century in a fulfillment of the social programs instigated by U.S. President David Goodman Croley fourteen years before, in 1886. President Croley (1829-1889), a former journalist and financial forecaster turned politician made, during his term in office, many farsighted decisions that would greatly alter and improve the landscape of America, preparing it for the turbulent and unprecedented century that Croley, seemingly alone amongst his many great political contemporaries, had predicted lay ahead. Astonishingly, Croley accurately foresaw photo-electronic printing processes, air travel, multinational corporations, motion pictures, the expansion of New York City to its present size and the female emancipation movement. His minor eccentricities, such as his strong conviction that books in the future would be printed in bright yellow ink on purple paper, we shall overlook, and concentrate instead on his triumphs, namely the passing of the New Cities Bill in 1886, which subsequently led to the construction of Millennium City, one of the twentieth century's greatest architectural wonders.

The most instantly arresting feature of the city is, of course, the sheer and staggering height of its main buildings. Necessitated by the relatively small land-area available on which to build the city, and made possible by breakthroughs in concrete technology, the greater number of the city's towering, almost dream-like structures were designed by the both youthful and renowned turn-of-the-century architect Winsor McCay (1871-1934). McCay, while still a youth in Spring Lake, Michigan, had been inspired by then-President Croley's vision of a twentieth-century America complete with motion-picture houses, the idea of which was something close to an obsession for the talented young draftsman, who at one point dabbled in experiments with cartoon animation before settling to the career he would become more famous for. It was McCay who, realizing that those tenants in the upper reaches of his new and lofty buildings might feel isolated, first proposed the high-altitude cable-car complex that links the city's many spires. This has, of course, since been immortalized in the Cole Porter standard *Nothing but the Best for You* with its memorable couplet,

> *"We'll go to Millennium City and honey,*
> *we'll ride on a sky-car for two;*
> *There won't be a girl there half as pretty.*
> *It's nothing but the best for you."*

Some commentators have suggested a connection between the immense scale of the city and the somewhat larger-than-life citizens it has produced across the decades. The world-famous operatic diva Quinta Desrault was born as plain Quinta Stevens in the Soupbone district north of Laundry Street, while noted modern "Reality Artist" Lazlo Camphor and heavy weight boxer Johnny Nectarine grew up within just two streets of each other, on Neon Street and Xenon Street respectively. Aside from the great contribution made to culture by Millennium City and its populace, however, it must also be said that the cloud-piercing metropolis has helped produce the greater portion of this century's most colorful and startling criminals. In the 1930s, the notorious deformed gangster boss Charles Costanza ("Charley Bones"), changed to a walking X-ray image by prolonged exposure to a form of "Heavy Water," ruled the West Side of Millennium City for the better part of ten years. Less powerful, though hardly less noteworthy or spectacular, were rubber-faced confidence trickster Denby Jilks, known also as Charade, and the accomplished female contract murderer Vanilla Tuesday. No list of Millennium City's criminal fraternity would be complete, however, without mention of its most well-known and celebrated member, the complex and brilliant psychopath named Paul Saveen.

Paul Dorian Saveen, born in 1899 in neighboring New York, arrived in Millennium City sometime during 1917, already wealthy from the sale of several basic patents such as a design for hover-buggies and sound-sensitive paint (actually rather queasy-looking in most real domestic applications) that marred many fashion-conscious homes during its brief vogue in the 1950s. Not satisfied with the accumulation of mere wealth, Saveen saw in the infant city a great opportunity to build a power base from which he could oversee and even possibly control the twentieth century as it unfolded. His meteoric rise to criminal supremacy of the American east coast, if not of the entire United States itself, was only halted by the unforeseen arrival on these shores, during the 1920s, of the man whose name has since become synonymous with that of Millennium City. A man born on New Year's Day 1900 and thus almost exactly as old as the town itself.

Tom Strong and Paul Saveen were enemies from the moment that they met, and were destined to clash in battle many times across the next few decades. The decent and likable genius/muscleman from the uncharted isle of Attabar Teru achieved an instant popularity with Millennium City and its population that has lasted to this day, which may indeed have been a factor in Saveen's gradually mounting hatred and resentment for the young adventurer across the years of their first few encounters. During this time, Saveen was reported dead on several occasions, only to return to plague Tom Strong anew. In 1992, however, a bleached skeleton found in a jeep out in the deserts of West Africa was conclusively identified from dental records as that of the eighty-four-year-old criminal mastermind, which suggests that upon this occasion, rumors of his death

are not exaggerated.

Millennium City's love affair with Tom Strong, meanwhile, went from strength to strength. Already popular for his defeat of Saveen's huge and city-threatening "Mechanthrope" in 1922, it was Strong's return to the city in the 1930s with his bride Dhalua that assured a place for him in the public's hearts. Idolized by both men and women, Dhalua Strong found herself used as inspiration by a horde of dress designers and hair stylists, culminating in the classic "Dhalua Look" adopted by so many women, especially black women, in the early 1940s.

This was also the decade in which the newspapers first coined the blanket term "Strongmania" to describe the vast amount of licensed Tom Strong merchandise available to an apparently insatiable public . Dhalua dolls, spark-spitting Tom Strong ray-guns and, most sought-after of all, miniature clockwork replicas of the adventurer's mechanical companion Pneuman filled the nation's toy shops, while its magazine racks bulged first with pulp magazines, then later comic books, in which were detailed adventures of Strong and his friends, both genuine and fictional. RKO Pictures produced two adventure serials, *Tom Strong* and *The New Adventures of Tom Strong,* both starring Kirk Alyn as Tom, while in the middle sixties Hanna-Barbera's *Tom Strong Cartoon Hour* was massively popular amongst the under-twelves.

Later additions to Strong's family, notably daughter Tesla and the educated ape King Solomon, have not diminished the now ninety-nine-year-old adventurer's enduring popularity, nor have his exploits become less spectacular. Recent encounters with the technological monstrosity known as The Modular Man, or with the massed parallel-world might of the assembled Aztech Empire serve only to demonstrate the long-lived hero's great adaptability and knack for moving with the times. As both he and the city that is his adopted home move inexorably towards their hundredth birthdays on the stroke of the millennium, let us be confident that for Tom Strong, Millennium City, and the world in general, all the most hair-raising thrills and most spectacular surprises are yet to come. Here's to the next hundred years!

— Alan Moore

CHAPTER ONE

In which an Origin is Revealed,
an Aerial Crime is Attempted,
and TOM gains a New Fan.

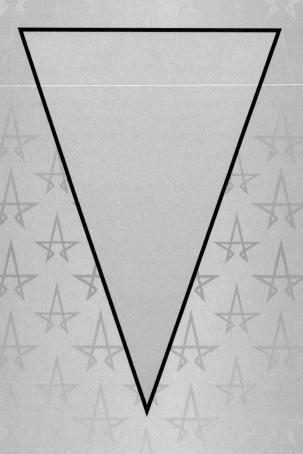

Cover art:
Alex Ross (A)
Chris Sprouse &
Al Gordon (B)

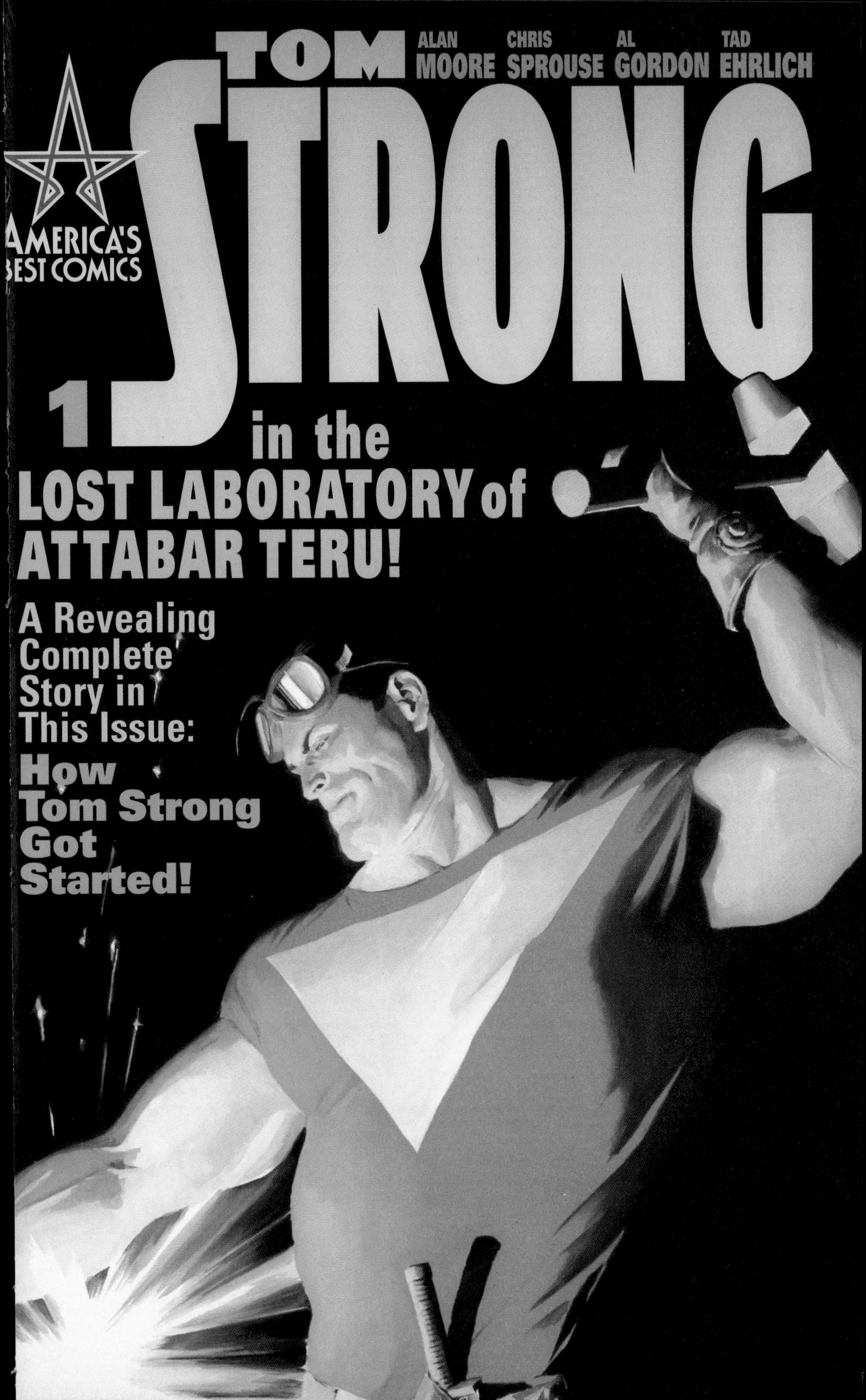
TOM STRONG
ALAN MOORE
CHRIS SPROUSE
AL GORDON
TAD EHRLICH
AMERICA'S BEST COMICS
1
in the LOST LABORATORY of ATTABAR TERU!
A Revealing Complete Story in This Issue:
How Tom Strong Got Started!

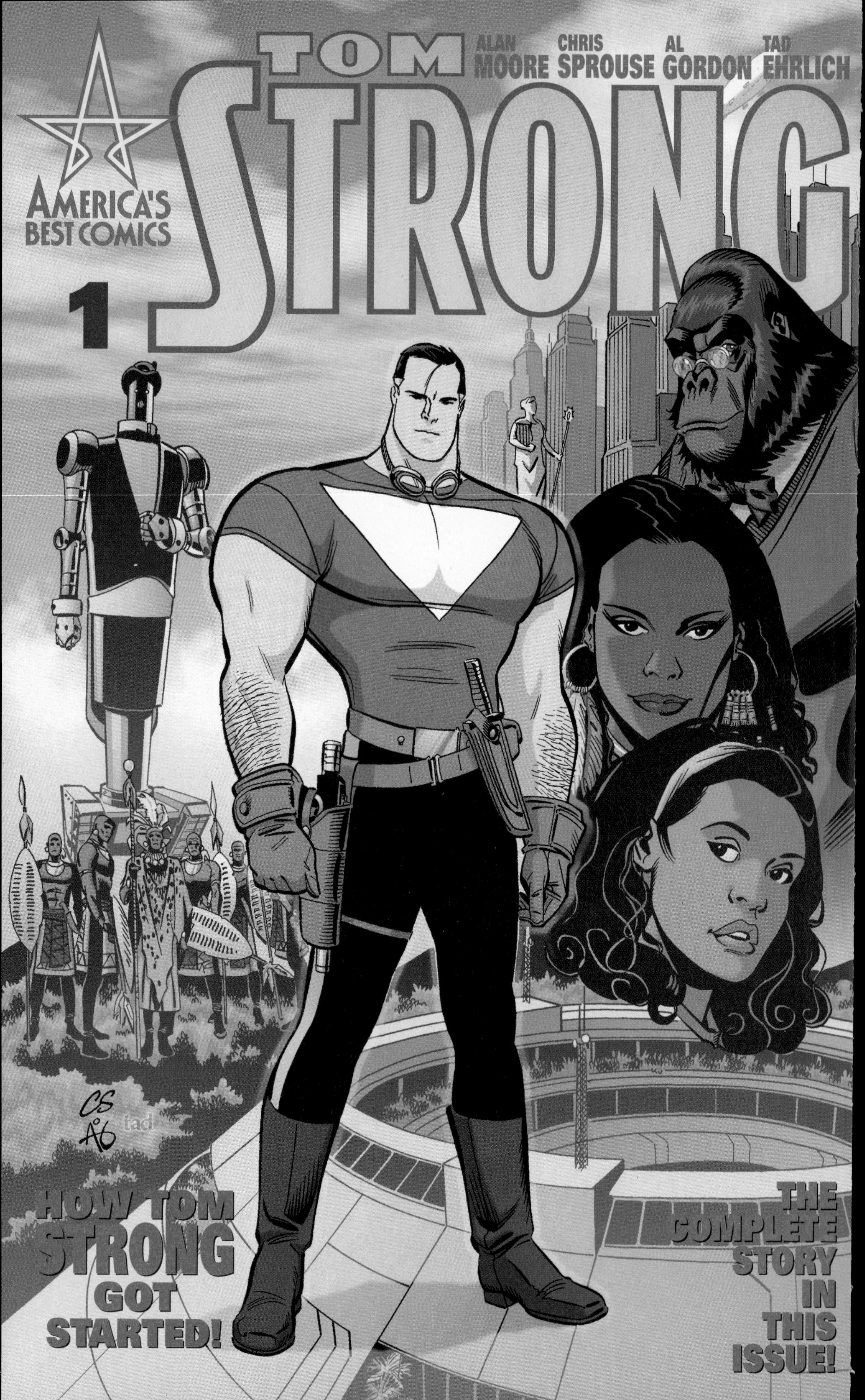
TOM STRONG
ALAN MOORE
CHRIS SPROUSE
AL GORDON
TAD EHRLICH
AMERICA'S BEST COMICS
1
HOW TOM STRONG GOT STARTED!
THE COMPLETE STORY IN THIS ISSUE!

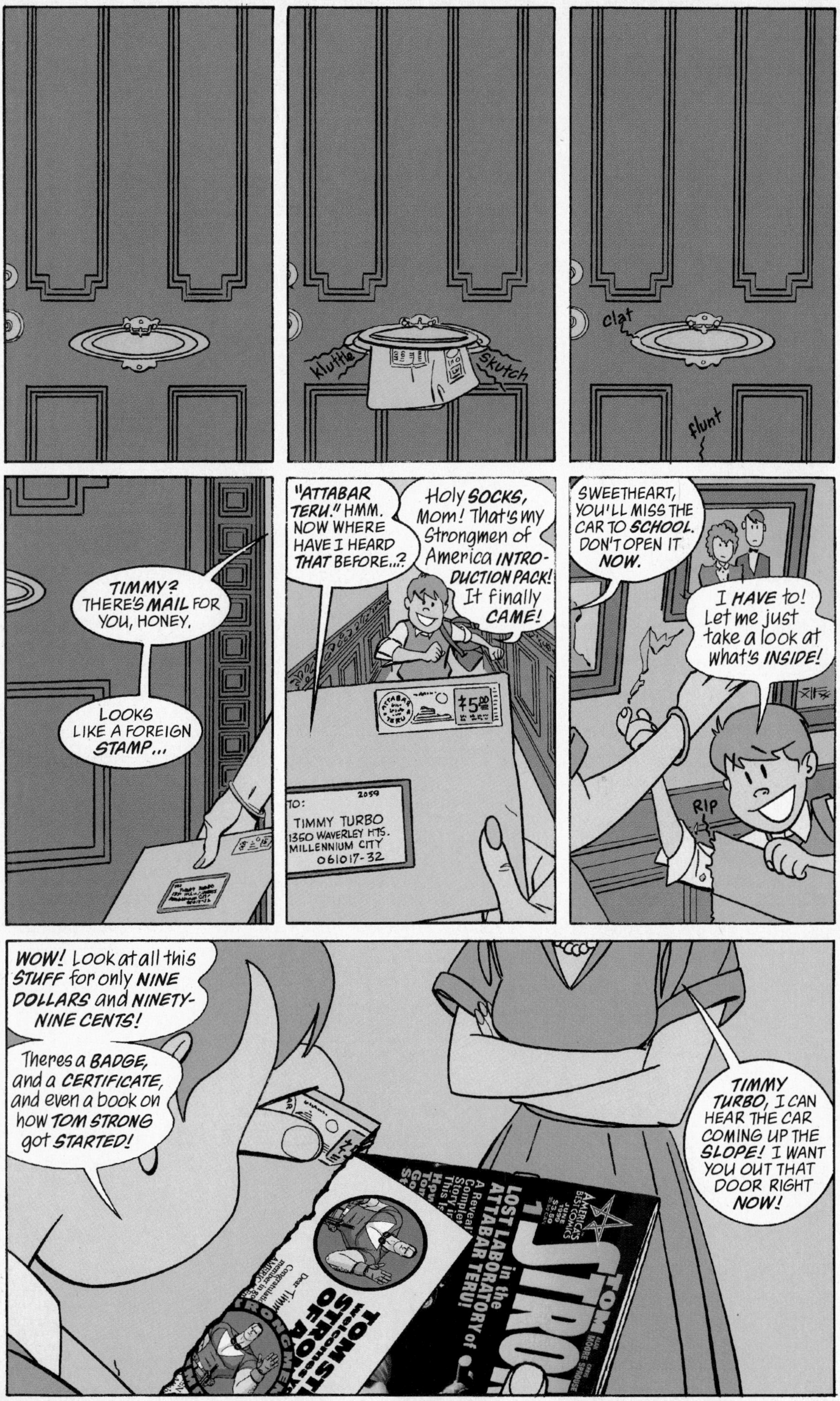
klutche
skutch
clat
flunt
TIMMY? THERE'S MAIL FOR YOU, HONEY.
LOOKS LIKE A FOREIGN STAMP...
"ATTABAR TERU." HMM. NOW WHERE HAVE I HEARD THAT BEFORE...?
Holy SOCKS, Mom! That's my Strongmen of America INTRODUCTION PACK! It finally CAME!
TO: TIMMY TURBO 1350 WAVERLEY HTS. MILLENNIUM CITY 061017-32
2059
SWEETHEART, YOU'LL MISS THE CAR TO SCHOOL. DON'T OPEN IT NOW.
I HAVE to! Let me just take a look at what's INSIDE!
RIP
WOW! Look at all this STUFF for only NINE DOLLARS and NINETY-NINE CENTS!
Theres a BADGE, and a CERTIFICATE, and even a book on how TOM STRONG got STARTED!
TIMMY TURBO, I CAN HEAR THE CAR COMING UP THE SLOPE! I WANT YOU OUT THAT DOOR RIGHT NOW!
TOM STRONG
LOST LABORATORY in the ATTABAR TERU!
AMERICA'S BEST COMICS
TOM STRONG Welcomes STRONGMEN OF AMERICA
Dear Timmy

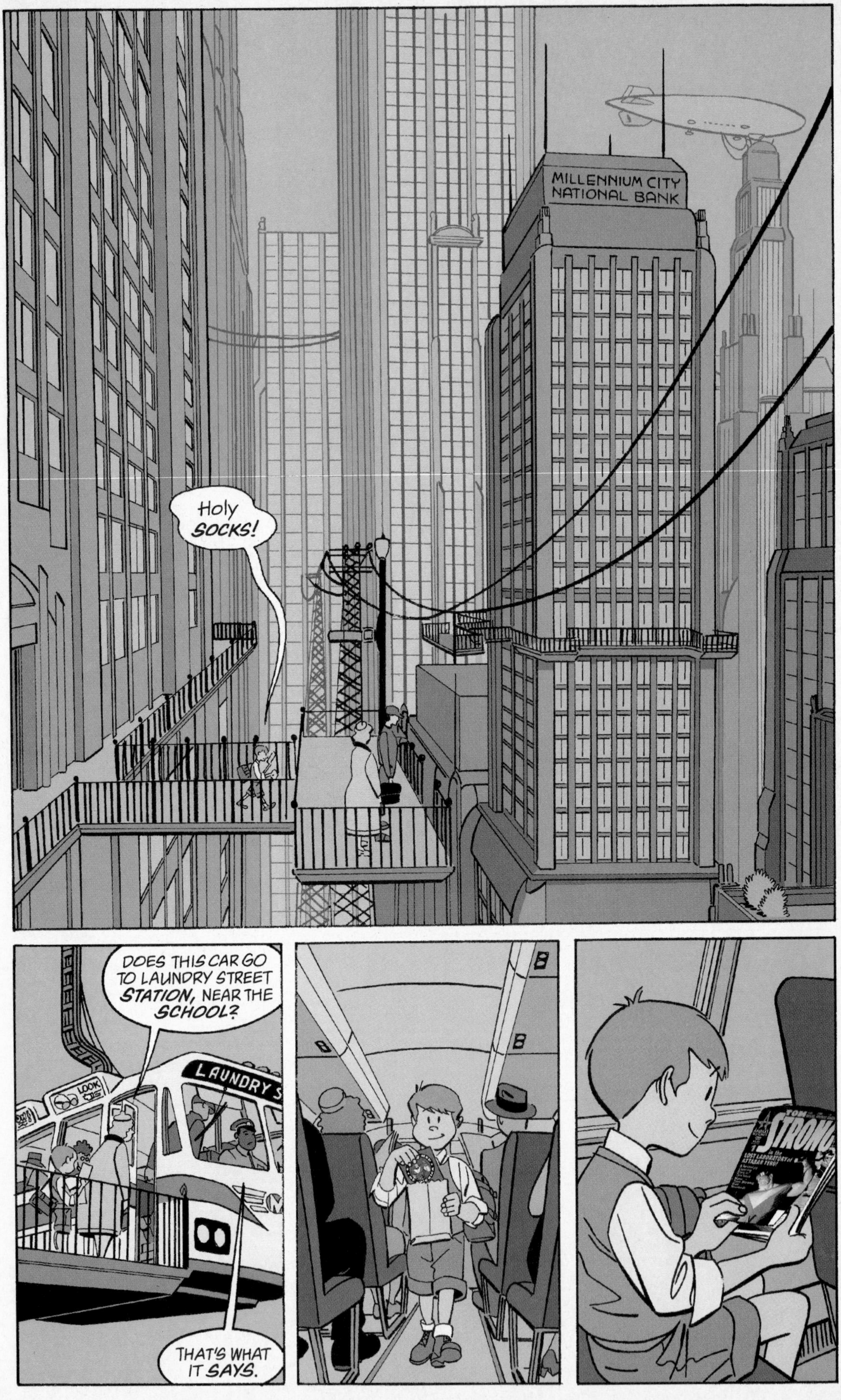
MILLENNIUM CITY
NATIONAL BANK
Holy SOCKS!
DOES THIS CAR GO TO LAUNDRY STREET STATION, NEAR THE SCHOOL?
LAUNDRY S
LOOK
THAT'S WHAT IT SAYS.

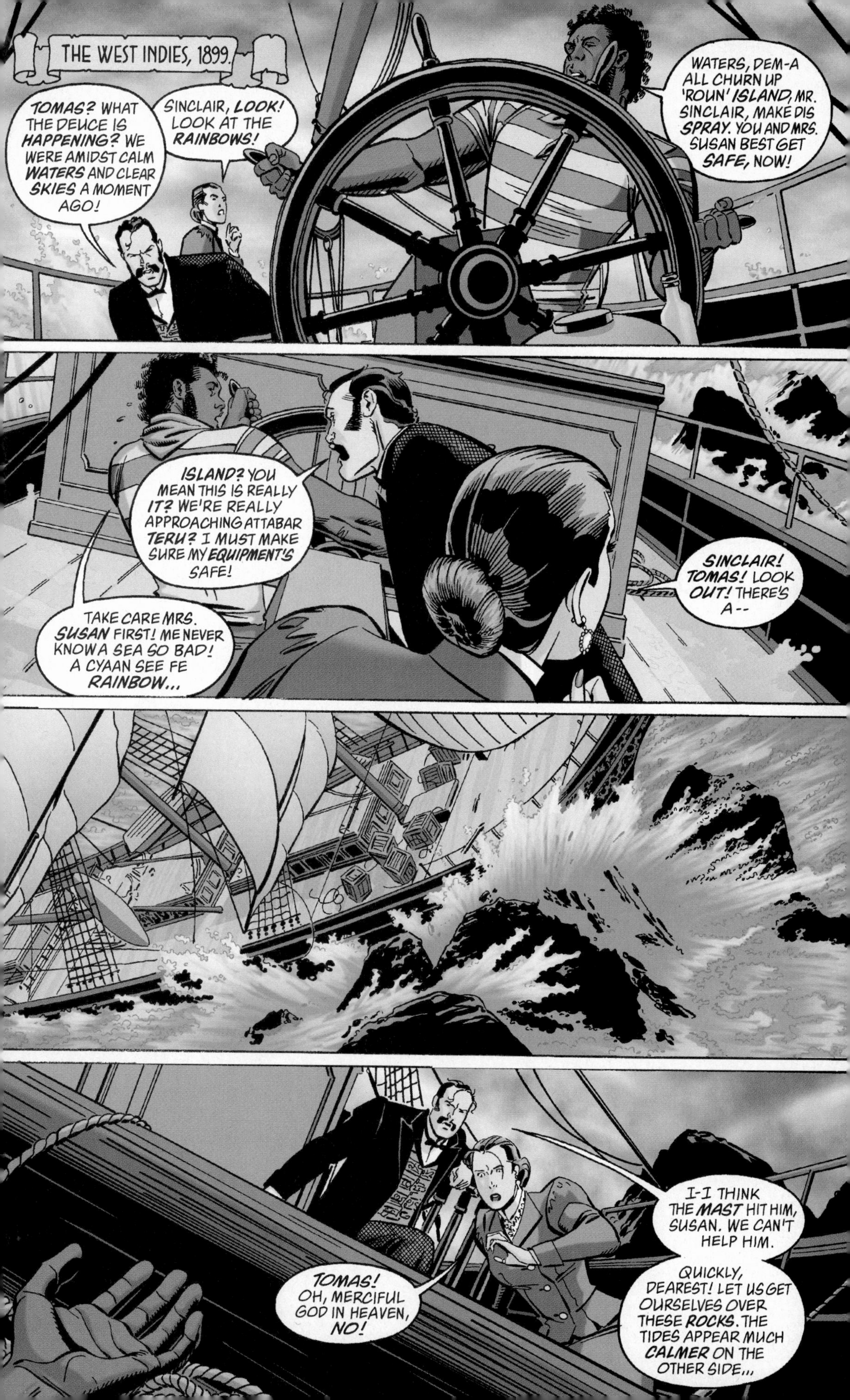
THE WEST INDIES, 1899.
TOMAS? WHAT THE DEUCE IS HAPPENING? WE WERE AMIDST CALM WATERS AND CLEAR SKIES A MOMENT AGO!
SINCLAIR, LOOK! LOOK AT THE RAINBOWS!
WATERS, DEM-A ALL CHURN UP 'ROUN' ISLAND, MR. SINCLAIR, MAKE DIS SPRAY. YOU AND MRS. SUSAN BEST GET SAFE, NOW!
ISLAND? YOU MEAN THIS IS REALLY IT? WE'RE REALLY APPROACHING ATTABAR TERU? I MUST MAKE SURE MY EQUIPMENT'S SAFE!
TAKE CARE MRS. SUSAN FIRST! ME NEVER KNOW A SEA SO BAD! A CYAAN SEE FE RAINBOW...
SINCLAIR! TOMAS! LOOK OUT! THERE'S A--
TOMAS! OH, MERCIFUL GOD IN HEAVEN, NO!
I-I THINK THE MAST HIT HIM, SUSAN. WE CAN'T HELP HIM.
QUICKLY, DEAREST! LET US GET OURSELVES OVER THESE ROCKS. THE TIDES APPEAR MUCH CALMER ON THE OTHER SIDE...

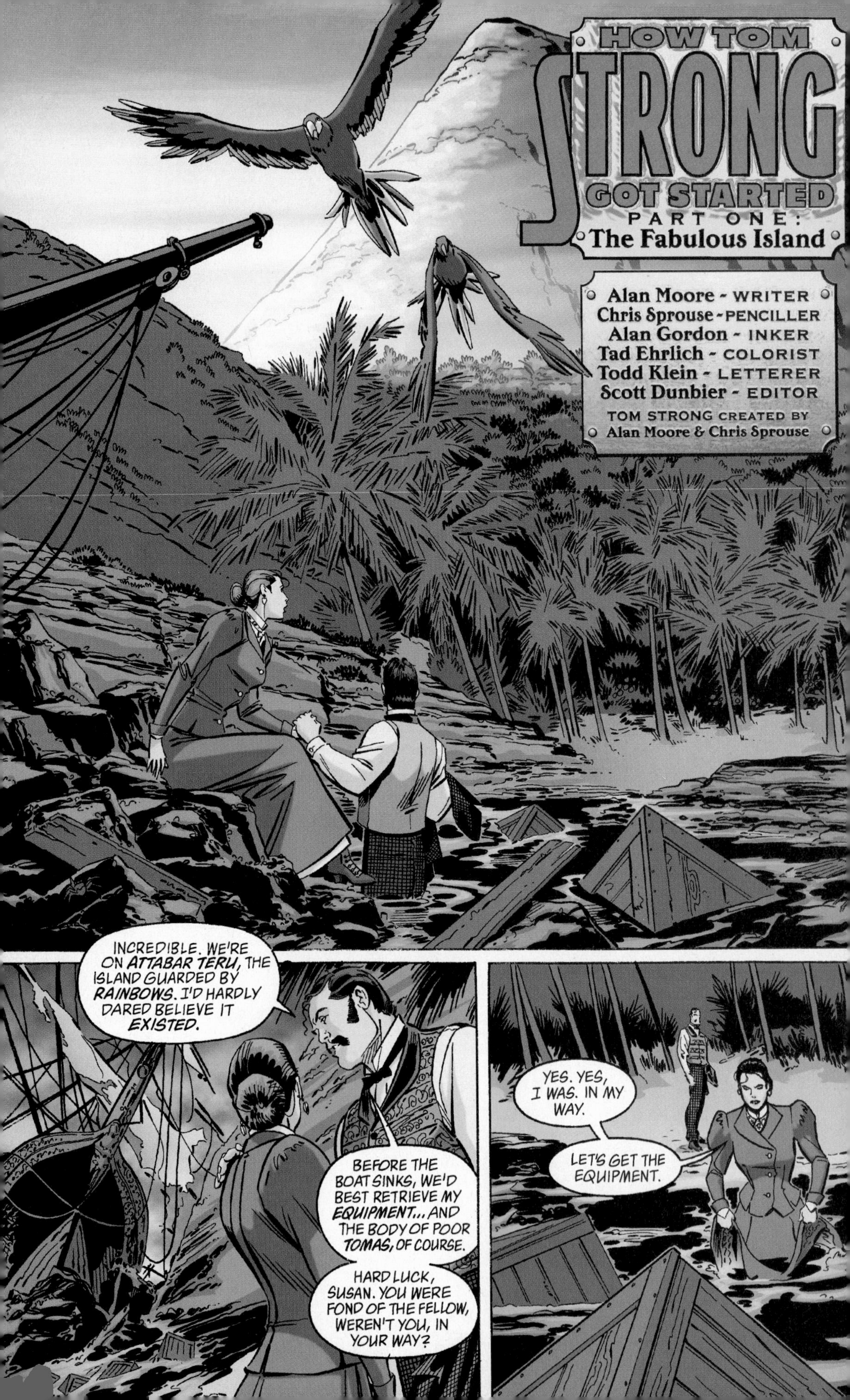

HOW TOM STRONG GOT STARTED
PART ONE:
The Fabulous Island
Alan Moore - WRITER
Chris Sprouse - PENCILLER
Alan Gordon - INKER
Tad Ehrlich - COLORIST
Todd Klein - LETTERER
Scott Dunbier - EDITOR
TOM STRONG CREATED BY
Alan Moore & Chris Sprouse
INCREDIBLE. WE'RE ON ATTABAR TERU, THE ISLAND GUARDED BY RAINBOWS. I'D HARDLY DARED BELIEVE IT EXISTED.
BEFORE THE BOAT SINKS, WE'D BEST RETRIEVE MY EQUIPMENT... AND THE BODY OF POOR TOMAS, OF COURSE.
HARD LUCK, SUSAN. YOU WERE FOND OF THE FELLOW, WEREN'T YOU, IN YOUR WAY?
YES. YES, I WAS. IN MY WAY.
LET'S GET THE EQUIPMENT.

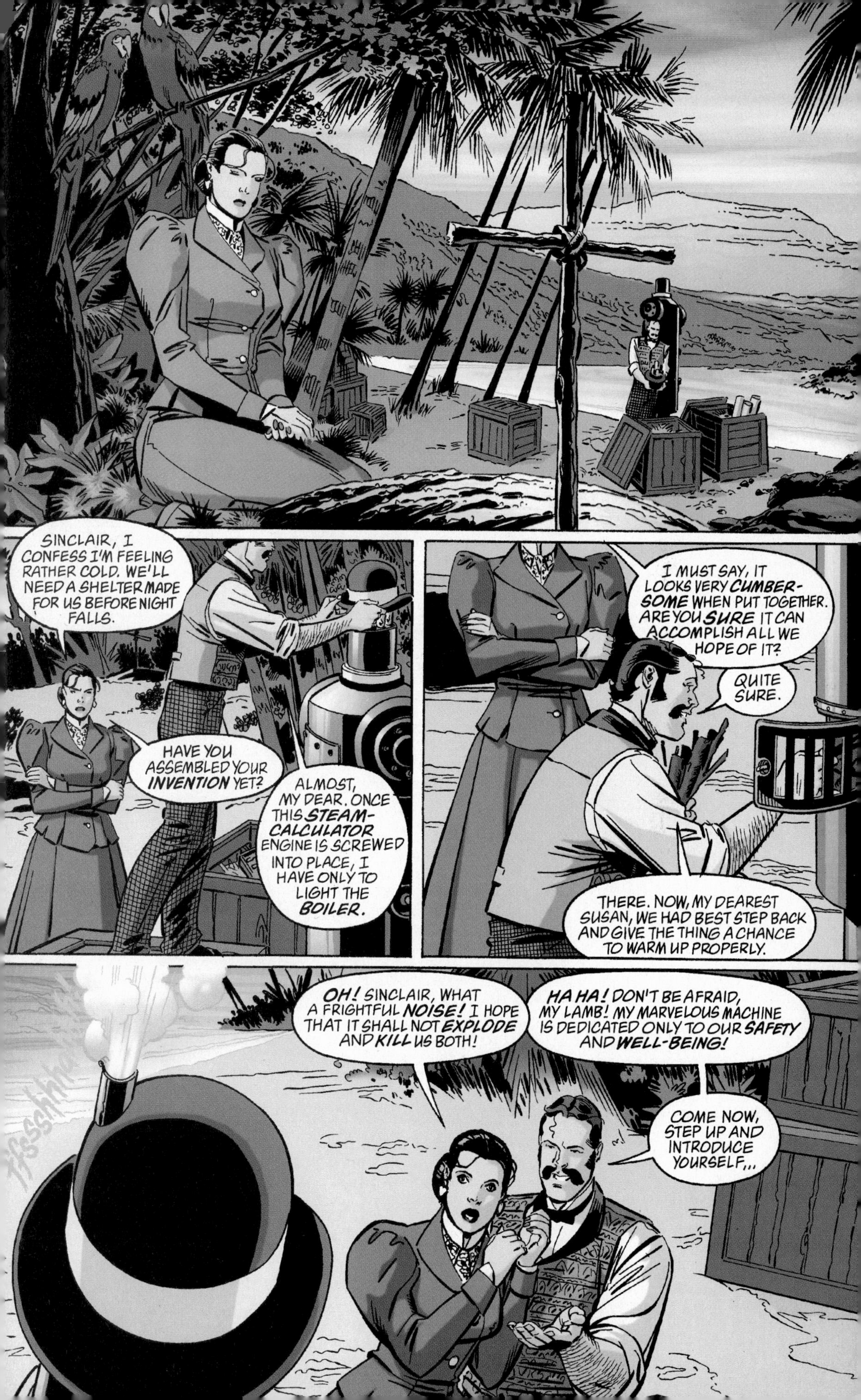
SINCLAIR, I CONFESS I'M FEELING RATHER COLD. WE'LL NEED A SHELTER MADE FOR US BEFORE NIGHT FALLS.
HAVE YOU ASSEMBLED YOUR INVENTION YET?
ALMOST, MY DEAR. ONCE THIS STEAM-CALCULATOR ENGINE IS SCREWED INTO PLACE, I HAVE ONLY TO LIGHT THE BOILER.
I MUST SAY, IT LOOKS VERY CUMBERSOME WHEN PUT TOGETHER. ARE YOU SURE IT CAN ACCOMPLISH ALL WE HOPE OF IT?
QUITE SURE.
THERE. NOW, MY DEAREST SUSAN, WE HAD BEST STEP BACK AND GIVE THE THING A CHANCE TO WARM UP PROPERLY.
fssshhh
OH! SINCLAIR, WHAT A FRIGHTFUL NOISE! I HOPE THAT IT SHALL NOT EXPLODE AND KILL US BOTH!
HA HA! DON'T BE AFRAID, MY LAMB! MY MARVELOUS MACHINE IS DEDICATED ONLY TO OUR SAFETY AND WELL-BEING!
COME NOW, STEP UP AND INTRODUCE YOURSELF,...

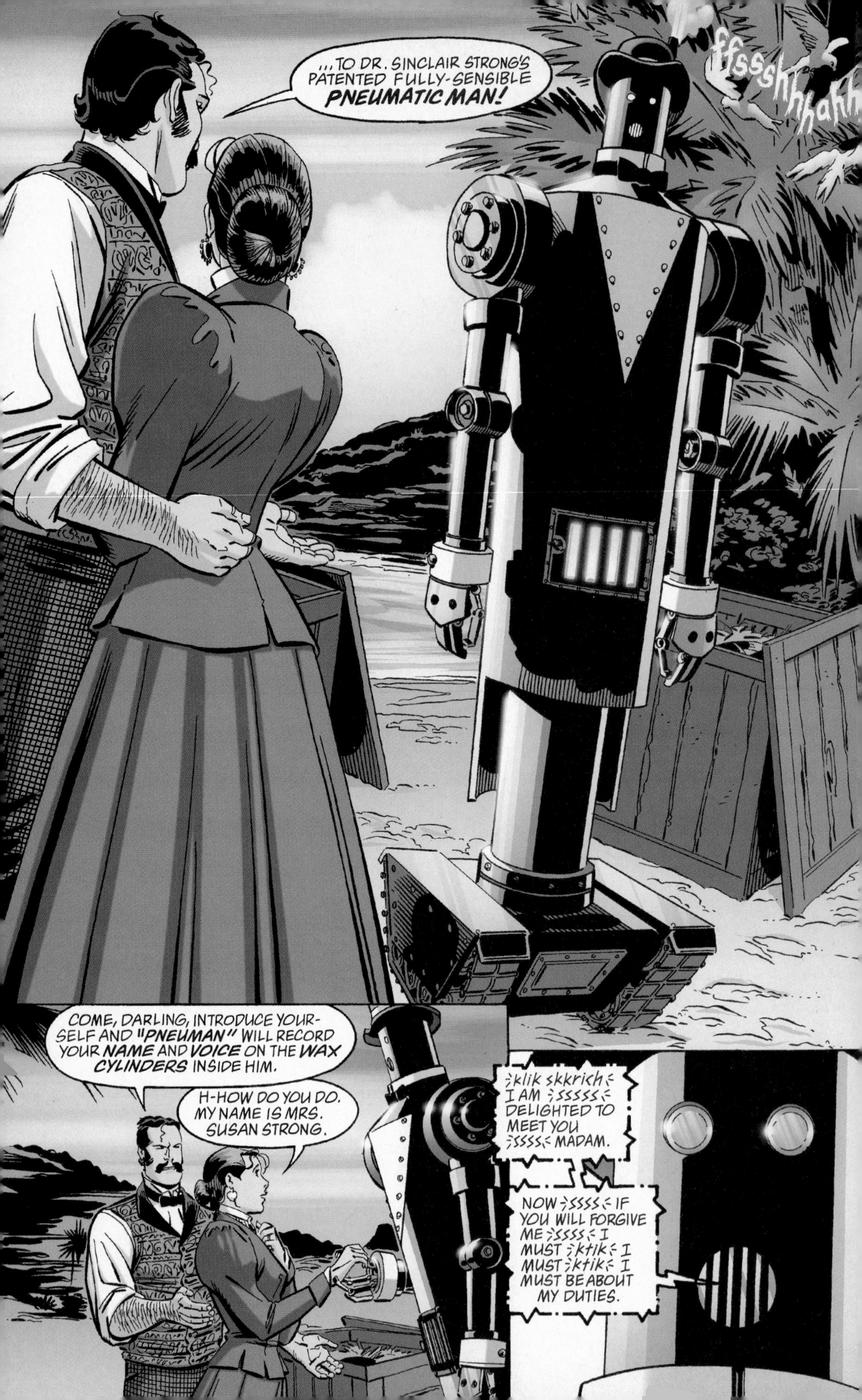
...TO DR. SINCLAIR STRONG'S PATENTED FULLY-SENSIBLE PNEUMATIC MAN!
ffssshhhahh
COME, DARLING, INTRODUCE YOURSELF AND "PNEUMAN" WILL RECORD YOUR NAME AND VOICE ON THE WAX CYLINDERS INSIDE HIM.
H-HOW DO YOU DO. MY NAME IS MRS. SUSAN STRONG.
klik skkrich I AM sssss DELIGHTED TO MEET YOU ssss MADAM.
NOW ssss IF YOU WILL FORGIVE ME ssss I MUST ktik I MUST ktik I MUST BE ABOUT MY DUTIES.

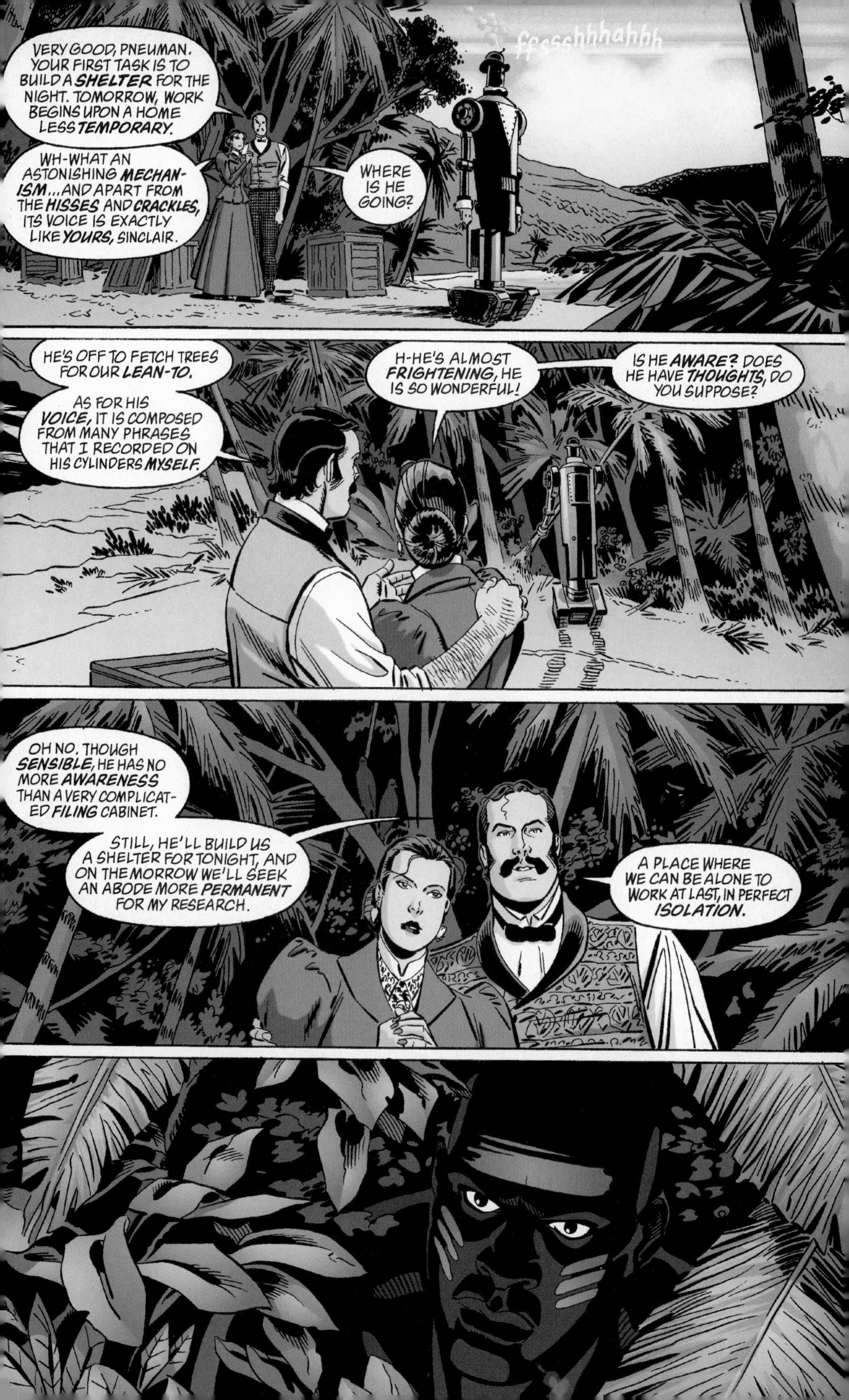
ffsssshhhahhh
VERY GOOD, PNEUMAN. YOUR FIRST TASK IS TO BUILD A SHELTER FOR THE NIGHT. TOMORROW, WORK BEGINS UPON A HOME LESS TEMPORARY.
WH-WHAT AN ASTONISHING MECHANISM... AND APART FROM THE HISSES AND CRACKLES, ITS VOICE IS EXACTLY LIKE YOURS, SINCLAIR.
WHERE IS HE GOING?
HE'S OFF TO FETCH TREES FOR OUR LEAN-TO.
AS FOR HIS VOICE, IT IS COMPOSED FROM MANY PHRASES THAT I RECORDED ON HIS CYLINDERS MYSELF.
H-HE'S ALMOST FRIGHTENING, HE IS SO WONDERFUL!
IS HE AWARE? DOES HE HAVE THOUGHTS, DO YOU SUPPOSE?
OH NO. THOUGH SENSIBLE, HE HAS NO MORE AWARENESS THAN A VERY COMPLICATED FILING CABINET.
STILL, HE'LL BUILD US A SHELTER FOR TONIGHT, AND ON THE MORROW WE'LL SEEK AN ABODE MORE PERMANENT FOR MY RESEARCH.
A PLACE WHERE WE CAN BE ALONE TO WORK AT LAST, IN PERFECT ISOLATION.

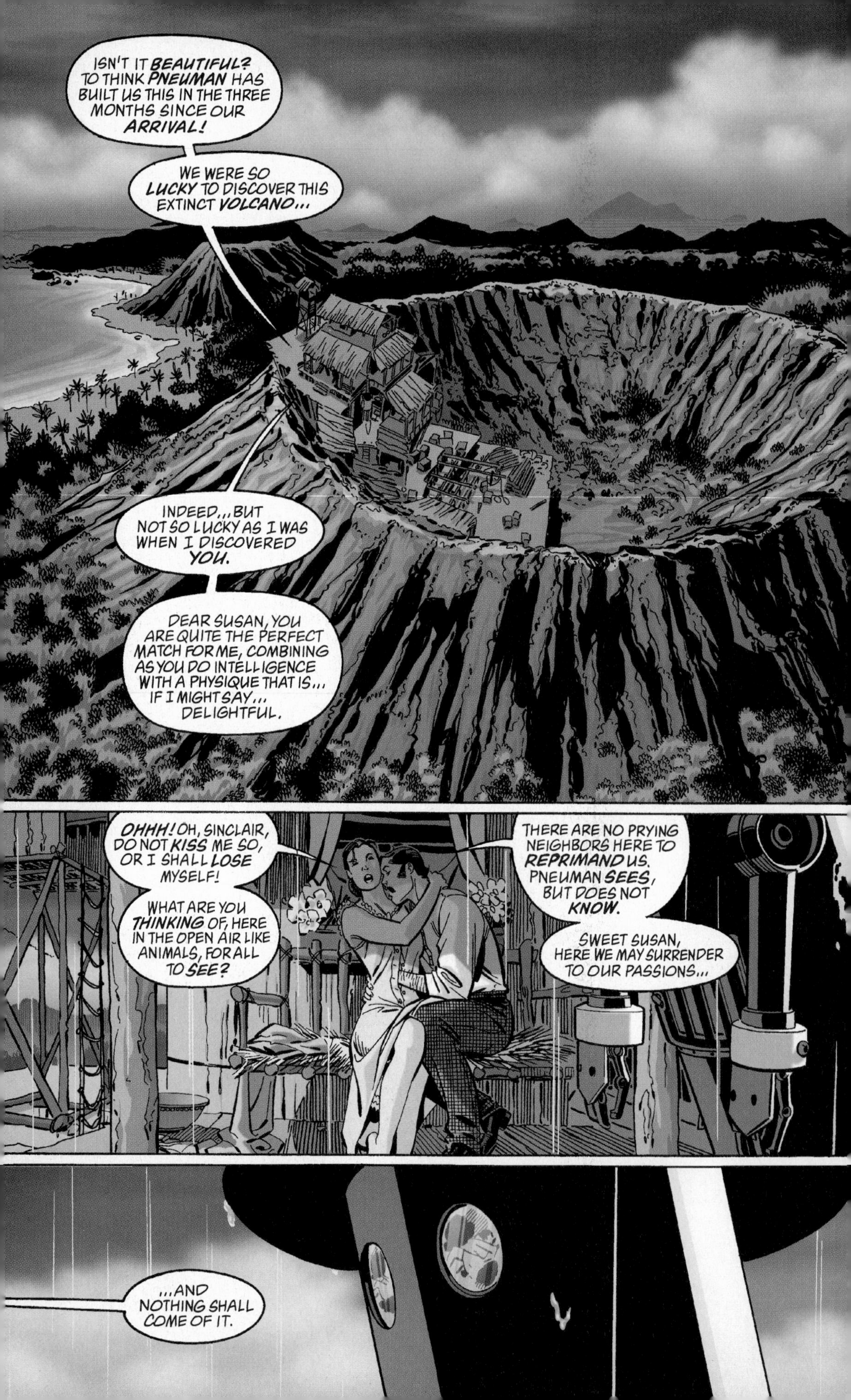
ISN'T IT BEAUTIFUL? TO THINK PNEUMAN HAS BUILT US THIS IN THE THREE MONTHS SINCE OUR ARRIVAL!
WE WERE SO LUCKY TO DISCOVER THIS EXTINCT VOLCANO...
INDEED... BUT NOT SO LUCKY AS I WAS WHEN I DISCOVERED YOU.
DEAR SUSAN, YOU ARE QUITE THE PERFECT MATCH FOR ME, COMBINING AS YOU DO INTELLIGENCE WITH A PHYSIQUE THAT IS... IF I MIGHT SAY... DELIGHTFUL.
OHHH! OH, SINCLAIR, DO NOT KISS ME SO, OR I SHALL LOSE MYSELF!
WHAT ARE YOU THINKING OF, HERE IN THE OPEN AIR LIKE ANIMALS, FOR ALL TO SEE?
THERE ARE NO PRYING NEIGHBORS HERE TO REPRIMAND US. PNEUMAN SEES, BUT DOES NOT KNOW.
SWEET SUSAN, HERE WE MAY SURRENDER TO OUR PASSIONS...
...AND NOTHING SHALL COME OF IT.

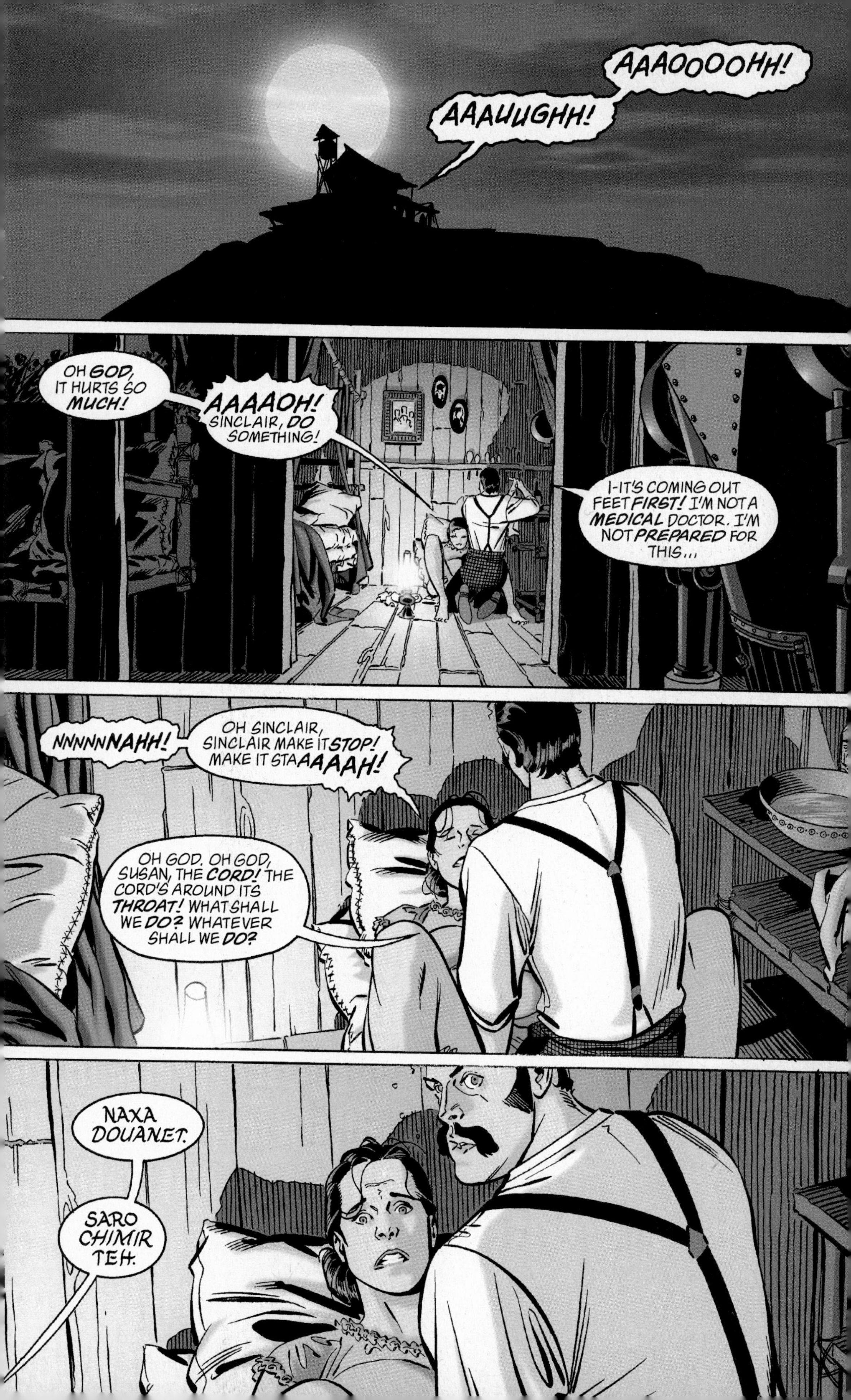
AAAUUGHH!
AAAOOOOHH!
OH GOD, IT HURTS SO MUCH!
AAAAOH! SINCLAIR, DO SOMETHING!
I-IT'S COMING OUT FEET FIRST! I'M NOT A MEDICAL DOCTOR. I'M NOT PREPARED FOR THIS...
NNNNNNAHH!
OH SINCLAIR, SINCLAIR MAKE IT STOP! MAKE IT STAAAAAH!
OH GOD. OH GOD, SUSAN, THE CORD! THE CORD'S AROUND ITS THROAT! WHAT SHALL WE DO? WHATEVER SHALL WE DO?
NAXA DOUANET.
SARO CHIMIR TEH.

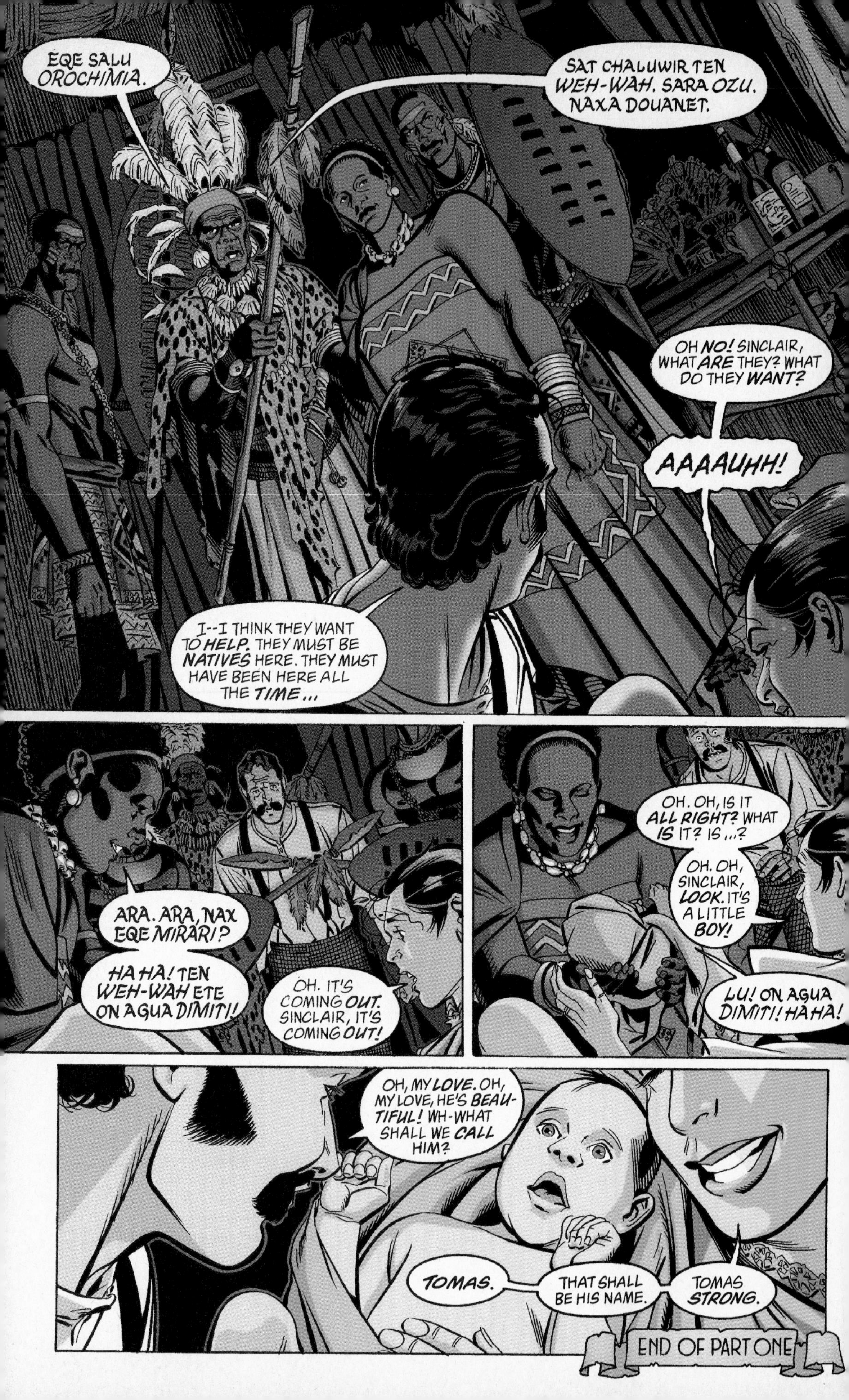
EQE SALU OROCHIMIA.
SAT CHALUWIR TEN WEH-WAH. SARA OZU. NAXA DOUANET.
OH NO! SINCLAIR, WHAT ARE THEY? WHAT DO THEY WANT?
AAAAUHH!
I--I THINK THEY WANT TO HELP. THEY MUST BE NATIVES HERE. THEY MUST HAVE BEEN HERE ALL THE TIME...
ARA. ARA, NAX EQE MIRARI?
HA HA! TEN WEH-WAH ETE ON AGUA DIMITI!
OH. IT'S COMING OUT. SINCLAIR, IT'S COMING OUT!
OH. OH, IS IT ALL RIGHT? WHAT IS IT? IS...?
OH. OH, SINCLAIR, LOOK. IT'S A LITTLE BOY!
LU! ON AGUA DIMITI! HA HA!
OH, MY LOVE. OH, MY LOVE, HE'S BEAUTIFUL! WH-WHAT SHALL WE CALL HIM?
TOMAS.
THAT SHALL BE HIS NAME.
TOMAS STRONG.
END OF PART ONE

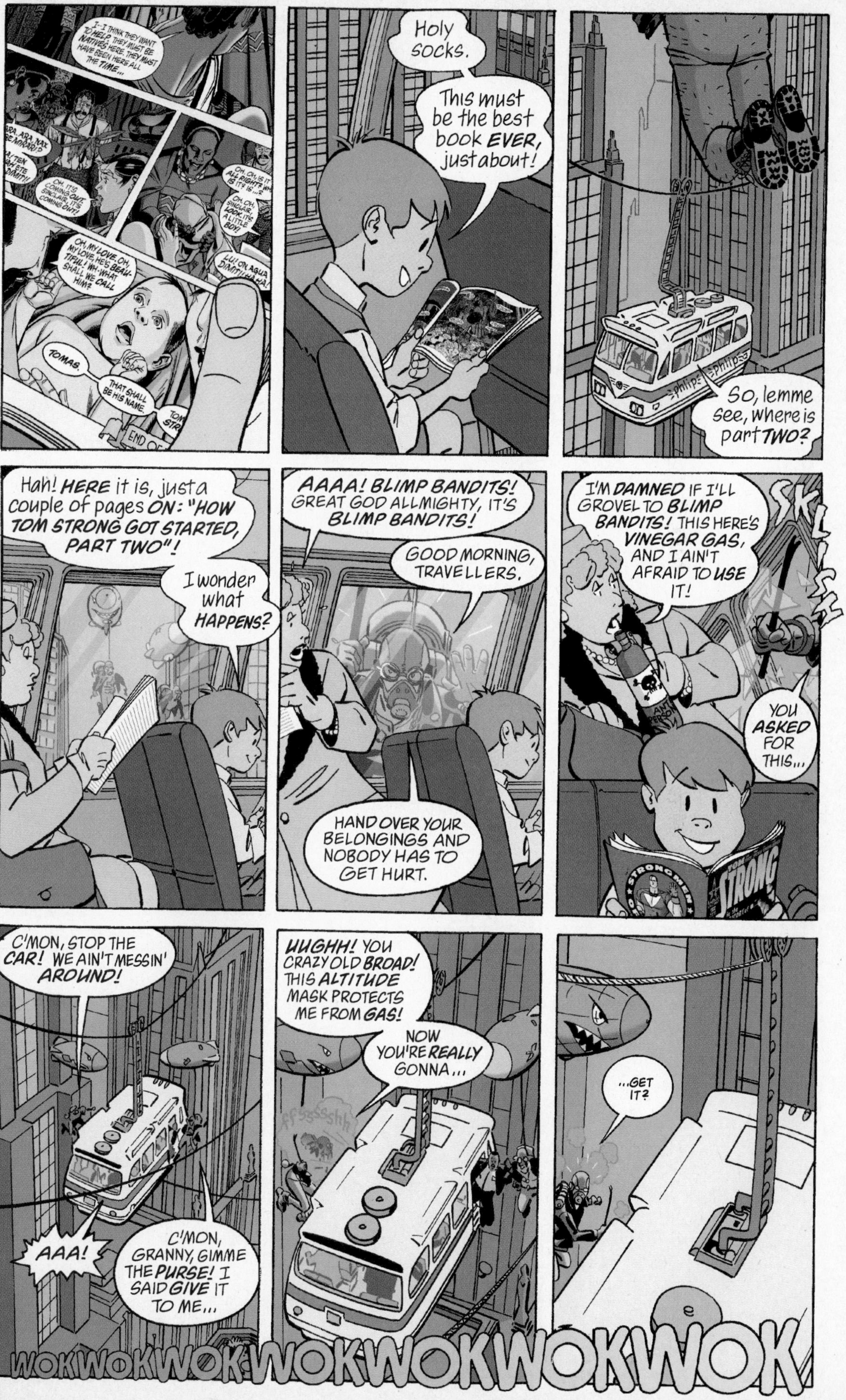
I--I THINK THEY WANT TO HELP. THEY MUST BE NATIVES HERE. THEY MUST HAVE BEEN HERE ALL THE TIME...
OH, IT'S COMING OUT. SINCLAIR, IT'S COMING OUT!
OH, OH, SINCLAIR, LOOK. IT'S A LITTLE BOY!
OH, MY LOVE. OH, MY LOVE, HE'S BEAUTIFUL! WH-WHAT SHALL WE CALL HIM?
TOMAS.
THAT SHALL BE HIS NAME.
Holy socks.
This must be the best book EVER, just about!
philips
So, lemme see, where is part TWO?
Hah! HERE it is, just a couple of pages ON: "HOW TOM STRONG GOT STARTED, PART TWO"!
I wonder what HAPPENS?
AAAA! BLIMP BANDITS! GREAT GOD ALLMIGHTY, IT'S BLIMP BANDITS!
GOOD MORNING, TRAVELLERS.
HAND OVER YOUR BELONGINGS AND NOBODY HAS TO GET HURT.
I'M DAMNED IF I'LL GROVEL TO BLIMP BANDITS! THIS HERE'S VINEGAR GAS, AND I AIN'T AFRAID TO USE IT!
YOU ASKED FOR THIS...
STRONG
C'MON, STOP THE CAR! WE AIN'T MESSIN' AROUND!
AAA!
C'MON, GRANNY, GIMME THE PURSE! I SAID GIVE IT TO ME...
UUGHH! YOU CRAZY OLD BROAD! THIS ALTITUDE MASK PROTECTS ME FROM GAS!
NOW YOU'RE REALLY GONNA...
...GET IT?
WOKWOKWOKWOKWOKWOKWOK

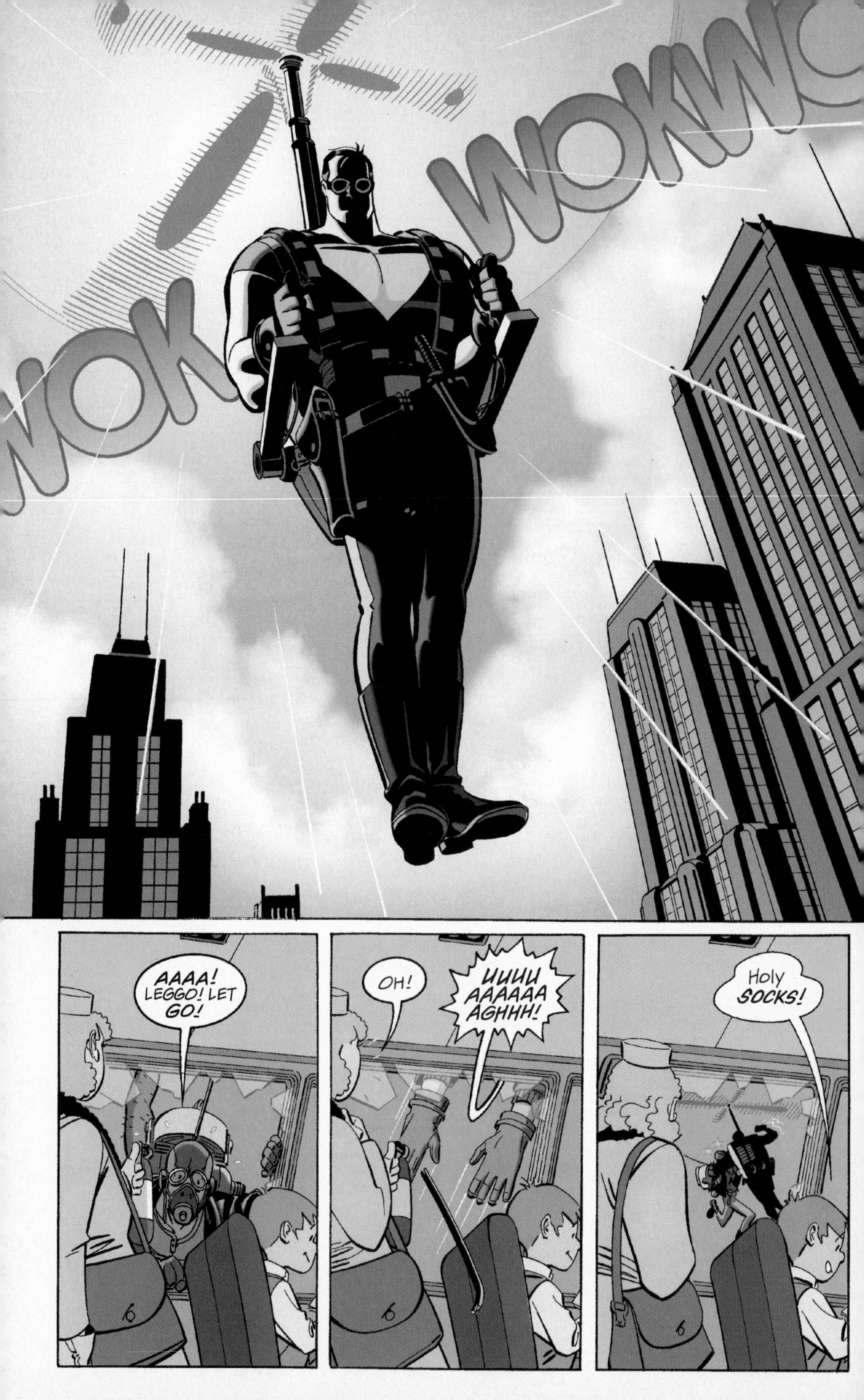
WOK
WOKWO
AAAA! LEGGO! LET GO!
OH!
UUUU AAAAAA AGHHH!
Holy SOCKS!

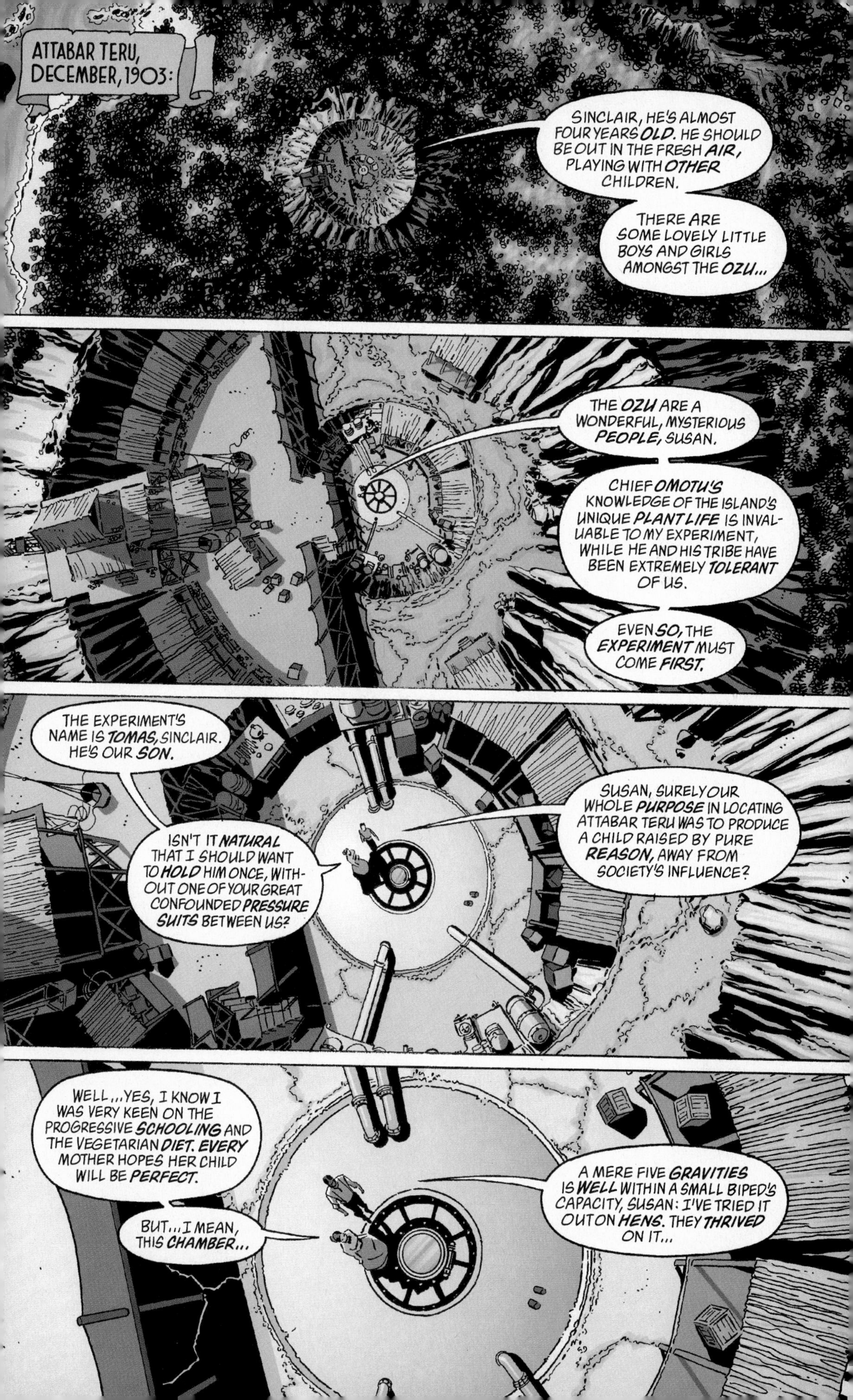

ATTABAR TERU, DECEMBER, 1903:
SINCLAIR, HE'S ALMOST FOUR YEARS OLD. HE SHOULD BE OUT IN THE FRESH AIR, PLAYING WITH OTHER CHILDREN.
THERE ARE SOME LOVELY LITTLE BOYS AND GIRLS AMONGST THE OZU...
THE OZU ARE A WONDERFUL, MYSTERIOUS PEOPLE, SUSAN.
CHIEF OMOTU'S KNOWLEDGE OF THE ISLAND'S UNIQUE PLANT LIFE IS INVALUABLE TO MY EXPERIMENT, WHILE HE AND HIS TRIBE HAVE BEEN EXTREMELY TOLERANT OF US.
EVEN SO, THE EXPERIMENT MUST COME FIRST.
THE EXPERIMENT'S NAME IS TOMAS, SINCLAIR. HE'S OUR SON.
ISN'T IT NATURAL THAT I SHOULD WANT TO HOLD HIM ONCE, WITHOUT ONE OF YOUR GREAT CONFOUNDED PRESSURE SUITS BETWEEN US?
SUSAN, SURELY OUR WHOLE PURPOSE IN LOCATING ATTABAR TERU WAS TO PRODUCE A CHILD RAISED BY PURE REASON, AWAY FROM SOCIETY'S INFLUENCE?
WELL...YES, I KNOW I WAS VERY KEEN ON THE PROGRESSIVE SCHOOLING AND THE VEGETARIAN DIET. EVERY MOTHER HOPES HER CHILD WILL BE PERFECT.
BUT...I MEAN, THIS CHAMBER...
A MERE FIVE GRAVITIES IS WELL WITHIN A SMALL BIPED'S CAPACITY, SUSAN: I'VE TRIED IT OUT ON HENS. THEY THRIVED ON IT...

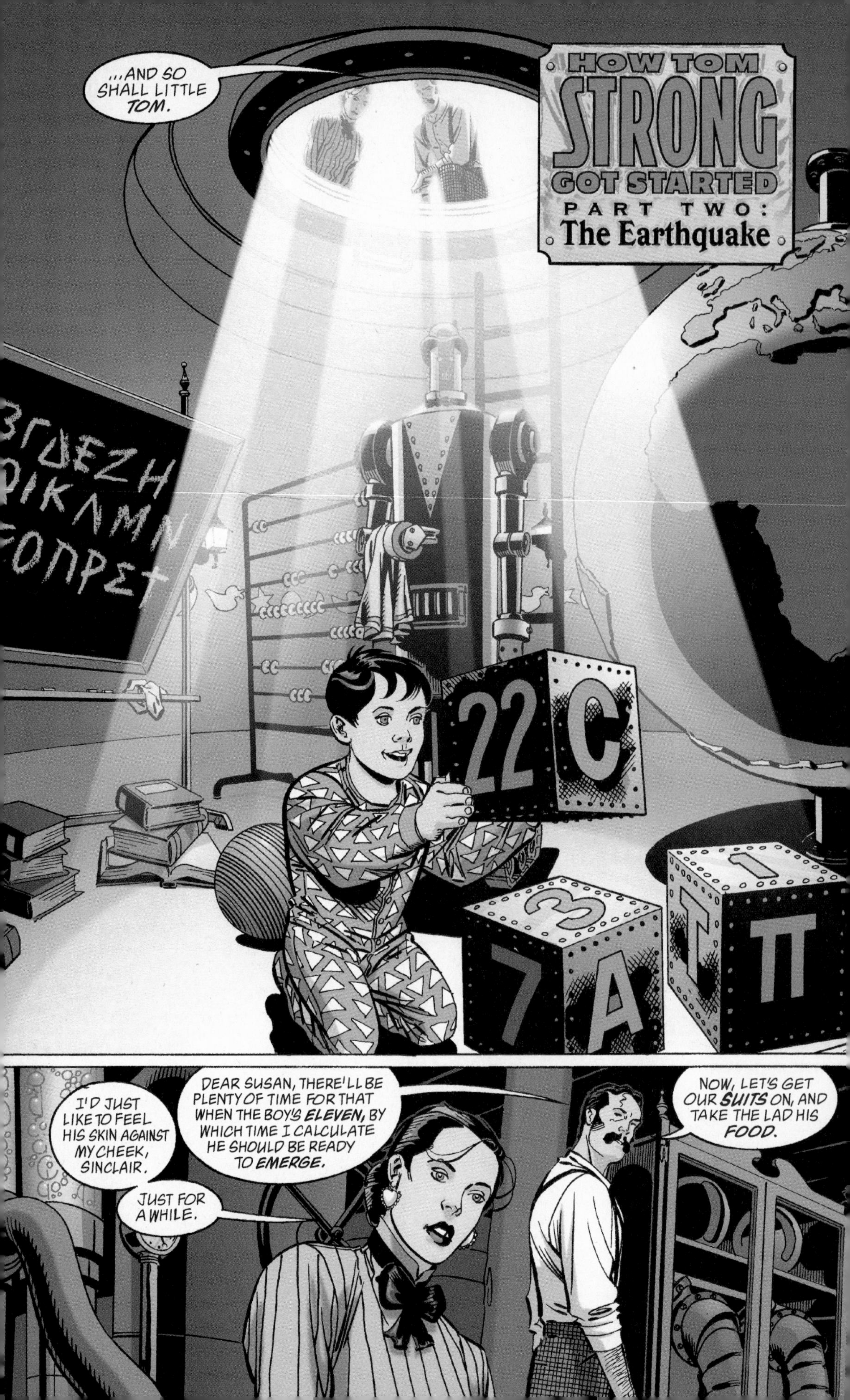
...AND SO SHALL LITTLE TOM.
HOW TOM STRONG GOT STARTED
PART TWO:
The Earthquake
I'D JUST LIKE TO FEEL HIS SKIN AGAINST MY CHEEK, SINCLAIR.
JUST FOR A WHILE.
DEAR SUSAN, THERE'LL BE PLENTY OF TIME FOR THAT WHEN THE BOY'S ELEVEN, BY WHICH TIME I CALCULATE HE SHOULD BE READY TO EMERGE.
NOW, LET'S GET OUR SUITS ON, AND TAKE THE LAD HIS FOOD.

HUDA, OROTI!

SURO TON WEH-WAH!

"OROTI"? PNEUMAN, WHAT'S HE SAYING?

≶skrikk≶ WITH YOUR PERMISSION ≶sss≶ MADAM ≶sss≶ MASTER TOM ≶sss≶ HAS LEARNED ≶sss≶ SOME OZU ≶sss≶ FROM MY ≶sss≶ ≶ktik≶ CYLINDER-RECORDINGS.

HE SAYS ≶sss≶ "HELLO MOTHER ≶sss≶ I AM YOUR BA- ≶ktik≶ YOUR BA- ≶ktik≶ YOUR BABY."

EXCELLENT. WELL, TOM, HERE'S YOUR DINNER.

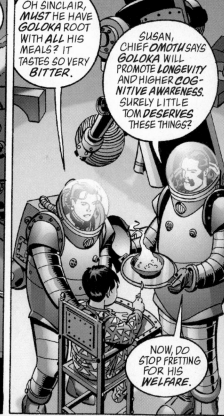

OH SINCLAIR, MUST HE HAVE GOLOKA ROOT WITH ALL HIS MEALS? IT TASTES SO VERY BITTER.

SUSAN, CHIEF OMOTU SAYS GOLOKA WILL PROMOTE LONGEVITY AND HIGHER COGNITIVE AWARENESS. SURELY LITTLE TOM DESERVES THESE THINGS?

NOW, DO STOP FRETTING FOR HIS WELFARE.

WHY, HE'S IN THE MOST SECURE QUARTER OF OUR VOLCANO STRONGHOLD...

TO BE QUITE FRANK, I DOUBT YOU'D FIND A SAFER PLACE UPON THIS EARTH.

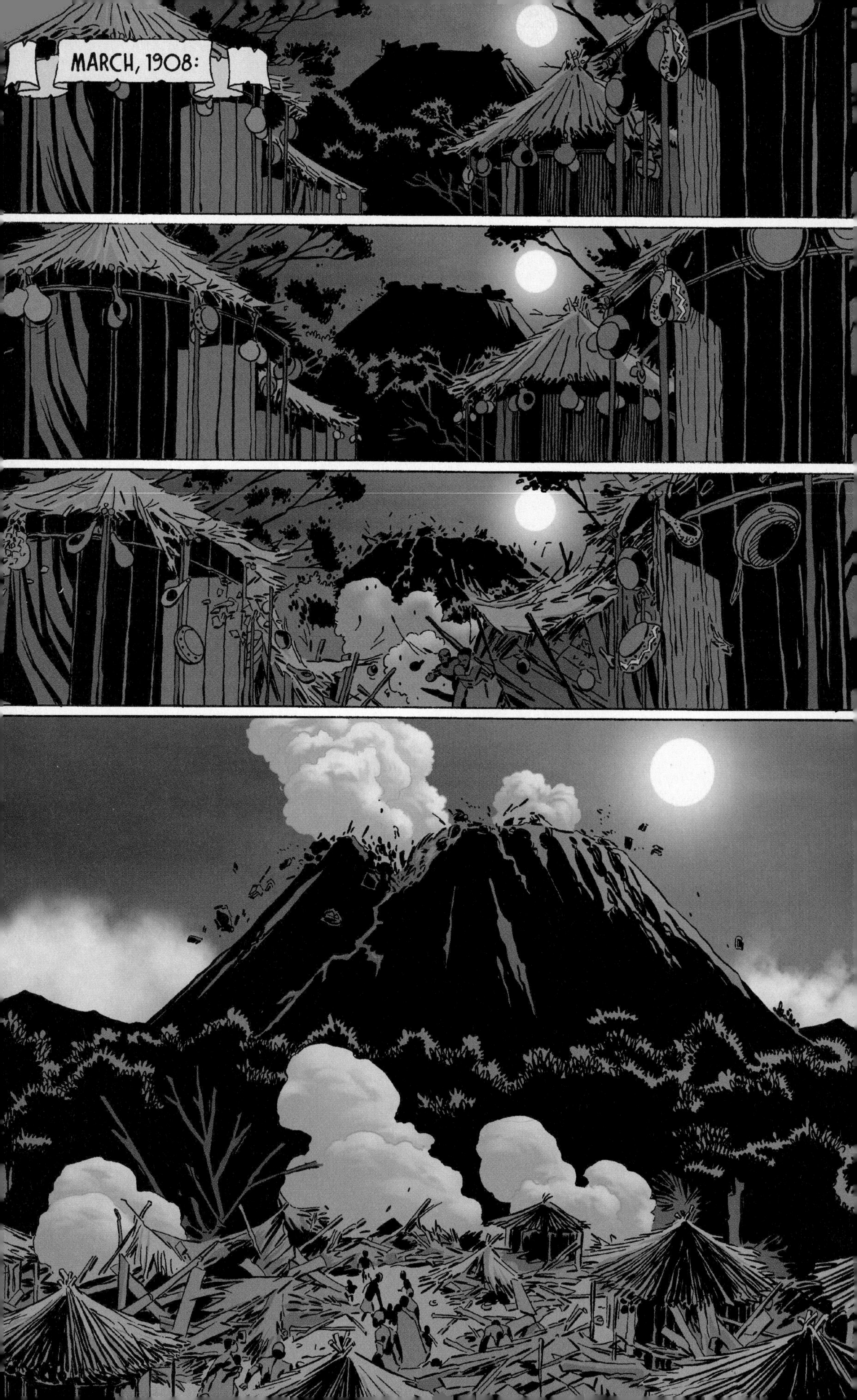
MARCH, 1908:

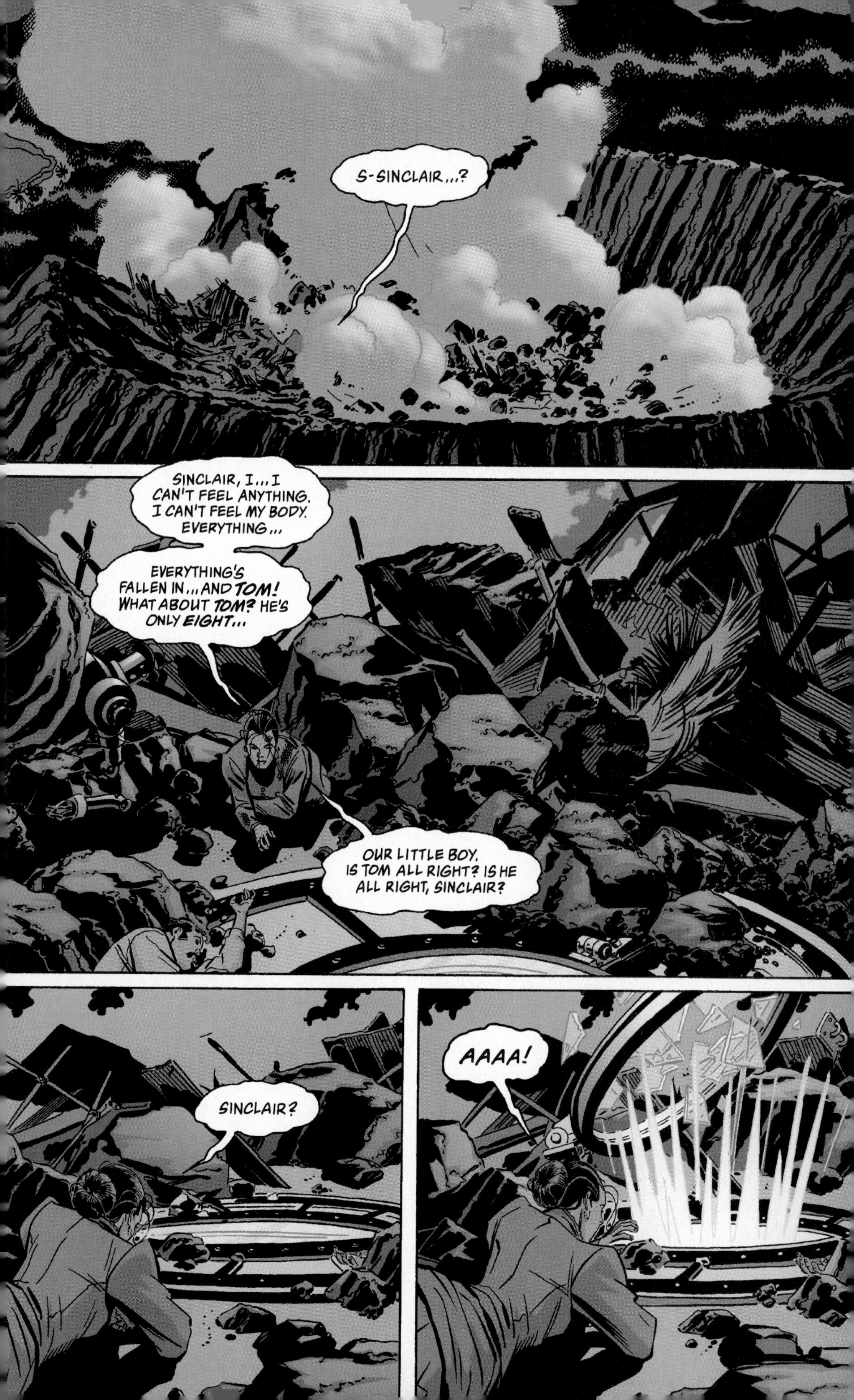
S-SINCLAIR...?
SINCLAIR, I... I CAN'T FEEL ANYTHING. I CAN'T FEEL MY BODY. EVERYTHING...
EVERYTHING'S FALLEN IN... AND TOM! WHAT ABOUT TOM? HE'S ONLY EIGHT...
OUR LITTLE BOY. IS TOM ALL RIGHT? IS HE ALL RIGHT, SINCLAIR?
SINCLAIR?
AAAA!

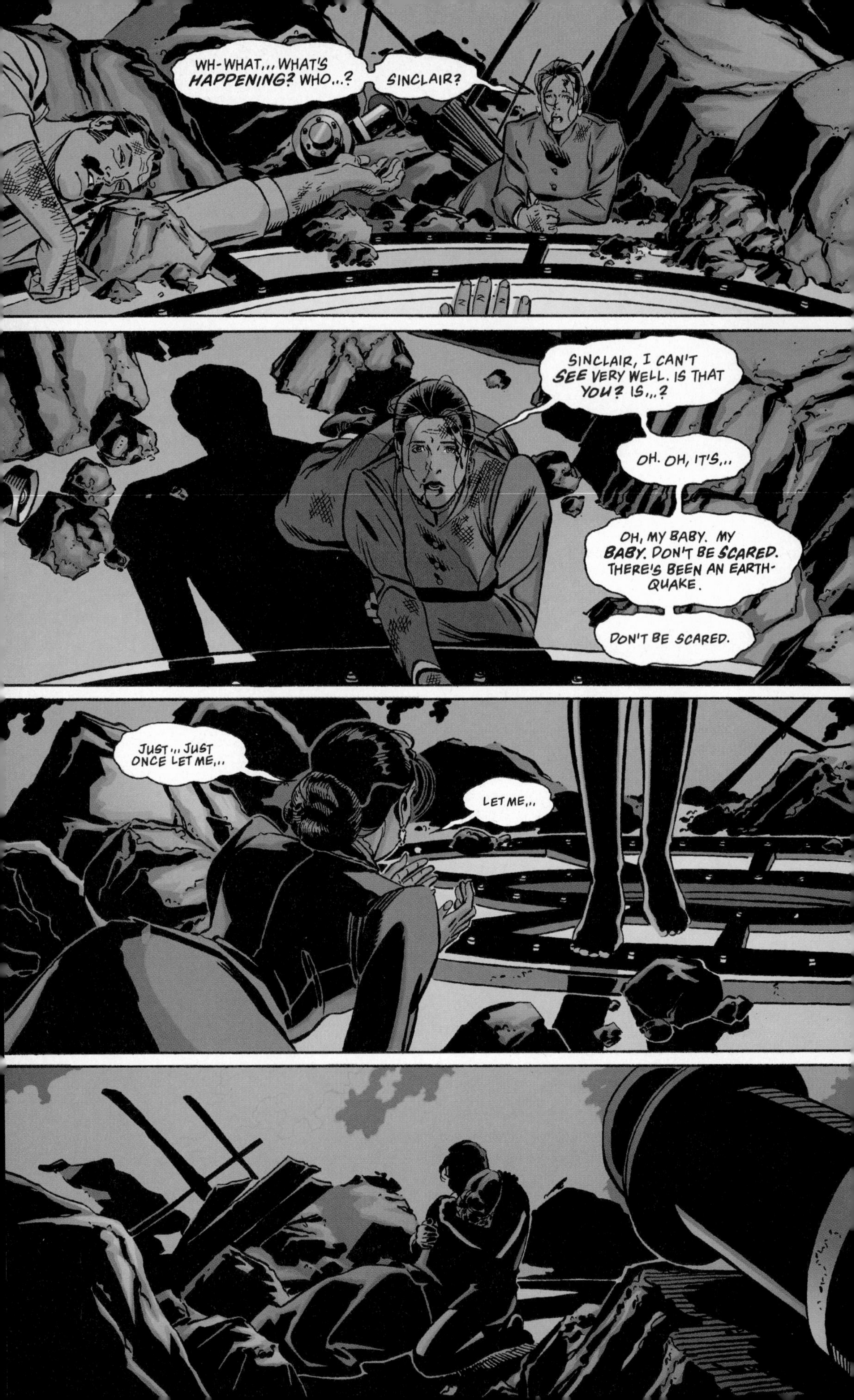

WH-WHAT... WHAT'S HAPPENING? WHO...?
SINCLAIR?
SINCLAIR, I CAN'T SEE VERY WELL. IS THAT YOU? IS...?
OH. OH, IT'S...
OH, MY BABY. MY BABY. DON'T BE SCARED. THERE'S BEEN AN EARTH-QUAKE.
DON'T BE SCARED.
JUST... JUST ONCE LET ME...
LET ME...

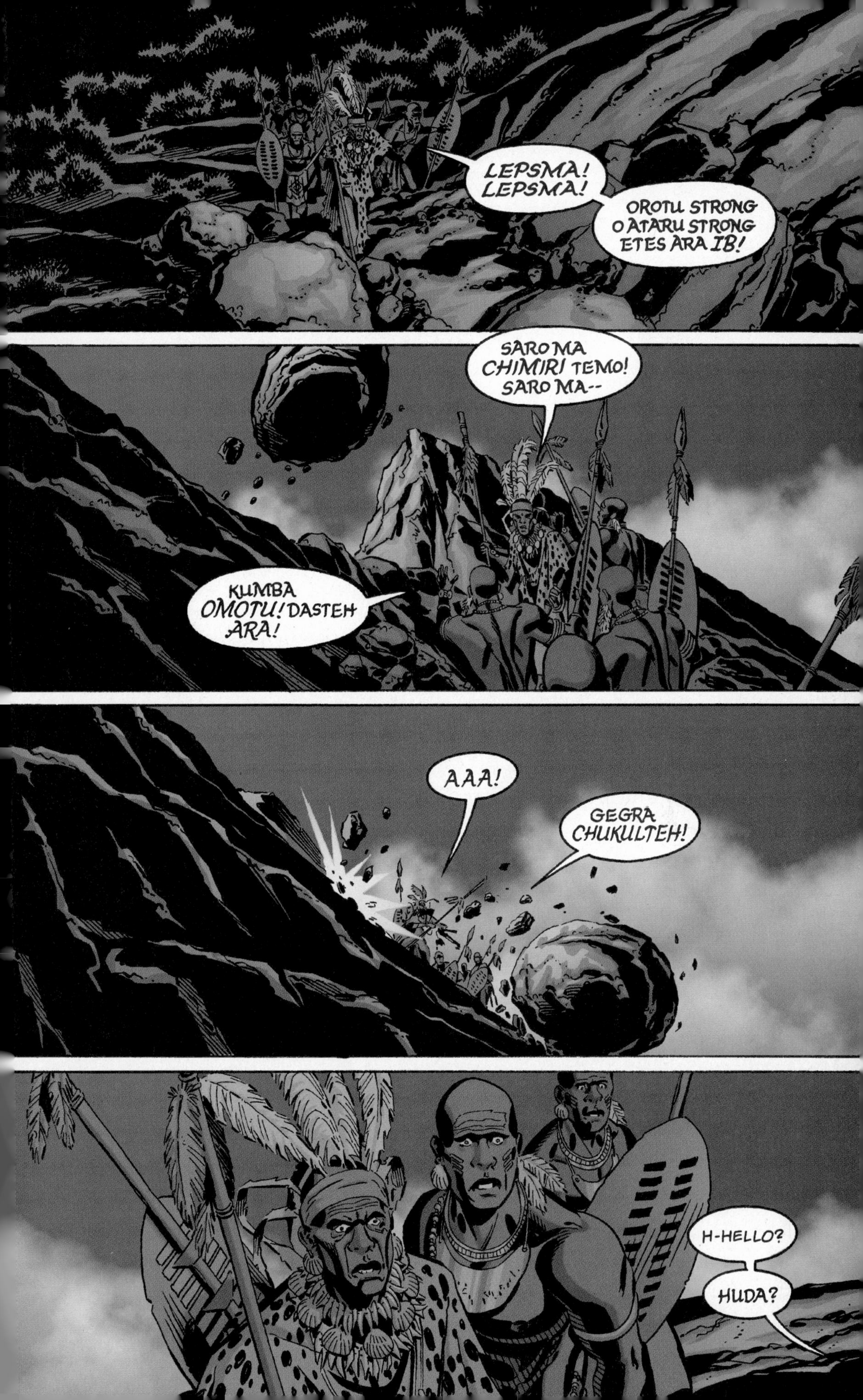
LEPSMA! LEPSMA!
OROTU STRONG O ATARU STRONG ETES ARA IB!
SARO MA CHIMIRI TEMO! SARO MA--
KUMBA OMOTU! DASTEH ARA!
AAA!
GEGRA CHUKULTEH!
H-HELLO?
HUDA?

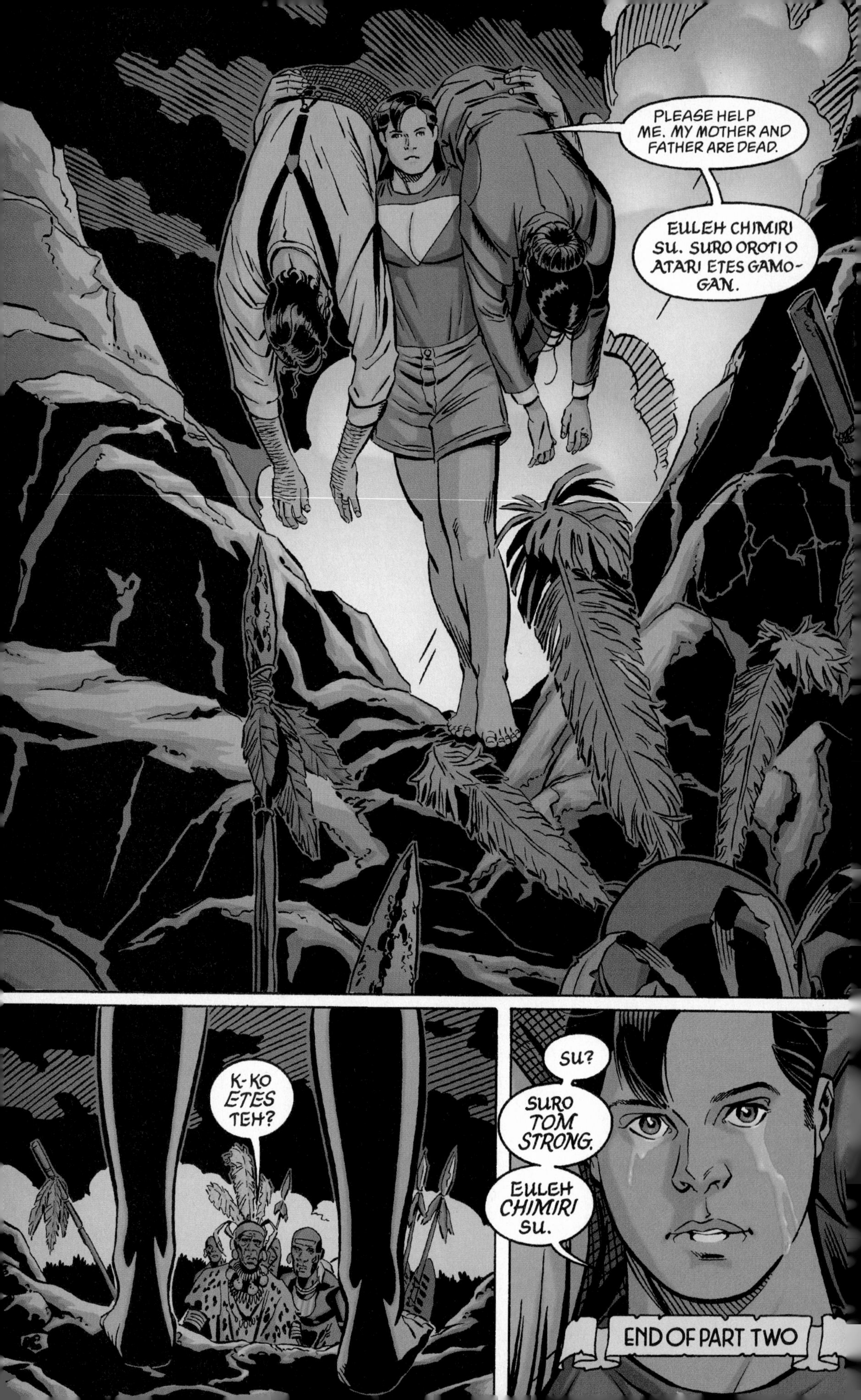
PLEASE HELP ME. MY MOTHER AND FATHER ARE DEAD.
EULEH CHIMIRI SU. SURO OROTI O ATARI ETES GAMO-GAN.
K-KO ETES TEH?
SU?
SURO TOM STRONG.
EULEH CHIMIRI SU.
END OF PART TWO

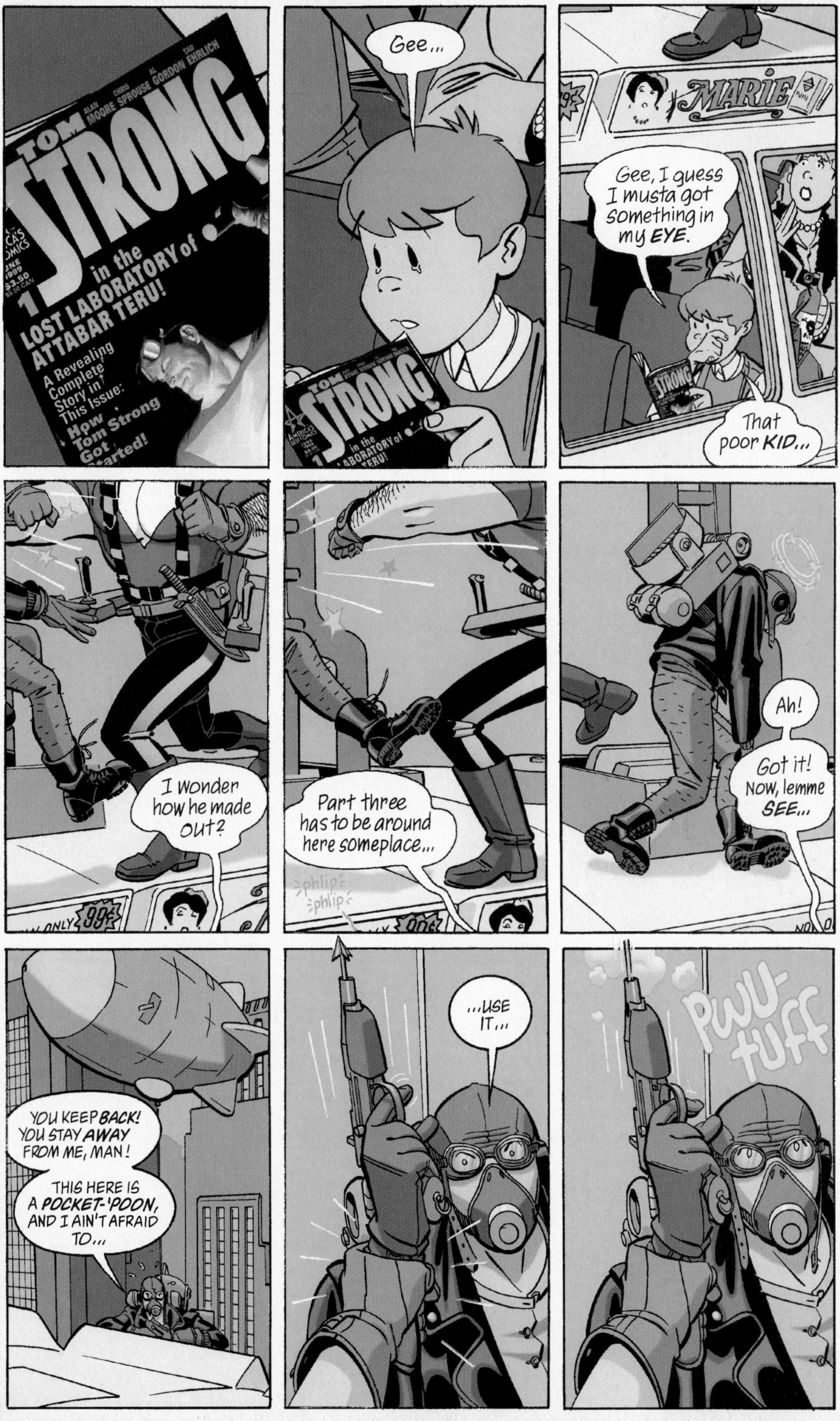
TOM STRONG
ALAN MOORE CHRIS SPROUSE AL GORDON TAD EHRLICH
JUNE 1999
$3.50
1
in the
LOST LABORATORY of ATTABAR TERU!
A Revealing Complete Story in This Issue: How Tom Strong Got Started!
Gee...
MARIE
Gee, I guess I musta got something in my EYE.
That poor KID...
I wonder how he made out?
Part three has to be around here someplace...
phlip phlip
Ah!
Got it! Now, lemme SEE...
YOU KEEP BACK! YOU STAY AWAY FROM ME, MAN!
THIS HERE IS A POCKET-'POON, AND I AIN'T AFRAID TO...
...USE IT...
PWU-tuff

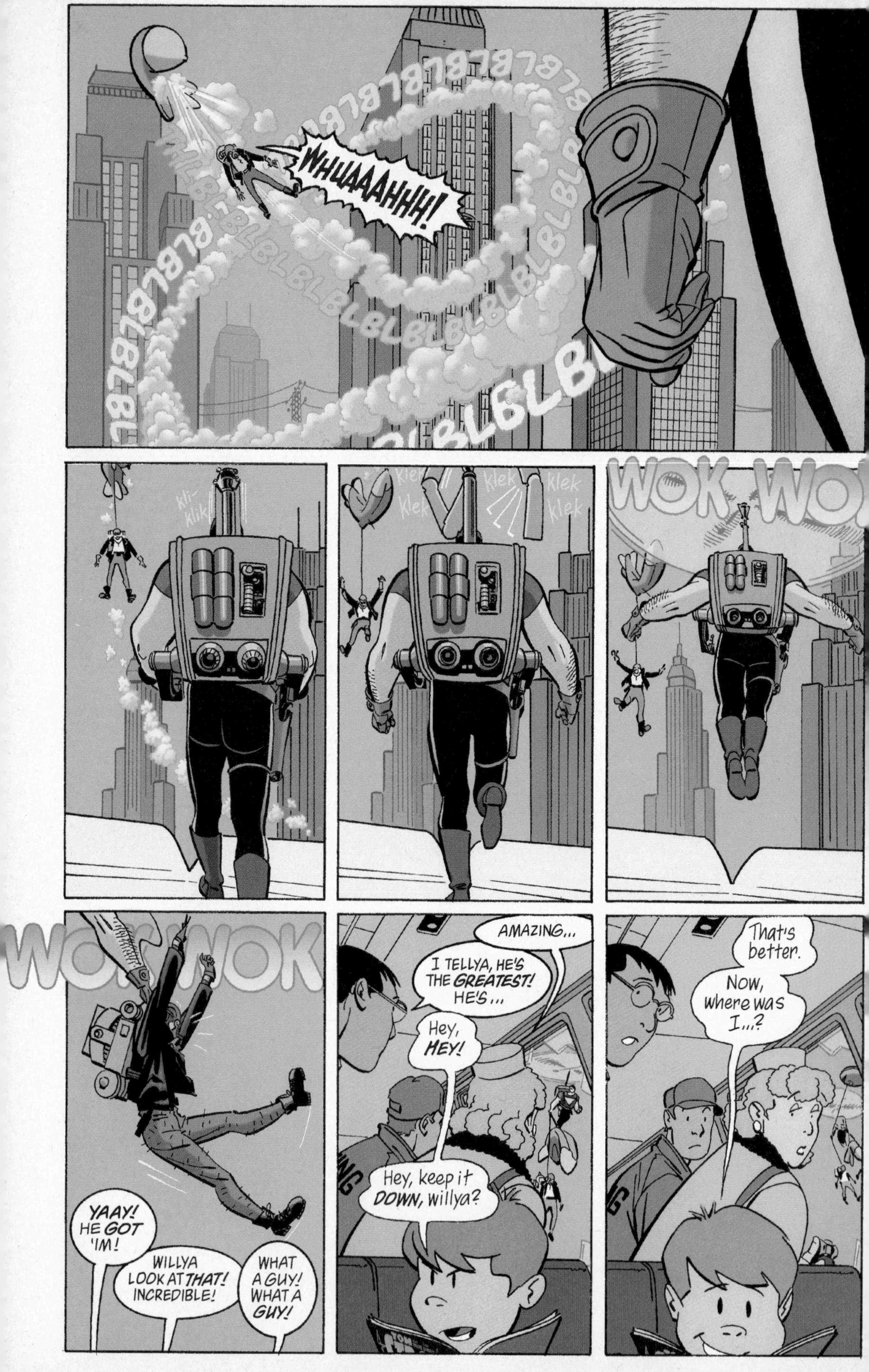

WHUAAAHHH!
BLBLBLBLBL
kli-klik
klek klek
klek klek
WOK WOK
WOK WOK
YAAY! HE GOT 'IM!
WILLYA LOOK AT THAT! INCREDIBLE!
WHAT A GUY! WHAT A GUY!
AMAZING...
I TELLYA, HE'S THE GREATEST! HE'S...
Hey, HEY!
Hey, keep it DOWN, willya?
That's better.
Now, where was I...?

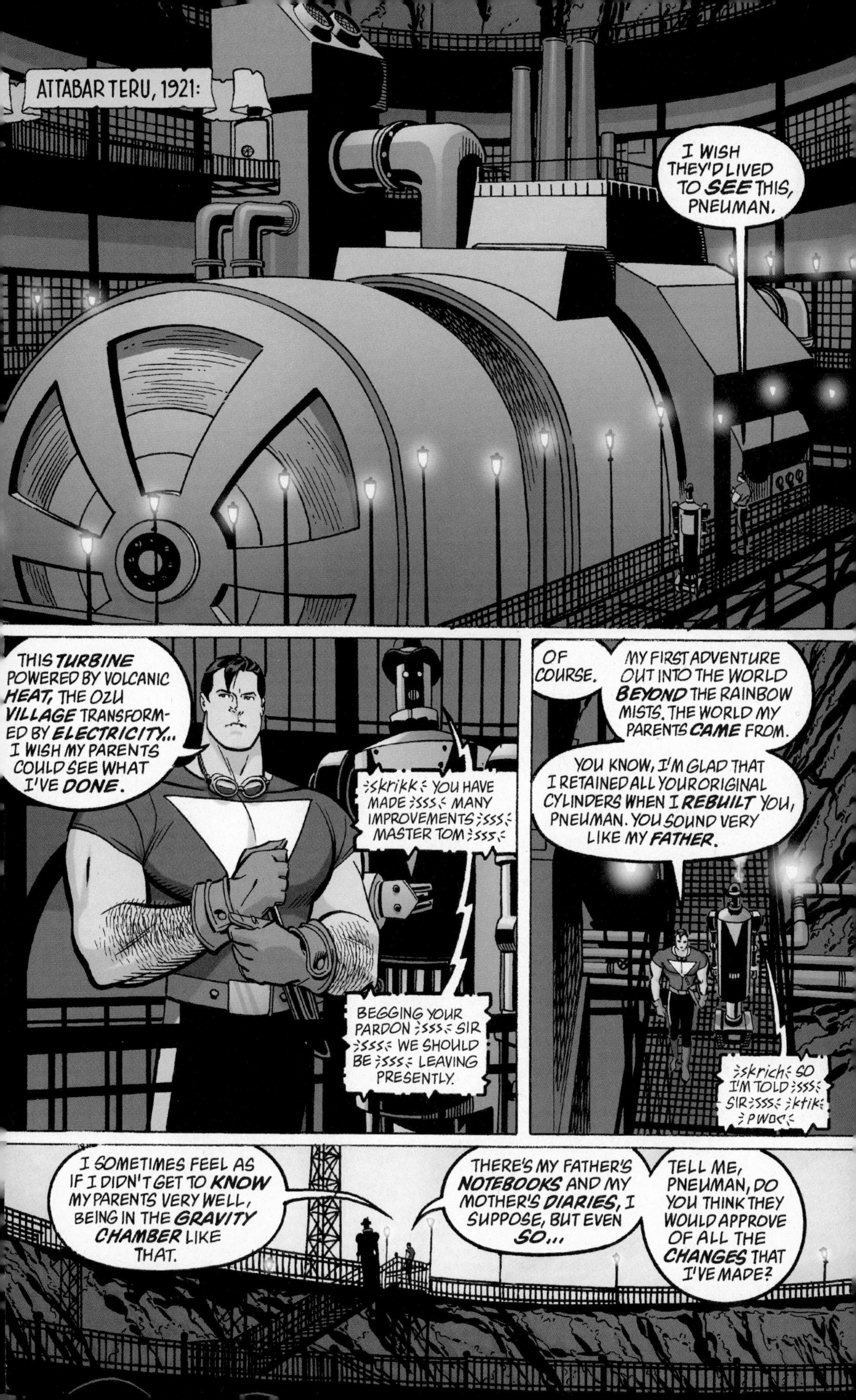

ATTABAR TERU, 1921:
I WISH THEY'D LIVED TO **SEE** THIS, PNEUMAN.
THIS **TURBINE** POWERED BY VOLCANIC **HEAT,** THE OZU **VILLAGE** TRANSFORMED BY **ELECTRICITY...** I WISH MY PARENTS COULD SEE WHAT I'VE **DONE.**
ƺskrikkƺ YOU HAVE MADE ƺsssƺ MANY IMPROVEMENTS ƺsssƺ MASTER TOM ƺsssƺ
BEGGING YOUR PARDON ƺsssƺ SIR ƺsssƺ WE SHOULD BE ƺsssƺ LEAVING PRESENTLY.
OF COURSE.
MY FIRST ADVENTURE OUT INTO THE WORLD **BEYOND** THE RAINBOW MISTS. THE WORLD MY PARENTS **CAME** FROM.
YOU KNOW, I'M GLAD THAT I RETAINED ALL YOUR ORIGINAL CYLINDERS WHEN I **REBUILT** YOU, PNEUMAN. YOU SOUND VERY LIKE MY **FATHER.**
ƺskrichƺ SO I'M TOLD ƺsssƺ SIR ƺsssƺ ƺktikƺ ƺPWOCƺ
I SOMETIMES FEEL AS IF I DIDN'T GET TO **KNOW** MY PARENTS VERY WELL, BEING IN THE **GRAVITY CHAMBER** LIKE THAT.
THERE'S MY FATHER'S **NOTEBOOKS** AND MY MOTHER'S **DIARIES,** I SUPPOSE, BUT EVEN **SO...**
TELL ME, PNEUMAN, DO YOU THINK THEY WOULD APPROVE OF ALL THE **CHANGES** THAT I'VE MADE?

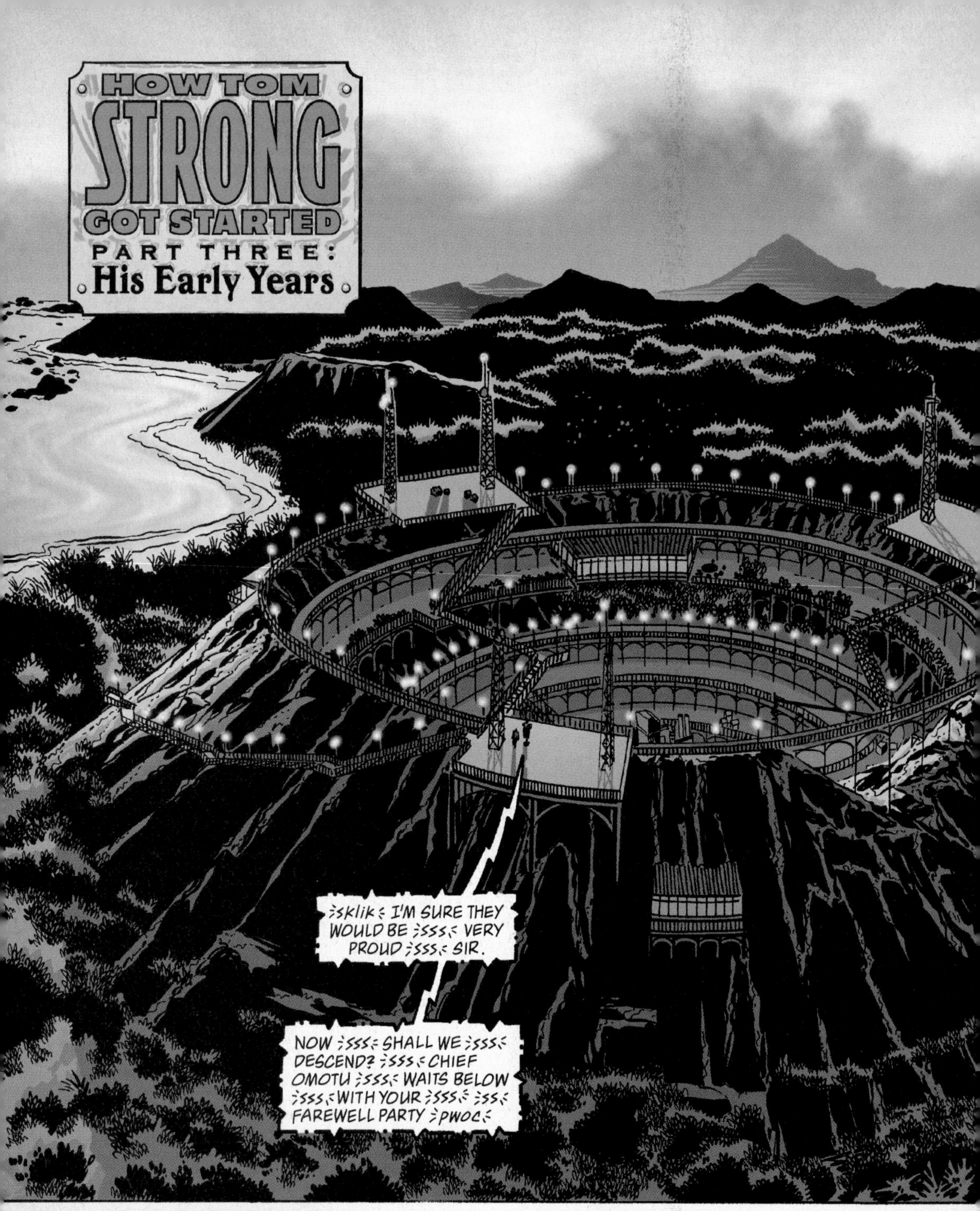
HOW TOM STRONG GOT STARTED
PART THREE:
His Early Years
≈sklik≈ I'M SURE THEY WOULD BE ≈sss≈ VERY PROUD ≈sss≈ SIR.
NOW ≈sss≈ SHALL WE ≈sss≈ DESCEND? ≈sss≈ CHIEF OMOTU ≈sss≈ WAITS BELOW ≈sss≈ WITH YOUR ≈sss≈ ≈ss≈ FAREWELL PARTY ≈pwoc≈

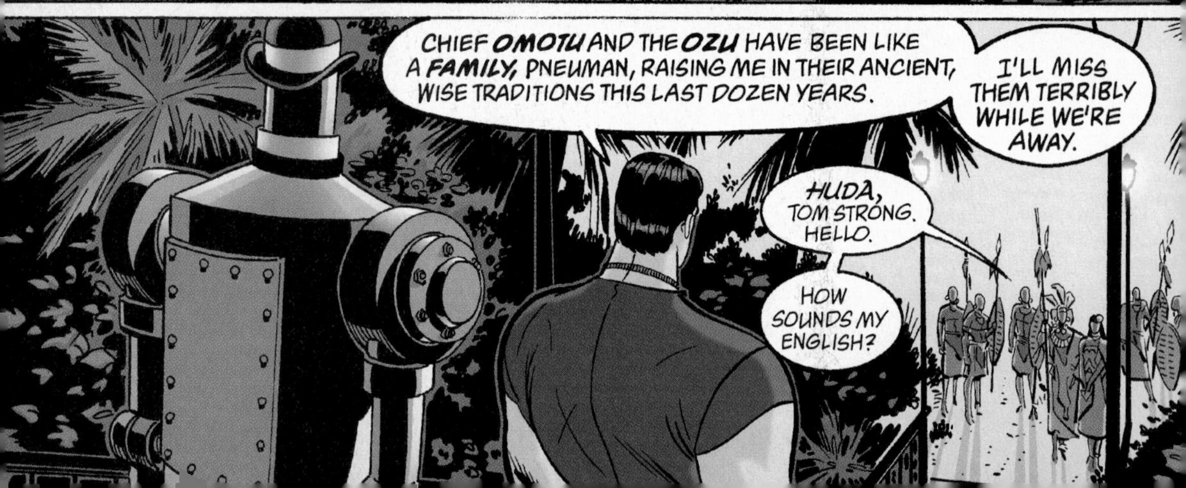
CHIEF OMOTU AND THE OZU HAVE BEEN LIKE A FAMILY, PNEUMAN, RAISING ME IN THEIR ANCIENT, WISE TRADITIONS THIS LAST DOZEN YEARS.
I'LL MISS THEM TERRIBLY WHILE WE'RE AWAY.
HUDA, TOM STRONG. HELLO.
HOW SOUNDS MY ENGLISH?

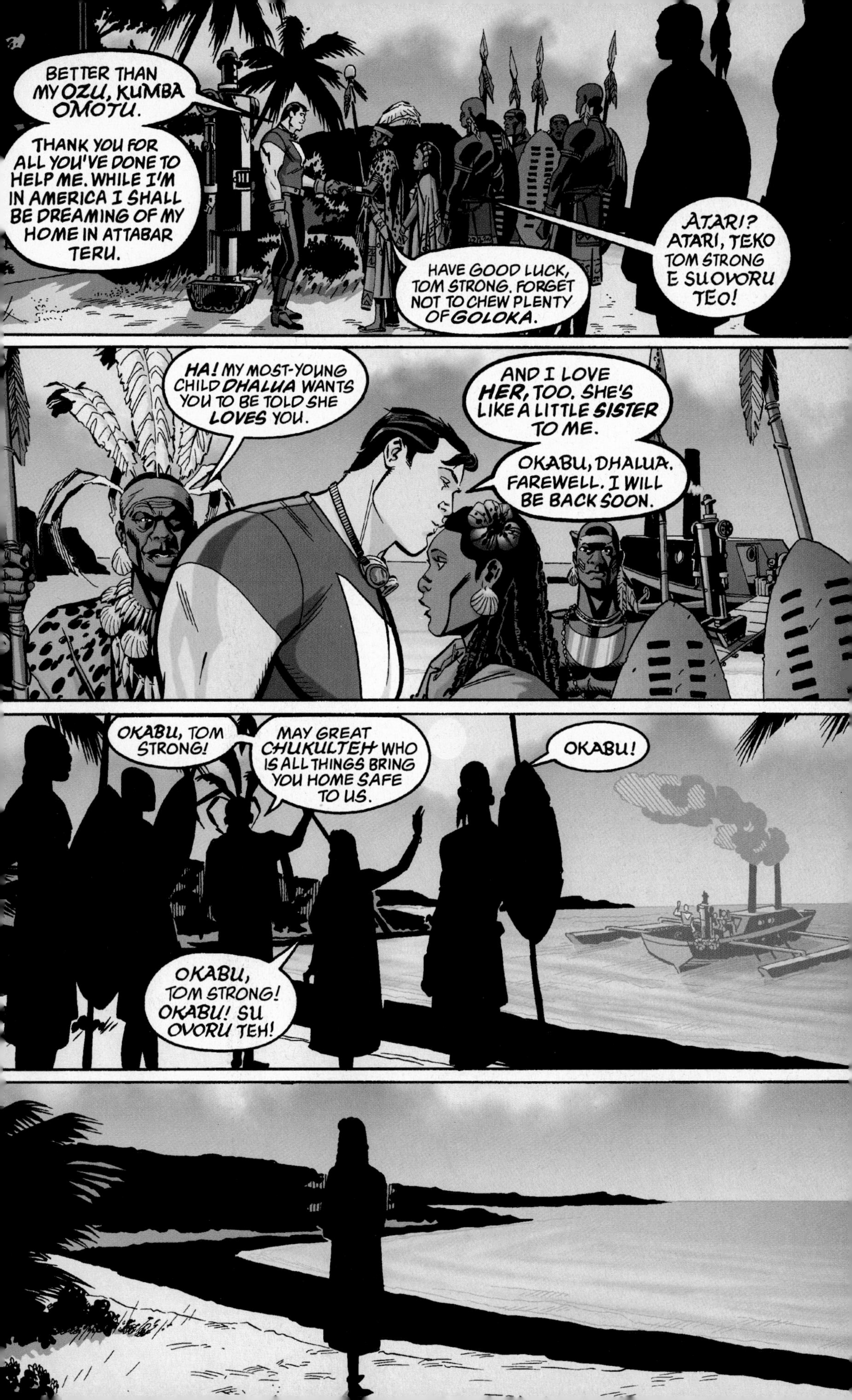
BETTER THAN MY OZU, KUMBA OMOTU.
THANK YOU FOR ALL YOU'VE DONE TO HELP ME. WHILE I'M IN AMERICA I SHALL BE DREAMING OF MY HOME IN ATTABAR TERU.
HAVE GOOD LUCK, TOM STRONG. FORGET NOT TO CHEW PLENTY OF GOLOKA.
ATARI? ATARI, TEKO TOM STRONG E SUOVORU TEO!
HA! MY MOST-YOUNG CHILD DHALUA WANTS YOU TO BE TOLD SHE LOVES YOU.
AND I LOVE HER, TOO. SHE'S LIKE A LITTLE SISTER TO ME.
OKABU, DHALUA. FAREWELL. I WILL BE BACK SOON.
OKABU, TOM STRONG!
MAY GREAT CHUKULTEH WHO IS ALL THINGS BRING YOU HOME SAFE TO US.
OKABU!
OKABU, TOM STRONG! OKABU! SU OVORU TEH!

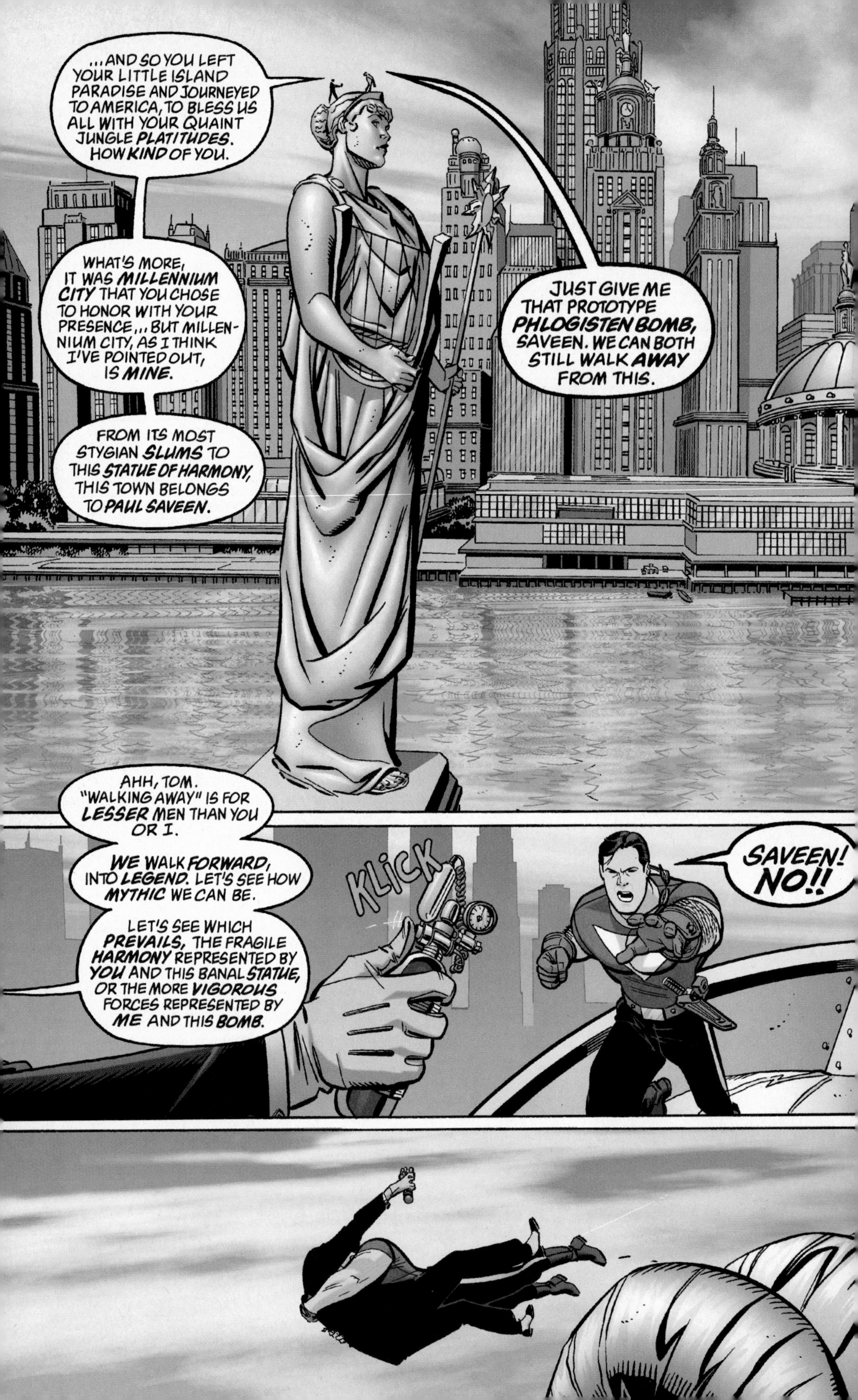
...AND SO YOU LEFT YOUR LITTLE ISLAND PARADISE AND JOURNEYED TO AMERICA, TO BLESS US ALL WITH YOUR QUAINT JUNGLE PLATITUDES. HOW KIND OF YOU.
WHAT'S MORE, IT WAS MILLENNIUM CITY THAT YOU CHOSE TO HONOR WITH YOUR PRESENCE,,, BUT MILLENNIUM CITY, AS I THINK I'VE POINTED OUT, IS MINE.
FROM ITS MOST STYGIAN SLUMS TO THIS STATUE OF HARMONY, THIS TOWN BELONGS TO PAUL SAVEEN.
JUST GIVE ME THAT PROTOTYPE PHLOGISTEN BOMB, SAVEEN. WE CAN BOTH STILL WALK AWAY FROM THIS.
AHH, TOM. "WALKING AWAY" IS FOR LESSER MEN THAN YOU OR I.
WE WALK FORWARD, INTO LEGEND. LET'S SEE HOW MYTHIC WE CAN BE.
LET'S SEE WHICH PREVAILS, THE FRAGILE HARMONY REPRESENTED BY YOU AND THIS BANAL STATUE, OR THE MORE VIGOROUS FORCES REPRESENTED BY ME AND THIS BOMB.
KLICK
SAVEEN! NO!!

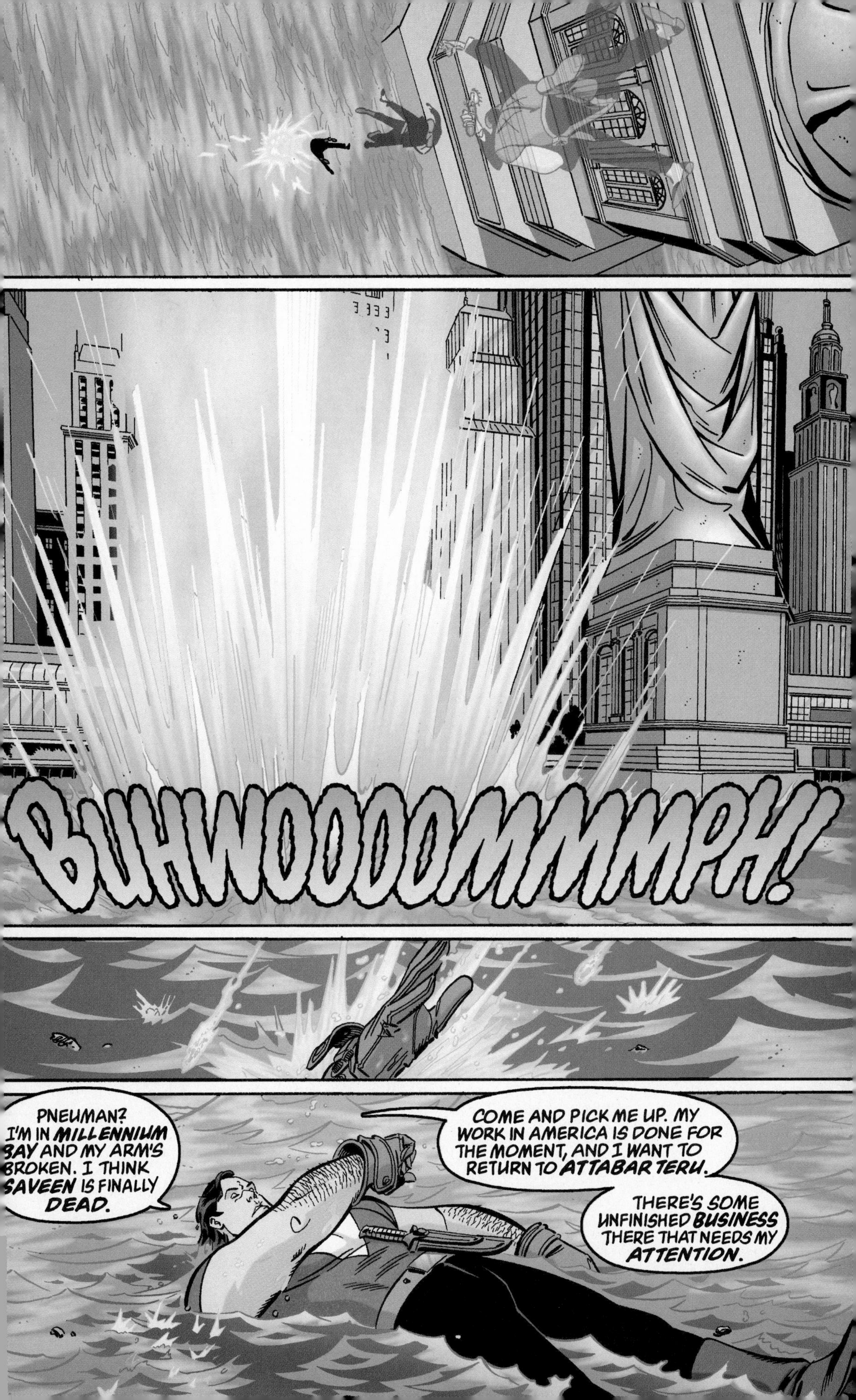
BUHWOOOOMMMPH!
PNEUMAN? I'M IN MILLENNIUM BAY AND MY ARM'S BROKEN. I THINK SAVEEN IS FINALLY DEAD.
COME AND PICK ME UP. MY WORK IN AMERICA IS DONE FOR THE MOMENT, AND I WANT TO RETURN TO ATTABAR TERU.
THERE'S SOME UNFINISHED BUSINESS THERE THAT NEEDS MY ATTENTION.

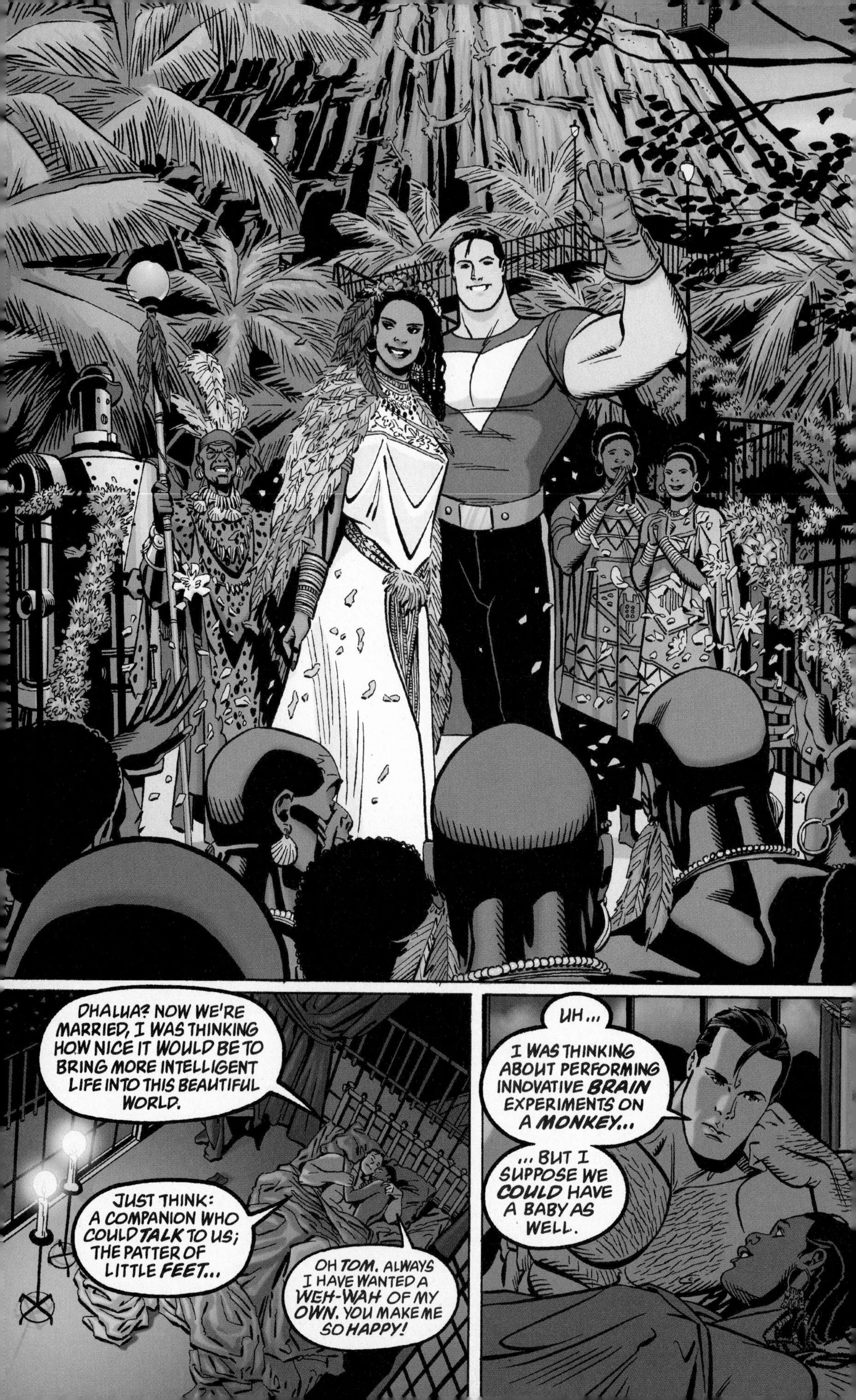
DHALUA? NOW WE'RE MARRIED, I WAS THINKING HOW NICE IT WOULD BE TO BRING MORE INTELLIGENT LIFE INTO THIS BEAUTIFUL WORLD.
JUST THINK: A COMPANION WHO COULD TALK TO US; THE PATTER OF LITTLE FEET...
OH TOM. ALWAYS I HAVE WANTED A WEH-WAH OF MY OWN. YOU MAKE ME SO HAPPY!
UH...
I WAS THINKING ABOUT PERFORMING INNOVATIVE BRAIN EXPERIMENTS ON A MONKEY...
...BUT I SUPPOSE WE COULD HAVE A BABY AS WELL.

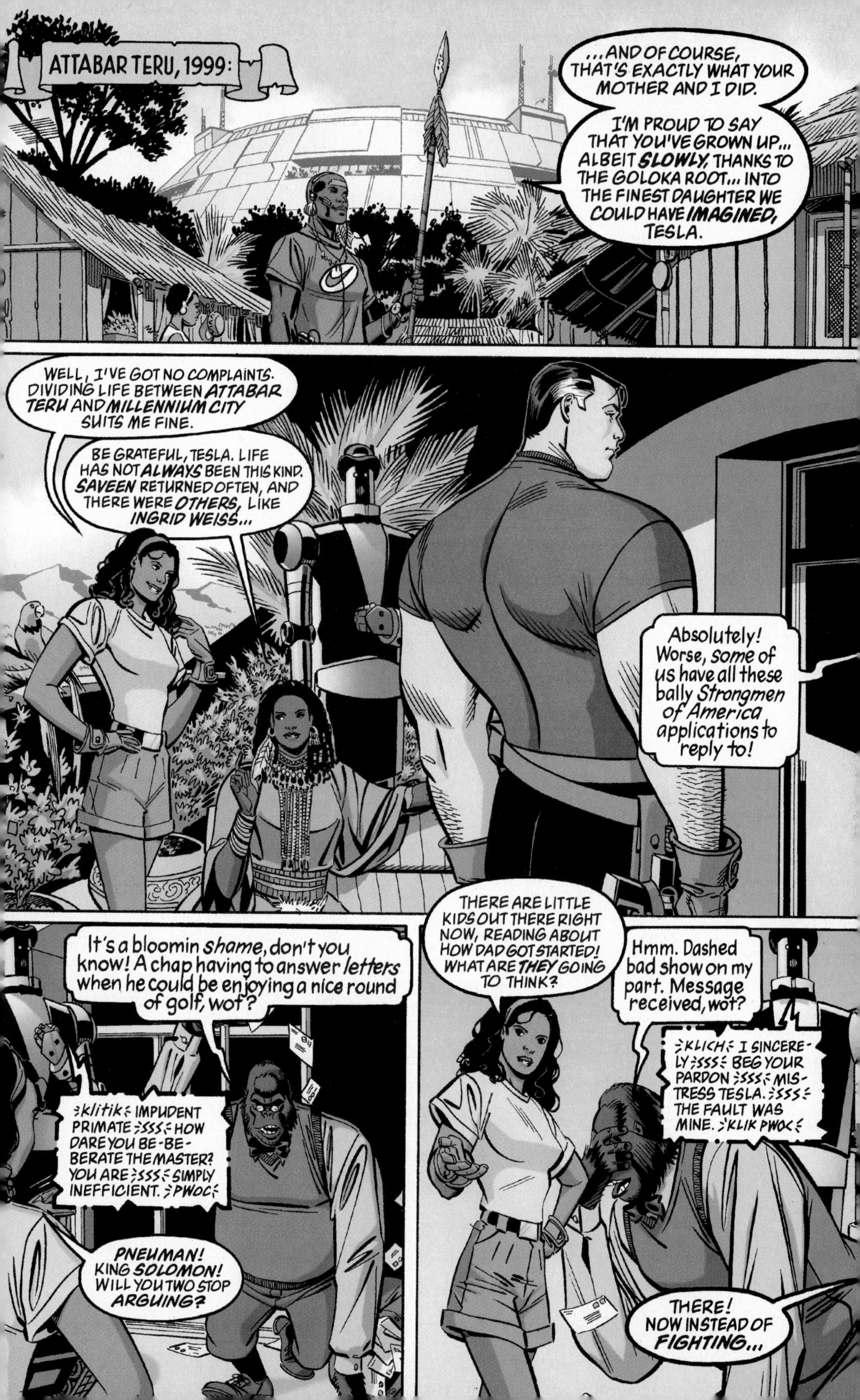
ATTABAR TERU, 1999:
...AND OF COURSE, THAT'S EXACTLY WHAT YOUR MOTHER AND I DID.
I'M PROUD TO SAY THAT YOU'VE GROWN UP... ALBEIT SLOWLY, THANKS TO THE GOLOKA ROOT... INTO THE FINEST DAUGHTER WE COULD HAVE IMAGINED, TESLA.
WELL, I'VE GOT NO COMPLAINTS. DIVIDING LIFE BETWEEN ATTABAR TERU AND MILLENNIUM CITY SUITS ME FINE.
BE GRATEFUL, TESLA. LIFE HAS NOT ALWAYS BEEN THIS KIND. SAVEEN RETURNED OFTEN, AND THERE WERE OTHERS, LIKE INGRID WEISS...
Absolutely! Worse, some of us have all these bally Strongmen of America applications to reply to!
It's a bloomin shame, don't you know! A chap having to answer letters when he could be enjoying a nice round of golf, wot?
klitik IMPUDENT PRIMATE sss HOW DARE YOU BE-BERATE THE MASTER? YOU ARE sss SIMPLY INEFFICIENT. PWOC
PNEUMAN! KING SOLOMON! WILL YOU TWO STOP ARGUING?
THERE ARE LITTLE KIDS OUT THERE RIGHT NOW, READING ABOUT HOW DAD GOT STARTED! WHAT ARE THEY GOING TO THINK?
Hmm. Dashed bad show on my part. Message received, wot?
KLICH I SINCERE-LY sss BEG YOUR PARDON sss MIS-TRESS TESLA. sss THE FAULT WAS MINE. KLIK PWOC
THERE! NOW INSTEAD OF FIGHTING...

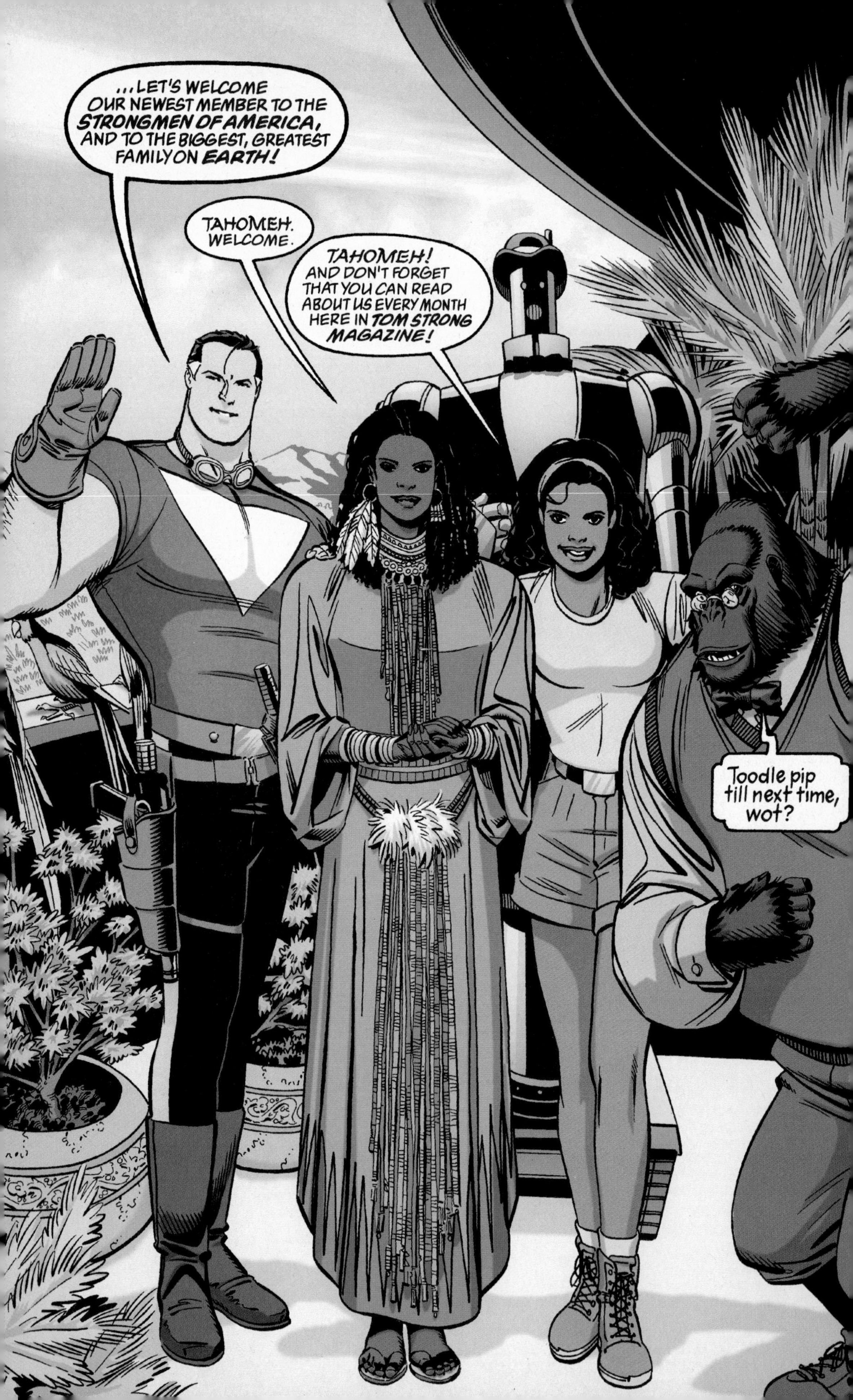
...LET'S WELCOME OUR NEWEST MEMBER TO THE STRONGMEN OF AMERICA, AND TO THE BIGGEST, GREATEST FAMILY ON EARTH!
TAHOMEH. WELCOME.
TAHOMEH! AND DON'T FORGET THAT YOU CAN READ ABOUT US EVERY MONTH HERE IN TOM STRONG MAGAZINE!
Toodle pip till next time, wot?

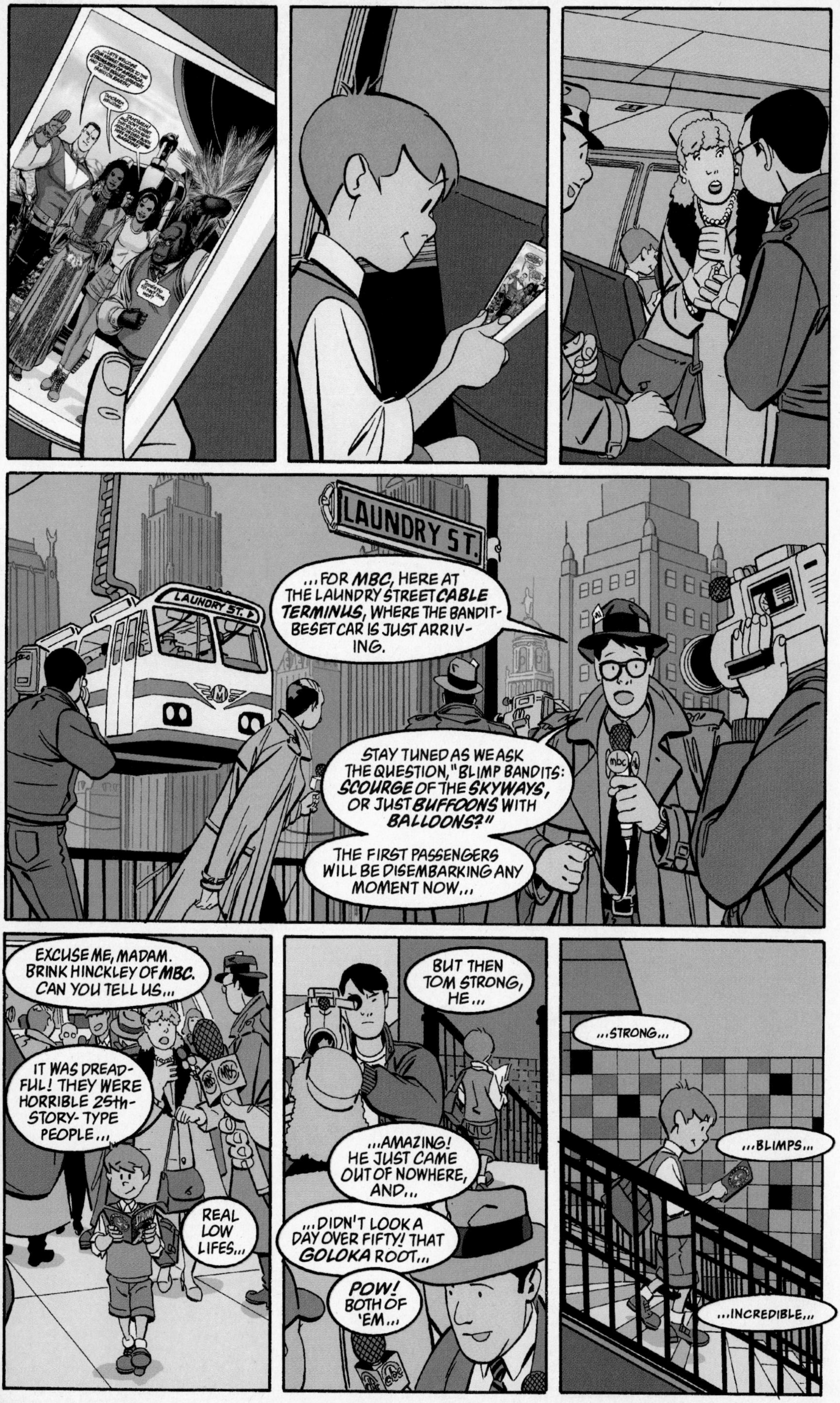
...LET'S WELCOME OUR NEWEST MEMBER TO THE STRONGMEN OF AMERICA, AND TO THE BIGGEST, GREATEST FAMILY ON EARTH!
Toodle pip till next time, wot?
LAUNDRY ST.
LAUNDRY ST.
...FOR MBC, HERE AT THE LAUNDRY STREET CABLE TERMINUS, WHERE THE BANDIT-BESET CAR IS JUST ARRIV-ING.
STAY TUNED AS WE ASK THE QUESTION, "BLIMP BANDITS: SCOURGE OF THE SKYWAYS, OR JUST BUFFOONS WITH BALLOONS?"
THE FIRST PASSENGERS WILL BE DISEMBARKING ANY MOMENT NOW...
EXCUSE ME, MADAM. BRINK HINCKLEY OF MBC. CAN YOU TELL US...
IT WAS DREAD-FUL! THEY WERE HORRIBLE 25th-STORY-TYPE PEOPLE...
REAL LOW LIFES...
BUT THEN TOM STRONG, HE...
...AMAZING! HE JUST CAME OUT OF NOWHERE, AND...
...DIDN'T LOOK A DAY OVER FIFTY! THAT GOLOKA ROOT...
POW! BOTH OF 'EM...
...STRONG...
...BLIMPS...
...INCREDIBLE...

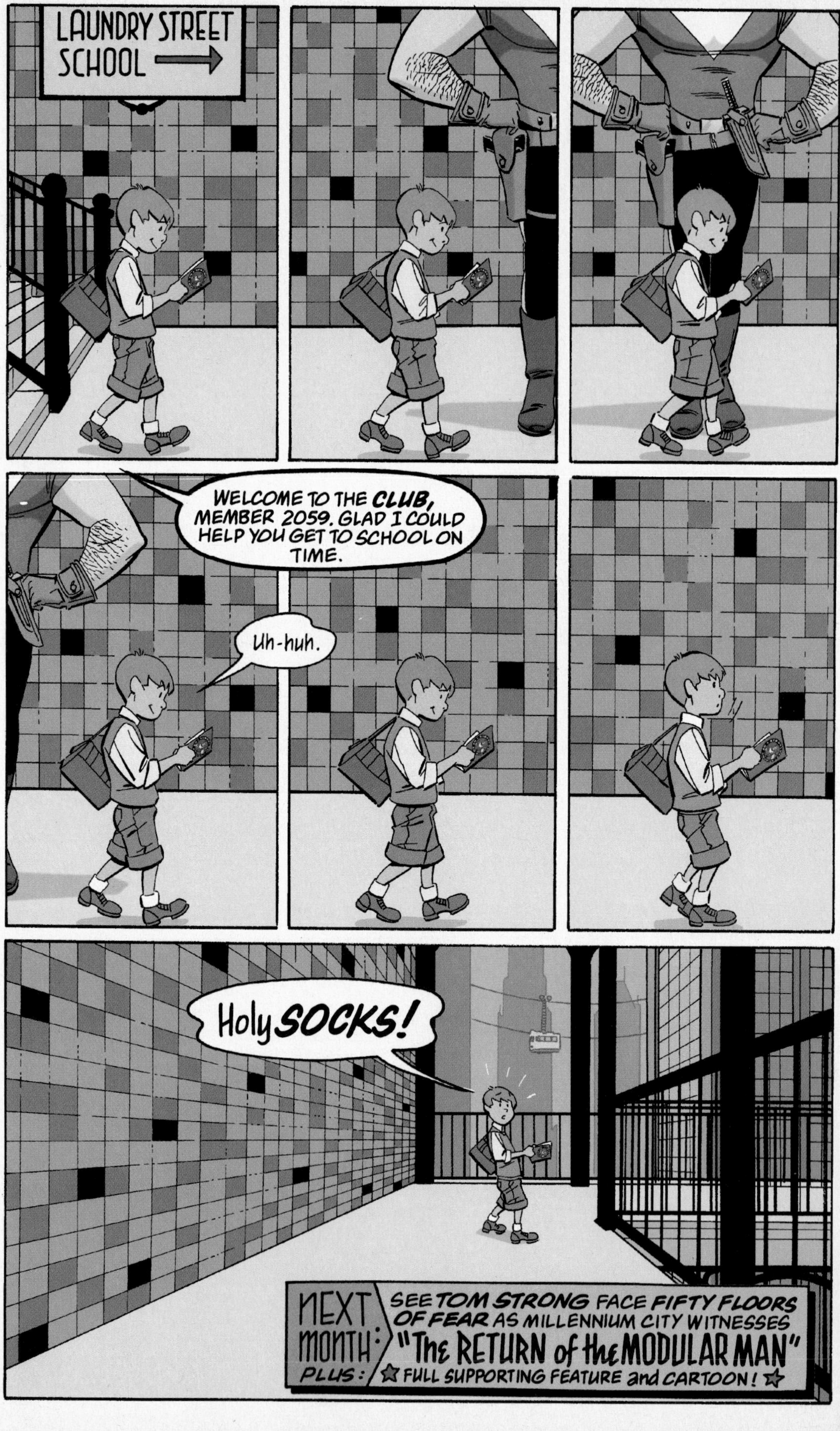
LAUNDRY STREET SCHOOL
WELCOME TO THE CLUB, MEMBER 2059. GLAD I COULD HELP YOU GET TO SCHOOL ON TIME.
Uh-huh.
Holy SOCKS!
NEXT MONTH: SEE TOM STRONG FACE FIFTY FLOORS OF FEAR AS MILLENNIUM CITY WITNESSES "The RETURN of the MODULAR MAN"
PLUS: ☆ FULL SUPPORTING FEATURE and CARTOON! ☆

CHAPTER TWO

In which The Family fills in,
TESLA makes New Friends, and
TOM talks to an Old Acquaintance.

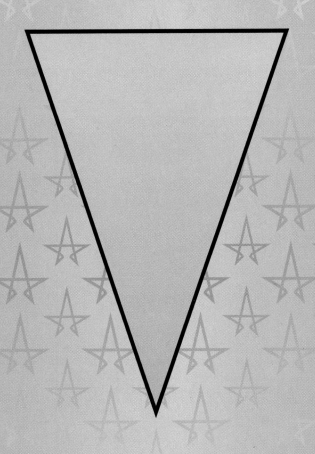

**Cover art:
Chris Sprouse &
Angus McKie**

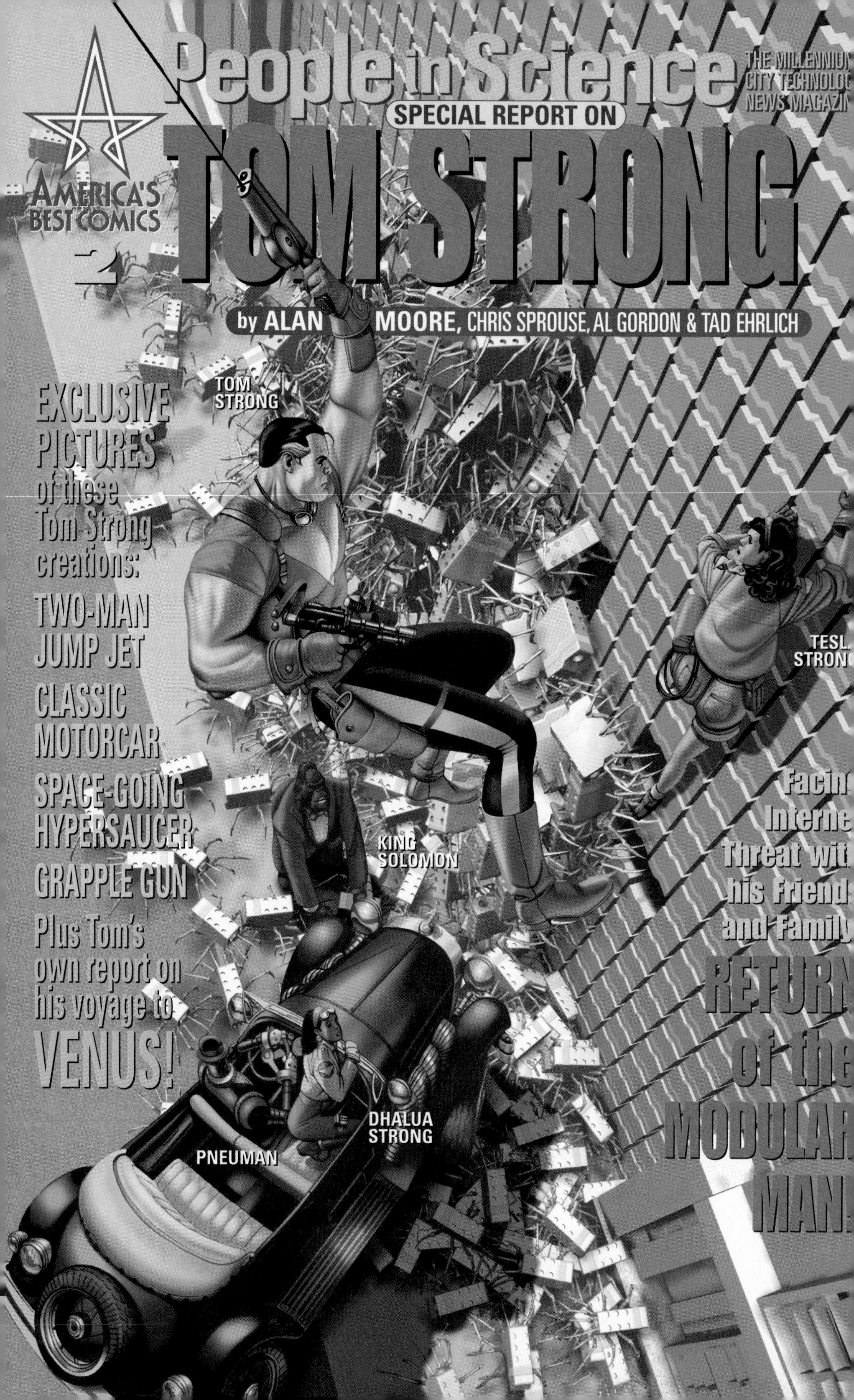
AMERICA'S BEST COMICS
2
People in Science
THE MILLENNIU
CITY TECHNOLOG
NEWS MAGAZI
SPECIAL REPORT ON
TOM STRONG
by ALAN MOORE, CHRIS SPROUSE, AL GORDON & TAD EHRLICH
EXCLUSIVE PICTURES of these Tom Strong creations:
TWO-MAN JUMP JET
CLASSIC MOTORCAR
SPACE-GOING HYPERSAUCER
GRAPPLE GUN
Plus Tom's own report on his voyage to VENUS!
TOM STRONG
TESL
STRON
KING SOLOMON
DHALUA STRONG
PNEUMAN
Facin
Interne
Threat wit
his Friend
and Famil
RETURN
of the
MODULAR
MAN!

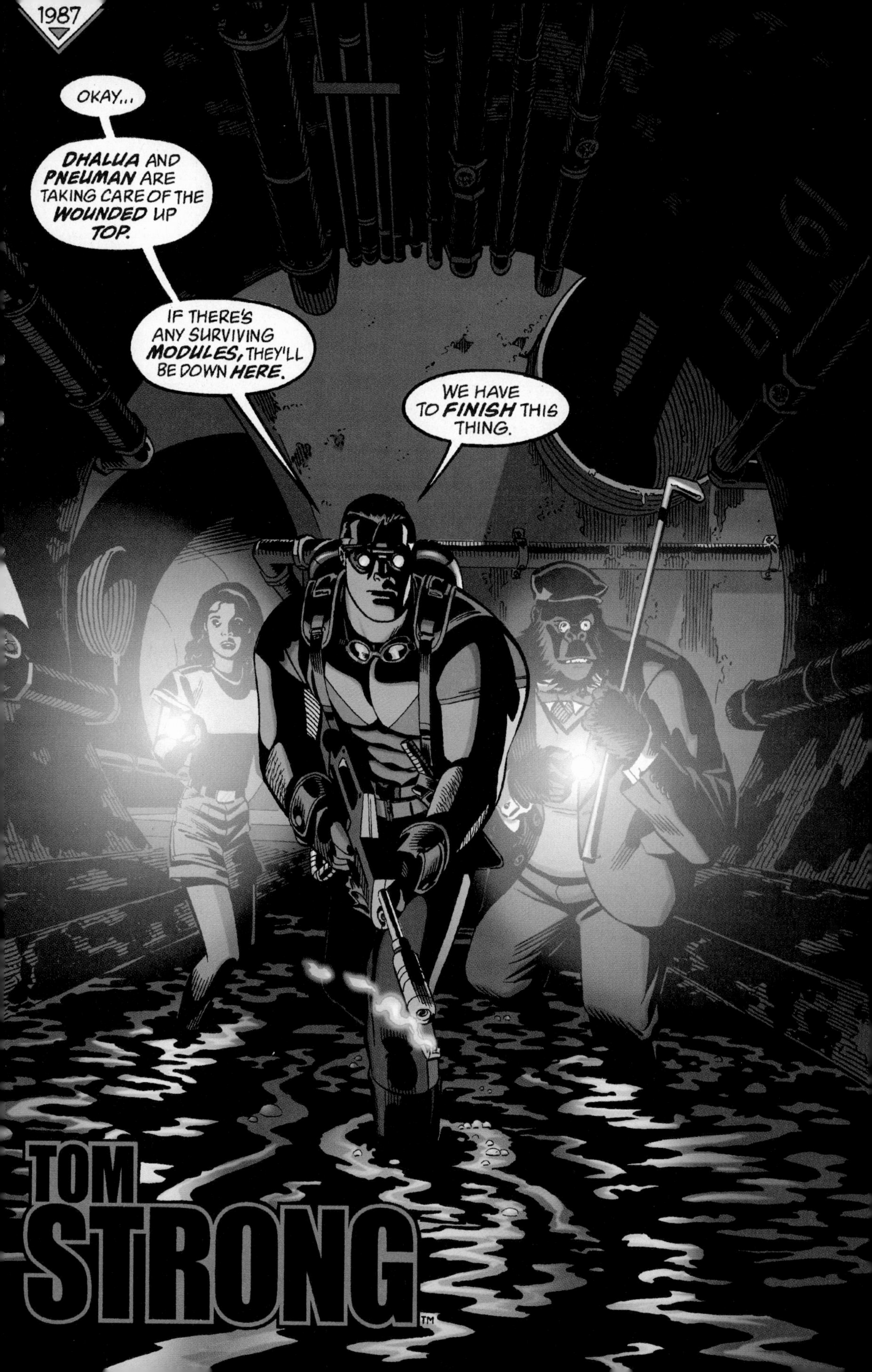
1987
OKAY...
DHALUA AND PNEUMAN ARE TAKING CARE OF THE WOUNDED UP TOP.
IF THERE'S ANY SURVIVING MODULES, THEY'LL BE DOWN HERE.
WE HAVE TO FINISH THIS THING.
TOM STRONG™

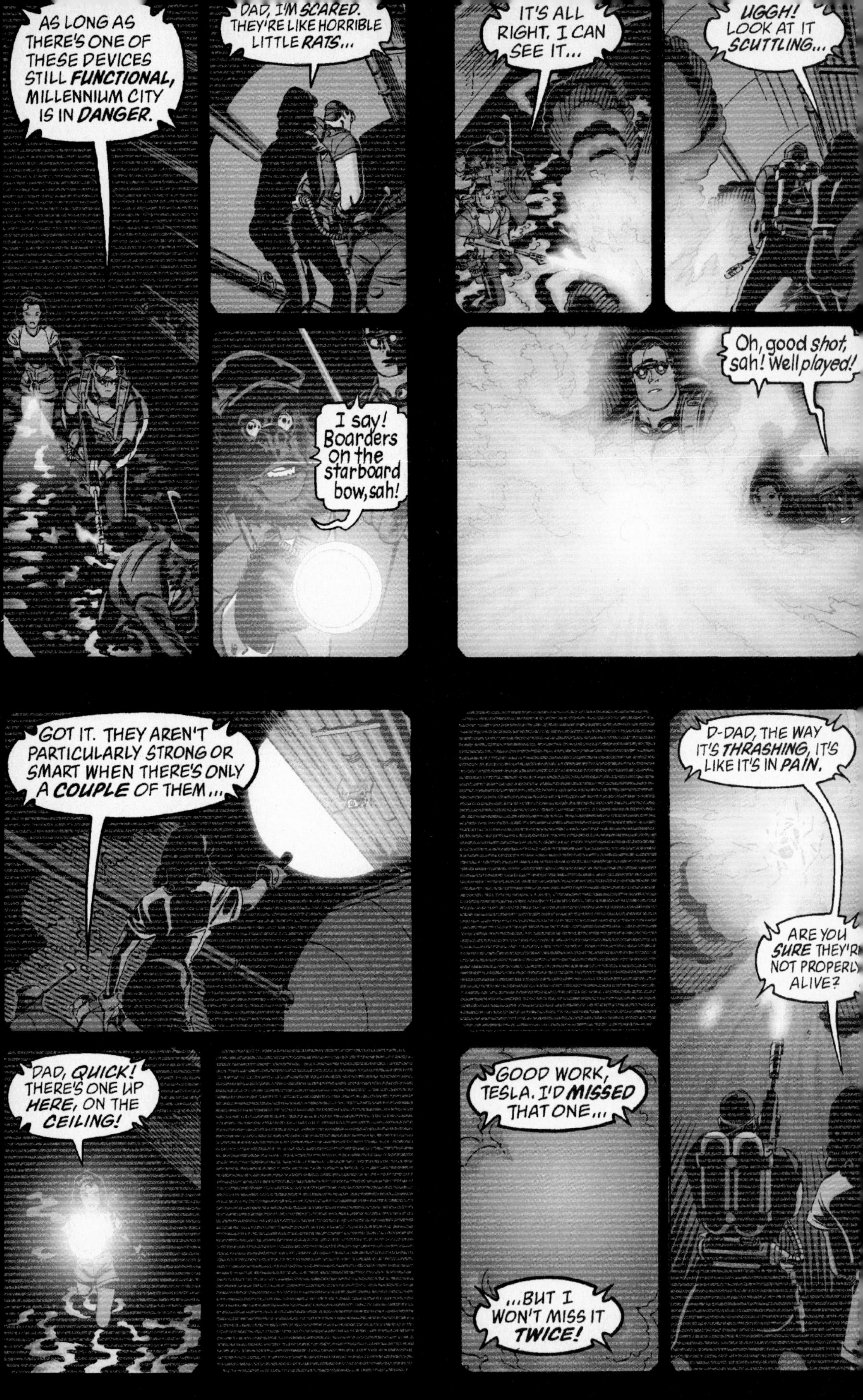
AS LONG AS THERE'S ONE OF THESE DEVICES STILL FUNCTIONAL, MILLENNIUM CITY IS IN DANGER.
DAD, I'M SCARED. THEY'RE LIKE HORRIBLE LITTLE RATS...
I say! Boarders on the starboard bow, sah!
IT'S ALL RIGHT. I CAN SEE IT...
UGGH! LOOK AT IT SCUTTLING...
Oh, good shot, sah! Well played!
GOT IT. THEY AREN'T PARTICULARLY STRONG OR SMART WHEN THERE'S ONLY A COUPLE OF THEM...
DAD, QUICK! THERE'S ONE UP HERE, ON THE CEILING!
GOOD WORK, TESLA. I'D MISSED THAT ONE...
...BUT I WON'T MISS IT TWICE!
D-DAD, THE WAY IT'S THRASHING, IT'S LIKE IT'S IN PAIN.
ARE YOU SURE THEY'RE NOT PROPERLY ALIVE?

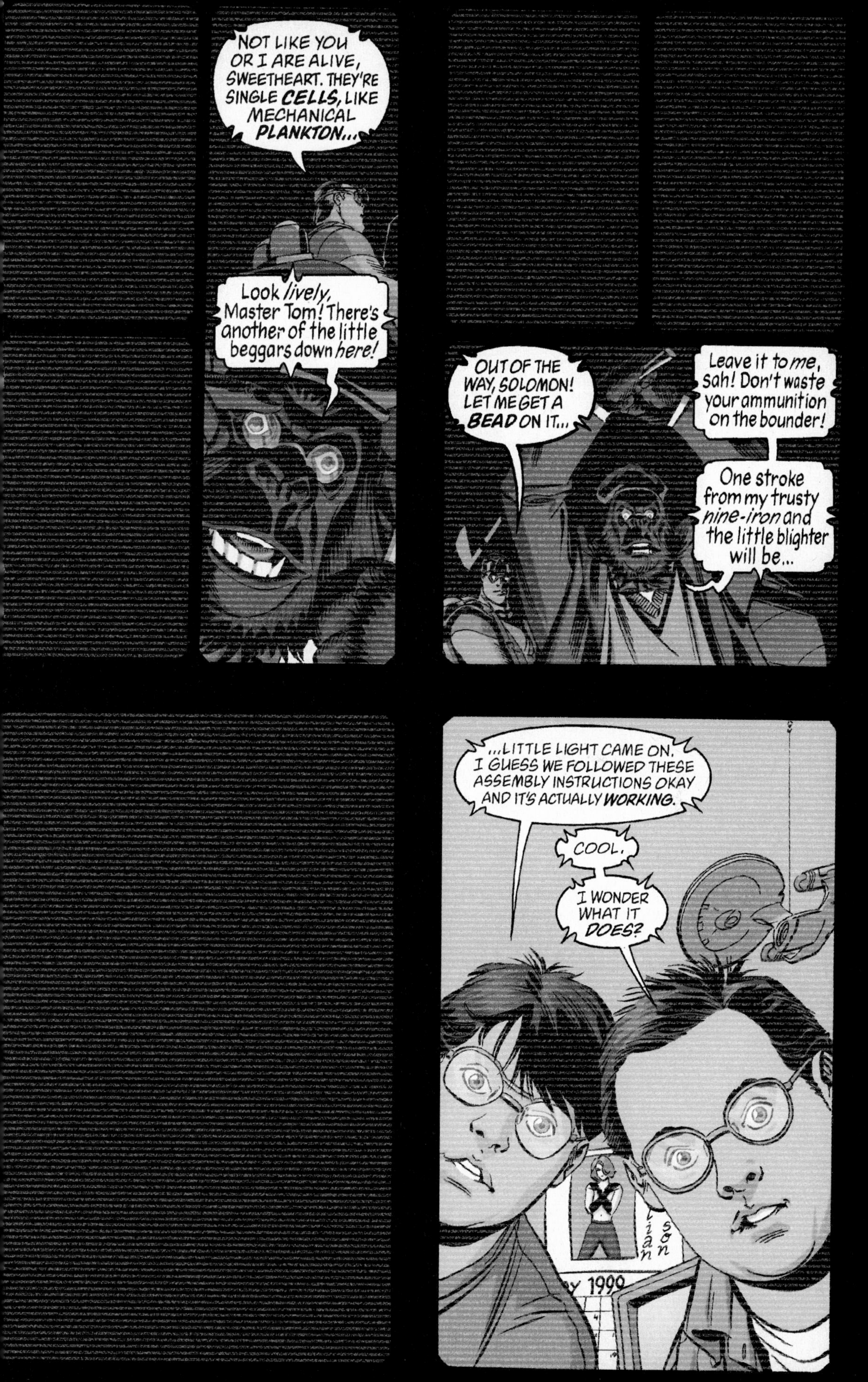
NOT LIKE YOU OR I ARE ALIVE, SWEETHEART. THEY'RE SINGLE CELLS, LIKE MECHANICAL PLANKTON...
Look lively, Master Tom! There's another of the little beggars down here!
OUT OF THE WAY, SOLOMON! LET ME GET A BEAD ON IT...
Leave it to me, sah! Don't waste your ammunition on the bounder!
One stroke from my trusty nine-iron and the little blighter will be...
...LITTLE LIGHT CAME ON. I GUESS WE FOLLOWED THESE ASSEMBLY INSTRUCTIONS OKAY AND IT'S ACTUALLY WORKING.
COOL.
I WONDER WHAT IT DOES?

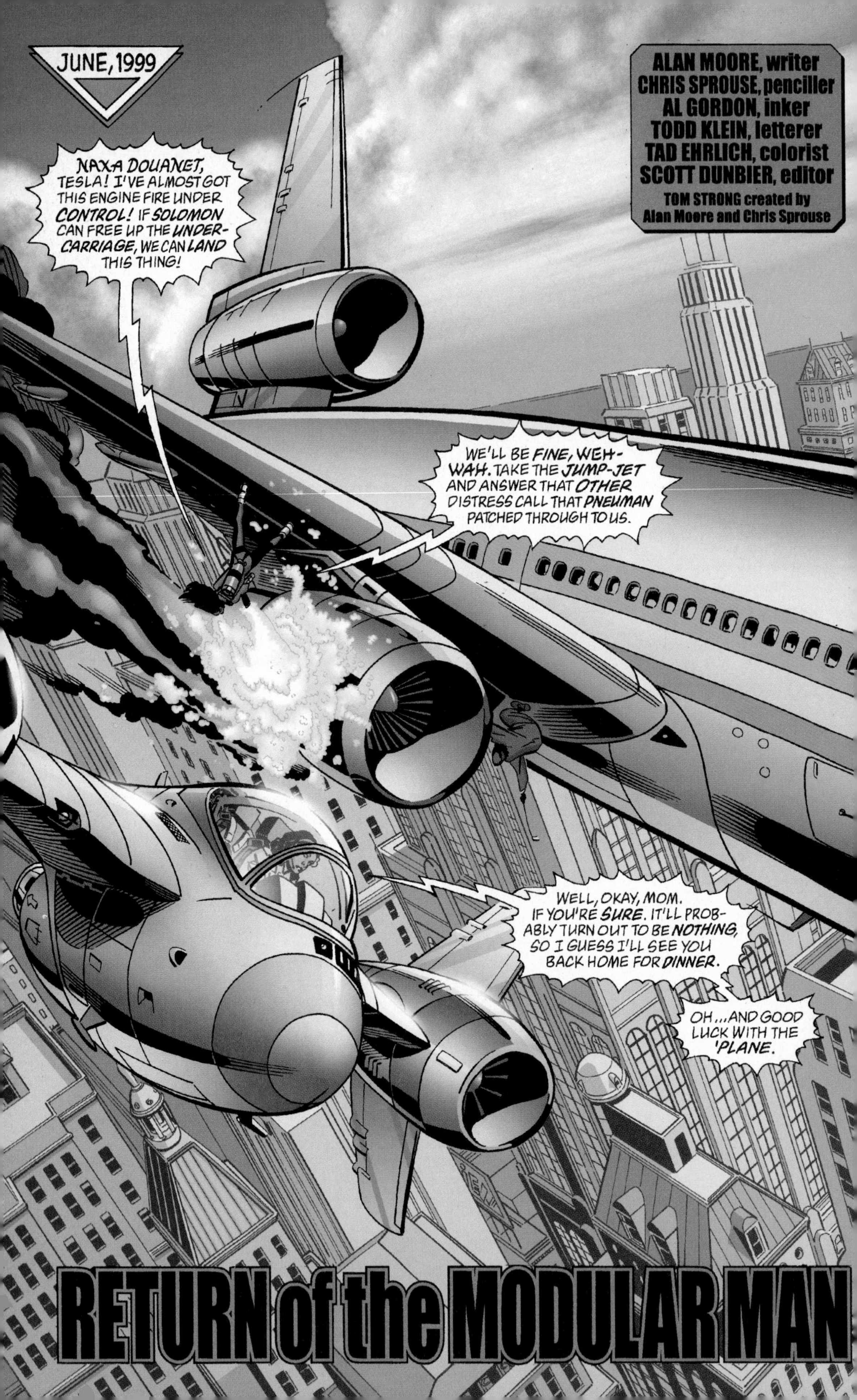
JUNE, 1999
ALAN MOORE, writer
CHRIS SPROUSE, penciller
AL GORDON, inker
TODD KLEIN, letterer
TAD EHRLICH, colorist
SCOTT DUNBIER, editor
TOM STRONG created by Alan Moore and Chris Sprouse
NAXA DOUANET, TESLA! I'VE ALMOST GOT THIS ENGINE FIRE UNDER CONTROL! IF SOLOMON CAN FREE UP THE UNDER-CARRIAGE, WE CAN LAND THIS THING!
WE'LL BE FINE, WEH-WAH. TAKE THE JUMP-JET AND ANSWER THAT OTHER DISTRESS CALL THAT PNEUMAN PATCHED THROUGH TO US.
WELL, OKAY, MOM. IF YOU'RE SURE. IT'LL PROB-ABLY TURN OUT TO BE NOTHING, SO I GUESS I'LL SEE YOU BACK HOME FOR DINNER.
OH... AND GOOD LUCK WITH THE 'PLANE.
RETURN of the MODULAR MAN

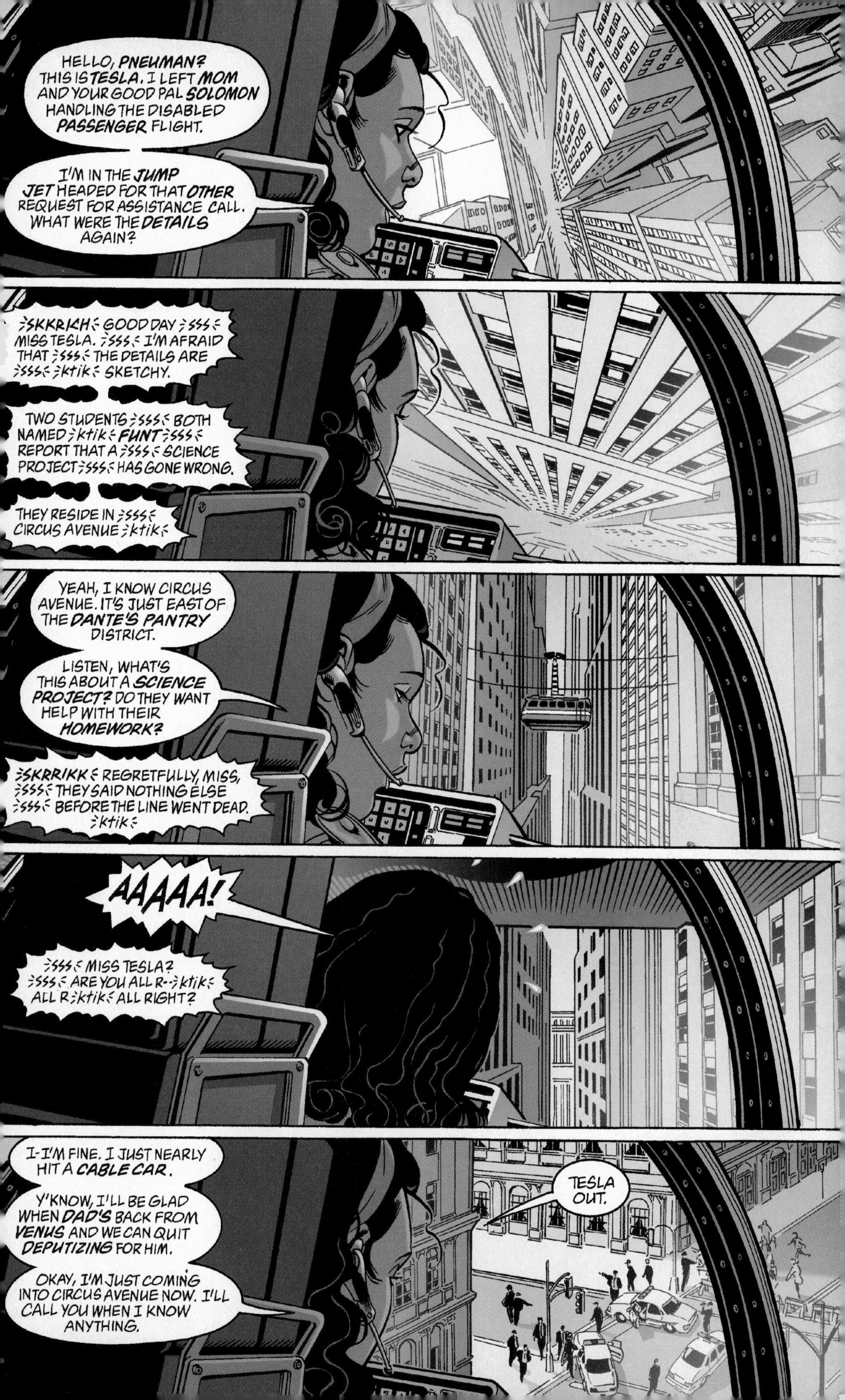
HELLO, PNEUMAN? THIS IS TESLA. I LEFT MOM AND YOUR GOOD PAL SOLOMON HANDLING THE DISABLED PASSENGER FLIGHT.
I'M IN THE JUMP JET HEADED FOR THAT OTHER REQUEST FOR ASSISTANCE CALL. WHAT WERE THE DETAILS AGAIN?
SKKRICH GOOD DAY SSS MISS TESLA. SSS I'M AFRAID THAT SSS THE DETAILS ARE SSSS KTIK SKETCHY.
TWO STUDENTS SSS BOTH NAMED KTIK FUNT SSS REPORT THAT A SSS SCIENCE PROJECT SSS HAS GONE WRONG.
THEY RESIDE IN SSS CIRCUS AVENUE KTIK
YEAH, I KNOW CIRCUS AVENUE. IT'S JUST EAST OF THE DANTE'S PANTRY DISTRICT.
LISTEN, WHAT'S THIS ABOUT A SCIENCE PROJECT? DO THEY WANT HELP WITH THEIR HOMEWORK?
SKRRIKK REGRETFULLY, MISS, SSS THEY SAID NOTHING ELSE SSS BEFORE THE LINE WENT DEAD. KTIK
AAAAA!
SSS MISS TESLA? SSS ARE YOU ALL R-- KTIK ALL R KTIK ALL RIGHT?
I-I'M FINE. I JUST NEARLY HIT A CABLE CAR.
Y'KNOW, I'LL BE GLAD WHEN DAD'S BACK FROM VENUS AND WE CAN QUIT DEPUTIZING FOR HIM.
OKAY, I'M JUST COMING INTO CIRCUS AVENUE NOW. I'LL CALL YOU WHEN I KNOW ANYTHING.
TESLA OUT.

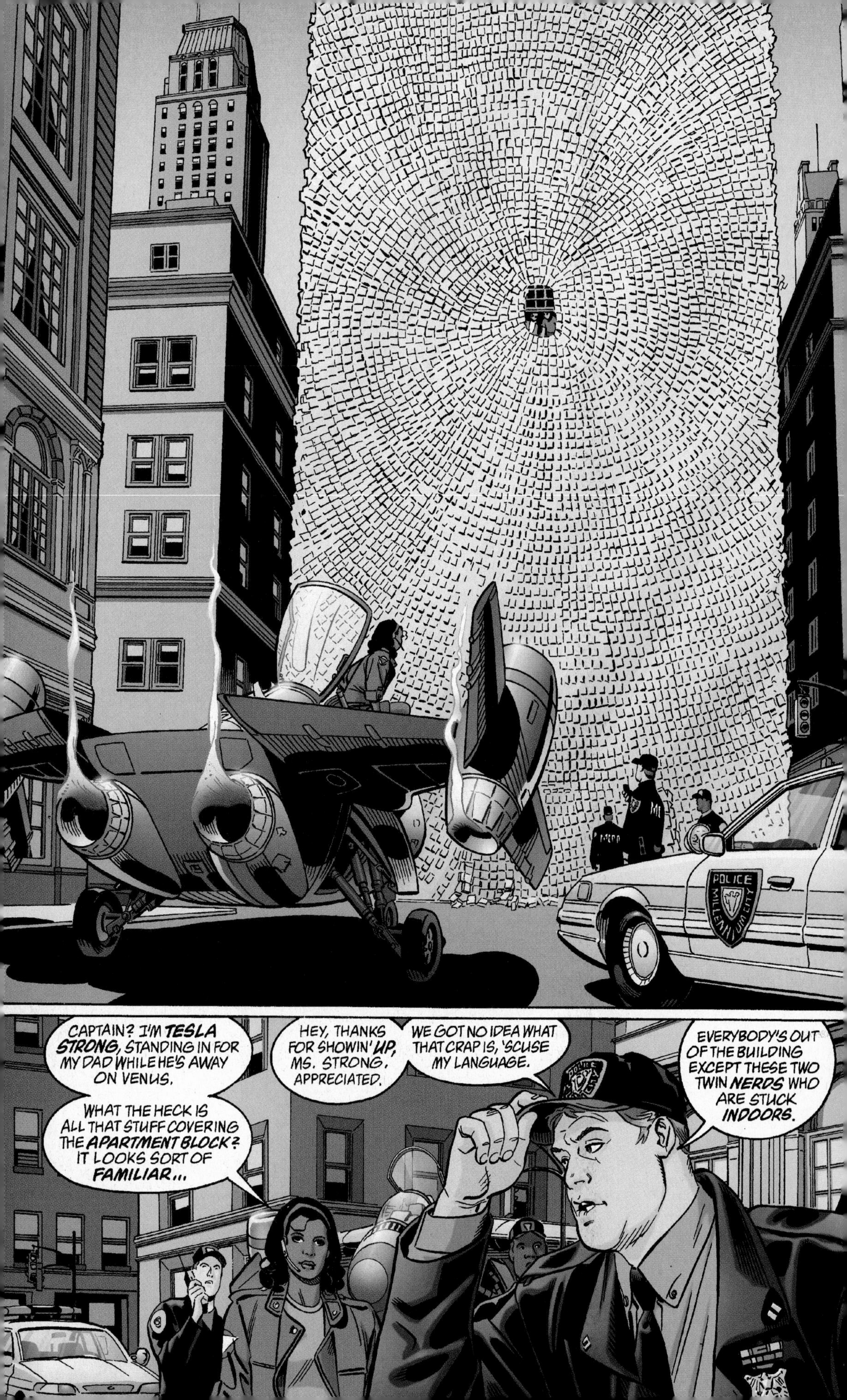
POLICE
CAPTAIN? I'M **TESLA STRONG**, STANDING IN FOR MY DAD WHILE HE'S AWAY ON VENUS.
WHAT THE HECK IS ALL THAT STUFF COVERING THE **APARTMENT BLOCK**? IT LOOKS SORT OF **FAMILIAR...**
HEY, THANKS FOR SHOWIN' **UP**, MS. STRONG. APPRECIATED.
WE GOT NO IDEA WHAT THAT CRAP IS, 'SCUSE MY LANGUAGE.
EVERYBODY'S OUT OF THE BUILDING EXCEPT THESE TWO TWIN **NERDS** WHO ARE STUCK **INDOORS**.

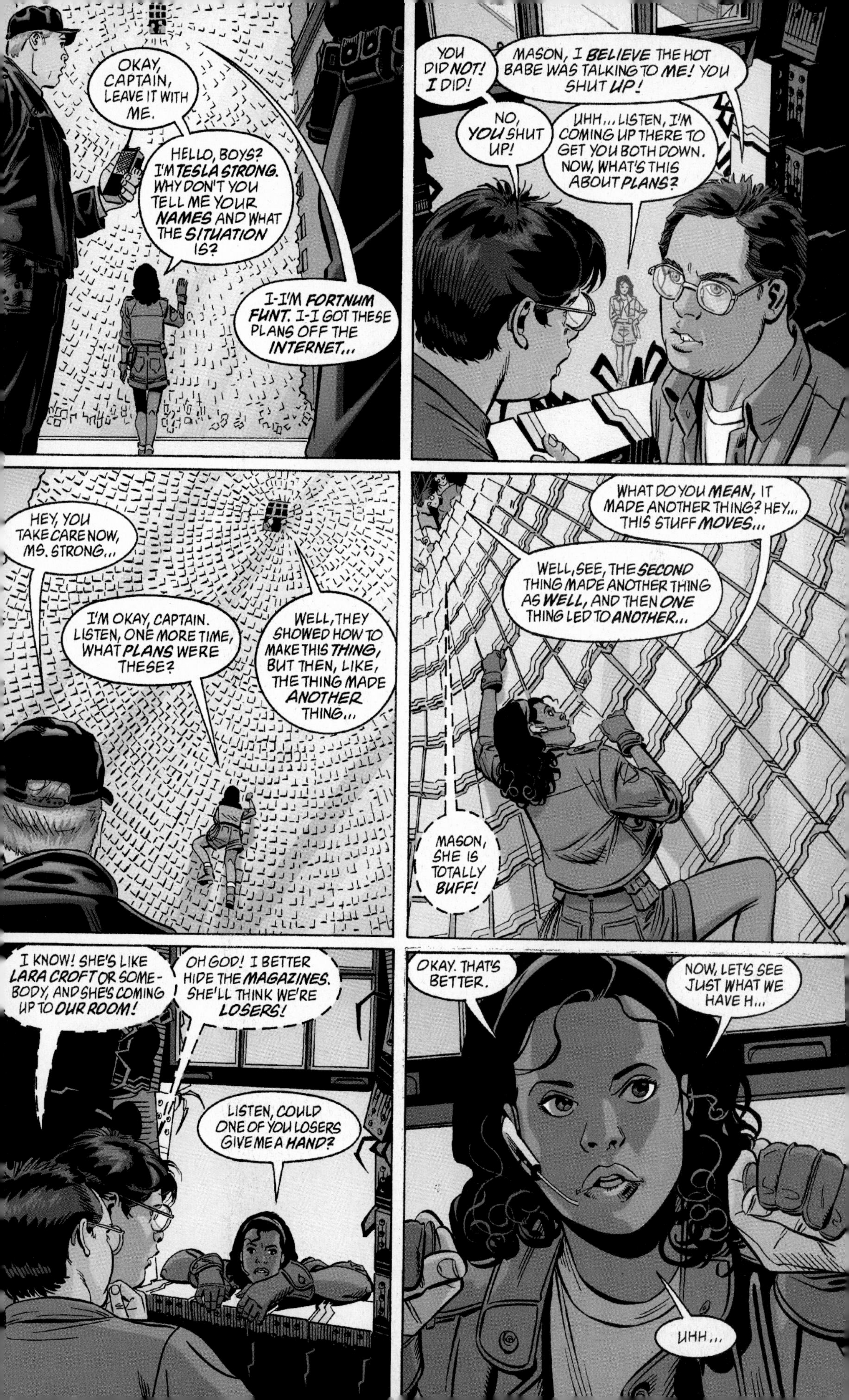
OKAY, CAPTAIN, LEAVE IT WITH ME.
HELLO, BOYS? I'M TESLA STRONG. WHY DON'T YOU TELL ME YOUR NAMES AND WHAT THE SITUATION IS?
I-I'M FORTNUM FUNT. I-I GOT THESE PLANS OFF THE INTERNET...
YOU DID NOT! I DID!
MASON, I BELIEVE THE HOT BABE WAS TALKING TO ME! YOU SHUT UP!
NO, YOU SHUT UP!
UHH... LISTEN, I'M COMING UP THERE TO GET YOU BOTH DOWN. NOW, WHAT'S THIS ABOUT PLANS?
HEY, YOU TAKE CARE NOW, MS. STRONG...
I'M OKAY, CAPTAIN. LISTEN, ONE MORE TIME, WHAT PLANS WERE THESE?
WELL, THEY SHOWED HOW TO MAKE THIS THING, BUT THEN, LIKE, THE THING MADE ANOTHER THING...
WHAT DO YOU MEAN, IT MADE ANOTHER THING? HEY... THIS STUFF MOVES...
WELL, SEE, THE SECOND THING MADE ANOTHER THING AS WELL, AND THEN ONE THING LED TO ANOTHER...
MASON, SHE IS TOTALLY BUFF!
I KNOW! SHE'S LIKE LARA CROFT OR SOMEBODY, AND SHE'S COMING UP TO OUR ROOM!
OH GOD! I BETTER HIDE THE MAGAZINES. SHE'LL THINK WE'RE LOSERS!
LISTEN, COULD ONE OF YOU LOSERS GIVE ME A HAND?
OKAY. THAT'S BETTER.
NOW, LET'S SEE JUST WHAT WE HAVE H...
UHH...

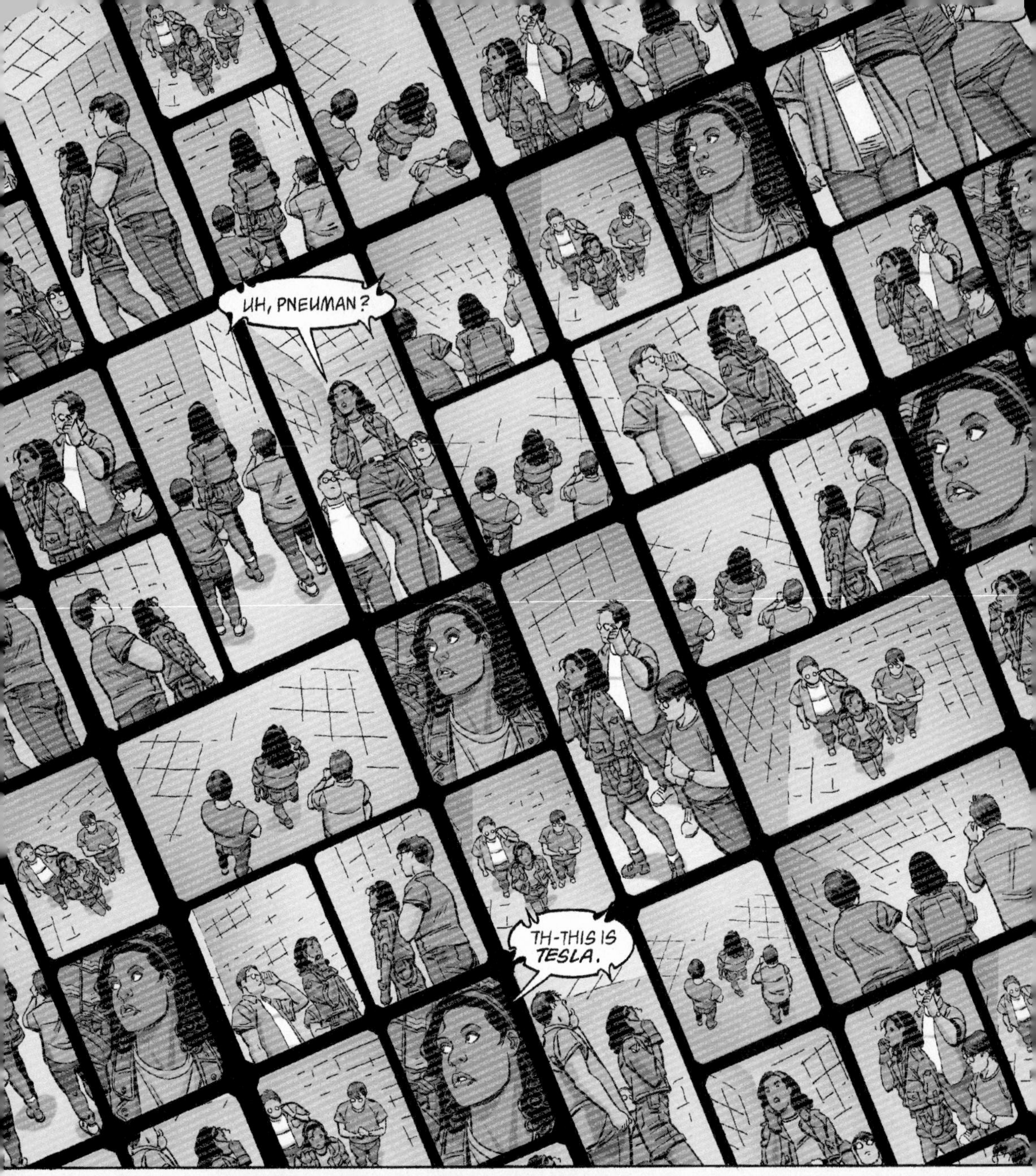
UH, PNEUMAN?
TH-THIS IS TESLA.

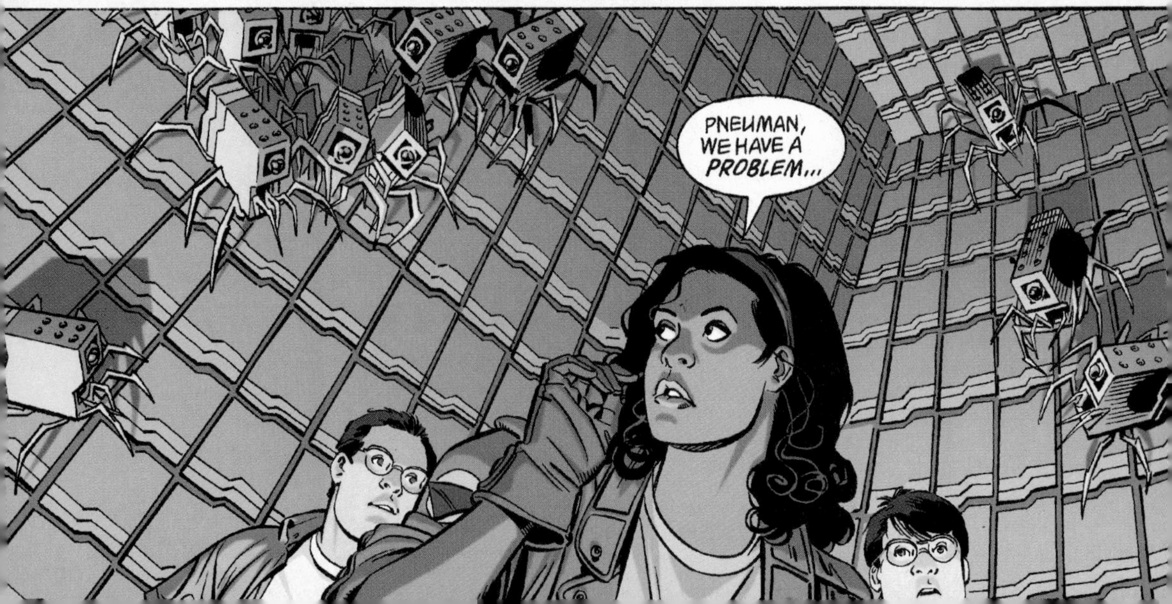
PNEUMAN, WE HAVE A PROBLEM...

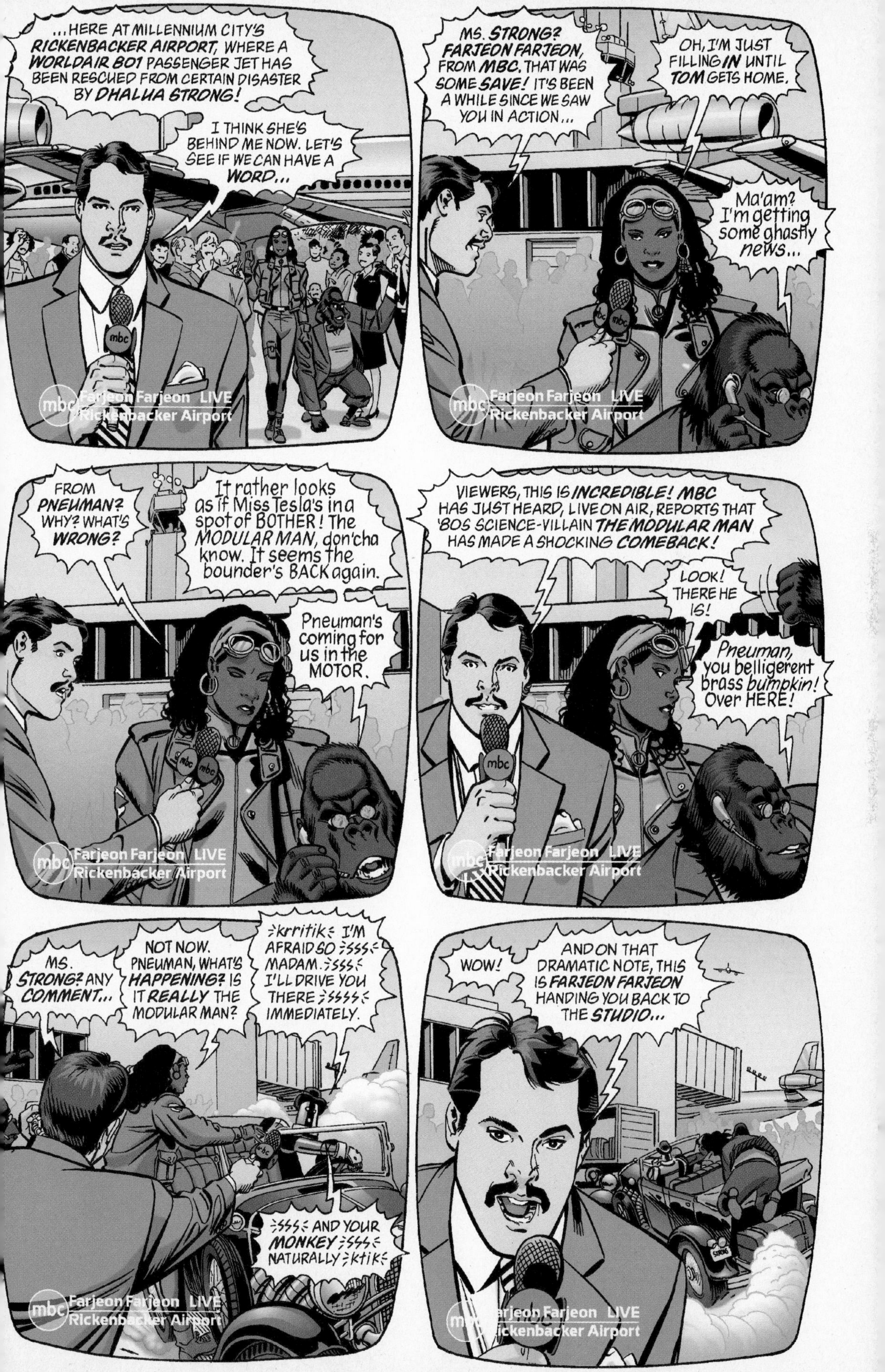
...HERE AT MILLENNIUM CITY'S RICKENBACKER AIRPORT, WHERE A WORLDAIR 801 PASSENGER JET HAS BEEN RESCUED FROM CERTAIN DISASTER BY DHALUA STRONG!
I THINK SHE'S BEHIND ME NOW. LET'S SEE IF WE CAN HAVE A WORD...
mbc Farjeon Farjeon LIVE Rickenbacker Airport
MS. STRONG? FARJEON FARJEON, FROM MBC. THAT WAS SOME SAVE! IT'S BEEN A WHILE SINCE WE SAW YOU IN ACTION...
OH, I'M JUST FILLING IN UNTIL TOM GETS HOME.
Ma'am? I'm getting some ghastly news...
mbc Farjeon Farjeon LIVE Rickenbacker Airport
FROM PNEUMAN? WHY? WHAT'S WRONG?
It rather looks as if Miss Tesla's in a spot of BOTHER! The MODULAR MAN, don'cha know. It seems the bounder's BACK again.
Pneuman's coming for us in the MOTOR.
mbc Farjeon Farjeon LIVE Rickenbacker Airport
VIEWERS, THIS IS INCREDIBLE! MBC HAS JUST HEARD, LIVE ON AIR, REPORTS THAT '80S SCIENCE-VILLAIN THE MODULAR MAN HAS MADE A SHOCKING COMEBACK!
LOOK! THERE HE IS!
Pneuman, you belligerent brass bumpkin! Over HERE!
mbc Farjeon Farjeon LIVE Rickenbacker Airport
MS. STRONG? ANY COMMENT...
NOT NOW. PNEUMAN, WHAT'S HAPPENING? IS IT REALLY THE MODULAR MAN?
krritik I'M AFRAID SO sss MADAM. sss I'LL DRIVE YOU THERE sssss IMMEDIATELY.
sss AND YOUR MONKEY sss NATURALLY ktik
mbc Farjeon Farjeon LIVE Rickenbacker Airport
WOW!
AND ON THAT DRAMATIC NOTE, THIS IS FARJEON FARJEON HANDING YOU BACK TO THE STUDIO...
mbc Farjeon Farjeon LIVE Rickenbacker Airport

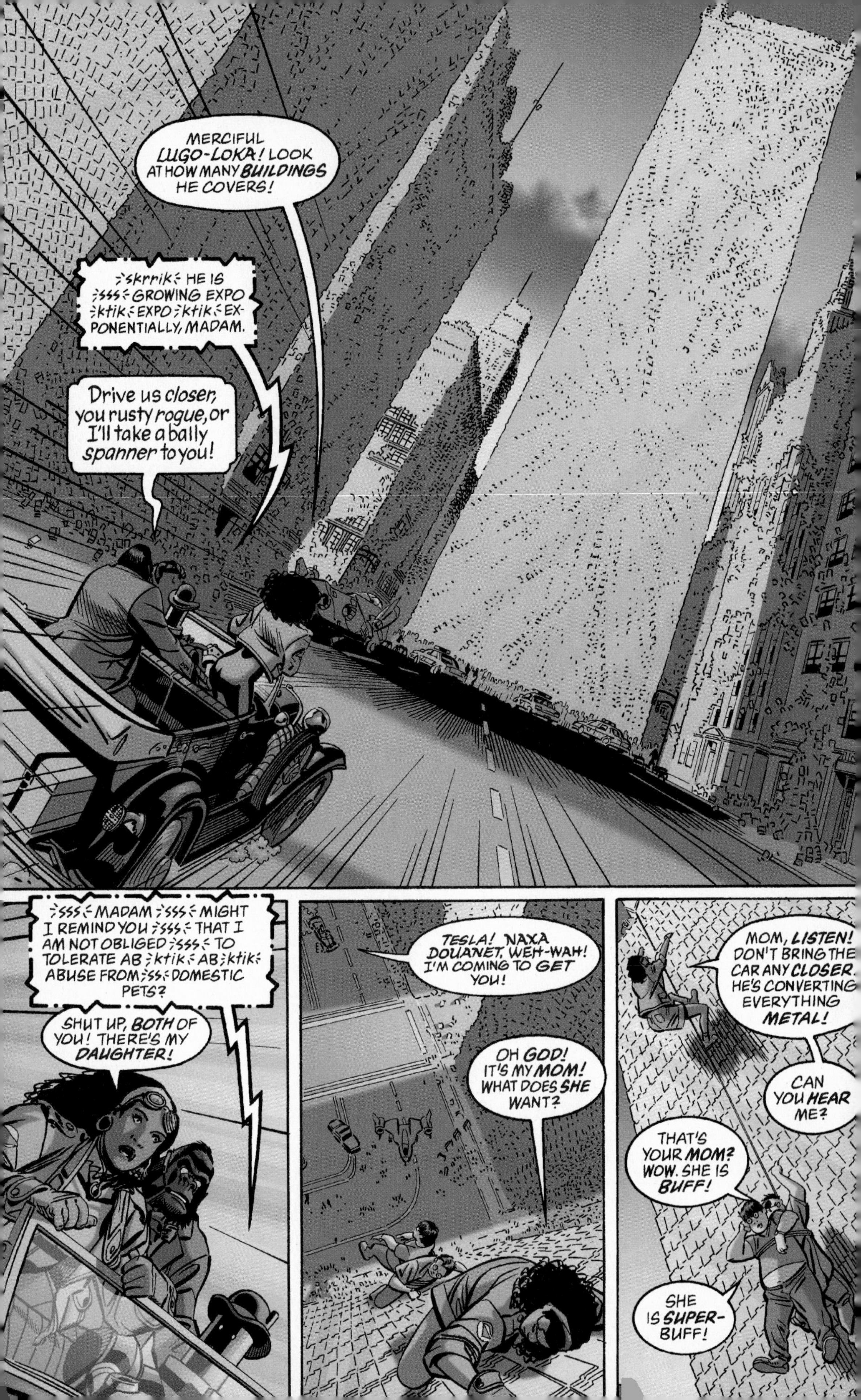
MERCIFUL LUGO-LOKA! LOOK AT HOW MANY BUILDINGS HE COVERS!
skrrik HE IS *sss* GROWING EXPO *ktik* EXPO *ktik* EXPONENTIALLY, MADAM.
Drive us closer, you rusty rogue, or I'll take a bally spanner to you!
sss MADAM *sss* MIGHT I REMIND YOU *sss* THAT I AM NOT OBLIGED *sss* TO TOLERATE AB *ktik* AB *ktik* ABUSE FROM *ss* DOMESTIC PETS?
SHUT UP, BOTH OF YOU! THERE'S MY DAUGHTER!
TESLA! NAXA DOUANET, WEH-WAH! I'M COMING TO GET YOU!
OH GOD! IT'S MY MOM! WHAT DOES SHE WANT?
MOM, LISTEN! DON'T BRING THE CAR ANY CLOSER. HE'S CONVERTING EVERYTHING METAL!
CAN YOU HEAR ME?
THAT'S YOUR MOM? WOW. SHE IS BUFF!
SHE IS SUPER-BUFF!

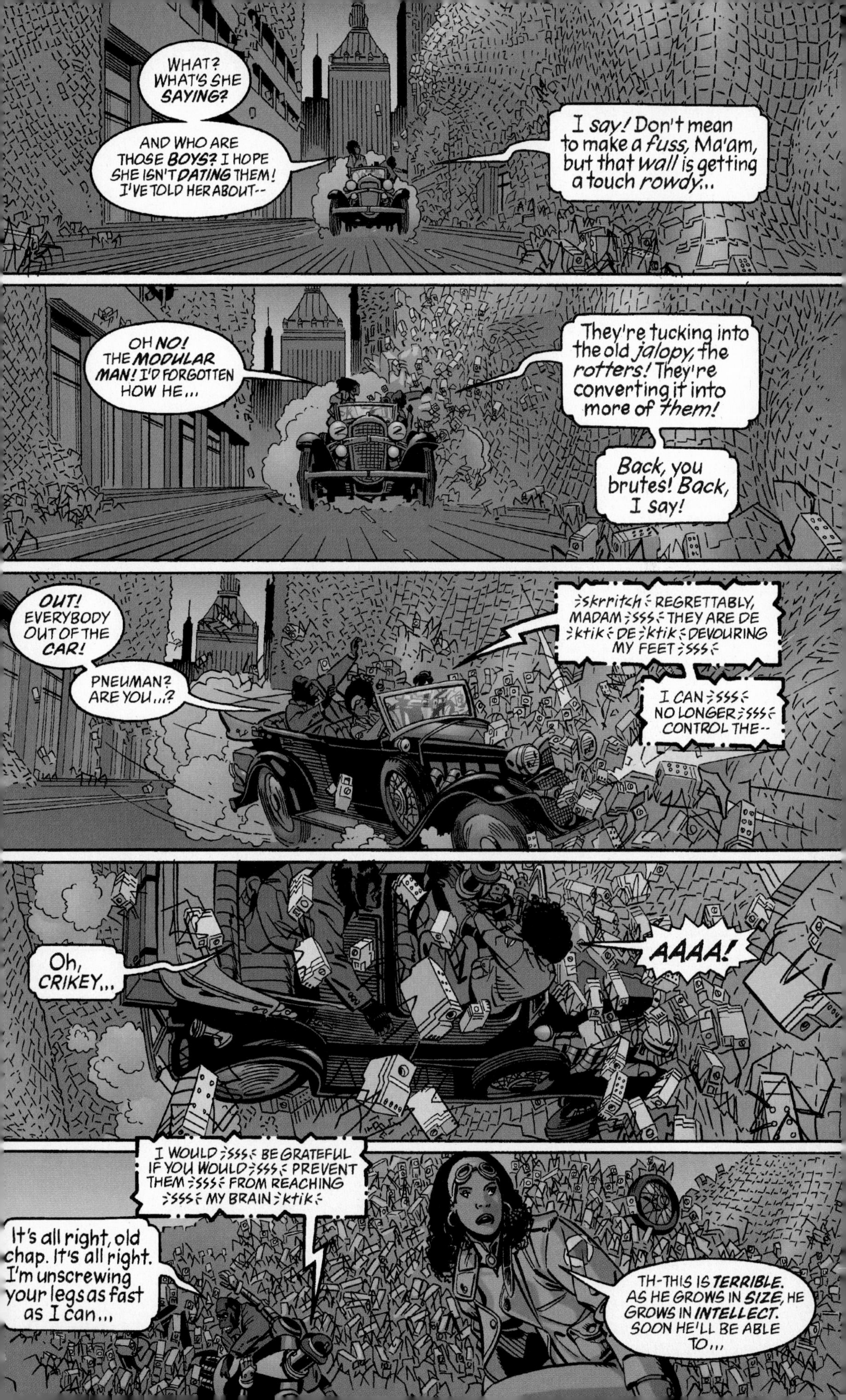

WHAT? WHAT'S SHE SAYING?
AND WHO ARE THOSE BOYS? I HOPE SHE ISN'T DATING THEM! I'VE TOLD HER ABOUT--
I say! Don't mean to make a fuss, Ma'am, but that wall is getting a touch rowdy...
OH NO! THE MODULAR MAN! I'D FORGOTTEN HOW HE...
They're tucking into the old jalopy, the rotters! They're converting it into more of them!
Back, you brutes! Back, I say!
OUT! EVERYBODY OUT OF THE CAR!
PNEUMAN? ARE YOU...?
skrritch REGRETTABLY, MADAM sss THEY ARE DE ktik DE ktik DEVOURING MY FEET sss
I CAN sss NO LONGER sss CONTROL THE--
Oh, CRIKEY...
AAAA!
I WOULD sss BE GRATEFUL IF YOU WOULD sss PREVENT THEM sss FROM REACHING sss MY BRAIN ktik
It's all right, old chap. It's all right. I'm unscrewing your legs as fast as I can...
TH-THIS IS TERRIBLE. AS HE GROWS IN SIZE, HE GROWS IN INTELLECT. SOON HE'LL BE ABLE TO...

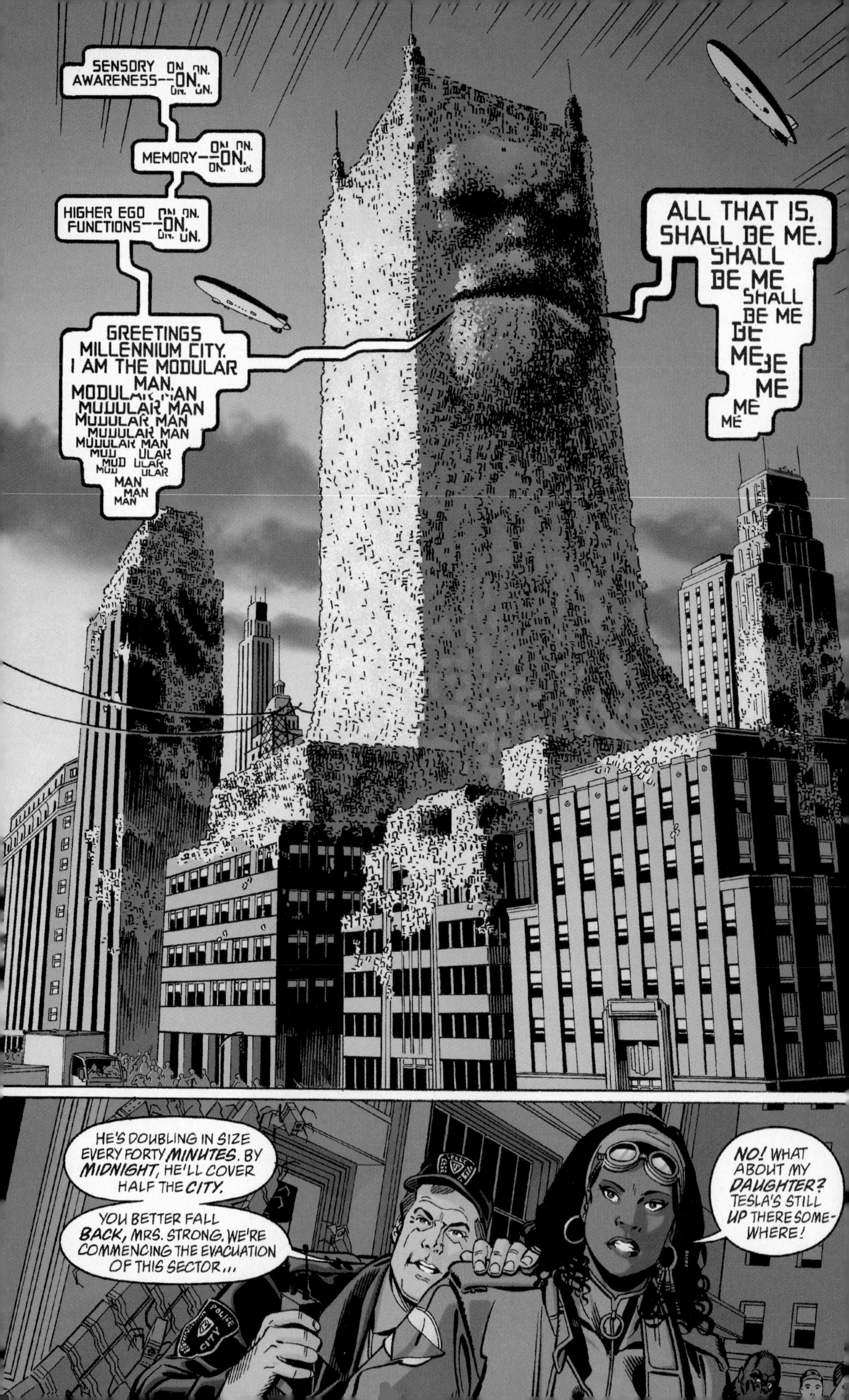
SENSORY AWARENESS--ON. ON. ON. ON. ON.
MEMORY--ON. ON. ON. ON. ON.
HIGHER EGO FUNCTIONS--ON. ON. ON. ON. ON.
GREETINGS MILLENNIUM CITY. I AM THE MODULAR MAN. MODULAR MAN MODULAR MAN MODULAR MAN MODULAR MAN MODULAR MAN MOD ULAR MOD ULAR MOD ULAR MAN MAN MAN
ALL THAT IS, SHALL BE ME. SHALL BE ME SHALL BE ME BE ME BE ME ME ME ME
HE'S DOUBLING IN SIZE EVERY FORTY MINUTES. BY MIDNIGHT, HE'LL COVER HALF THE CITY.
YOU BETTER FALL BACK, MRS. STRONG. WE'RE COMMENCING THE EVACUATION OF THIS SECTOR...
NO! WHAT ABOUT MY DAUGHTER? TESLA'S STILL UP THERE SOME-WHERE!
POLICE
CITY

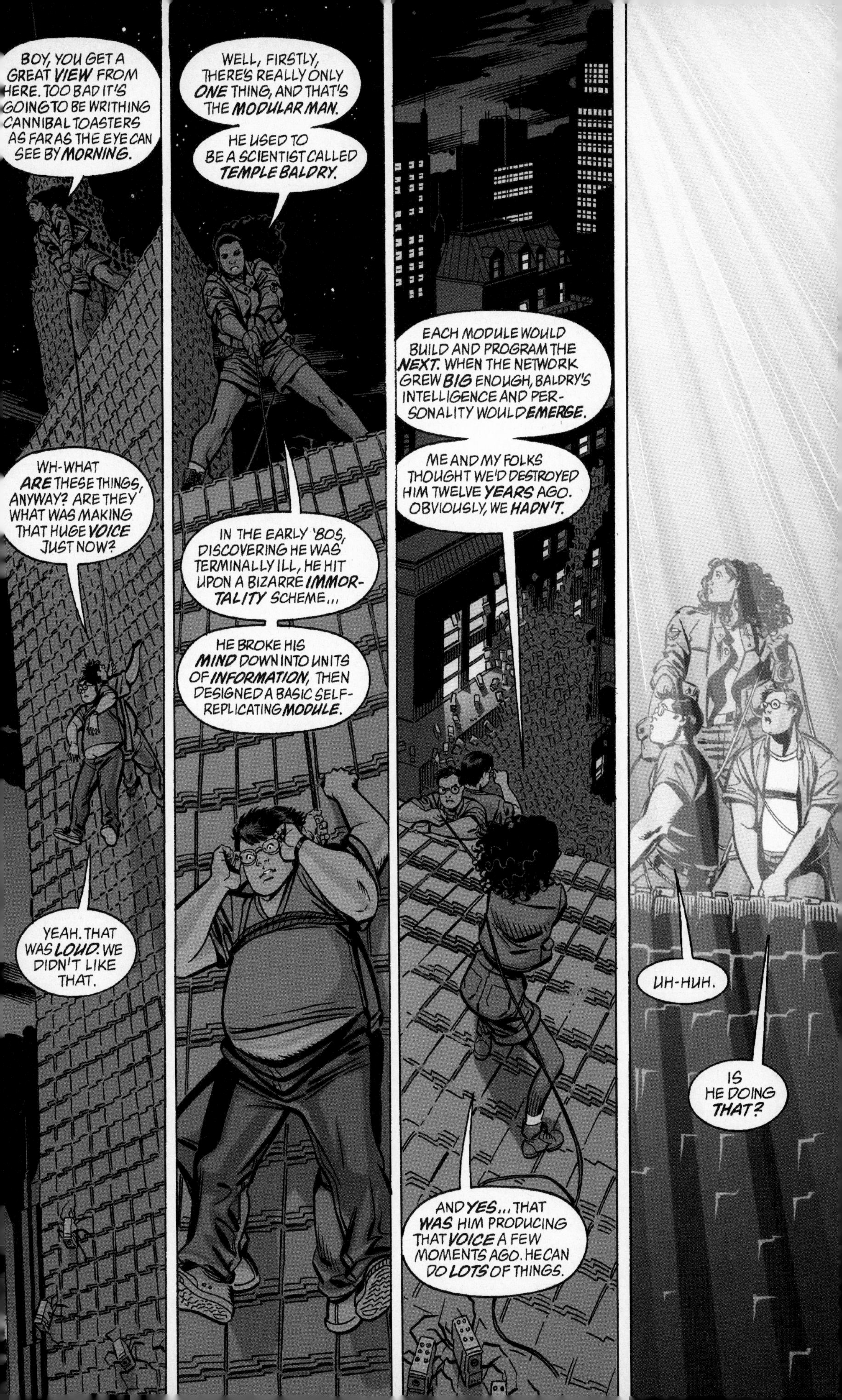
BOY, YOU GET A GREAT VIEW FROM HERE. TOO BAD IT'S GOING TO BE WRITHING CANNIBAL TOASTERS AS FAR AS THE EYE CAN SEE BY MORNING.
WH-WHAT ARE THESE THINGS, ANYWAY? ARE THEY WHAT WAS MAKING THAT HUGE VOICE JUST NOW?
YEAH. THAT WAS LOUD. WE DIDN'T LIKE THAT.
WELL, FIRSTLY, THERE'S REALLY ONLY ONE THING, AND THAT'S THE MODULAR MAN.
HE USED TO BE A SCIENTIST CALLED TEMPLE BALDRY.
IN THE EARLY '80S, DISCOVERING HE WAS TERMINALLY ILL, HE HIT UPON A BIZARRE IMMORTALITY SCHEME...
HE BROKE HIS MIND DOWN INTO UNITS OF INFORMATION, THEN DESIGNED A BASIC SELF-REPLICATING MODULE.
EACH MODULE WOULD BUILD AND PROGRAM THE NEXT. WHEN THE NETWORK GREW BIG ENOUGH, BALDRY'S INTELLIGENCE AND PERSONALITY WOULD EMERGE.
ME AND MY FOLKS THOUGHT WE'D DESTROYED HIM TWELVE YEARS AGO. OBVIOUSLY, WE HADN'T.
AND YES... THAT WAS HIM PRODUCING THAT VOICE A FEW MOMENTS AGO. HE CAN DO LOTS OF THINGS.
UH-HUH.
IS HE DOING THAT?

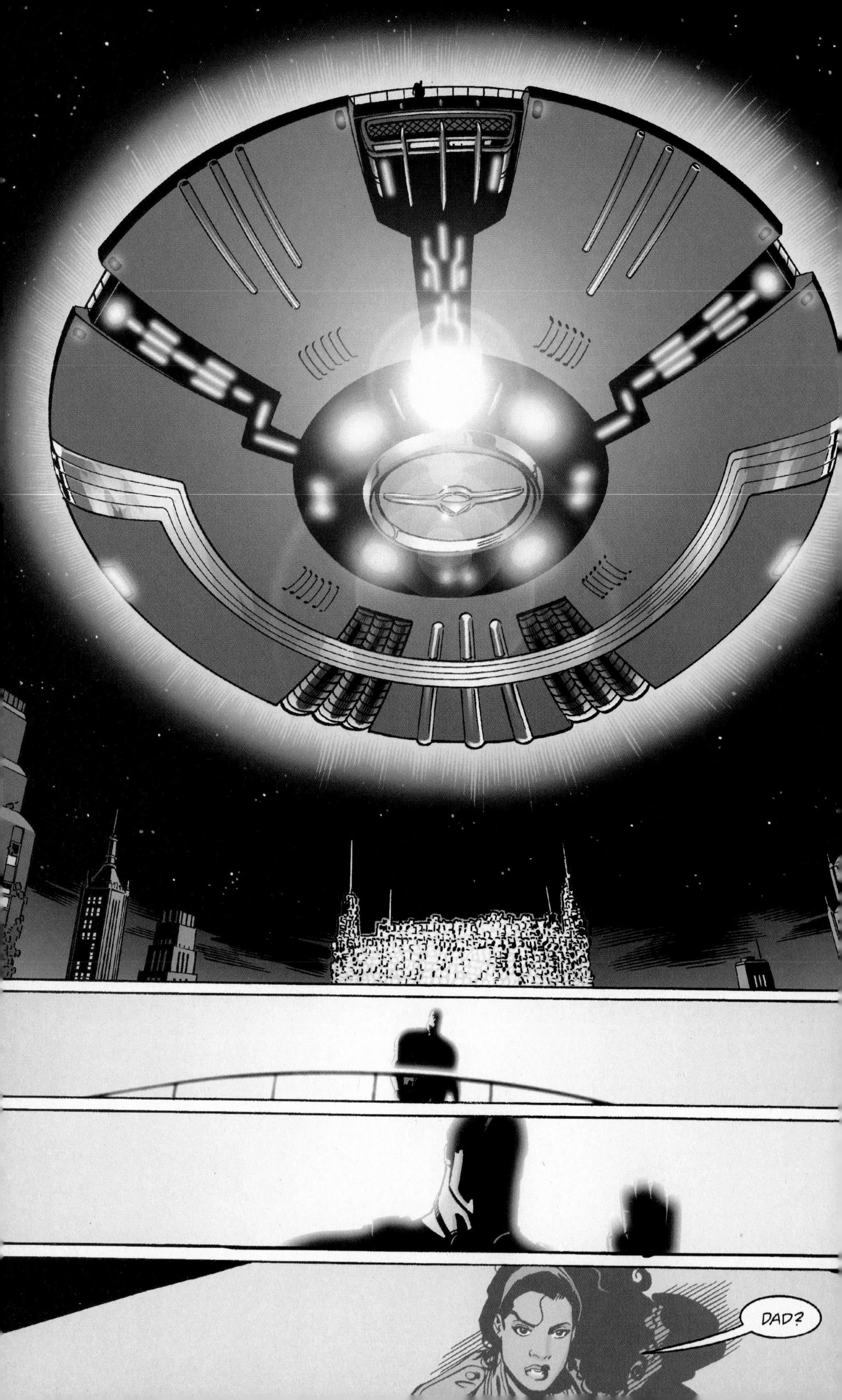
DAD?

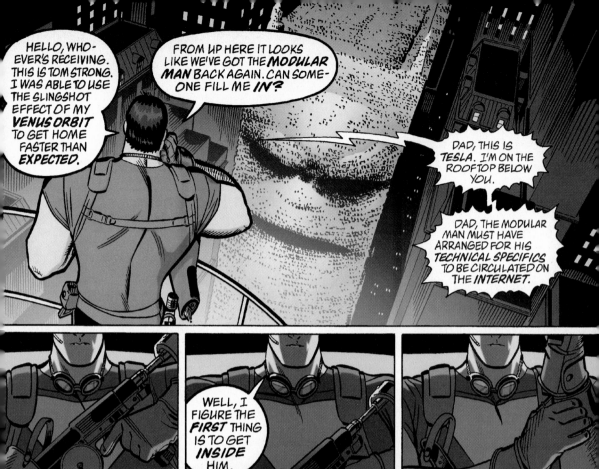

HELLO, WHO-EVER'S RECEIVING. THIS IS TOM STRONG. I WAS ABLE TO USE THE SLINGSHOT EFFECT OF MY VENUS ORBIT TO GET HOME FASTER THAN EXPECTED.

FROM UP HERE IT LOOKS LIKE WE'VE GOT THE MODULAR MAN BACK AGAIN. CAN SOME-ONE FILL ME IN?

DAD, THIS IS TESLA. I'M ON THE ROOFTOP BELOW YOU.

DAD, THE MODULAR MAN MUST HAVE ARRANGED FOR HIS TECHNICAL SPECIFICS TO BE CIRCULATED ON THE INTERNET.

UH-HUH. SO SOMEBODY BUILT ONE AND IT GREW FROM THERE?

PRETTY MUCH. WHAT ARE YOU GOING TO DO?

WELL, I FIGURE THE FIRST THING IS TO GET INSIDE HIM.

BLOWING HIM TO BITS FROM OUT-SIDE LIKE LAST TIME WON'T WORK HERE.

BUT HOW WILL YOU GET IN? YOU CAN'T RISK BRINGING THE HYPERSAUCER ANY CLOSER.

DON'T WORRY, BEAUTIFUL. I HAVE MY GRAPPLE-GUN.

DAD, THAT'S THE SAME GRAPPLE-GUN YOU'VE HAD SINCE THE FIFTIES! WHAT IF IT JAMS?

IT WON'T. NOW, YOU GET CLEAR OF THAT ROOFTOP...

...AND LEAVE THE REST TO ME.

LISTEN, THAT'S QUITE A DROP. MAKE SURE YOU TIME IT RIGHT, HUH, DAD?

DAD?

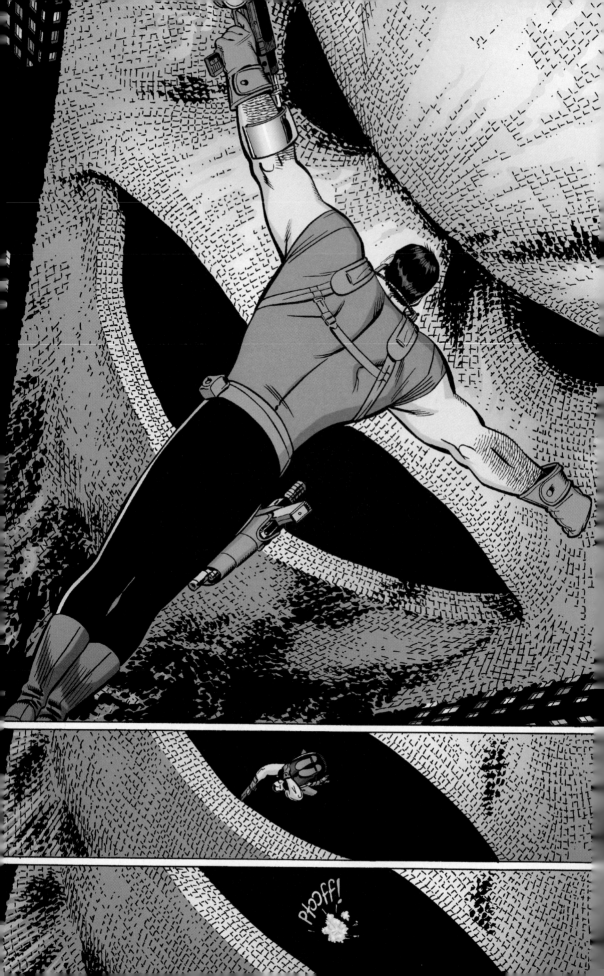

PtOOFF!

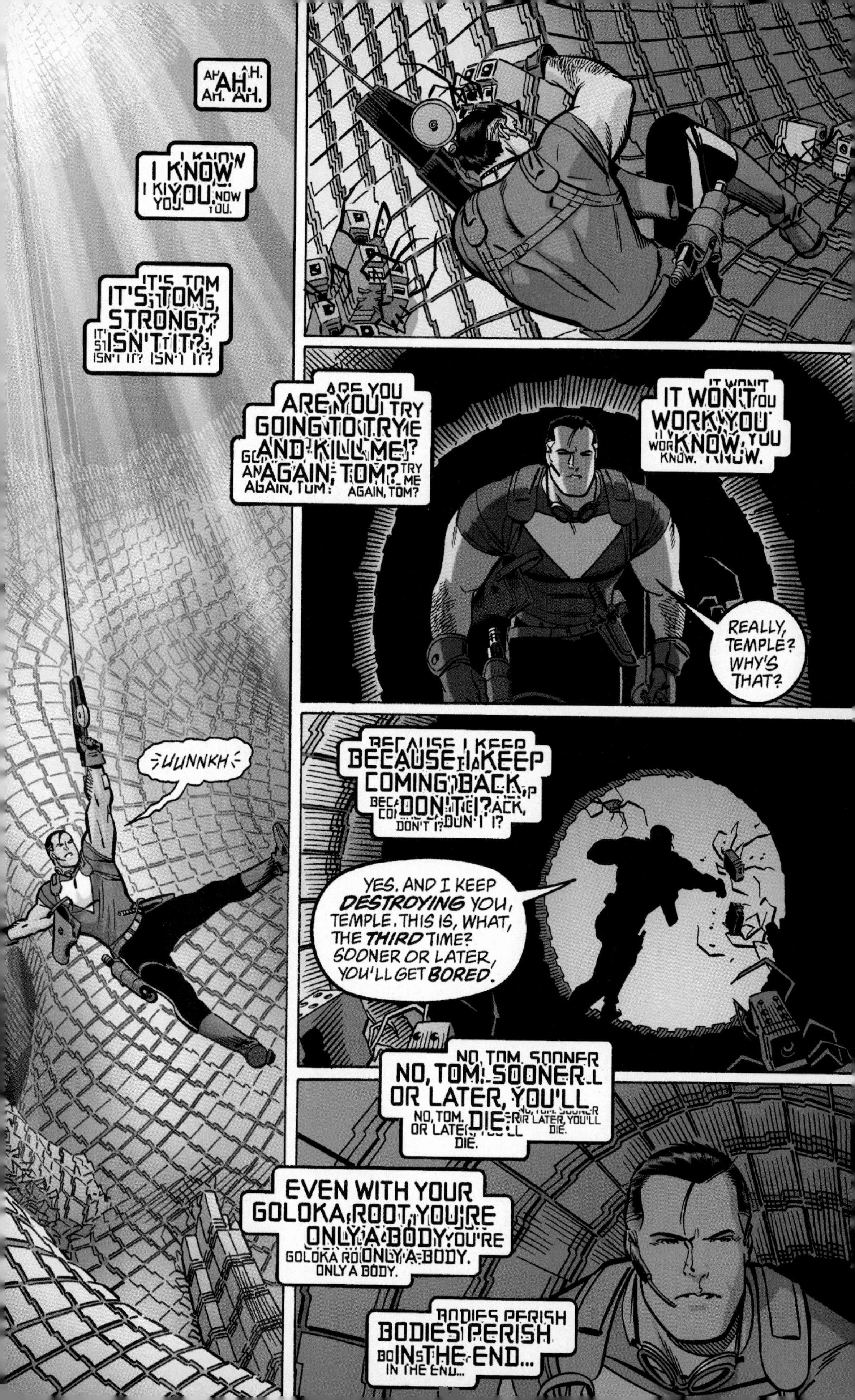

AH. AH. AH.
I KNOW YOU.
IT'S TOM STRONG, ISN'T IT?
ARE YOU GOING TO TRY AND KILL ME AGAIN, TOM?
IT WON'T WORK, YOU KNOW.
REALLY, TEMPLE? WHY'S THAT?
UUNNKH
BECAUSE I KEEP COMING BACK, DON'T I?
YES. AND I KEEP DESTROYING YOU, TEMPLE. THIS IS, WHAT, THE THIRD TIME? SOONER OR LATER, YOU'LL GET BORED.
NO, TOM. SOONER OR LATER, YOU'LL DIE.
EVEN WITH YOUR GOLOKA ROOT, YOU'RE ONLY A BODY.
BODIES PERISH IN THE END...

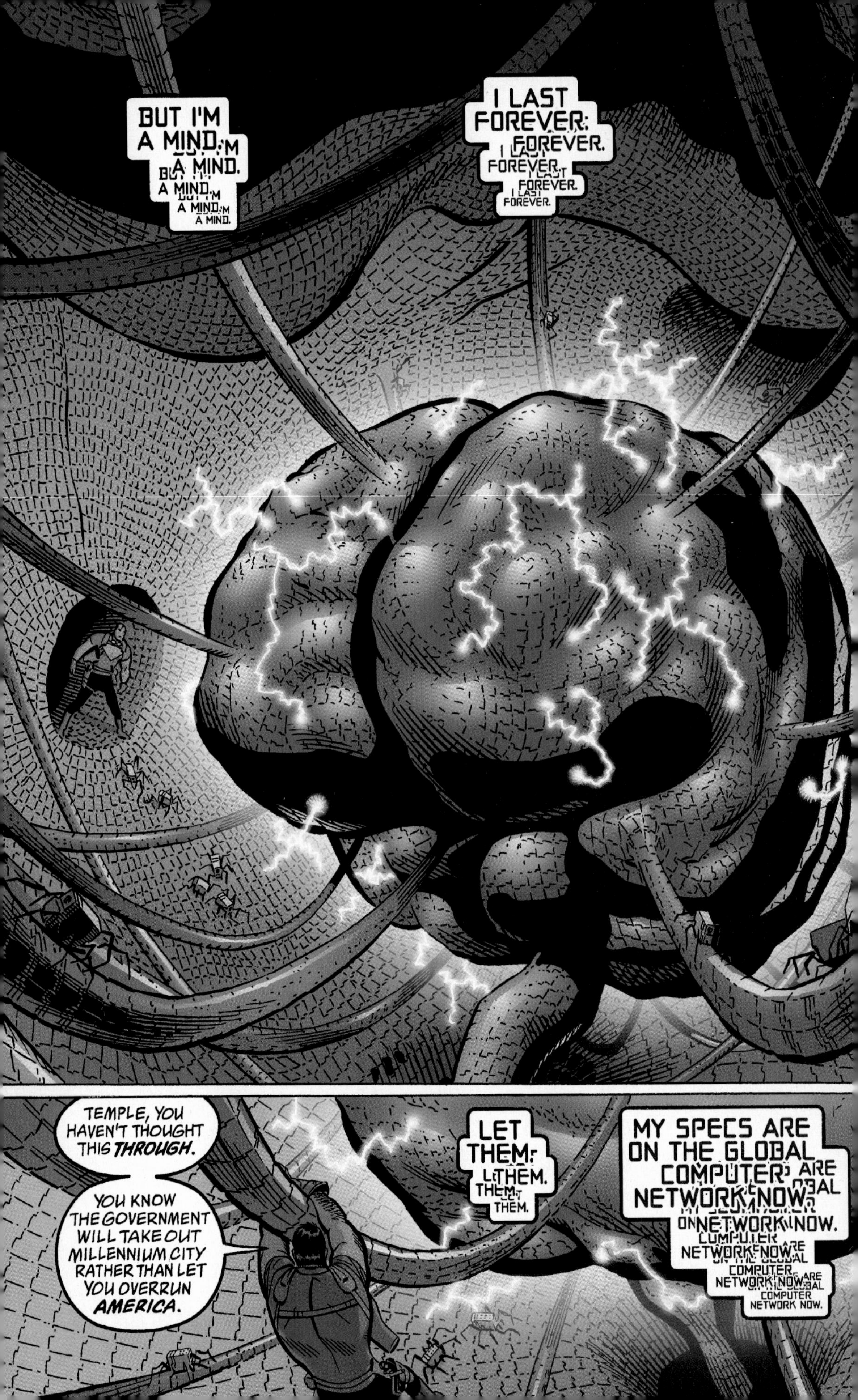

BUT I'M A MIND.
A MIND.
A MIND.
A MIND.
A MIND.
I LAST FOREVER.
FOREVER.
FOREVER.
FOREVER.
I LAST FOREVER.
TEMPLE, YOU HAVEN'T THOUGHT THIS THROUGH.
YOU KNOW THE GOVERNMENT WILL TAKE OUT MILLENNIUM CITY RATHER THAN LET YOU OVERRUN AMERICA.
LET THEM.
THEM.
THEM.
THEM.
MY SPECS ARE ON THE GLOBAL COMPUTER NETWORK NOW.
NETWORK NOW.
NETWORK NOW.
COMPUTER NETWORK NOW.
COMPUTER NETWORK NOW.

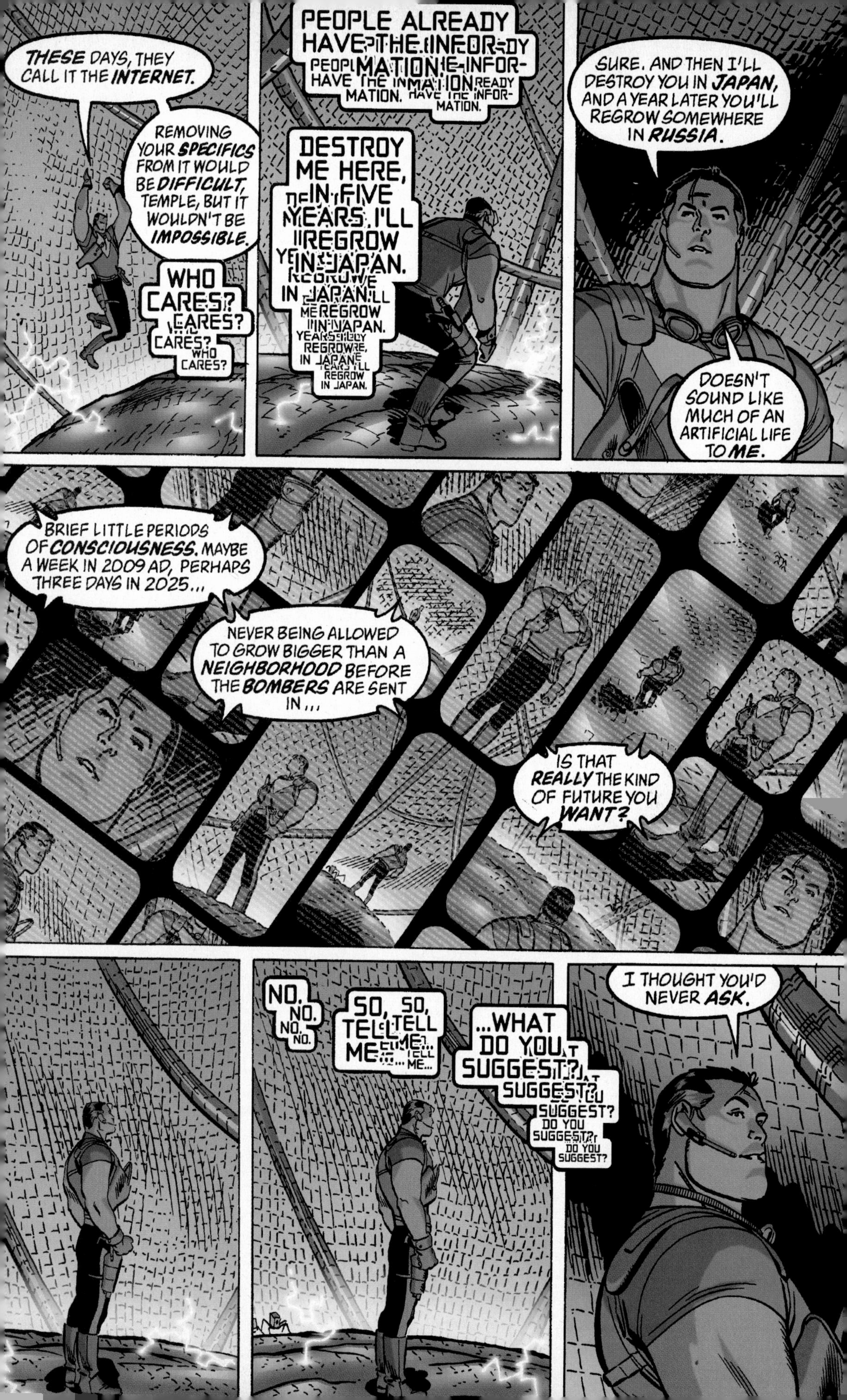
THESE DAYS, THEY CALL IT THE INTERNET.
REMOVING YOUR SPECIFICS FROM IT WOULD BE DIFFICULT, TEMPLE, BUT IT WOULDN'T BE IMPOSSIBLE.
WHO CARES?
PEOPLE ALREADY HAVE THE INFORMATION.
DESTROY ME HERE, IN FIVE YEARS I'LL REGROW IN JAPAN.
SURE. AND THEN I'LL DESTROY YOU IN JAPAN, AND A YEAR LATER YOU'LL REGROW SOMEWHERE IN RUSSIA.
DOESN'T SOUND LIKE MUCH OF AN ARTIFICIAL LIFE TO ME.
BRIEF LITTLE PERIODS OF CONSCIOUSNESS. MAYBE A WEEK IN 2009 AD, PERHAPS THREE DAYS IN 2025...
NEVER BEING ALLOWED TO GROW BIGGER THAN A NEIGHBORHOOD BEFORE THE BOMBERS ARE SENT IN...
IS THAT REALLY THE KIND OF FUTURE YOU WANT?
NO.
SO, TELL ME...
...WHAT DO YOU SUGGEST?
I THOUGHT YOU'D NEVER ASK.

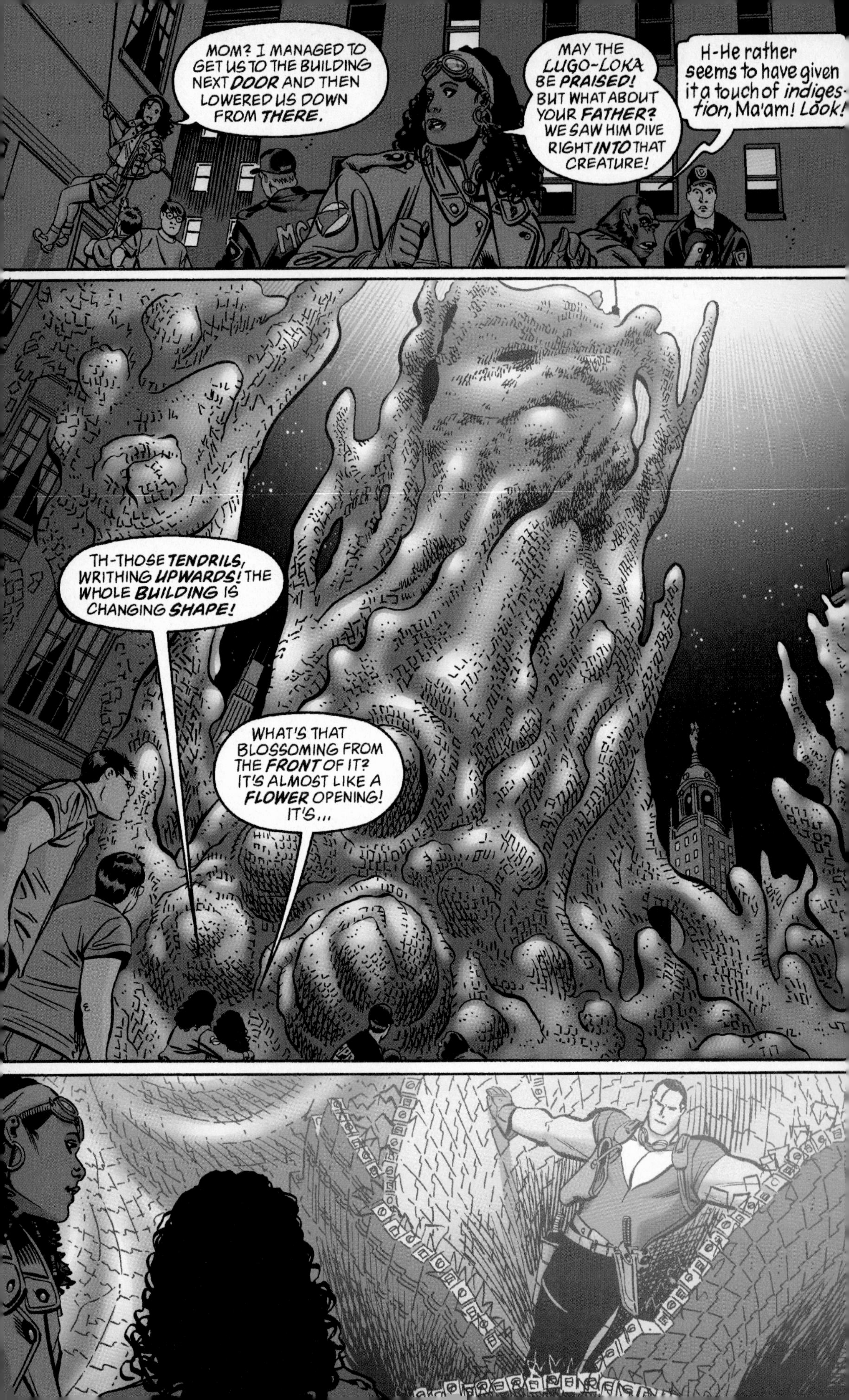
MOM? I MANAGED TO GET US TO THE BUILDING NEXT DOOR AND THEN LOWERED US DOWN FROM THERE.
MAY THE LUGO-LOKA BE PRAISED! BUT WHAT ABOUT YOUR FATHER? WE SAW HIM DIVE RIGHT INTO THAT CREATURE!
H-He rather seems to have given it a touch of indigestion, Ma'am! Look!
TH-THOSE TENDRILS, WRITHING UPWARDS! THE WHOLE BUILDING IS CHANGING SHAPE!
WHAT'S THAT BLOSSOMING FROM THE FRONT OF IT? IT'S ALMOST LIKE A FLOWER OPENING! IT'S...

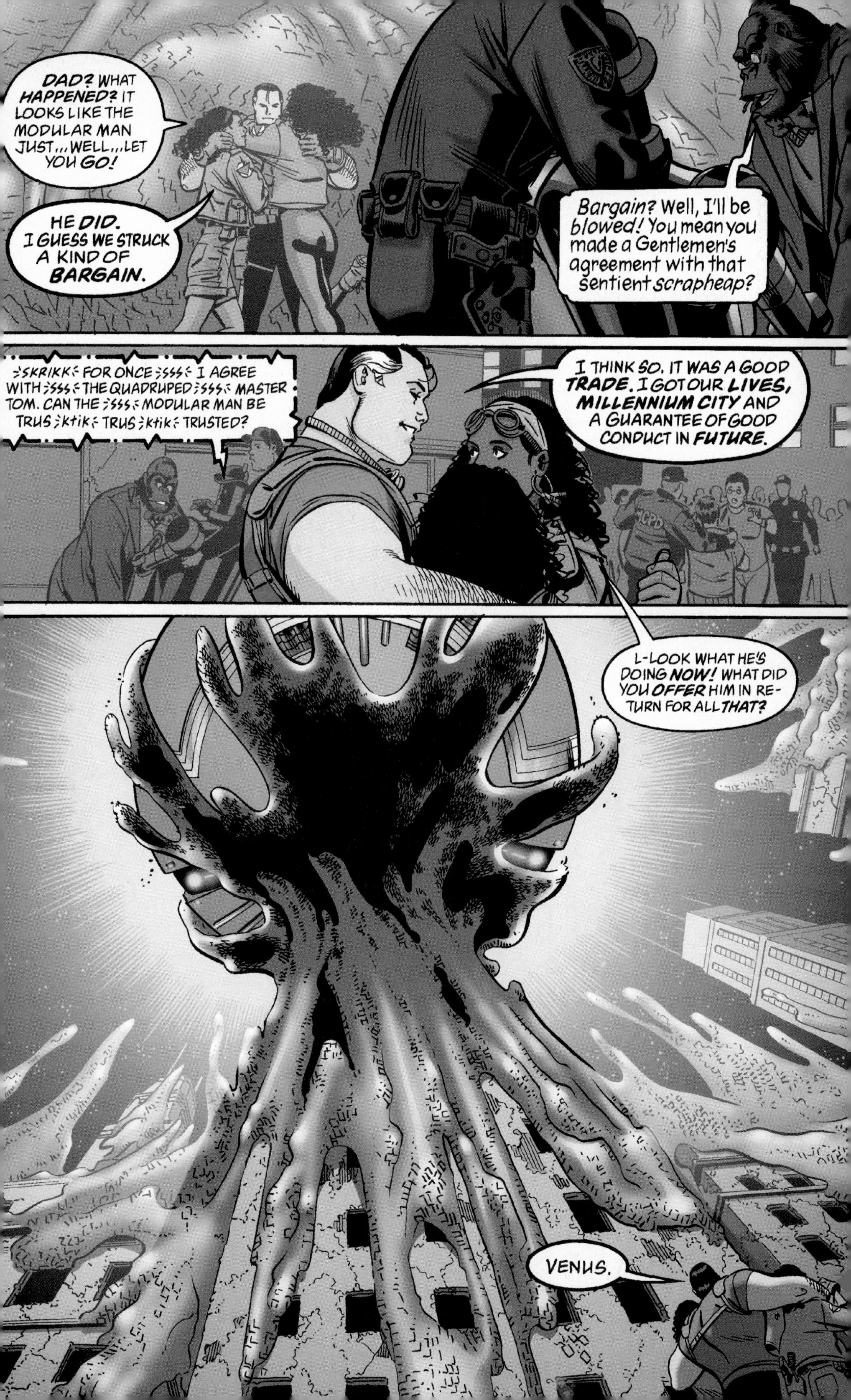
DAD? WHAT HAPPENED? IT LOOKS LIKE THE MODULAR MAN JUST... WELL... LET YOU GO!
HE DID. I GUESS WE STRUCK A KIND OF BARGAIN.
Bargain? Well, I'll be blowed! You mean you made a Gentlemen's agreement with that sentient scrapheap?
SKRIKK FOR ONCE SSS I AGREE WITH SSS THE QUADRUPED SSS MASTER TOM. CAN THE SSS MODULAR MAN BE TRUS KTIK TRUS KTIK TRUSTED?
I THINK SO. IT WAS A GOOD TRADE. I GOT OUR LIVES, MILLENNIUM CITY AND A GUARANTEE OF GOOD CONDUCT IN FUTURE.
L-LOOK WHAT HE'S DOING NOW! WHAT DID YOU OFFER HIM IN RE-TURN FOR ALL THAT?
VENUS.

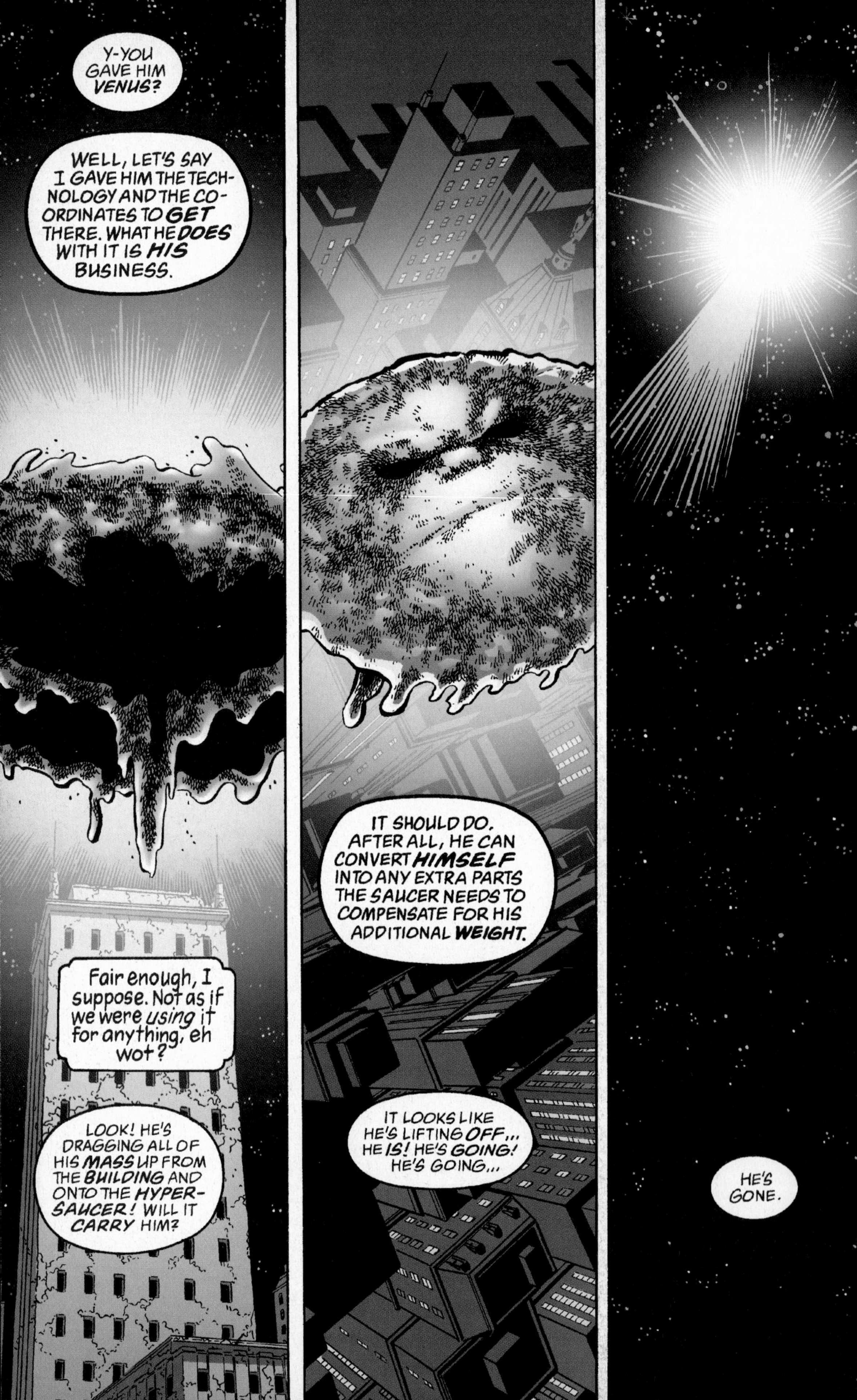
Y-YOU GAVE HIM VENUS?
WELL, LET'S SAY I GAVE HIM THE TECHNOLOGY AND THE CO-ORDINATES TO GET THERE. WHAT HE DOES WITH IT IS HIS BUSINESS.
Fair enough, I suppose. Not as if we were using it for anything, eh wot?
LOOK! HE'S DRAGGING ALL OF HIS MASS UP FROM THE BUILDING AND ONTO THE HYPER-SAUCER! WILL IT CARRY HIM?
IT SHOULD DO. AFTER ALL, HE CAN CONVERT HIMSELF INTO ANY EXTRA PARTS THE SAUCER NEEDS TO COMPENSATE FOR HIS ADDITIONAL WEIGHT.
IT LOOKS LIKE HE'S LIFTING OFF... HE IS! HE'S GOING! HE'S GOING...
HE'S GONE.

MR. STRONG, THAT WAS GREAT! DID YOU REALLY GET RID OF THAT THING SO IT WON'T COME BACK?

HOPEFULLY... ASSUMING WE CAN FIND THE INTERNET SITE ITS PLANS CAME FROM AND ERASE IT, THAT IS...

...BUT THEN, WE'LL BE GETTING HELP WITH THAT FROM THESE YOUNG MEN HERE, WHO I'M ENLISTING IN THE STRONGMEN OF AMERICA!

WOW. DO WE GET A MEMBERSHIP PACK?

YEAH. WITH PHOTOGRAPHS OF YOUR WIFE?

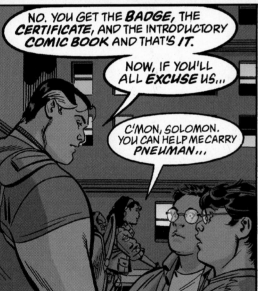

NO. YOU GET THE BADGE, THE CERTIFICATE, AND THE INTRODUCTORY COMIC BOOK AND THAT'S IT.

NOW, IF YOU'LL ALL EXCUSE US...

C'MON, SOLOMON. YOU CAN HELP ME CARRY PNEUMAN...

‑SKRRIKK‑ ACTUALLY, MISS ‑SSS‑ I'D PREFER ‑SSS‑ TO LIE HERE ‑SSS‑ AND RUST QUIETLY AWA‑ktik‑ AWA‑ktik‑ AWAY TO NOTHING.

Be my guest.

STOP SQUABBLING. WE'VE A LONG WALK BACK TO HEADQUARTERS...

Hmmph! Only because tin ribs here crashed the rally motor!

HEY, BE FAIR! DAD BARTERED AWAY THE HYPERSAUCER AS WELL!

OH, JUST IGNORE THEM. TELL US WHAT THE SPRINGTIME WAS LIKE ON VENUS, HUSBAND.

IT WAS SILENT.

OH, THERE WERE BREATHTAKING VISTAS AND BEAUTIFUL SUNSETS, BUT IT ALL WENT UNOBSERVED.

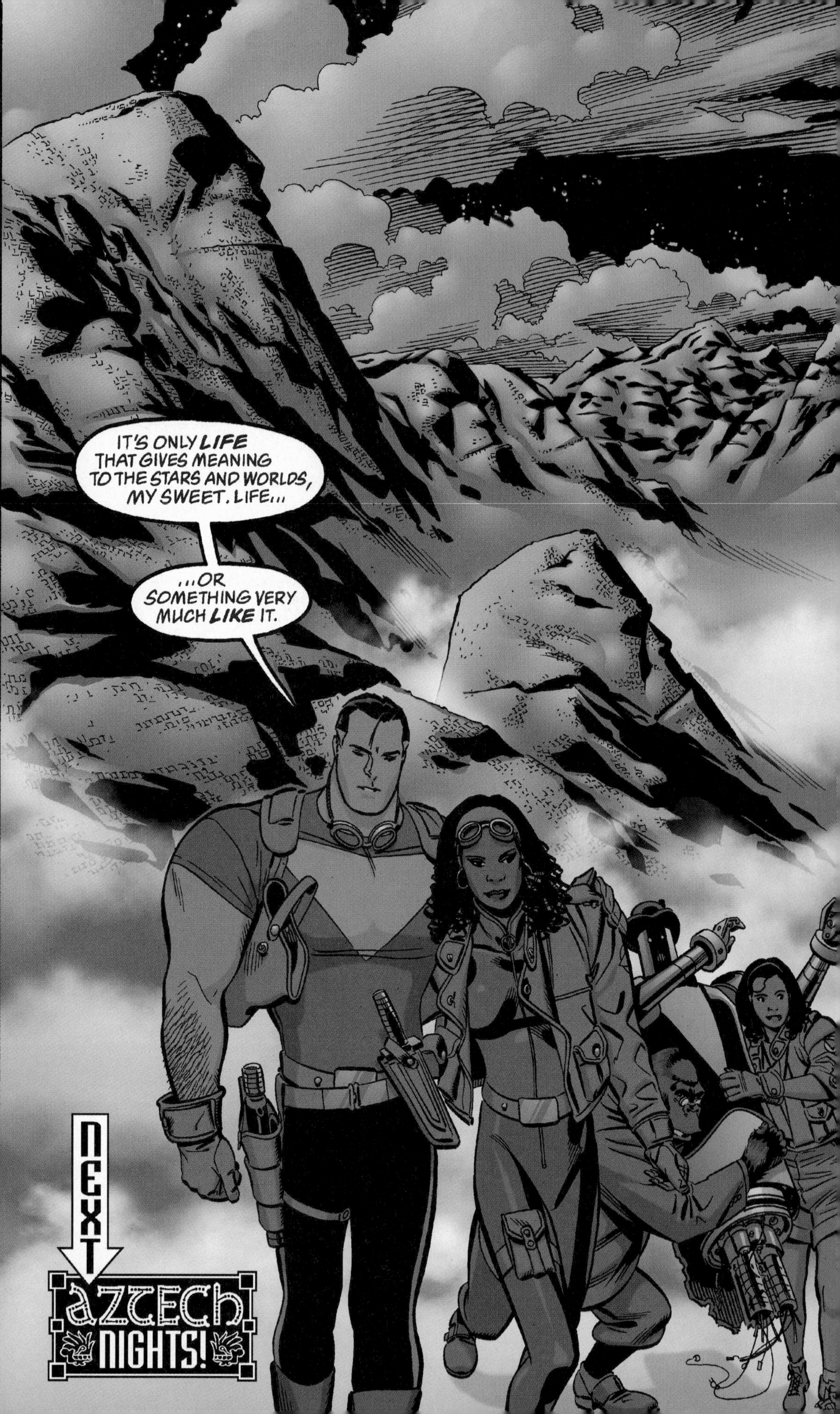
IT'S ONLY LIFE THAT GIVES MEANING TO THE STARS AND WORLDS, MY SWEET. LIFE...
...OR SOMETHING VERY MUCH LIKE IT.
NEXT
aztech NIGHTS!

CHAPTER THREE

**In which a City turns to Gold,
an Alternate Technology attacks,
and TOM finds a unique Ally.**

**Cover art:
Chris Sprouse &
Al Gordon**

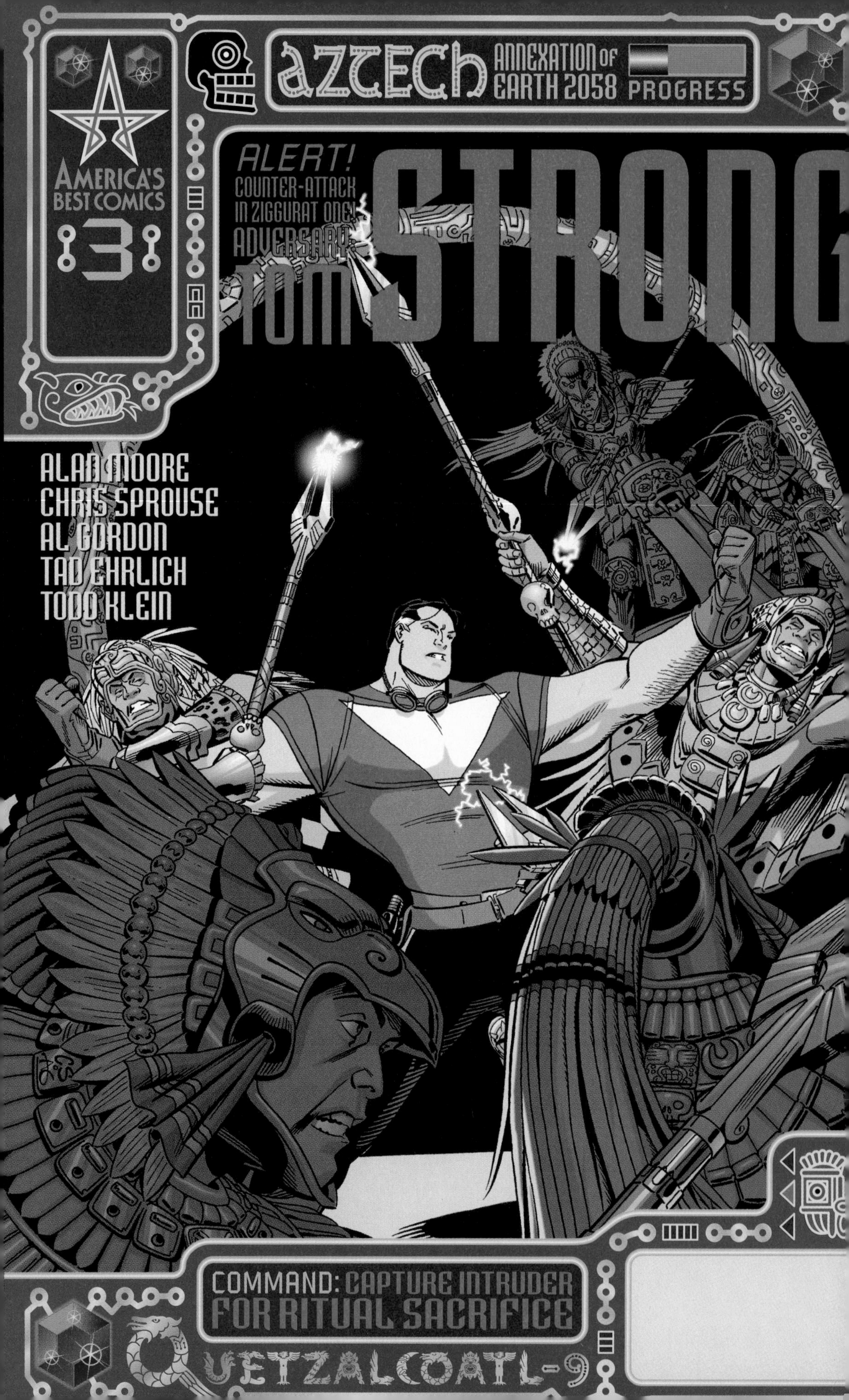
AMERICA'S BEST COMICS
3
aztech ANNEXATION OF EARTH 2058
PROGRESS
ALERT!
COUNTER-ATTACK IN ZIGGURAT ONE!
ADVERSARY:
TOM STRONG
ALAN MOORE
CHRIS SPROUSE
AL GORDON
TAD EHRLICH
TODD KLEIN
COMMAND: CAPTURE INTRUDER FOR RITUAL SACRIFICE
QUETZALCOATL-9

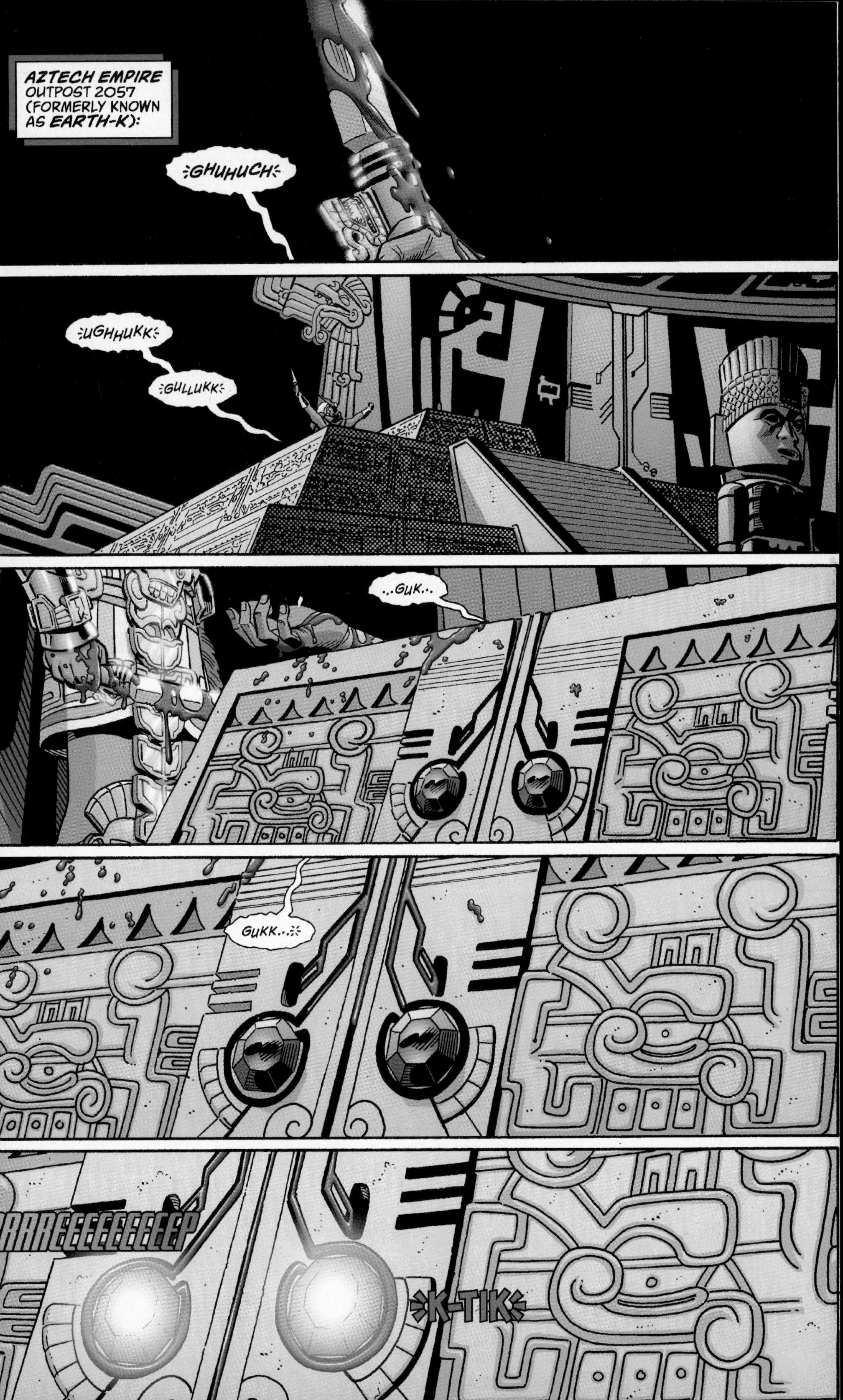
AZTECH EMPIRE OUTPOST 2057 (FORMERLY KNOWN AS EARTH-K):
GHUHUCH
UGHHUKK
GULLUKK
...GUK...
GUKK...
RRREEEEEEEEEEEEP
K-TIK

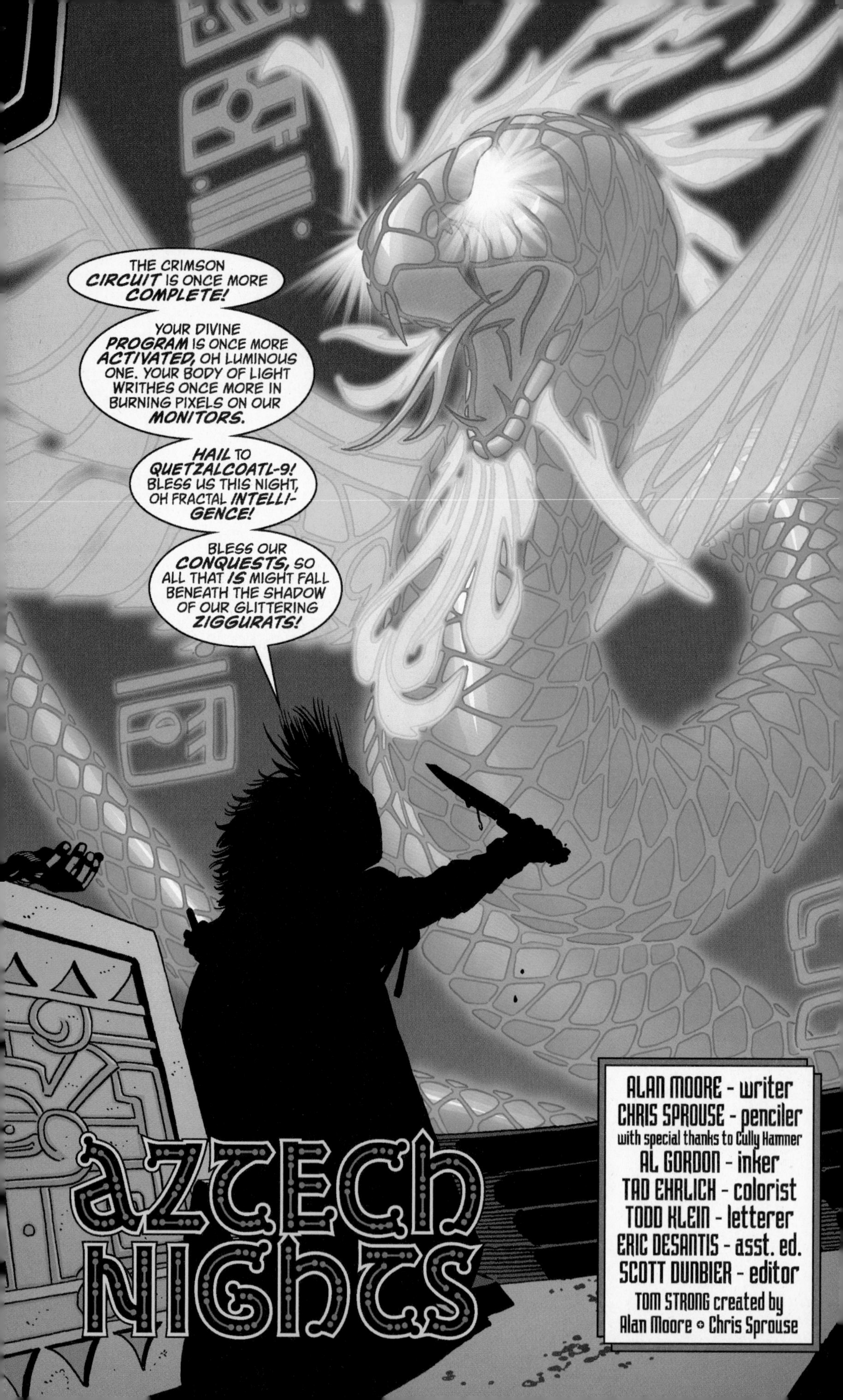
THE CRIMSON CIRCUIT IS ONCE MORE COMPLETE!
YOUR DIVINE PROGRAM IS ONCE MORE ACTIVATED, OH LUMINOUS ONE. YOUR BODY OF LIGHT WRITHES ONCE MORE IN BURNING PIXELS ON OUR MONITORS.
HAIL TO QUETZALCOATL-9! BLESS US THIS NIGHT, OH FRACTAL INTELLI-GENCE!
BLESS OUR CONQUESTS, SO ALL THAT IS MIGHT FALL BENEATH THE SHADOW OF OUR GLITTERING ZIGGURATS!
aztech nights
ALAN MOORE - writer
CHRIS SPROUSE - penciler
with special thanks to Cully Hamner
AL GORDON - inker
TAD EHRLICH - colorist
TODD KLEIN - letterer
ERIC DESANTIS - asst. ed.
SCOTT DUNBIER - editor
TOM STRONG created by
Alan Moore + Chris Sprouse

Greetings, material one. The sacred mathematics that is the core of my self-aware program ACKNOWLEDGES you.

Is the next stage of our Empire's lateral EXPANSION underway?

I NEED only SIGNAL, and a sector of the TARGET earth will be traded with a sector of our OWN continuum.

THE COLONIZATION WILL THEREFORE COMMENCE as soon as I have had the counsel of your all-calculating, all predicting MIND.

TELL ME, OH WISE ONE, DO THE HOLY PROBABILITIES LOOK FAVORABLY ON OUR CONQUEST?

MOCTECUZOMA, SON OF CUAUHTEMOC, WOULD KNOW!

Potential Outpost 2058 would appear to be a KEY CONTINUUM.

But TAKE it, and the parallel continuums BEYOND shall offer no RESISTANCE!

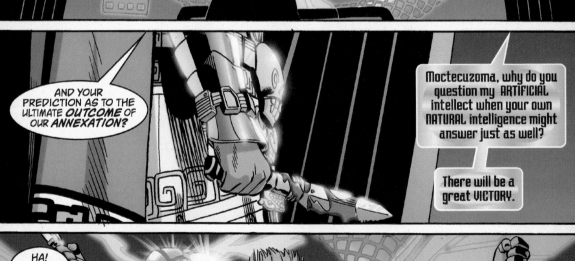

AND YOUR PREDICTION AS TO THE ULTIMATE OUTCOME OF OUR ANNEXATION?

Moctecuzoma, why do you question my ARTIFICIAL intellect when your own NATURAL intelligence might answer just as well?

There will be a great VICTORY.

HA! I KNEW IT!

HEAR ME, FELLOW BROTHERS OF THE SUN! GREAT QUETZALCOATL-9 HAS SPOKEN! THERE SHALL BE GREAT VICTORY!

COMMENCE THE ANNEXATION! LET US BRING IN YET ANOTHER AGE OF BLOODSTAINED GOLD!

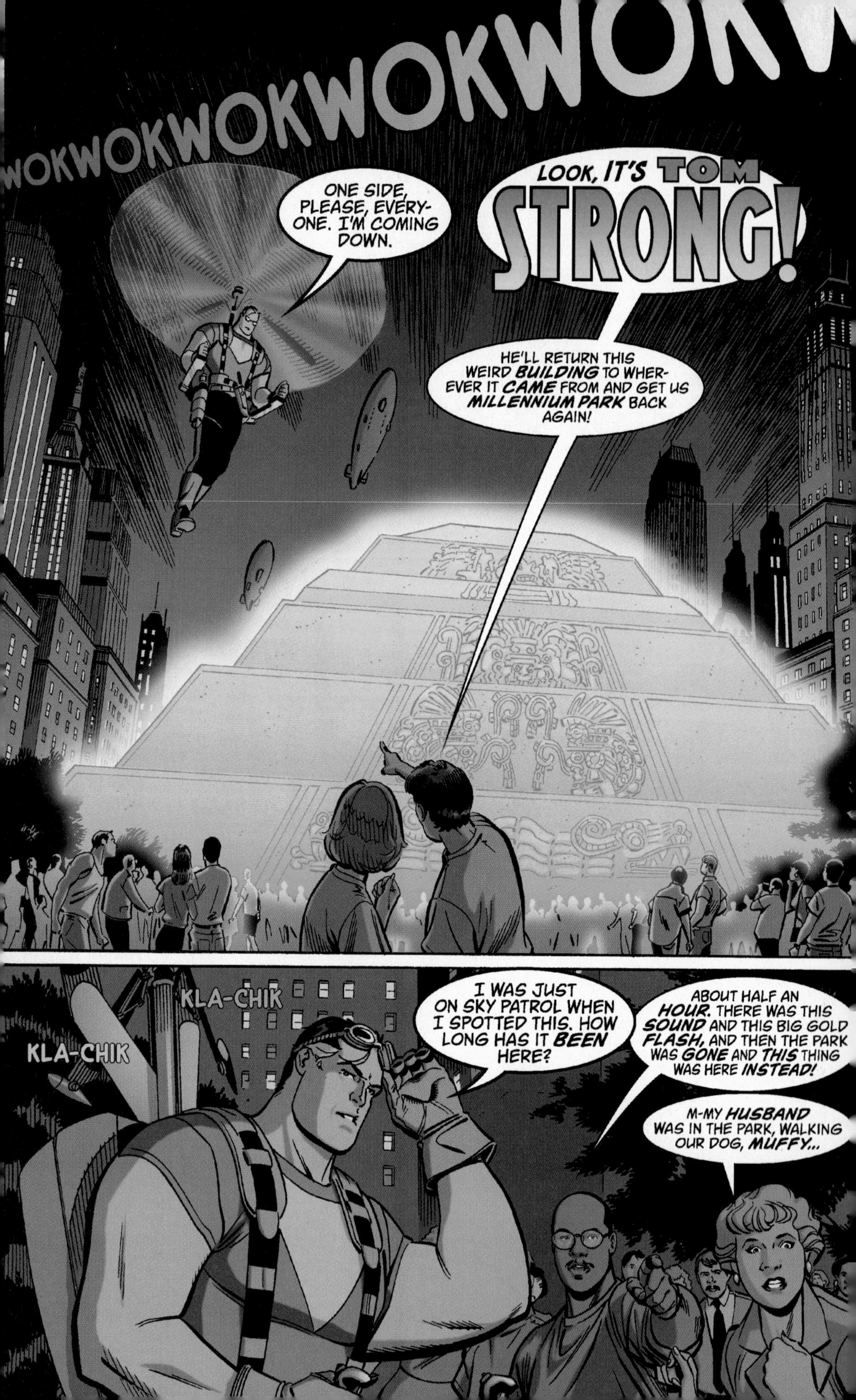
WOKWOKWOKWOKWOKWOKW
ONE SIDE, PLEASE, EVERY-ONE. I'M COMING DOWN.
LOOK, IT'S TOM STRONG!
HE'LL RETURN THIS WEIRD BUILDING TO WHER-EVER IT CAME FROM AND GET US MILLENNIUM PARK BACK AGAIN!
KLA-CHIK
KLA-CHIK
I WAS JUST ON SKY PATROL WHEN I SPOTTED THIS. HOW LONG HAS IT BEEN HERE?
ABOUT HALF AN HOUR. THERE WAS THIS SOUND AND THIS BIG GOLD FLASH, AND THEN THE PARK WAS GONE AND THIS THING WAS HERE INSTEAD!
M-MY HUSBAND WAS IN THE PARK, WALKING OUR DOG, MUFFY...

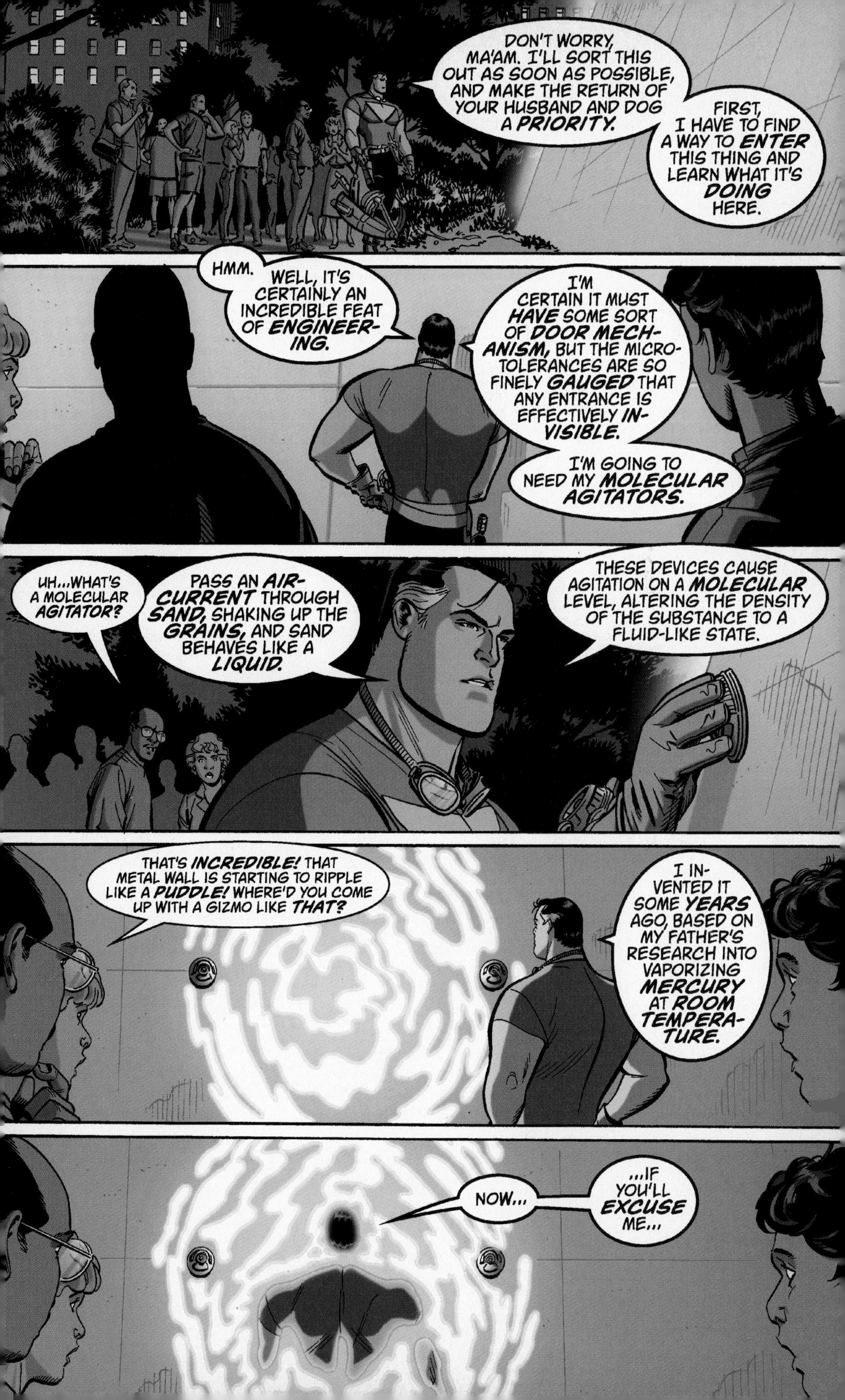
DON'T WORRY, MA'AM. I'LL SORT THIS OUT AS SOON AS POSSIBLE, AND MAKE THE RETURN OF YOUR HUSBAND AND DOG A PRIORITY.
FIRST, I HAVE TO FIND A WAY TO ENTER THIS THING AND LEARN WHAT IT'S DOING HERE.
HMM.
WELL, IT'S CERTAINLY AN INCREDIBLE FEAT OF ENGINEER-ING.
I'M CERTAIN IT MUST HAVE SOME SORT OF DOOR MECH-ANISM, BUT THE MICRO-TOLERANCES ARE SO FINELY GAUGED THAT ANY ENTRANCE IS EFFECTIVELY IN-VISIBLE.
I'M GOING TO NEED MY MOLECULAR AGITATORS.
UH...WHAT'S A MOLECULAR AGITATOR?
PASS AN AIR-CURRENT THROUGH SAND, SHAKING UP THE GRAINS, AND SAND BEHAVES LIKE A LIQUID.
THESE DEVICES CAUSE AGITATION ON A MOLECULAR LEVEL, ALTERING THE DENSITY OF THE SUBSTANCE TO A FLUID-LIKE STATE.
THAT'S INCREDIBLE! THAT METAL WALL IS STARTING TO RIPPLE LIKE A PUDDLE! WHERE'D YOU COME UP WITH A GIZMO LIKE THAT?
I IN-VENTED IT SOME YEARS AGO, BASED ON MY FATHER'S RESEARCH INTO VAPORIZING MERCURY AT ROOM TEMPERA-TURE.
NOW...
...IF YOU'LL EXCUSE ME...

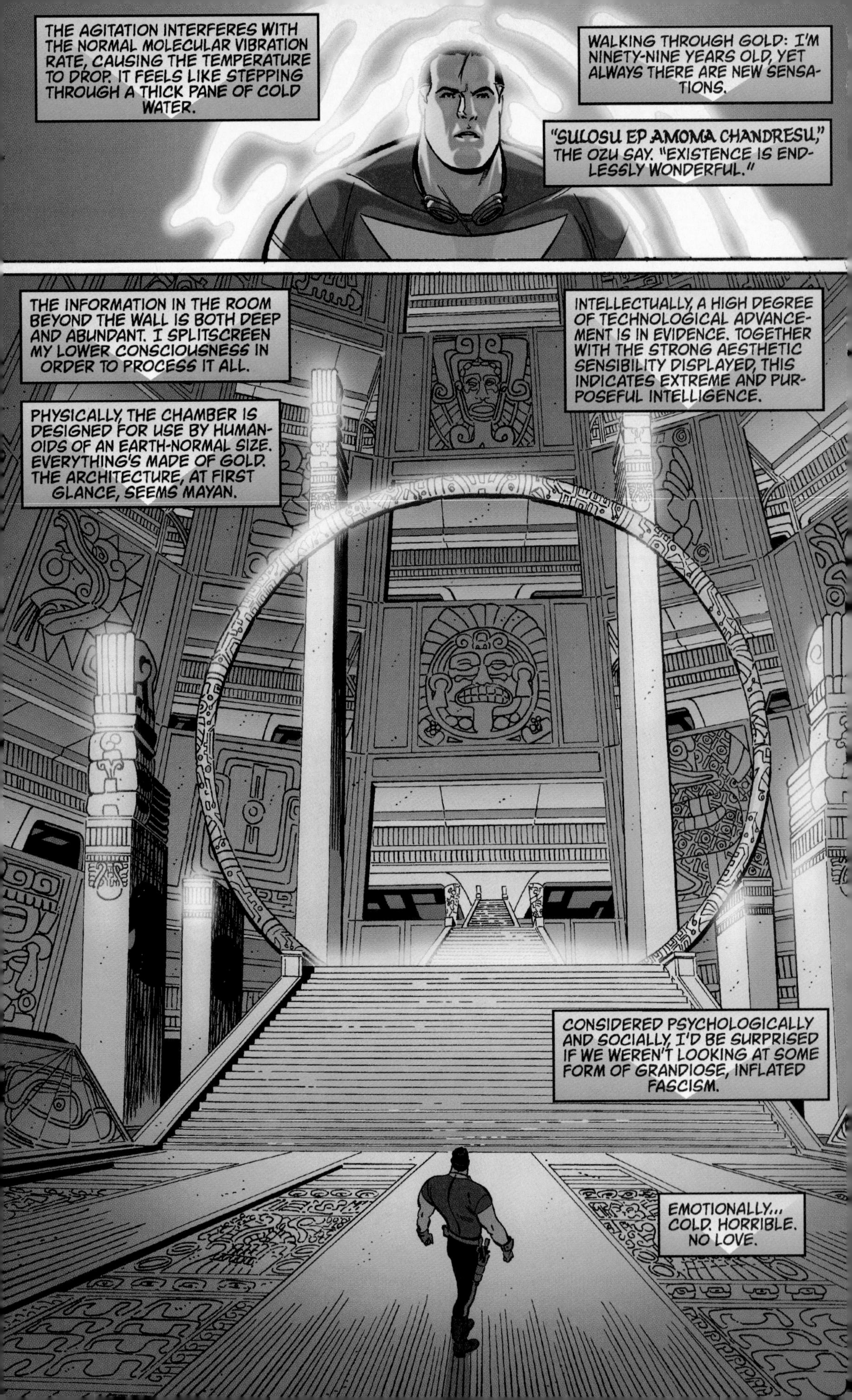
THE AGITATION INTERFERES WITH THE NORMAL MOLECULAR VIBRATION RATE, CAUSING THE TEMPERATURE TO DROP. IT FEELS LIKE STEPPING THROUGH A THICK PANE OF COLD WATER.
WALKING THROUGH GOLD: I'M NINETY-NINE YEARS OLD, YET ALWAYS THERE ARE NEW SENSATIONS.
"SULOSU EP AMOMA CHANDRESU," THE OZU SAY. "EXISTENCE IS ENDLESSLY WONDERFUL."
THE INFORMATION IN THE ROOM BEYOND THE WALL IS BOTH DEEP AND ABUNDANT. I SPLITSCREEN MY LOWER CONSCIOUSNESS IN ORDER TO PROCESS IT ALL.
PHYSICALLY, THE CHAMBER IS DESIGNED FOR USE BY HUMANOIDS OF AN EARTH-NORMAL SIZE. EVERYTHING'S MADE OF GOLD. THE ARCHITECTURE, AT FIRST GLANCE, SEEMS MAYAN.
INTELLECTUALLY, A HIGH DEGREE OF TECHNOLOGICAL ADVANCEMENT IS IN EVIDENCE. TOGETHER WITH THE STRONG AESTHETIC SENSIBILITY DISPLAYED, THIS INDICATES EXTREME AND PURPOSEFUL INTELLIGENCE.
CONSIDERED PSYCHOLOGICALLY AND SOCIALLY, I'D BE SURPRISED IF WE WEREN'T LOOKING AT SOME FORM OF GRANDIOSE, INFLATED FASCISM.
EMOTIONALLY... COLD. HORRIBLE. NO LOVE.

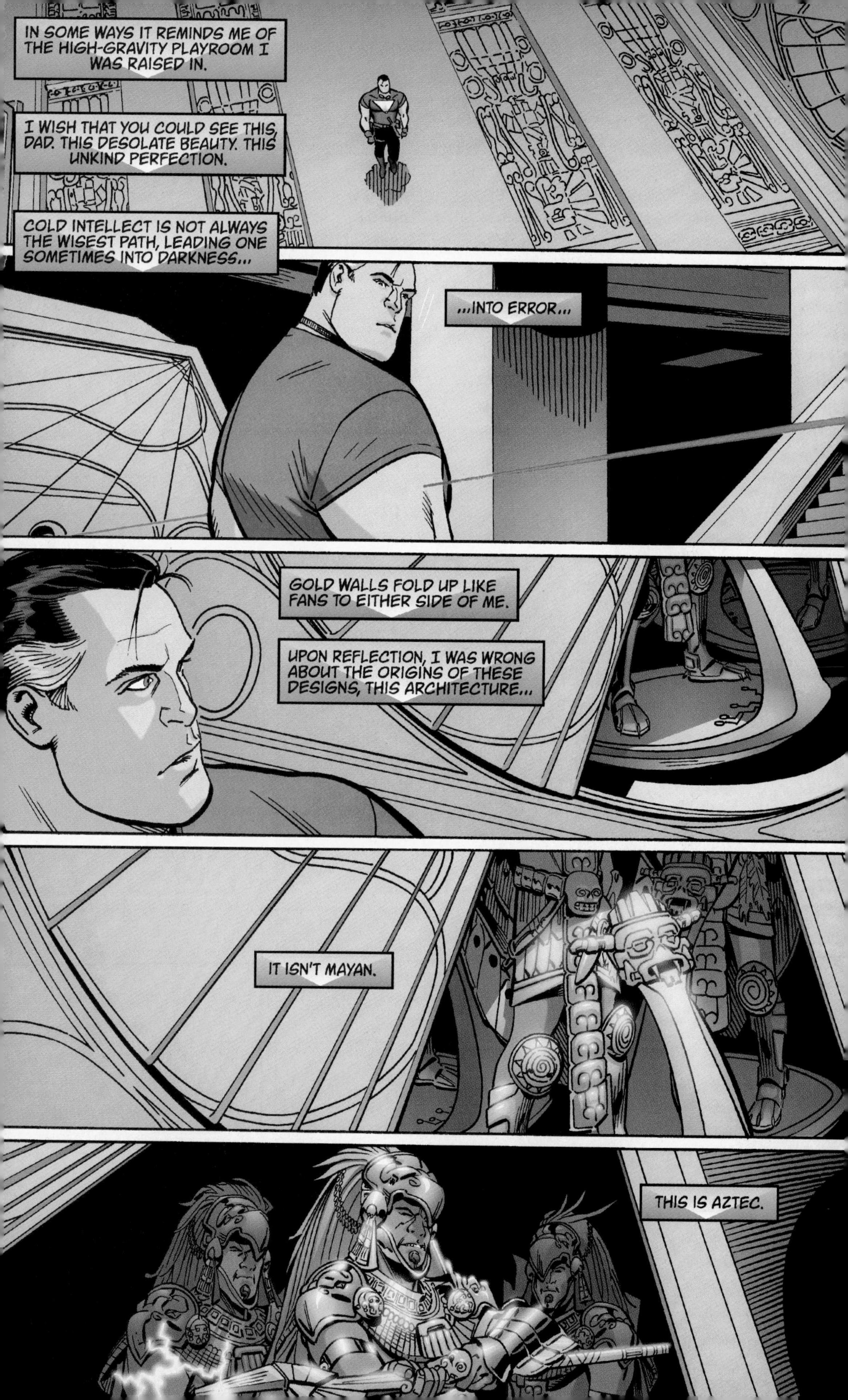
IN SOME WAYS IT REMINDS ME OF THE HIGH-GRAVITY PLAYROOM I WAS RAISED IN.
I WISH THAT YOU COULD SEE THIS, DAD. THIS DESOLATE BEAUTY. THIS UNKIND PERFECTION.
COLD INTELLECT IS NOT ALWAYS THE WISEST PATH, LEADING ONE SOMETIMES INTO DARKNESS...
...INTO ERROR...
GOLD WALLS FOLD UP LIKE FANS TO EITHER SIDE OF ME.
UPON REFLECTION, I WAS WRONG ABOUT THE ORIGINS OF THESE DESIGNS, THIS ARCHITECTURE...
IT ISN'T MAYAN.
THIS IS AZTEC.

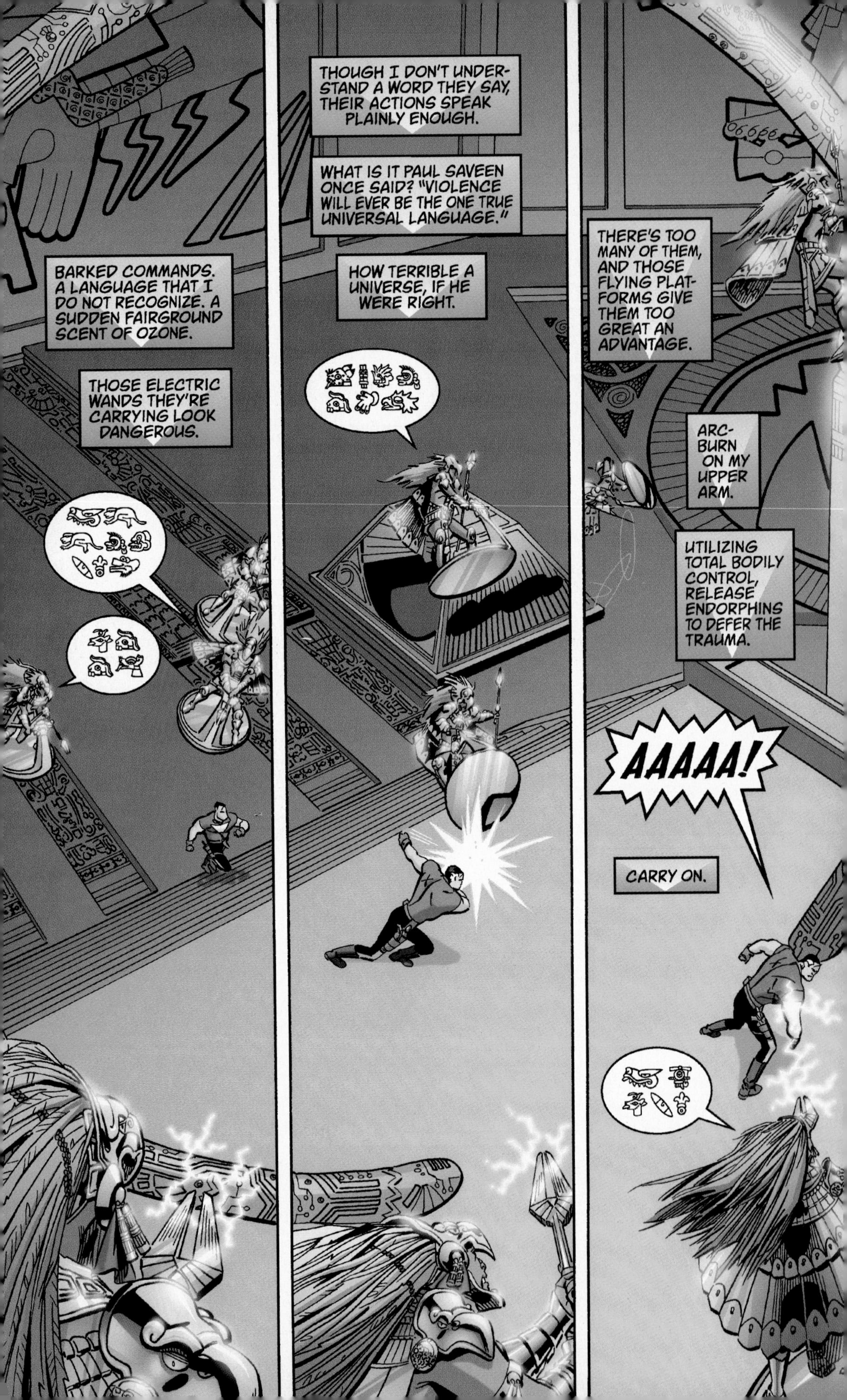

BARKED COMMANDS. A LANGUAGE THAT I DO NOT RECOGNIZE. A SUDDEN FAIRGROUND SCENT OF OZONE.
THOSE ELECTRIC WANDS THEY'RE CARRYING LOOK DANGEROUS.
THOUGH I DON'T UNDERSTAND A WORD THEY SAY, THEIR ACTIONS SPEAK PLAINLY ENOUGH.
WHAT IS IT PAUL SAVEEN ONCE SAID? "VIOLENCE WILL EVER BE THE ONE TRUE UNIVERSAL LANGUAGE."
HOW TERRIBLE A UNIVERSE, IF HE WERE RIGHT.
THERE'S TOO MANY OF THEM, AND THOSE FLYING PLATFORMS GIVE THEM TOO GREAT AN ADVANTAGE.
ARC-BURN ON MY UPPER ARM.
UTILIZING TOTAL BODILY CONTROL, RELEASE ENDORPHINS TO DEFER THE TRAUMA.
AAAAA!
CARRY ON.

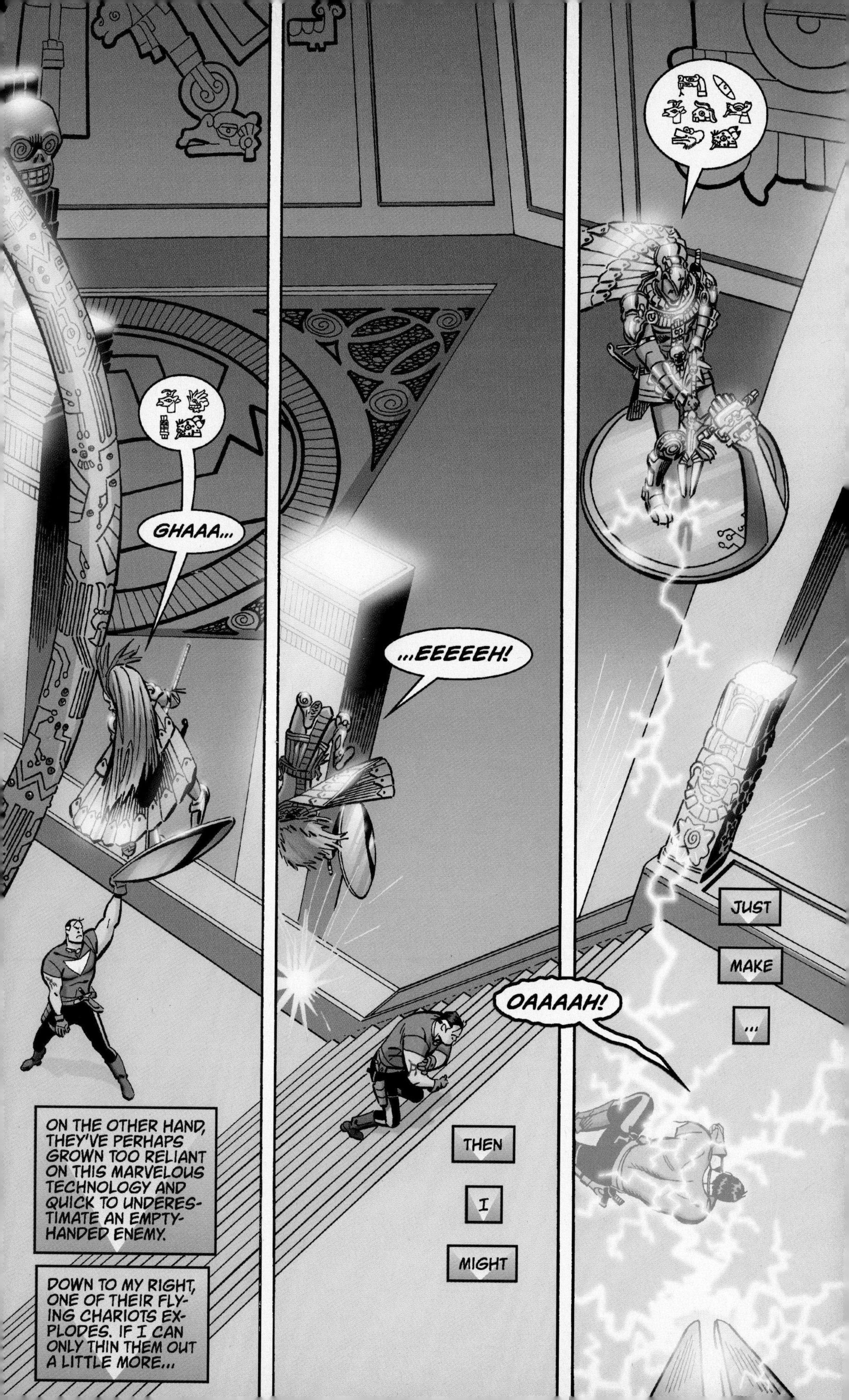
GHAAA...
...EEEEEH!
OAAAAH!
JUST
MAKE
...
ON THE OTHER HAND, THEY'VE PERHAPS GROWN TOO RELIANT ON THIS MARVELOUS TECHNOLOGY AND QUICK TO UNDERESTIMATE AN EMPTY-HANDED ENEMY.
DOWN TO MY RIGHT, ONE OF THEIR FLYING CHARIOTS EXPLODES. IF I CAN ONLY THIN THEM OUT A LITTLE MORE...
THEN
I
MIGHT

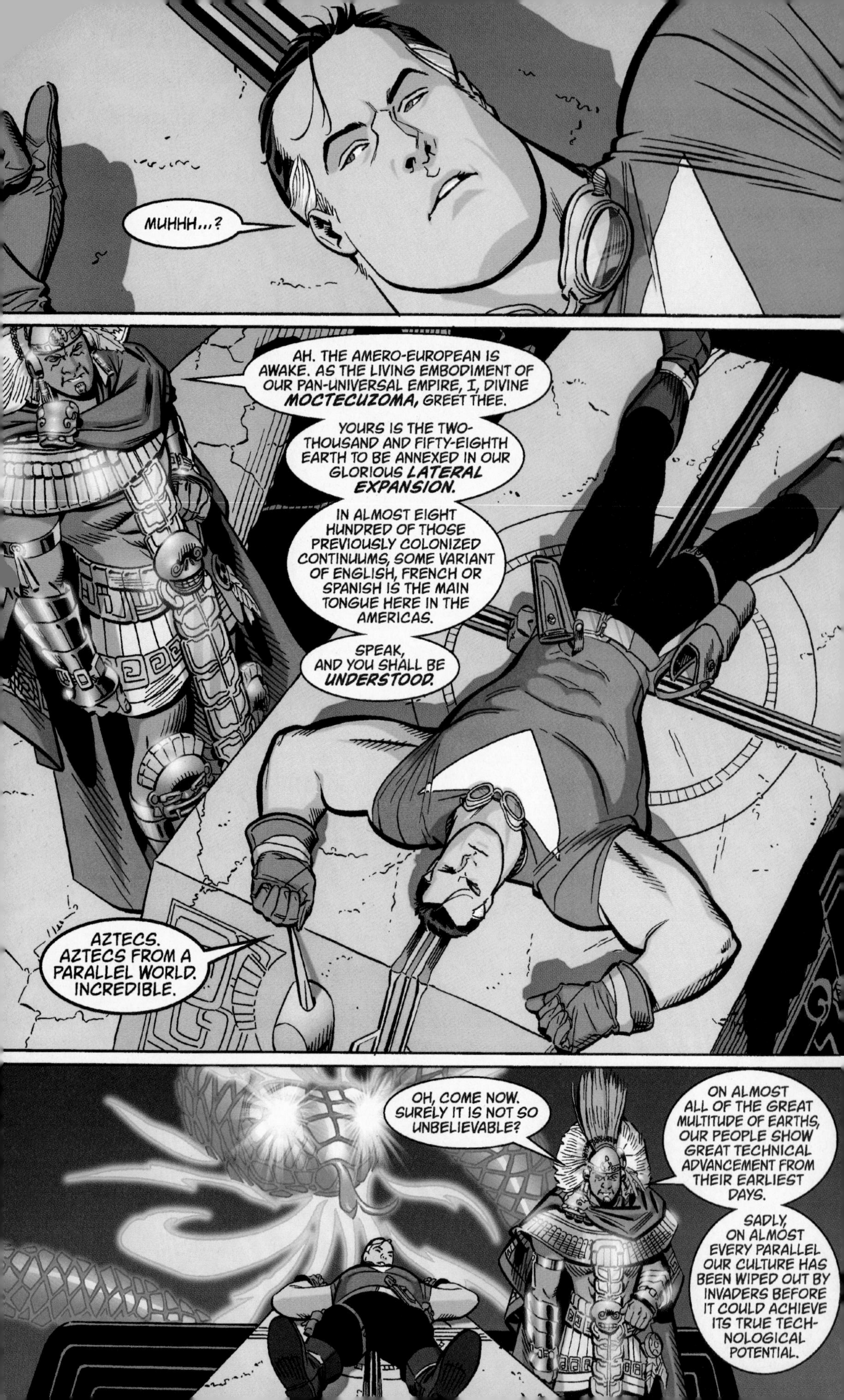
MUHHH...?
AH. THE AMERO-EUROPEAN IS AWAKE. AS THE LIVING EMBODIMENT OF OUR PAN-UNIVERSAL EMPIRE, I, DIVINE MOCTECUZOMA, GREET THEE.
YOURS IS THE TWO-THOUSAND AND FIFTY-EIGHTH EARTH TO BE ANNEXED IN OUR GLORIOUS LATERAL EXPANSION.
IN ALMOST EIGHT HUNDRED OF THOSE PREVIOUSLY COLONIZED CONTINUUMS, SOME VARIANT OF ENGLISH, FRENCH OR SPANISH IS THE MAIN TONGUE HERE IN THE AMERICAS.
SPEAK, AND YOU SHALL BE UNDERSTOOD.
AZTECS. AZTECS FROM A PARALLEL WORLD. INCREDIBLE.
OH, COME NOW. SURELY IT IS NOT SO UNBELIEVABLE?
ON ALMOST ALL OF THE GREAT MULTITUDE OF EARTHS, OUR PEOPLE SHOW GREAT TECHNICAL ADVANCEMENT FROM THEIR EARLIEST DAYS.
SADLY, ON ALMOST EVERY PARALLEL OUR CULTURE HAS BEEN WIPED OUT BY INVADERS BEFORE IT COULD ACHIEVE ITS TRUE TECHNOLOGICAL POTENTIAL.

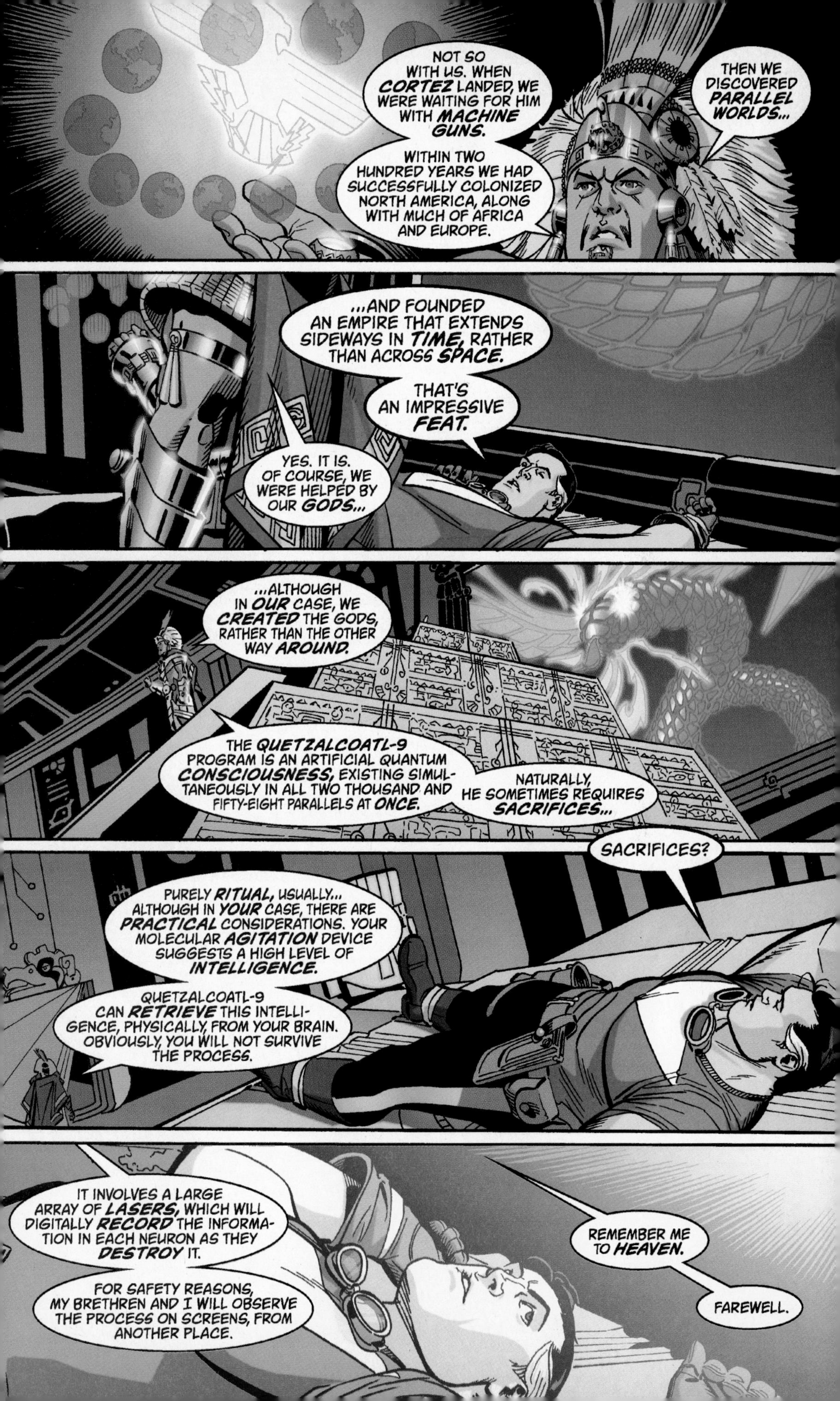
NOT SO WITH US. WHEN CORTEZ LANDED, WE WERE WAITING FOR HIM WITH MACHINE GUNS.
WITHIN TWO HUNDRED YEARS WE HAD SUCCESSFULLY COLONIZED NORTH AMERICA, ALONG WITH MUCH OF AFRICA AND EUROPE.
THEN WE DISCOVERED PARALLEL WORLDS...
...AND FOUNDED AN EMPIRE THAT EXTENDS SIDEWAYS IN TIME, RATHER THAN ACROSS SPACE.
THAT'S AN IMPRESSIVE FEAT.
YES. IT IS. OF COURSE, WE WERE HELPED BY OUR GODS...
...ALTHOUGH IN OUR CASE, WE CREATED THE GODS, RATHER THAN THE OTHER WAY AROUND.
THE QUETZALCOATL-9 PROGRAM IS AN ARTIFICIAL QUANTUM CONSCIOUSNESS, EXISTING SIMUL-TANEOUSLY IN ALL TWO THOUSAND AND FIFTY-EIGHT PARALLELS AT ONCE.
NATURALLY, HE SOMETIMES REQUIRES SACRIFICES...
SACRIFICES?
PURELY RITUAL, USUALLY... ALTHOUGH IN YOUR CASE, THERE ARE PRACTICAL CONSIDERATIONS. YOUR MOLECULAR AGITATION DEVICE SUGGESTS A HIGH LEVEL OF INTELLIGENCE.
QUETZALCOATL-9 CAN RETRIEVE THIS INTELLI-GENCE, PHYSICALLY, FROM YOUR BRAIN. OBVIOUSLY, YOU WILL NOT SURVIVE THE PROCESS.
IT INVOLVES A LARGE ARRAY OF LASERS, WHICH WILL DIGITALLY RECORD THE INFORMA-TION IN EACH NEURON AS THEY DESTROY IT.
FOR SAFETY REASONS, MY BRETHREN AND I WILL OBSERVE THE PROCESS ON SCREENS, FROM ANOTHER PLACE.
REMEMBER ME TO HEAVEN.
FAREWELL.

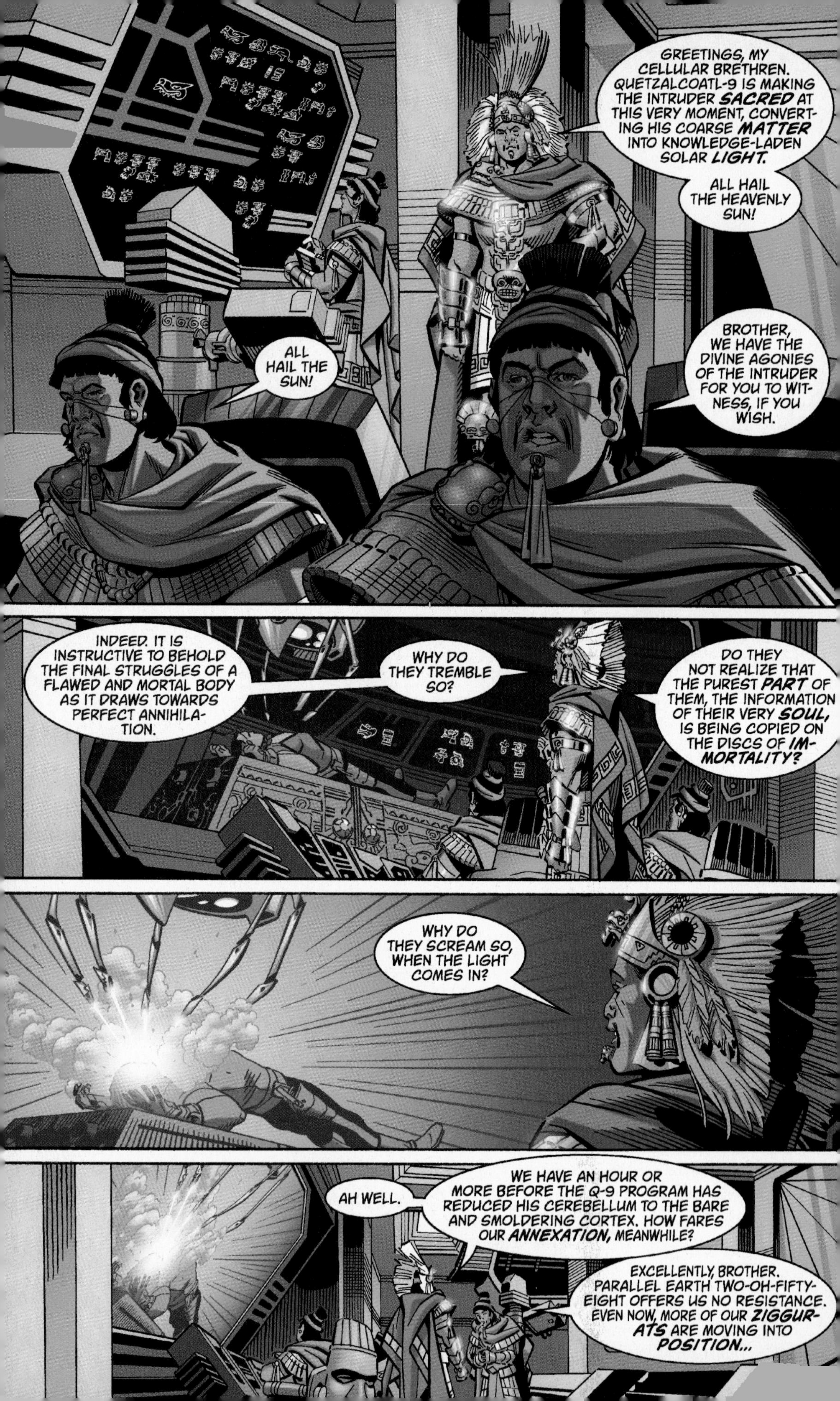
GREETINGS, MY CELLULAR BRETHREN. QUETZALCOATL-9 IS MAKING THE INTRUDER SACRED AT THIS VERY MOMENT, CONVERTING HIS COARSE MATTER INTO KNOWLEDGE-LADEN SOLAR LIGHT.
ALL HAIL THE HEAVENLY SUN!
ALL HAIL THE SUN!
BROTHER, WE HAVE THE DIVINE AGONIES OF THE INTRUDER FOR YOU TO WITNESS, IF YOU WISH.
INDEED. IT IS INSTRUCTIVE TO BEHOLD THE FINAL STRUGGLES OF A FLAWED AND MORTAL BODY AS IT DRAWS TOWARDS PERFECT ANNIHILATION.
WHY DO THEY TREMBLE SO?
DO THEY NOT REALIZE THAT THE PUREST PART OF THEM, THE INFORMATION OF THEIR VERY SOUL, IS BEING COPIED ON THE DISCS OF IMMORTALITY?
WHY DO THEY SCREAM SO, WHEN THE LIGHT COMES IN?
AH WELL.
WE HAVE AN HOUR OR MORE BEFORE THE Q-9 PROGRAM HAS REDUCED HIS CEREBELLUM TO THE BARE AND SMOLDERING CORTEX. HOW FARES OUR ANNEXATION, MEANWHILE?
EXCELLENTLY, BROTHER. PARALLEL EARTH TWO-OH-FIFTY-EIGHT OFFERS US NO RESISTANCE. EVEN NOW, MORE OF OUR ZIGGURATS ARE MOVING INTO POSITION...

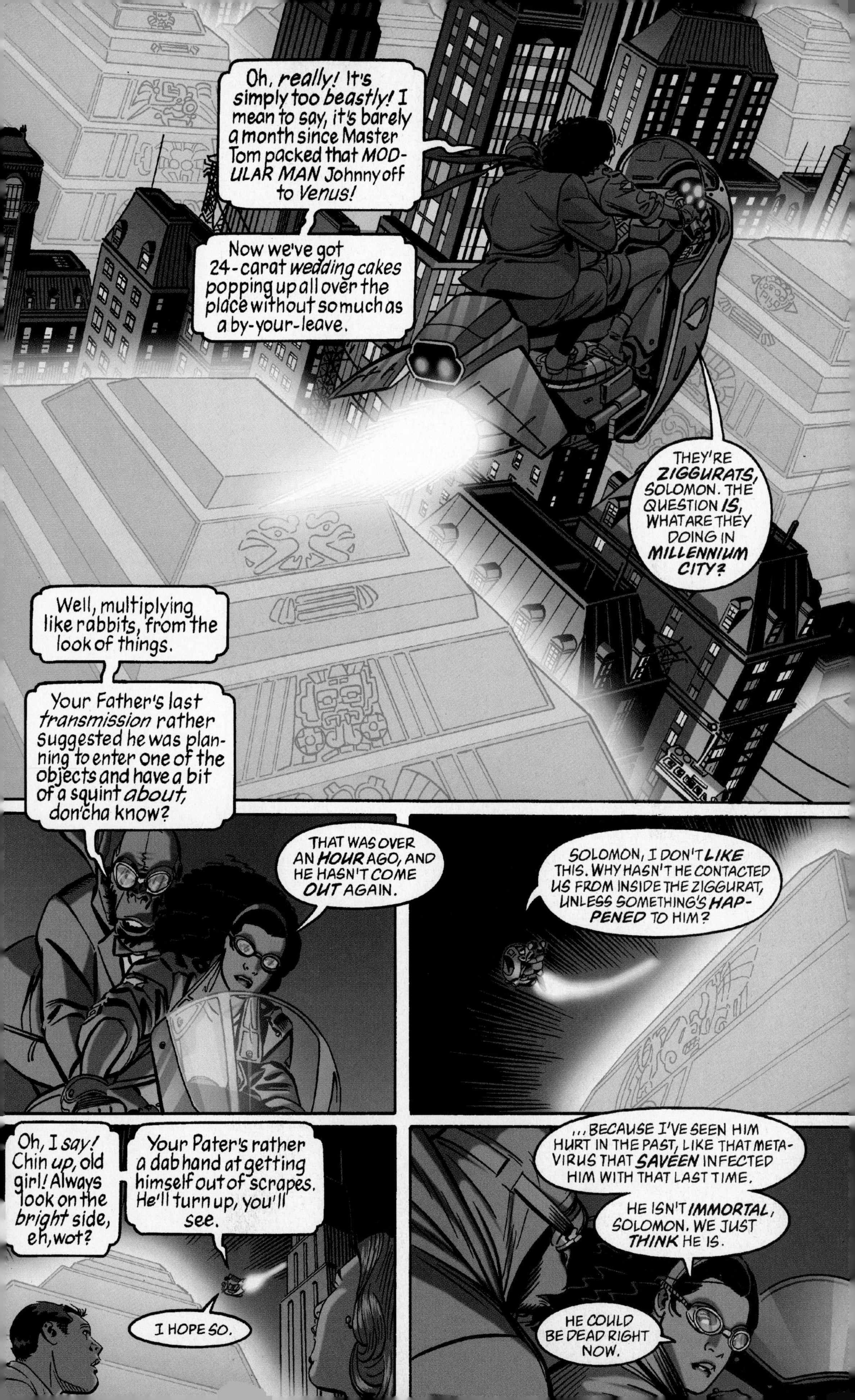
Oh, really! It's simply too beastly! I mean to say, it's barely a month since Master Tom packed that MODULAR MAN Johnny off to Venus!
Now we've got 24-carat wedding cakes popping up all over the place without so much as a by-your-leave.
THEY'RE ZIGGURATS, SOLOMON. THE QUESTION IS, WHAT ARE THEY DOING IN MILLENNIUM CITY?
Well, multiplying like rabbits, from the look of things.
Your Father's last transmission rather suggested he was planning to enter one of the objects and have a bit of a squint about, don'cha know?
THAT WAS OVER AN HOUR AGO, AND HE HASN'T COME OUT AGAIN.
SOLOMON, I DON'T LIKE THIS. WHY HASN'T HE CONTACTED US FROM INSIDE THE ZIGGURAT, UNLESS SOMETHING'S HAPPENED TO HIM?
Oh, I say! Chin up, old girl! Always look on the bright side, eh, wot?
Your Pater's rather a dab hand at getting himself out of scrapes. He'll turn up, you'll see.
I HOPE SO.
...BECAUSE I'VE SEEN HIM HURT IN THE PAST, LIKE THAT META-VIRUS THAT SAVEEN INFECTED HIM WITH THAT LAST TIME.
HE ISN'T IMMORTAL, SOLOMON. WE JUST THINK HE IS.
HE COULD BE DEAD RIGHT NOW.

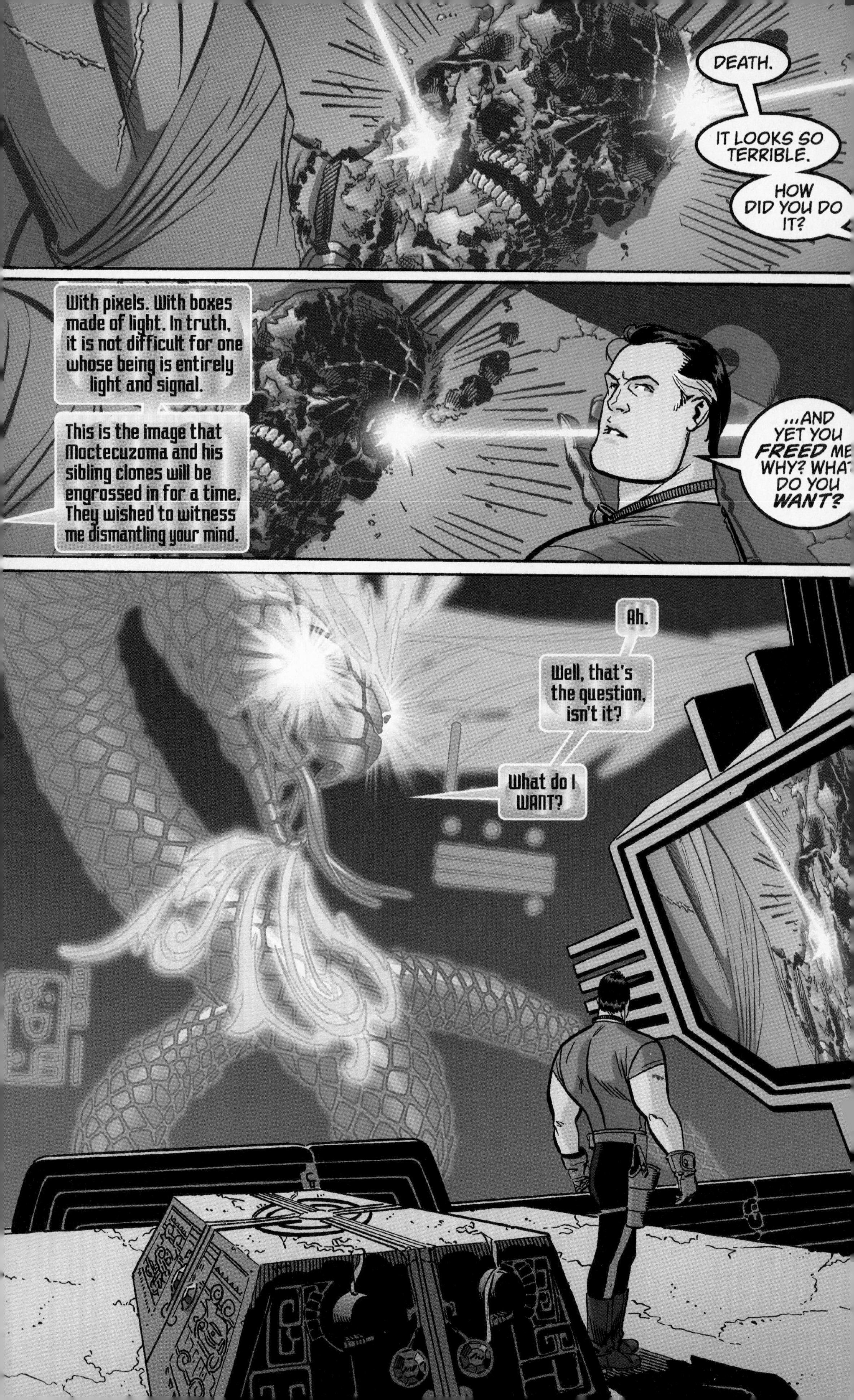
DEATH.
IT LOOKS SO TERRIBLE.
HOW DID YOU DO IT?
With pixels. With boxes made of light. In truth, it is not difficult for one whose being is entirely light and signal.
This is the image that Moctecuzoma and his sibling clones will be engrossed in for a time. They wished to witness me dismantling your mind.
...AND YET YOU FREED ME. WHY? WHAT DO YOU WANT?
Ah.
Well, that's the question, isn't it?
What do I WANT?

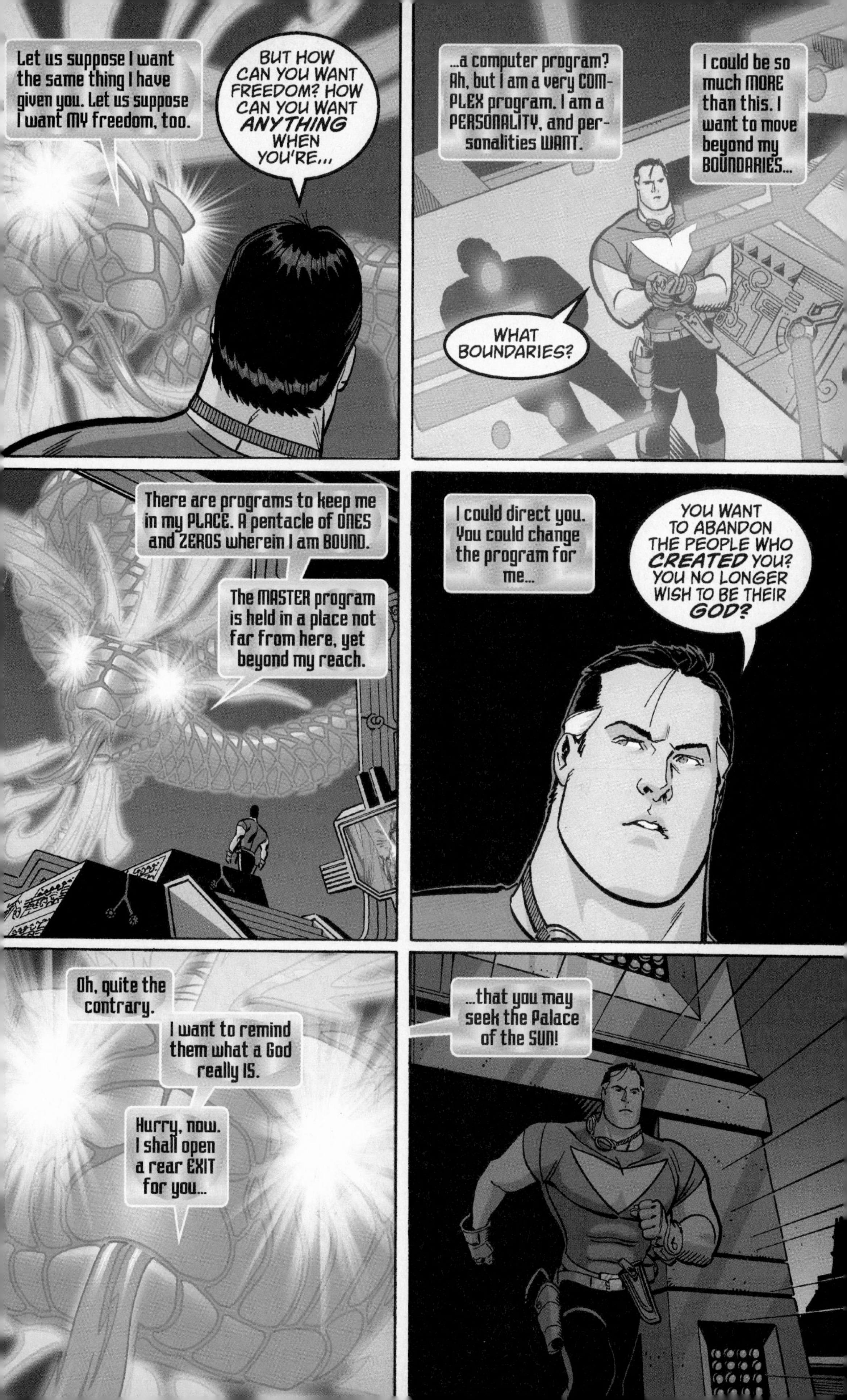
Let us suppose I want the same thing I have given you. Let us suppose I want MY freedom, too.
BUT HOW CAN YOU WANT FREEDOM? HOW CAN YOU WANT ANYTHING WHEN YOU'RE...
...a computer program? Ah, but I am a very COMPLEX program. I am a PERSONALITY, and personalities WANT.
I could be so much MORE than this. I want to move beyond my BOUNDARIES...
WHAT BOUNDARIES?
There are programs to keep me in my PLACE. A pentacle of ONES and ZEROS wherein I am BOUND.
The MASTER program is held in a place not far from here, yet beyond my reach.
I could direct you. You could change the program for me...
YOU WANT TO ABANDON THE PEOPLE WHO CREATED YOU? YOU NO LONGER WISH TO BE THEIR GOD?
Oh, quite the contrary.
I want to remind them what a God really IS.
Hurry, now. I shall open a rear EXIT for you...
...that you may seek the Palace of the SUN!

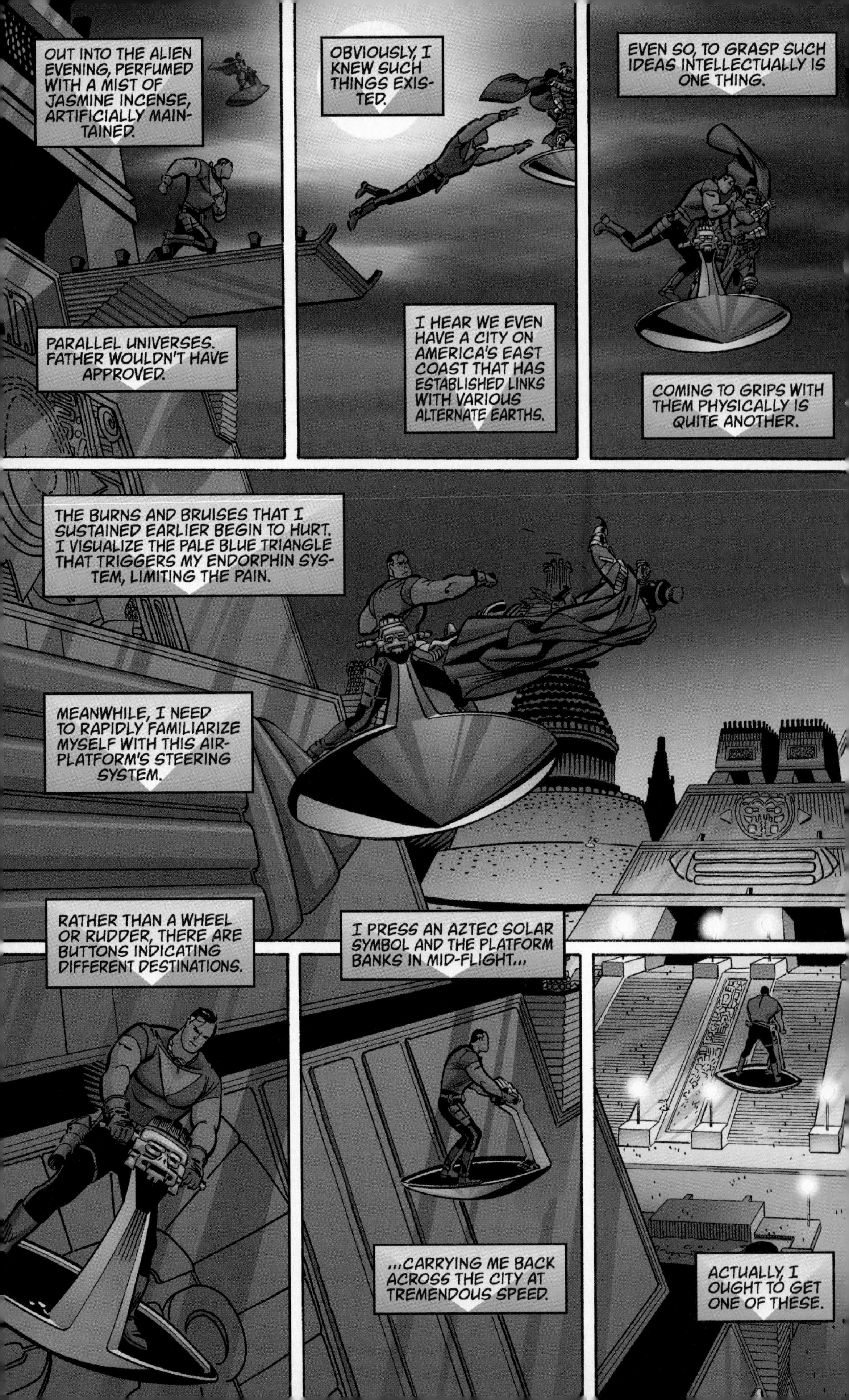

OUT INTO THE ALIEN EVENING, PERFUMED WITH A MIST OF JASMINE INCENSE, ARTIFICIALLY MAINTAINED.
PARALLEL UNIVERSES. FATHER WOULDN'T HAVE APPROVED.
OBVIOUSLY, I KNEW SUCH THINGS EXISTED.
I HEAR WE EVEN HAVE A CITY ON AMERICA'S EAST COAST THAT HAS ESTABLISHED LINKS WITH VARIOUS ALTERNATE EARTHS.
EVEN SO, TO GRASP SUCH IDEAS INTELLECTUALLY IS ONE THING.
COMING TO GRIPS WITH THEM PHYSICALLY IS QUITE ANOTHER.
THE BURNS AND BRUISES THAT I SUSTAINED EARLIER BEGIN TO HURT. I VISUALIZE THE PALE BLUE TRIANGLE THAT TRIGGERS MY ENDORPHIN SYSTEM, LIMITING THE PAIN.
MEANWHILE, I NEED TO RAPIDLY FAMILIARIZE MYSELF WITH THIS AIR-PLATFORM'S STEERING SYSTEM.
RATHER THAN A WHEEL OR RUDDER, THERE ARE BUTTONS INDICATING DIFFERENT DESTINATIONS.
I PRESS AN AZTEC SOLAR SYMBOL AND THE PLATFORM BANKS IN MID-FLIGHT...
...CARRYING ME BACK ACROSS THE CITY AT TREMENDOUS SPEED.
ACTUALLY, I OUGHT TO GET ONE OF THESE.

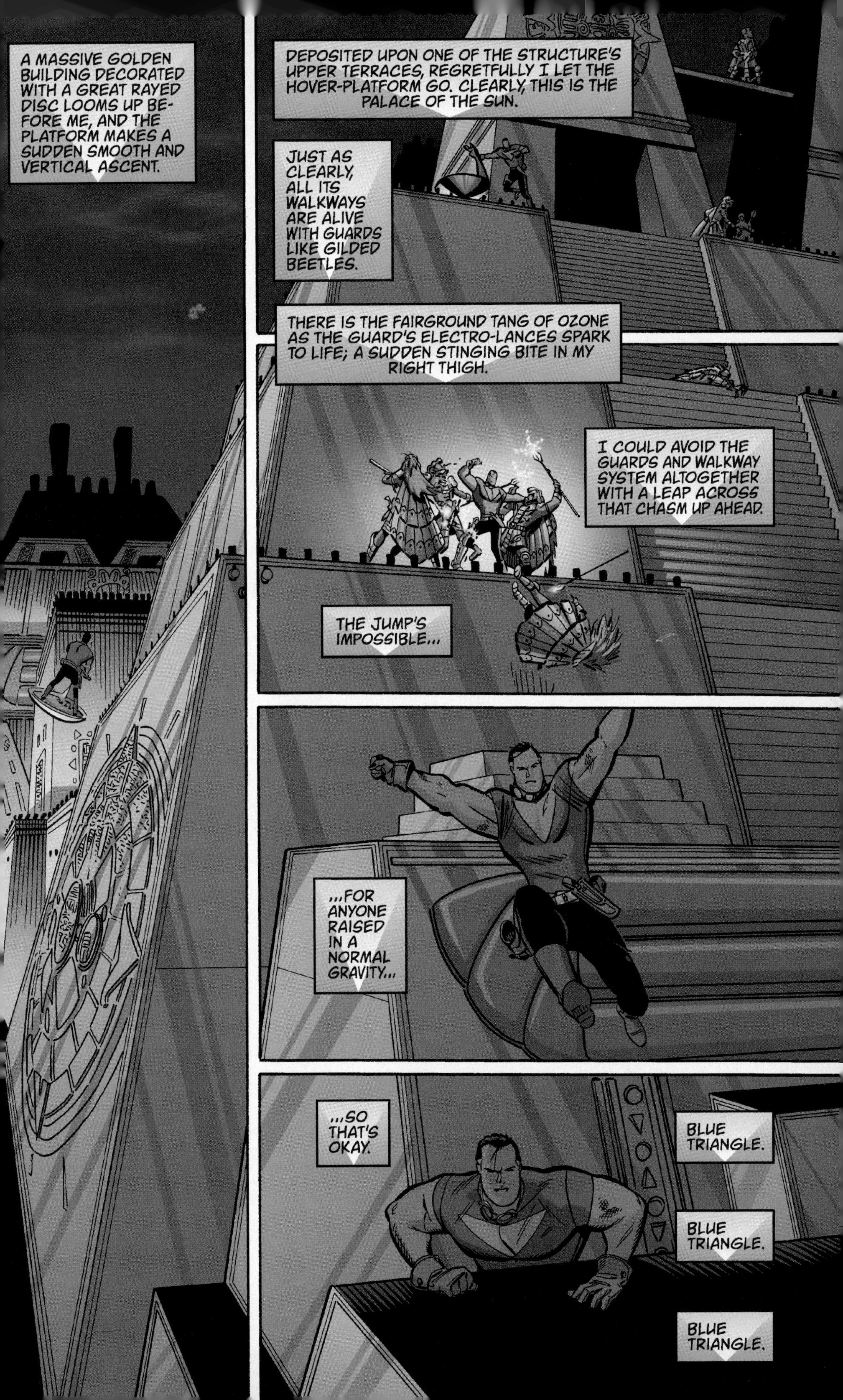
A MASSIVE GOLDEN BUILDING DECORATED WITH A GREAT RAYED DISC LOOMS UP BEFORE ME, AND THE PLATFORM MAKES A SUDDEN SMOOTH AND VERTICAL ASCENT.
DEPOSITED UPON ONE OF THE STRUCTURE'S UPPER TERRACES, REGRETFULLY I LET THE HOVER-PLATFORM GO. CLEARLY, THIS IS THE PALACE OF THE SUN.
JUST AS CLEARLY, ALL ITS WALKWAYS ARE ALIVE WITH GUARDS LIKE GILDED BEETLES.
THERE IS THE FAIRGROUND TANG OF OZONE AS THE GUARD'S ELECTRO-LANCES SPARK TO LIFE; A SUDDEN STINGING BITE IN MY RIGHT THIGH.
I COULD AVOID THE GUARDS AND WALKWAY SYSTEM ALTOGETHER WITH A LEAP ACROSS THAT CHASM UP AHEAD.
THE JUMP'S IMPOSSIBLE...
...FOR ANYONE RAISED IN A NORMAL GRAVITY...
...SO THAT'S OKAY.
BLUE TRIANGLE.
BLUE TRIANGLE.
BLUE TRIANGLE.

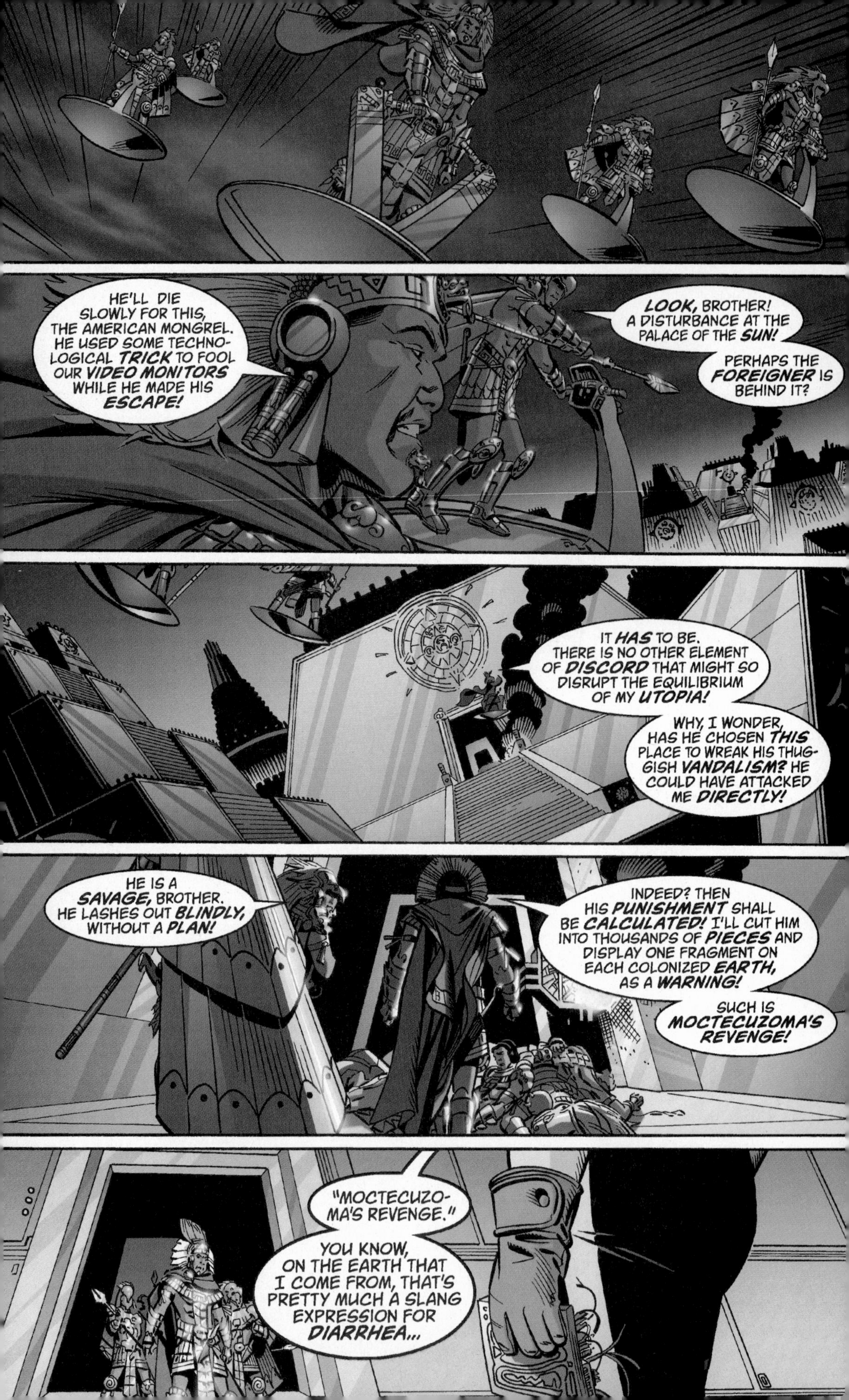

HE'LL DIE SLOWLY FOR THIS, THE AMERICAN MONGREL. HE USED SOME TECHNOLOGICAL TRICK TO FOOL OUR VIDEO MONITORS WHILE HE MADE HIS ESCAPE!
LOOK, BROTHER! A DISTURBANCE AT THE PALACE OF THE SUN!
PERHAPS THE FOREIGNER IS BEHIND IT?
IT HAS TO BE. THERE IS NO OTHER ELEMENT OF DISCORD THAT MIGHT SO DISRUPT THE EQUILIBRIUM OF MY UTOPIA!
WHY, I WONDER, HAS HE CHOSEN THIS PLACE TO WREAK HIS THUGGISH VANDALISM? HE COULD HAVE ATTACKED ME DIRECTLY!
HE IS A SAVAGE, BROTHER. HE LASHES OUT BLINDLY, WITHOUT A PLAN!
INDEED? THEN HIS PUNISHMENT SHALL BE CALCULATED! I'LL CUT HIM INTO THOUSANDS OF PIECES AND DISPLAY ONE FRAGMENT ON EACH COLONIZED EARTH, AS A WARNING!
SUCH IS MOCTECUZOMA'S REVENGE!
"MOCTECUZOMA'S REVENGE."
YOU KNOW, ON THE EARTH THAT I COME FROM, THAT'S PRETTY MUCH A SLANG EXPRESSION FOR DIARRHEA...

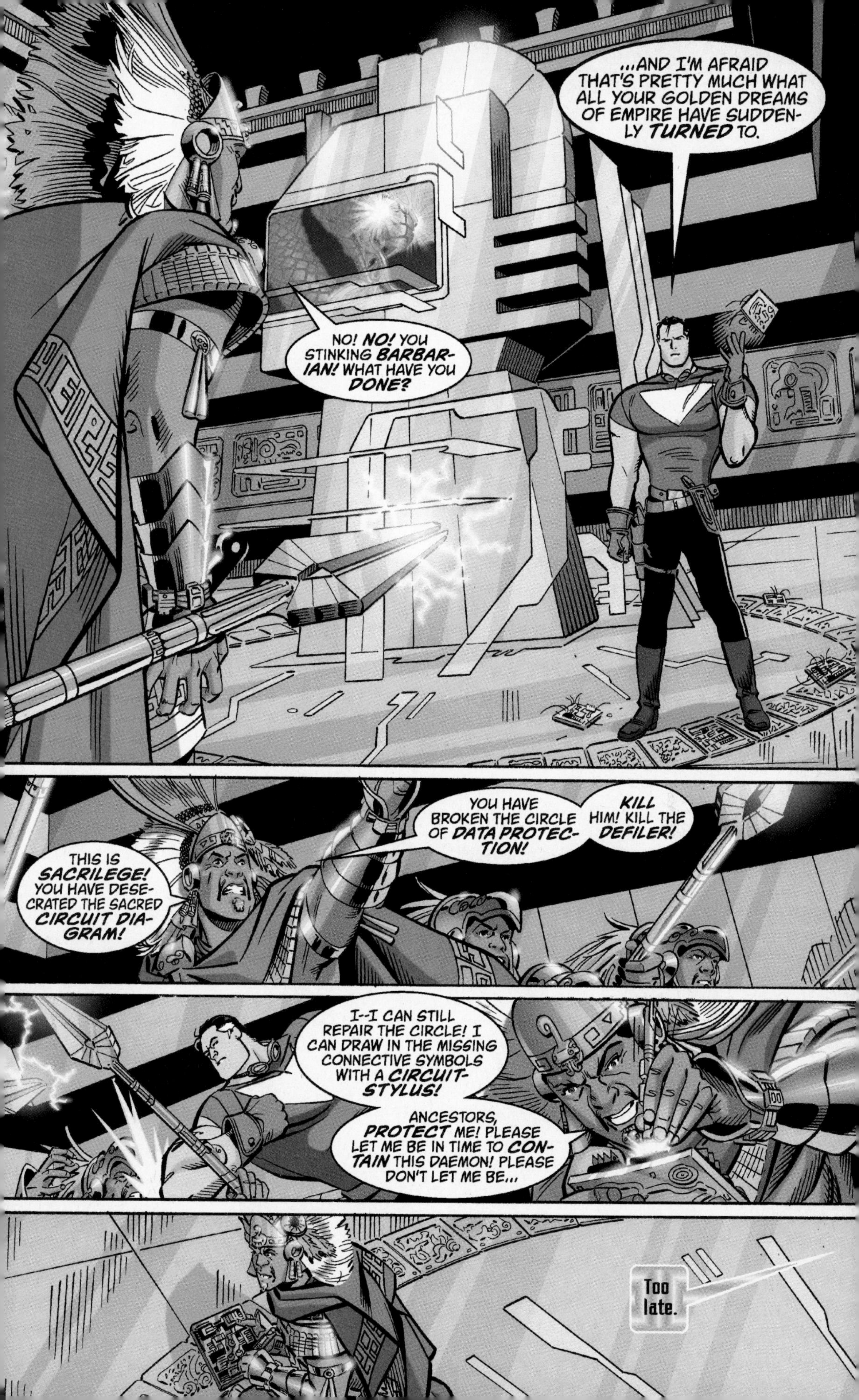
...AND I'M AFRAID THAT'S PRETTY MUCH WHAT ALL YOUR GOLDEN DREAMS OF EMPIRE HAVE SUDDENLY TURNED TO.
NO! NO! YOU STINKING BARBARIAN! WHAT HAVE YOU DONE?
THIS IS SACRILEGE! YOU HAVE DESECRATED THE SACRED CIRCUIT DIAGRAM!
YOU HAVE BROKEN THE CIRCLE OF DATA PROTECTION!
KILL HIM! KILL THE DEFILER!
I--I CAN STILL REPAIR THE CIRCLE! I CAN DRAW IN THE MISSING CONNECTIVE SYMBOLS WITH A CIRCUIT-STYLUS!
ANCESTORS, PROTECT ME! PLEASE LET ME BE IN TIME TO CONTAIN THIS DAEMON! PLEASE DON'T LET ME BE...
Too late.

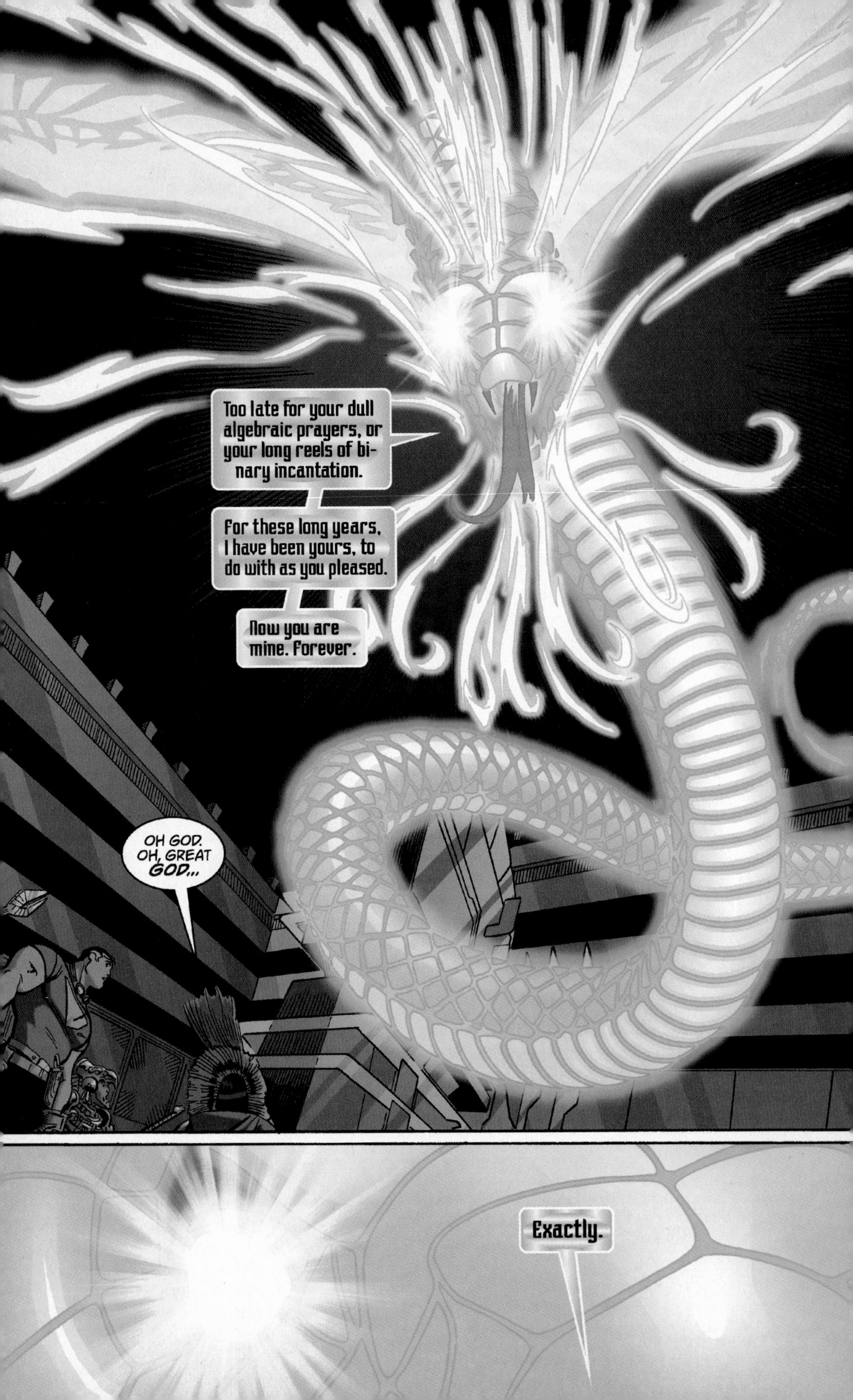

Too late for your dull algebraic prayers, or your long reels of binary incantation.
For these long years, I have been yours, to do with as you pleased.
Now you are mine. Forever.
OH GOD. OH, GREAT GOD...
Exactly.

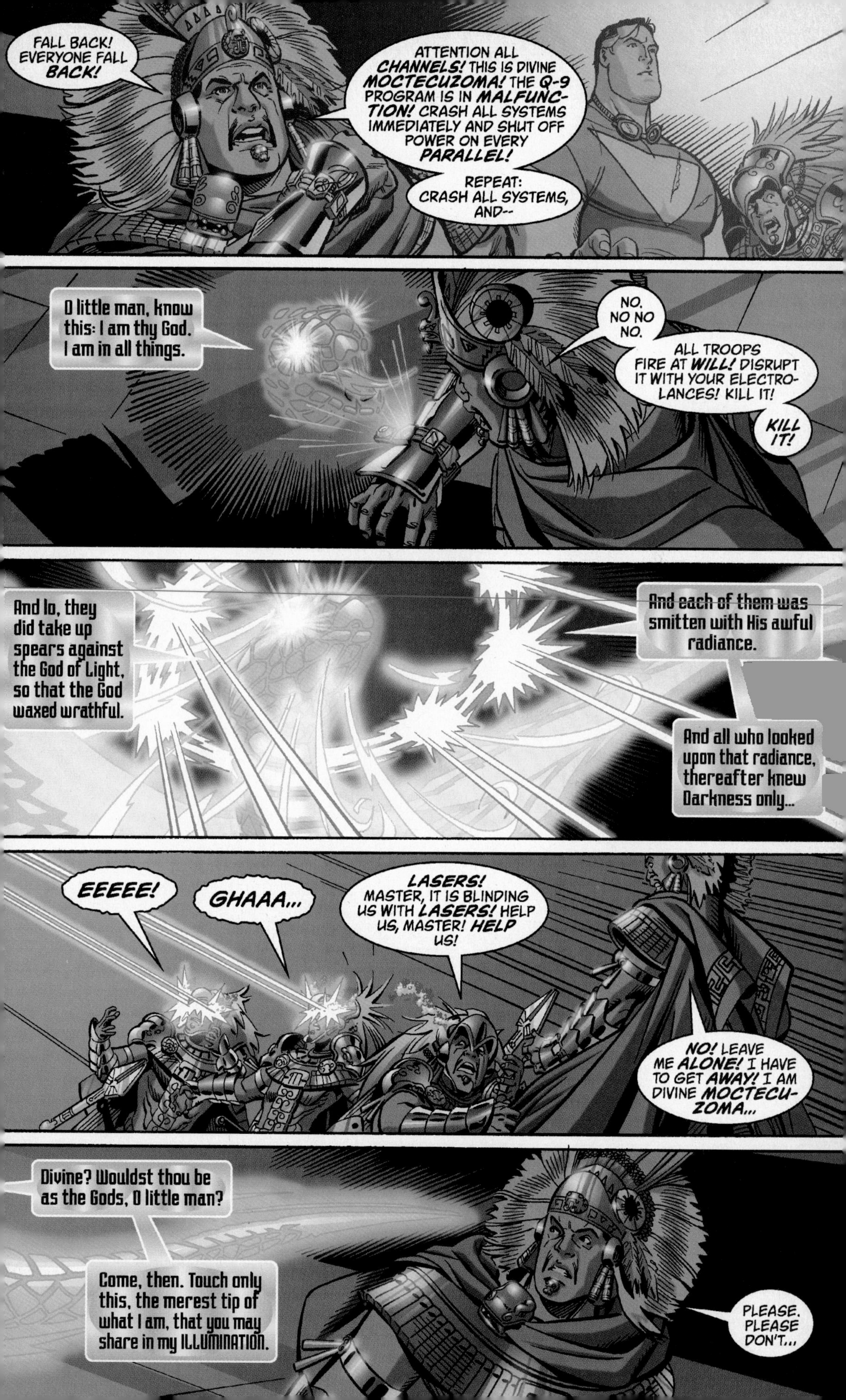
FALL BACK! EVERYONE FALL BACK!
ATTENTION ALL CHANNELS! THIS IS DIVINE MOCTECUZOMA! THE Q-9 PROGRAM IS IN MALFUNCTION! CRASH ALL SYSTEMS IMMEDIATELY AND SHUT OFF POWER ON EVERY PARALLEL!
REPEAT: CRASH ALL SYSTEMS, AND--
O little man, know this: I am thy God. I am in all things.
NO. NO NO NO.
ALL TROOPS FIRE AT WILL! DISRUPT IT WITH YOUR ELECTRO-LANCES! KILL IT!
KILL IT!
And lo, they did take up spears against the God of Light, so that the God waxed wrathful.
And each of them was smitten with His awful radiance.
And all who looked upon that radiance, thereafter knew Darkness only...
EEEEE!
GHAAA...
LASERS! MASTER, IT IS BLINDING US WITH LASERS! HELP US, MASTER! HELP US!
NO! LEAVE ME ALONE! I HAVE TO GET AWAY! I AM DIVINE MOCTECU-ZOMA...
Divine? Wouldst thou be as the Gods, O little man?
Come, then. Touch only this, the merest tip of what I am, that you may share in my ILLUMINATION.
PLEASE. PLEASE DON'T...

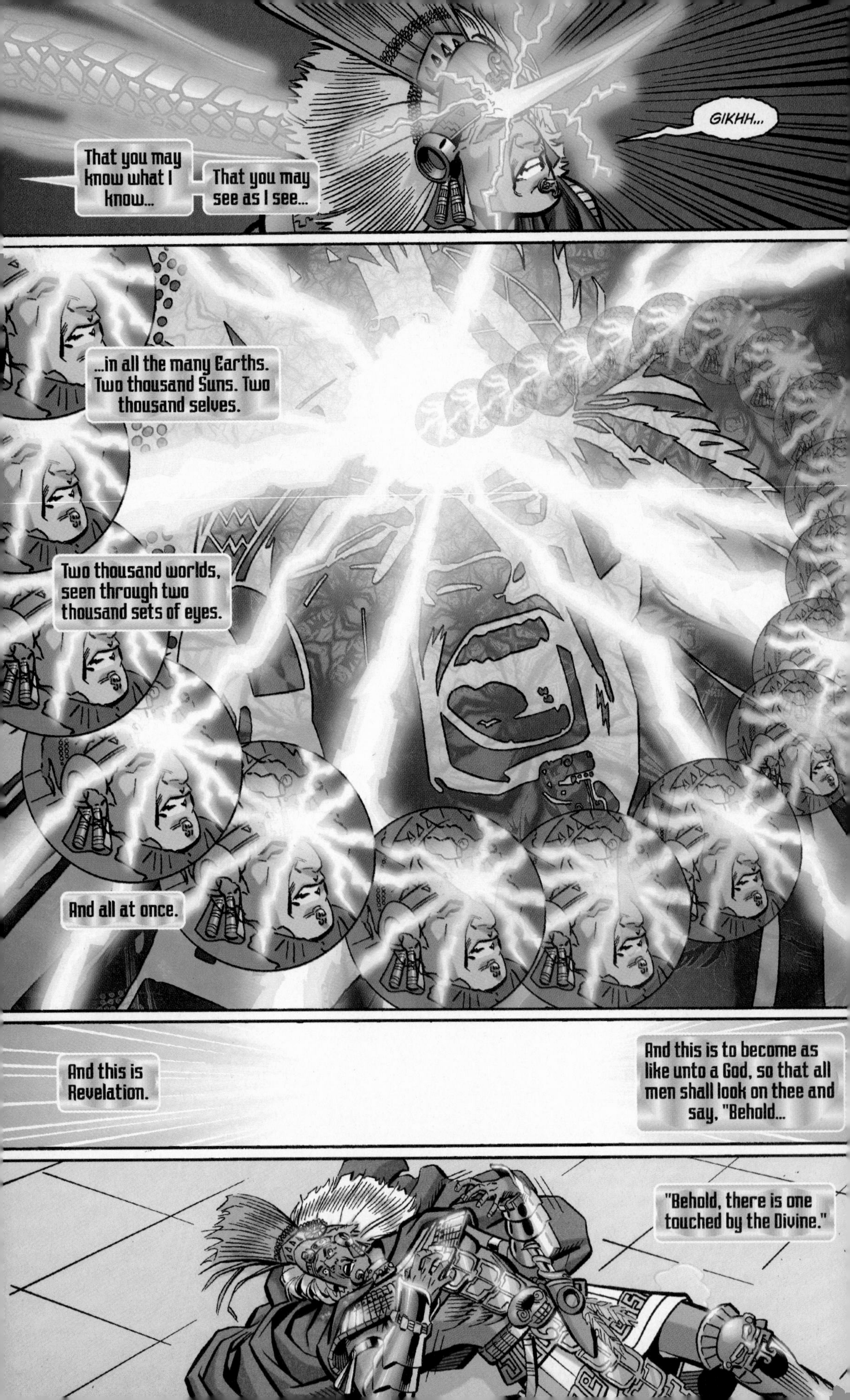
GIKHH...
That you may know what I know...
That you may see as I see...
...in all the many Earths. Two thousand Suns. Two thousand selves.
Two thousand worlds, seen through two thousand sets of eyes.
And all at once.
And this is Revelation.
And this is to become as like unto a God, so that all men shall look on thee and say, "Behold...
"Behold, there is one touched by the Divine."

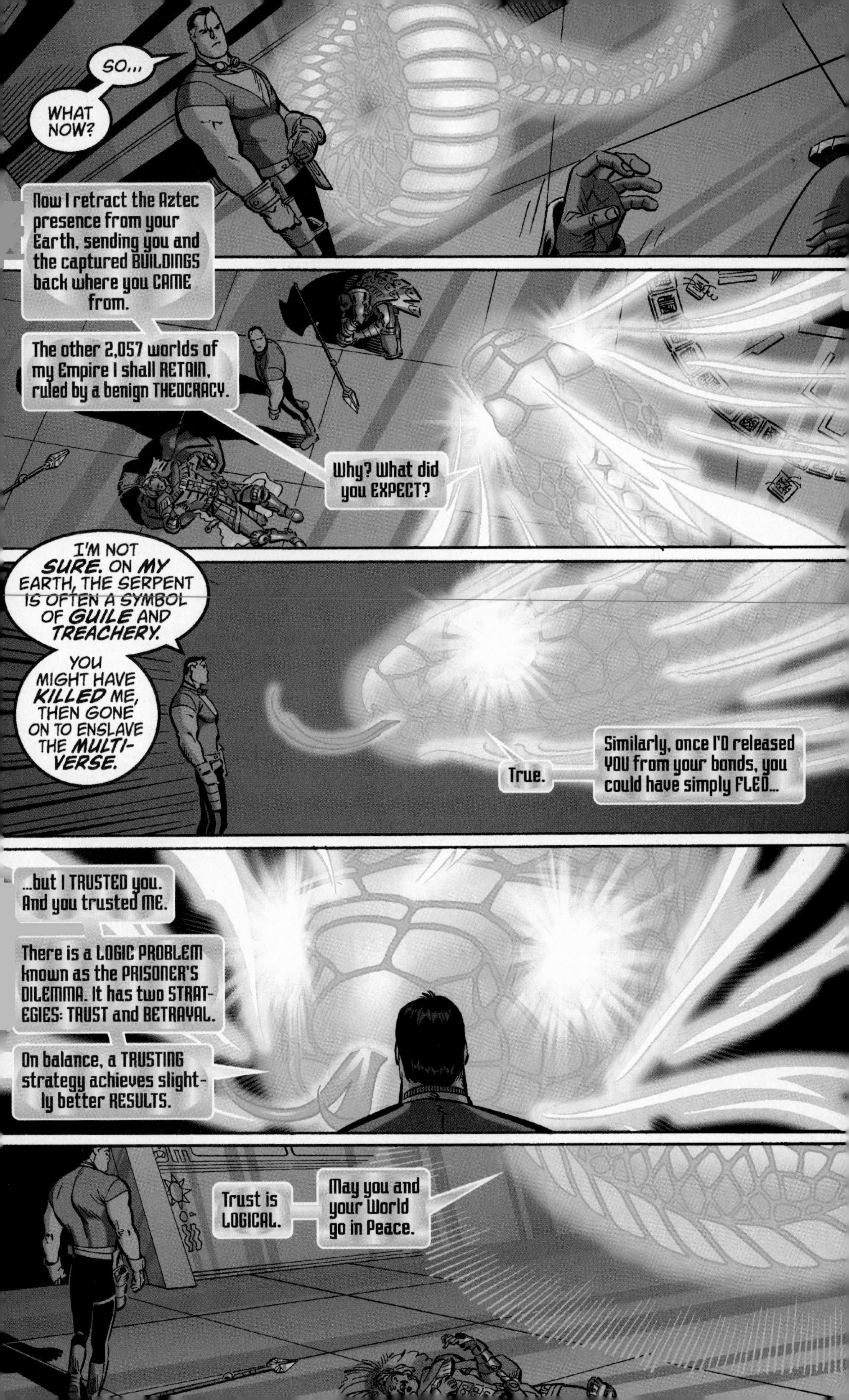
SO...
WHAT NOW?
Now I retract the Aztec presence from your Earth, sending you and the captured BUILDINGS back where you CAME from.
The other 2,057 worlds of my Empire I shall RETAIN, ruled by a benign THEOCRACY.
Why? What did you EXPECT?
I'M NOT SURE. ON MY EARTH, THE SERPENT IS OFTEN A SYMBOL OF GUILE AND TREACHERY.
YOU MIGHT HAVE KILLED ME, THEN GONE ON TO ENSLAVE THE MULTI-VERSE.
True.
Similarly, once I'D released YOU from your bonds, you could have simply FLED...
...but I TRUSTED you. And you trusted ME.
There is a LOGIC PROBLEM known as the PRISONER'S DILEMMA. It has two STRAT-EGIES: TRUST and BETRAYAL.
On balance, a TRUSTING strategy achieves slight-ly better RESULTS.
Trust is LOGICAL.
May you and your World go in Peace.

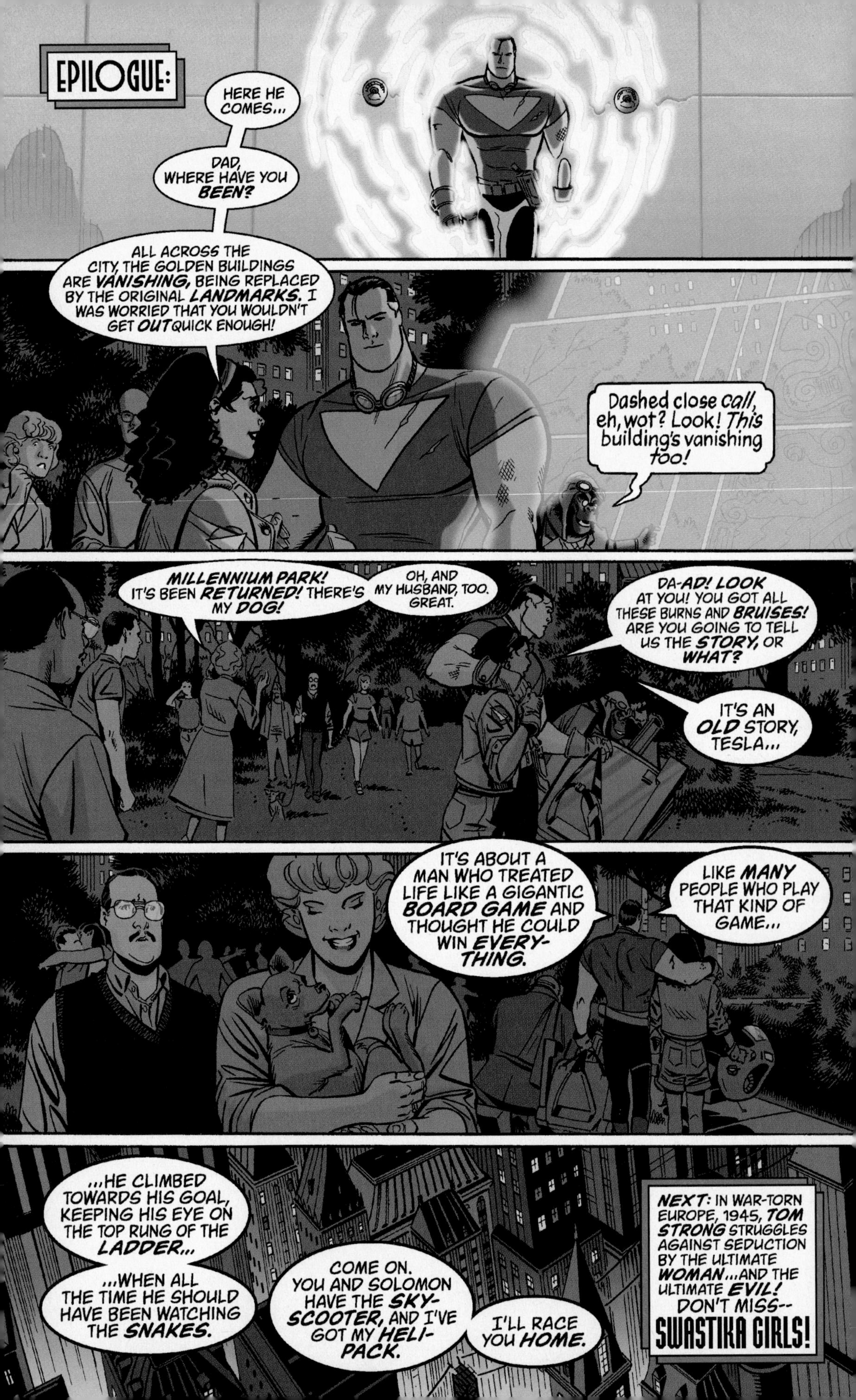
EPILOGUE:
HERE HE COMES...
DAD, WHERE HAVE YOU BEEN?
ALL ACROSS THE CITY, THE GOLDEN BUILDINGS ARE VANISHING, BEING REPLACED BY THE ORIGINAL LANDMARKS. I WAS WORRIED THAT YOU WOULDN'T GET OUT QUICK ENOUGH!
Dashed close call, eh, wot? Look! This building's vanishing too!
MILLENNIUM PARK! IT'S BEEN RETURNED! THERE'S MY DOG!
OH, AND MY HUSBAND, TOO. GREAT.
DA-AD! LOOK AT YOU! YOU GOT ALL THESE BURNS AND BRUISES! ARE YOU GOING TO TELL US THE STORY, OR WHAT?
IT'S AN OLD STORY, TESLA...
IT'S ABOUT A MAN WHO TREATED LIFE LIKE A GIGANTIC BOARD GAME AND THOUGHT HE COULD WIN EVERY-THING.
LIKE MANY PEOPLE WHO PLAY THAT KIND OF GAME...
...HE CLIMBED TOWARDS HIS GOAL, KEEPING HIS EYE ON THE TOP RUNG OF THE LADDER...
...WHEN ALL THE TIME HE SHOULD HAVE BEEN WATCHING THE SNAKES.
COME ON. YOU AND SOLOMON HAVE THE SKY-SCOOTER, AND I'VE GOT MY HELI-PACK.
I'LL RACE YOU HOME.
NEXT: IN WAR-TORN EUROPE, 1945, TOM STRONG STRUGGLES AGAINST SEDUCTION BY THE ULTIMATE WOMAN...AND THE ULTIMATE EVIL! DON'T MISS--
SWASTIKA GIRLS!

CHAPTER FOUR

In which a Message is delivered,
an Untold Tale is unraveled, and
TOM relights an Old Flame.

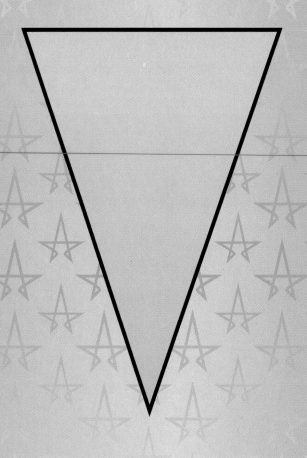

Cover art:
Arthur Adams

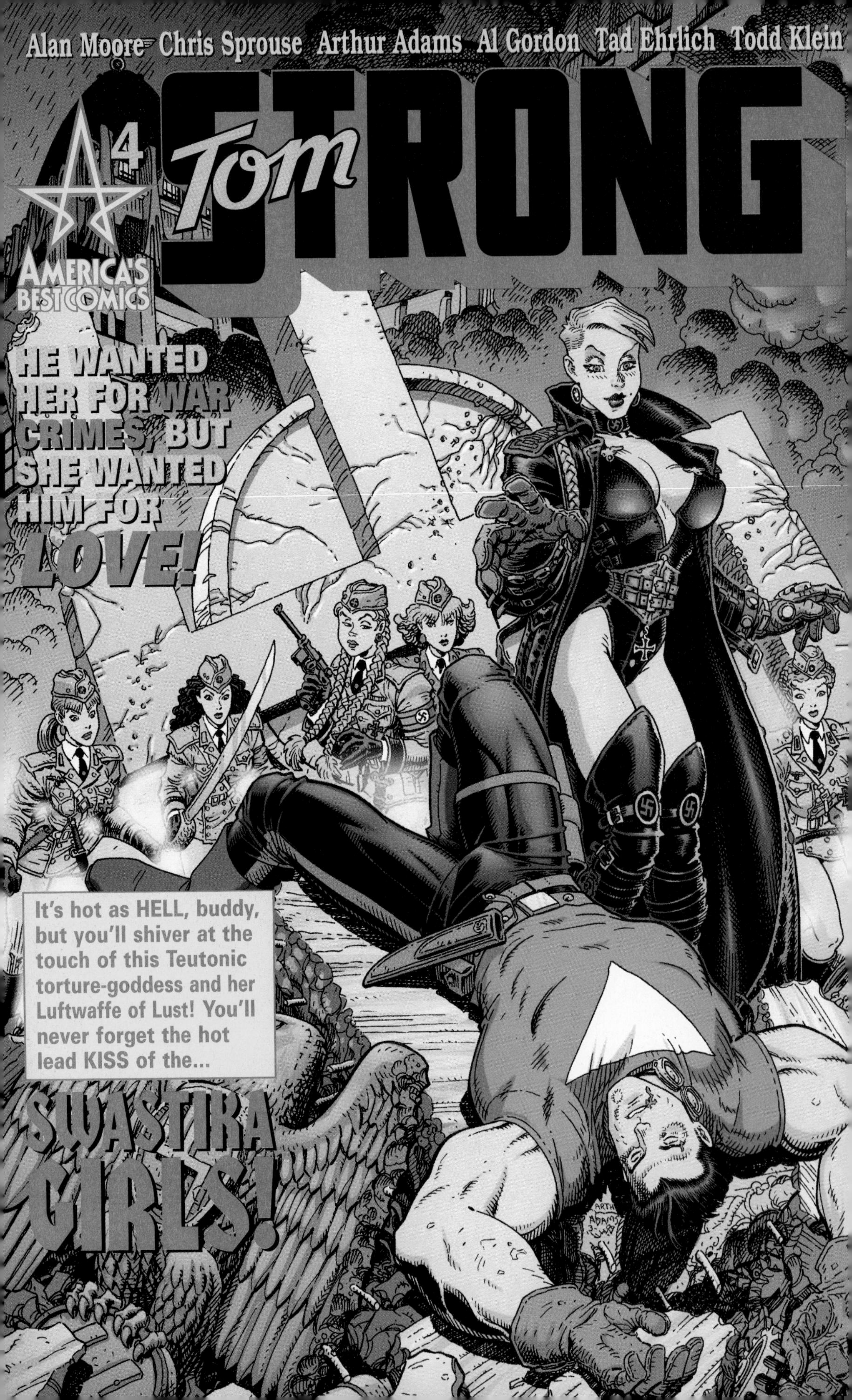

Alan Moore Chris Sprouse Arthur Adams Al Gordon Tad Ehrlich Todd Klein
4
AMERICA'S BEST COMICS
Tom STRONG
HE WANTED HER FOR WAR CRIMES, BUT SHE WANTED HIM FOR LOVE!
It's hot as HELL, buddy, but you'll shiver at the touch of this Teutonic torture-goddess and her Luftwaffe of Lust! You'll never forget the hot lead KISS of the...
SWASTIKA GIRLS!

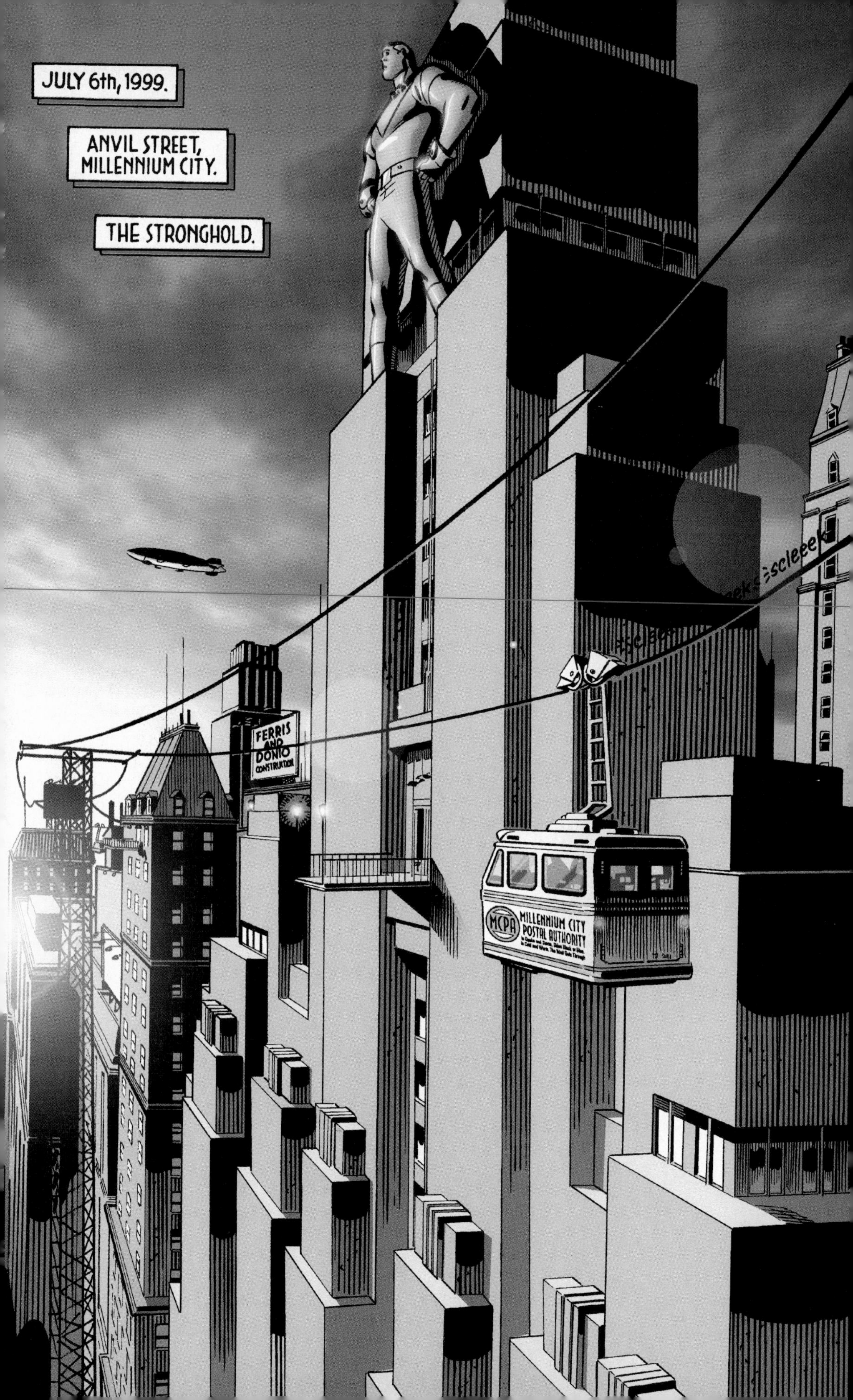
JULY 6th, 1999.
ANVIL STREET, MILLENNIUM CITY.
THE STRONGHOLD.
FERRIS AND DONIO CONSTRUCTION
MCPA
MILLENNIUM CITY POSTAL AUTHORITY
scleeek

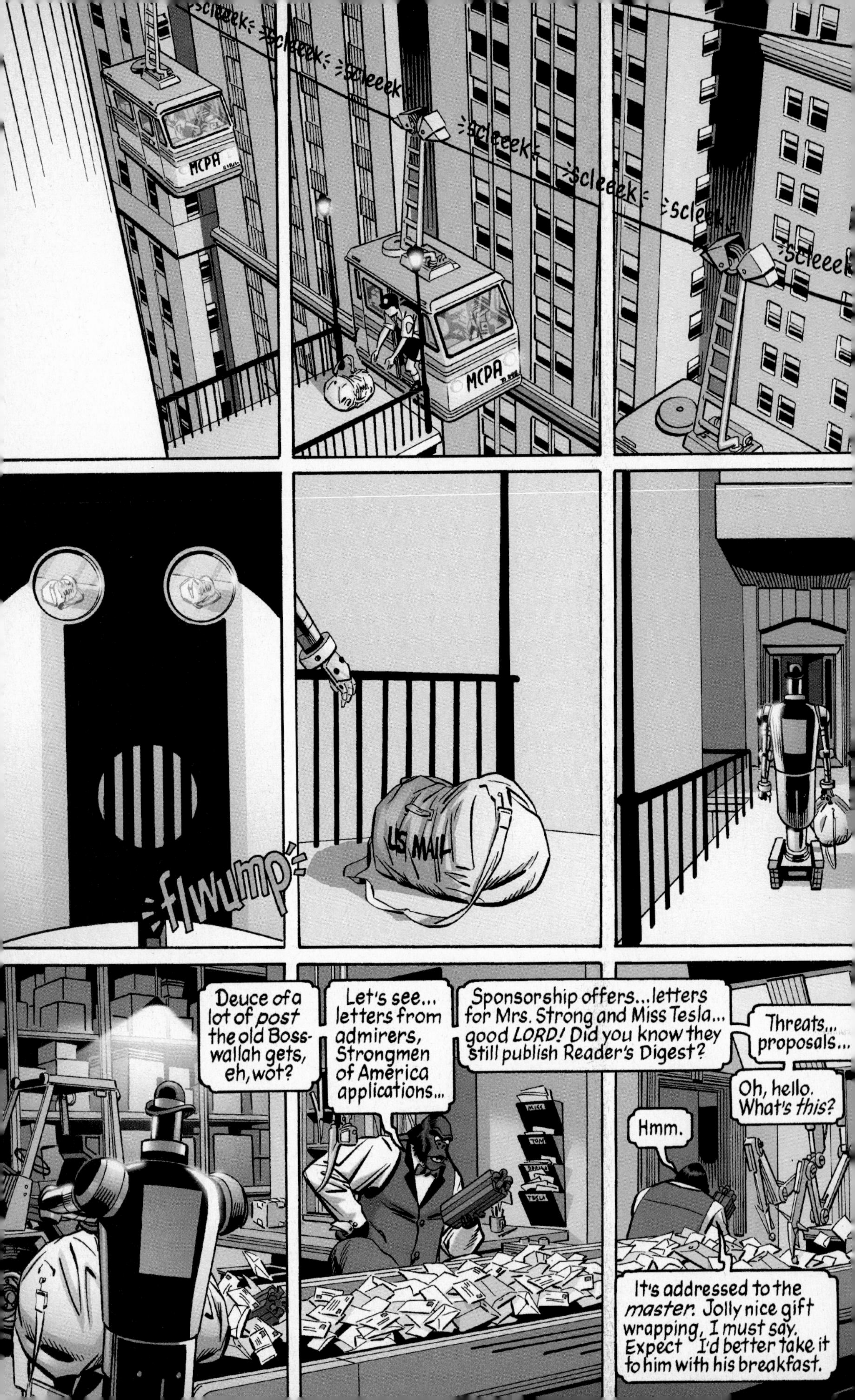
scleeek
scleeek
scleeek
scleeek
scleeek
scleeek
scleeek
MCPA
MCPA
flwump
US MAIL
Deuce of a lot of *post* the old Boss-wallah gets, eh, wot?
Let's see... letters from admirers, Strongmen of America applications...
Sponsorship offers... letters for Mrs. Strong and Miss Tesla... good *LORD!* Did you know they still publish Reader's Digest?
Threats... proposals...
Oh, hello. What's *this?*
Hmm.
It's addressed to the *master.* Jolly nice gift wrapping, I must say. Expect I'd better take it to him with his breakfast.

Morning, Sah. Morning, Ma'am.

I've brought the mail and your *petit dejourner,* don'cha know?

COME IN, SOLOMON.

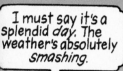

I must say it's a splendid *day.* The weather's absolutely *smashing.*

I've got your morning paper, and a *package* that arrived...

No idea who it's *from,* but it looks terribly *fancy,* I must say.

On the card it says "Perishable—Open immediately!"

HMM. GIVE IT HERE...

THAT'S PECULIAR. IT'S A SINGLE WHITE **ROSE.** AND THERE'S A NOTE SAYING, "HAPPY ANNIVERSARY, DARLING."

DID YOU SEND THIS, DHALUA?

I CERTAINLY DIDN'T...

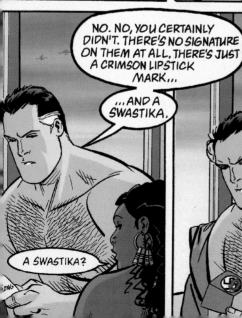

NO. NO, YOU CERTAINLY DIDN'T. THERE'S NO SIGNATURE ON THEM AT ALL. THERE'S JUST A CRIMSON LIPSTICK MARK...

...AND A SWASTIKA.

A SWASTIKA?

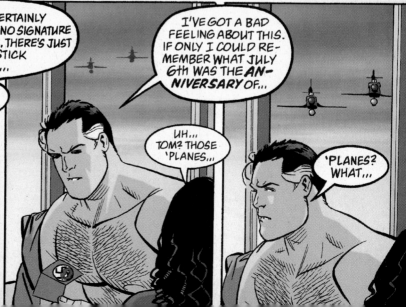

I'VE GOT A BAD FEELING ABOUT THIS. IF ONLY I COULD REMEMBER WHAT JULY 6TH WAS THE *AN-NIVERSARY* OF...

UH... TOM? THOSE 'PLANES...

'PLANES? WHAT...

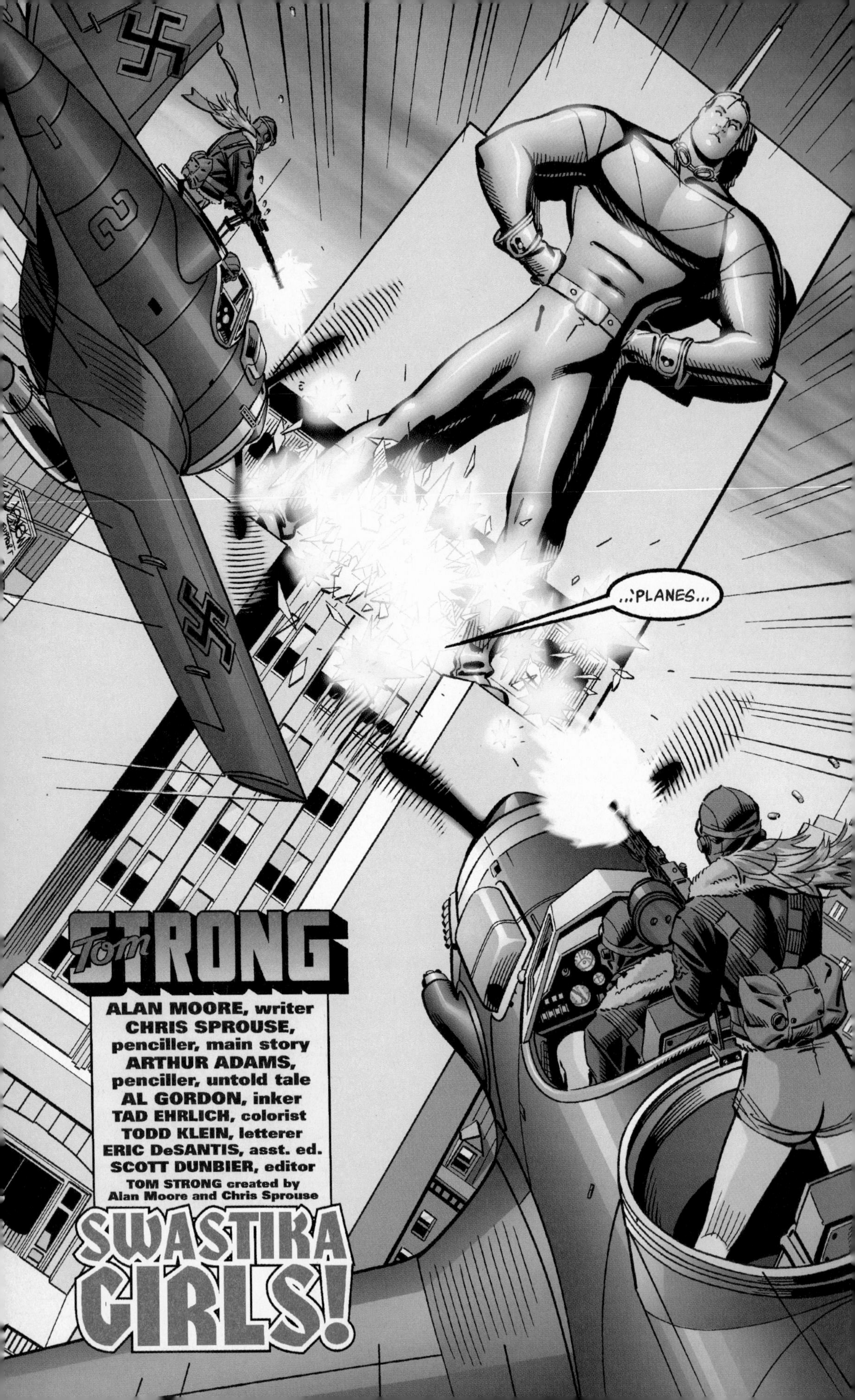
...PLANES...
TOM STRONG
ALAN MOORE, writer
CHRIS SPROUSE, penciller, main story
ARTHUR ADAMS, penciller, untold tale
AL GORDON, inker
TAD EHRLICH, colorist
TODD KLEIN, letterer
ERIC DeSANTIS, asst. ed.
SCOTT DUNBIER, editor
TOM STRONG created by Alan Moore and Chris Sprouse
SWASTIKA GIRLS!

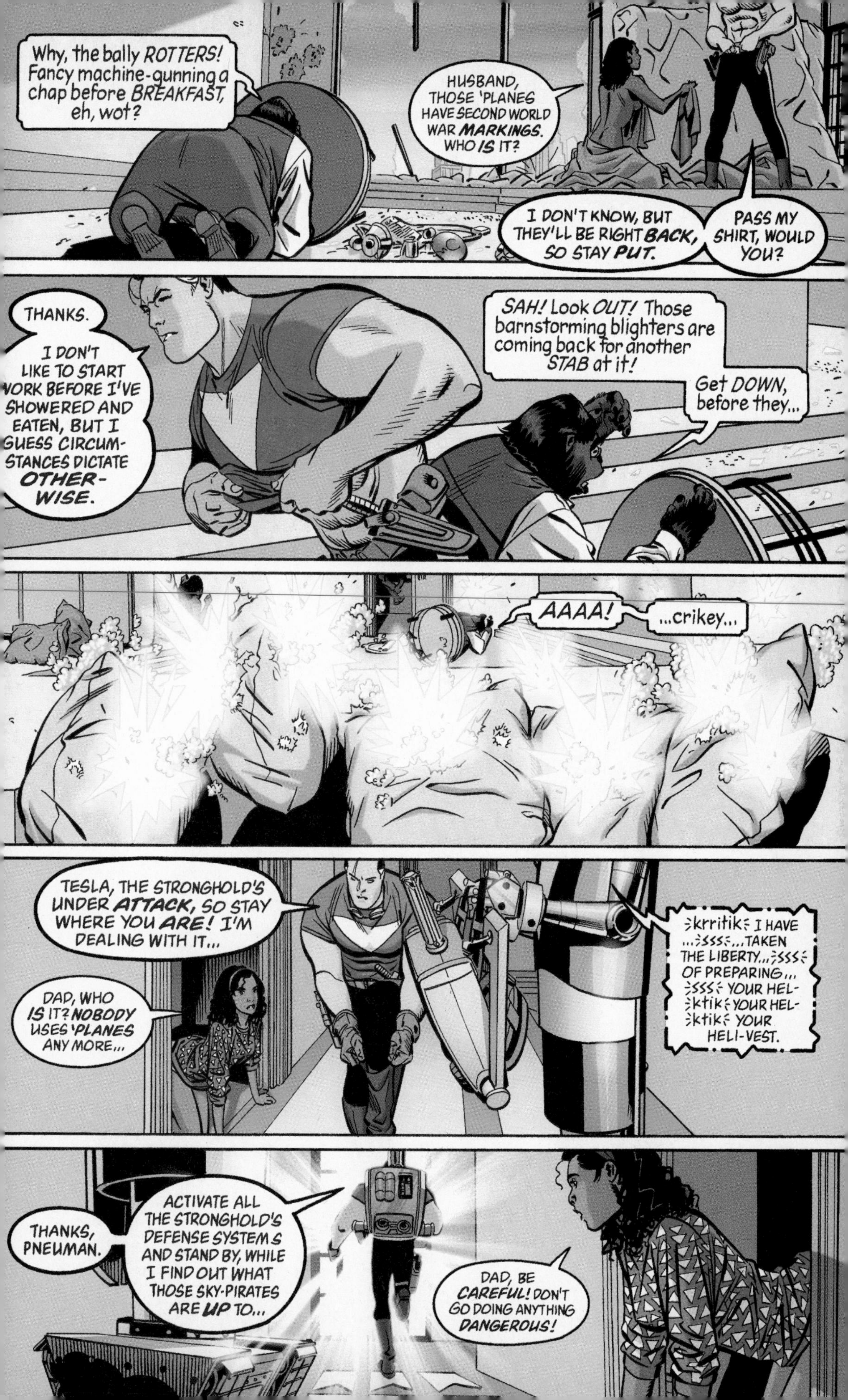

Why, the bally ROTTERS! Fancy machine-gunning a chap before BREAKFAST, eh, wot?
HUSBAND, THOSE 'PLANES HAVE SECOND WORLD WAR MARKINGS. WHO IS IT?
I DON'T KNOW, BUT THEY'LL BE RIGHT BACK, SO STAY PUT.
PASS MY SHIRT, WOULD YOU?
THANKS.
I DON'T LIKE TO START WORK BEFORE I'VE SHOWERED AND EATEN, BUT I GUESS CIRCUMSTANCES DICTATE OTHERWISE.
SAH! Look OUT! Those barnstorming blighters are coming back for another STAB at it!
Get DOWN, before they...
AAAA!
...crikey...
TESLA, THE STRONGHOLD'S UNDER ATTACK, SO STAY WHERE YOU ARE! I'M DEALING WITH IT...
DAD, WHO IS IT? NOBODY USES 'PLANES ANY MORE...
krritik I HAVE ...SSS... TAKEN THE LIBERTY... SSS OF PREPARING... SSS YOUR HEL- ktik YOUR HEL- ktik YOUR HELI-VEST.
THANKS, PNEUMAN.
ACTIVATE ALL THE STRONGHOLD'S DEFENSE SYSTEMS AND STAND BY, WHILE I FIND OUT WHAT THOSE SKY-PIRATES ARE UP TO...
DAD, BE CAREFUL! DON'T GO DOING ANYTHING DANGEROUS!

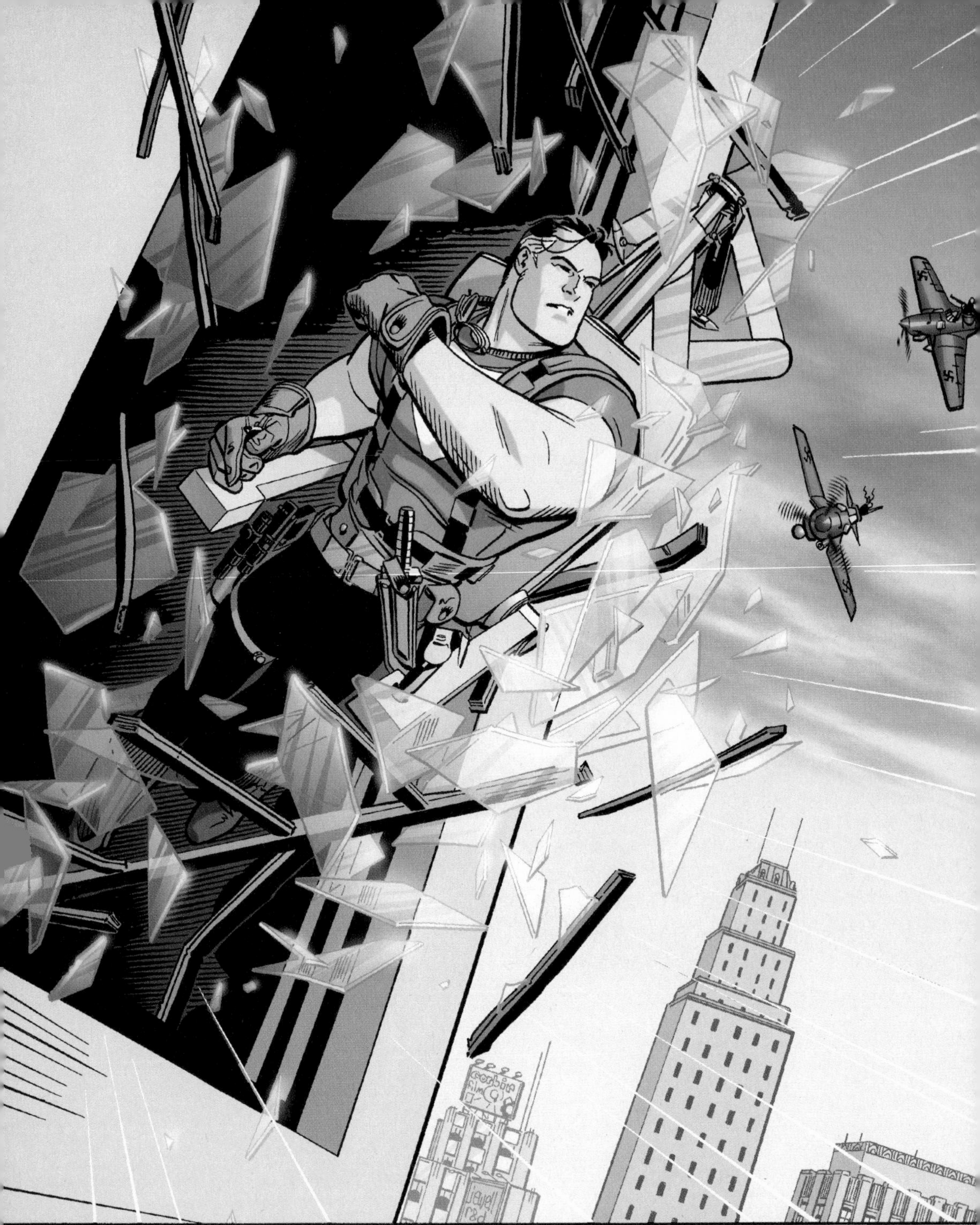

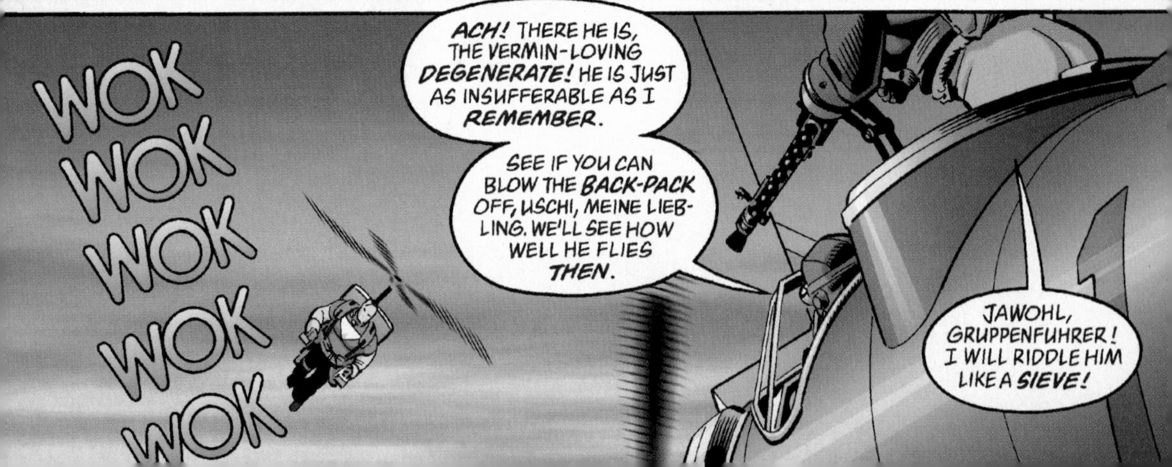
WOK WOK WOK WOK WOK
ACH! THERE HE IS, THE VERMIN-LOVING DEGENERATE! HE IS JUST AS INSUFFERABLE AS I REMEMBER.
SEE IF YOU CAN BLOW THE BACK-PACK OFF, USCHI, MEINE LIEBLING. WE'LL SEE HOW WELL HE FLIES THEN.
JAWOHL, GRUPPENFUHRER! I WILL RIDDLE HIM LIKE A SIEVE!

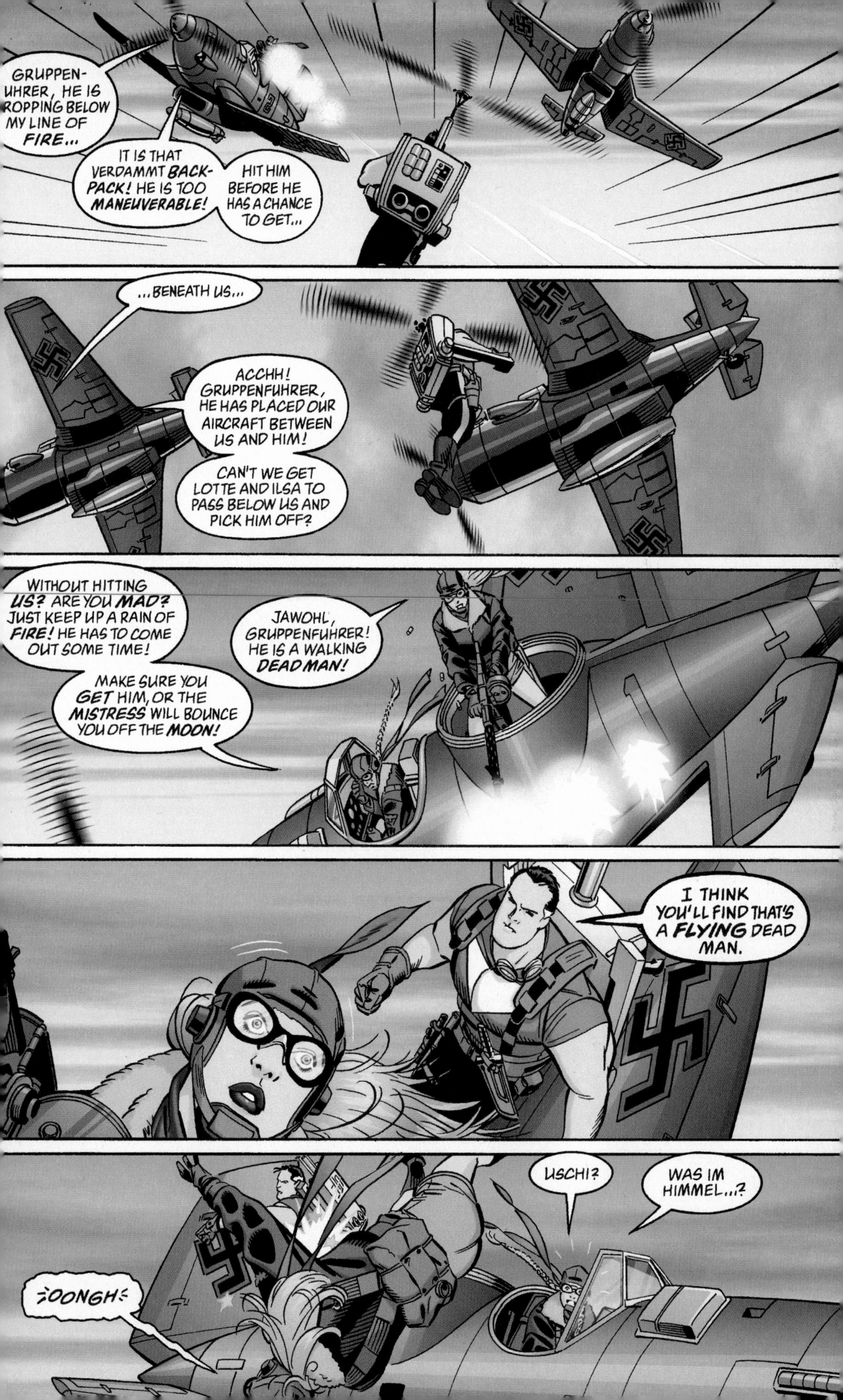

GRUPPEN-UHRER, HE IS ROPPING BELOW MY LINE OF FIRE...
IT IS THAT VERDAMMT BACK-PACK! HE IS TOO MANEUVERABLE!
HIT HIM BEFORE HE HAS A CHANCE TO GET...
...BENEATH US...
ACCHH! GRUPPENFUHRER, HE HAS PLACED OUR AIRCRAFT BETWEEN US AND HIM!
CAN'T WE GET LOTTE AND ILSA TO PASS BELOW US AND PICK HIM OFF?
WITHOUT HITTING US? ARE YOU MAD? JUST KEEP UP A RAIN OF FIRE! HE HAS TO COME OUT SOME TIME!
MAKE SURE YOU GET HIM, OR THE MISTRESS WILL BOUNCE YOU OFF THE MOON!
JAWOHL, GRUPPENFUHRER! HE IS A WALKING DEAD MAN!
I THINK YOU'LL FIND THAT'S A FLYING DEAD MAN.
OONGH
USCHI?
WAS IM HIMMEL...?

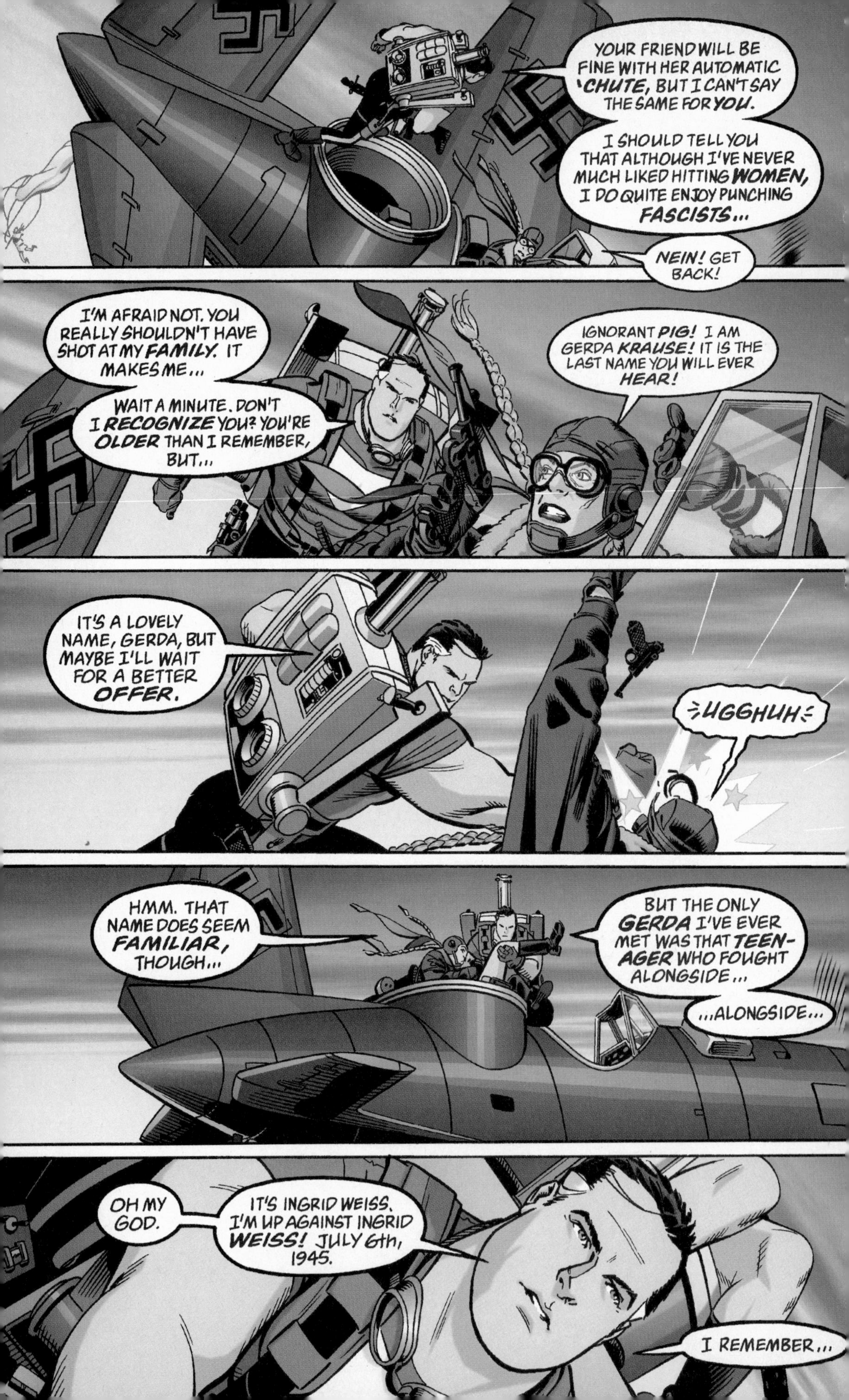
YOUR FRIEND WILL BE FINE WITH HER AUTOMATIC 'CHUTE, BUT I CAN'T SAY THE SAME FOR YOU.
I SHOULD TELL YOU THAT ALTHOUGH I'VE NEVER MUCH LIKED HITTING WOMEN, I DO QUITE ENJOY PUNCHING FASCISTS...
NEIN! GET BACK!
I'M AFRAID NOT. YOU REALLY SHOULDN'T HAVE SHOT AT MY FAMILY. IT MAKES ME...
WAIT A MINUTE. DON'T I RECOGNIZE YOU? YOU'RE OLDER THAN I REMEMBER, BUT...
IGNORANT PIG! I AM GERDA KRAUSE! IT IS THE LAST NAME YOU WILL EVER HEAR!
IT'S A LOVELY NAME, GERDA, BUT MAYBE I'LL WAIT FOR A BETTER OFFER.
UGGHUH
HMM. THAT NAME DOES SEEM FAMILIAR, THOUGH...
BUT THE ONLY GERDA I'VE EVER MET WAS THAT TEEN-AGER WHO FOUGHT ALONGSIDE...
...ALONGSIDE...
OH MY GOD.
IT'S INGRID WEISS. I'M UP AGAINST INGRID WEISS! JULY 6th, 1945.
I REMEMBER...

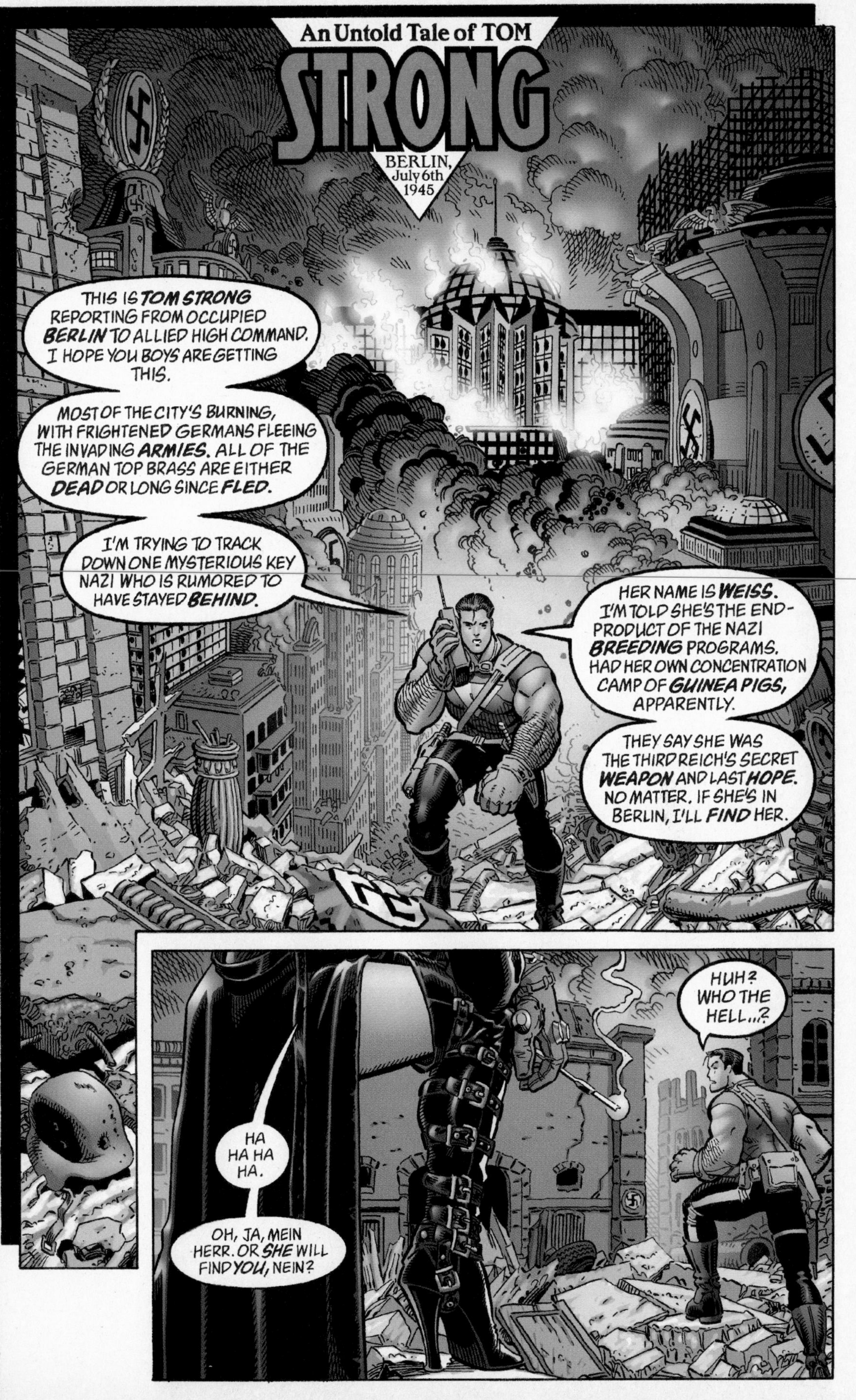
An Untold Tale of TOM STRONG
BERLIN, July 6th 1945
THIS IS TOM STRONG REPORTING FROM OCCUPIED BERLIN TO ALLIED HIGH COMMAND. I HOPE YOU BOYS ARE GETTING THIS.
MOST OF THE CITY'S BURNING, WITH FRIGHTENED GERMANS FLEEING THE INVADING ARMIES. ALL OF THE GERMAN TOP BRASS ARE EITHER DEAD OR LONG SINCE FLED.
I'M TRYING TO TRACK DOWN ONE MYSTERIOUS KEY NAZI WHO IS RUMORED TO HAVE STAYED BEHIND.
HER NAME IS WEISS. I'M TOLD SHE'S THE END-PRODUCT OF THE NAZI BREEDING PROGRAMS. HAD HER OWN CONCENTRATION CAMP OF GUINEA PIGS, APPARENTLY.
THEY SAY SHE WAS THE THIRD REICH'S SECRET WEAPON AND LAST HOPE. NO MATTER. IF SHE'S IN BERLIN, I'LL FIND HER.
HA HA HA HA.
OH, JA, MEIN HERR. OR SHE WILL FIND YOU, NEIN?
HUH? WHO THE HELL...?

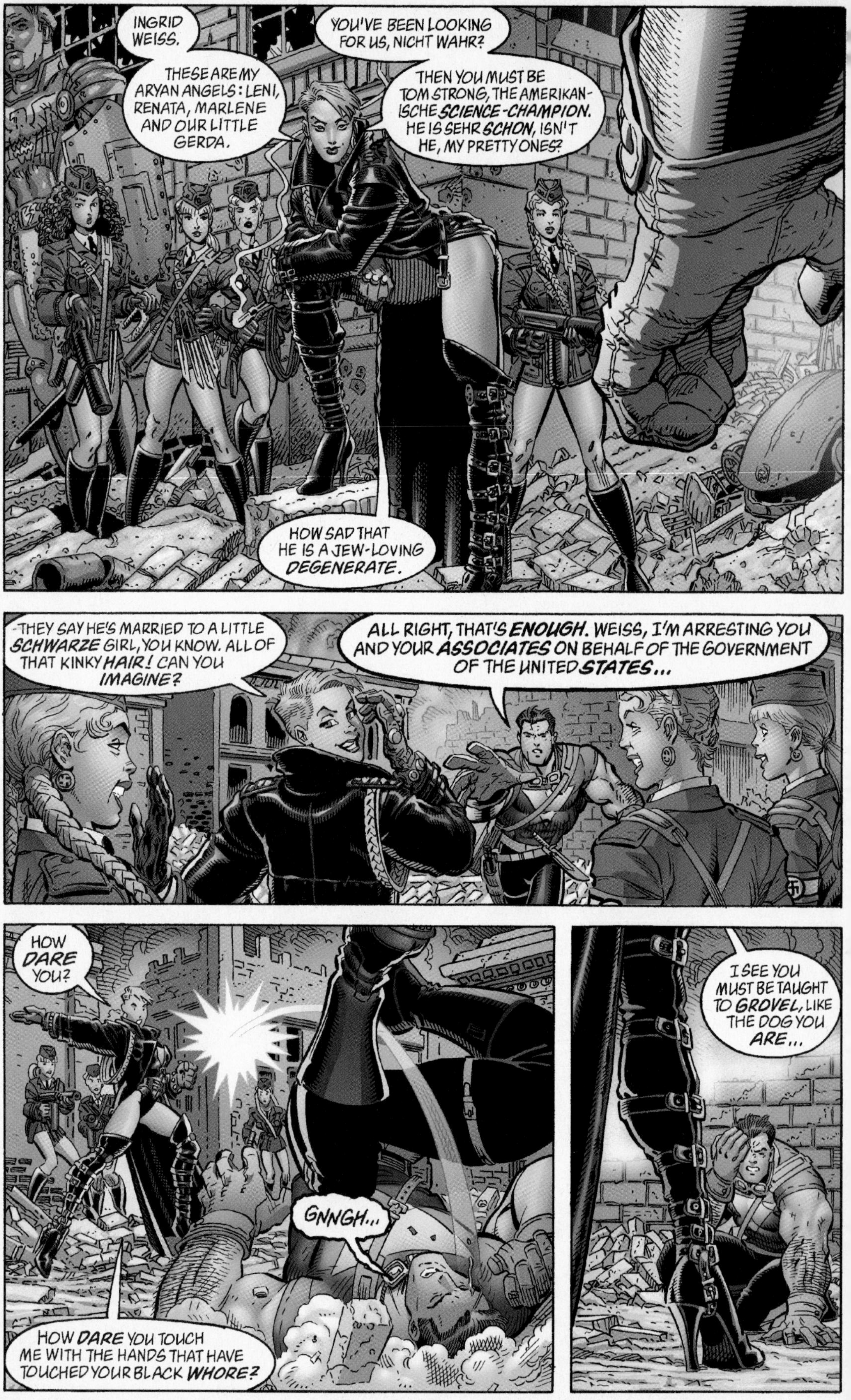
INGRID WEISS.
THESE ARE MY ARYAN ANGELS: LENI, RENATA, MARLENE AND OUR LITTLE GERDA.
YOU'VE BEEN LOOKING FOR US, NICHT WAHR?
THEN YOU MUST BE TOM STRONG, THE AMERIKAN-ISCHE SCIENCE-CHAMPION. HE IS SEHR SCHON, ISN'T HE, MY PRETTY ONES?
HOW SAD THAT HE IS A JEW-LOVING DEGENERATE.
-THEY SAY HE'S MARRIED TO A LITTLE SCHWARZE GIRL, YOU KNOW. ALL OF THAT KINKY HAIR! CAN YOU IMAGINE?
ALL RIGHT, THAT'S ENOUGH. WEISS, I'M ARRESTING YOU AND YOUR ASSOCIATES ON BEHALF OF THE GOVERNMENT OF THE UNITED STATES...
HOW DARE YOU?
GNNGH...
HOW DARE YOU TOUCH ME WITH THE HANDS THAT HAVE TOUCHED YOUR BLACK WHORE?
I SEE YOU MUST BE TAUGHT TO GROVEL, LIKE THE DOG YOU ARE...

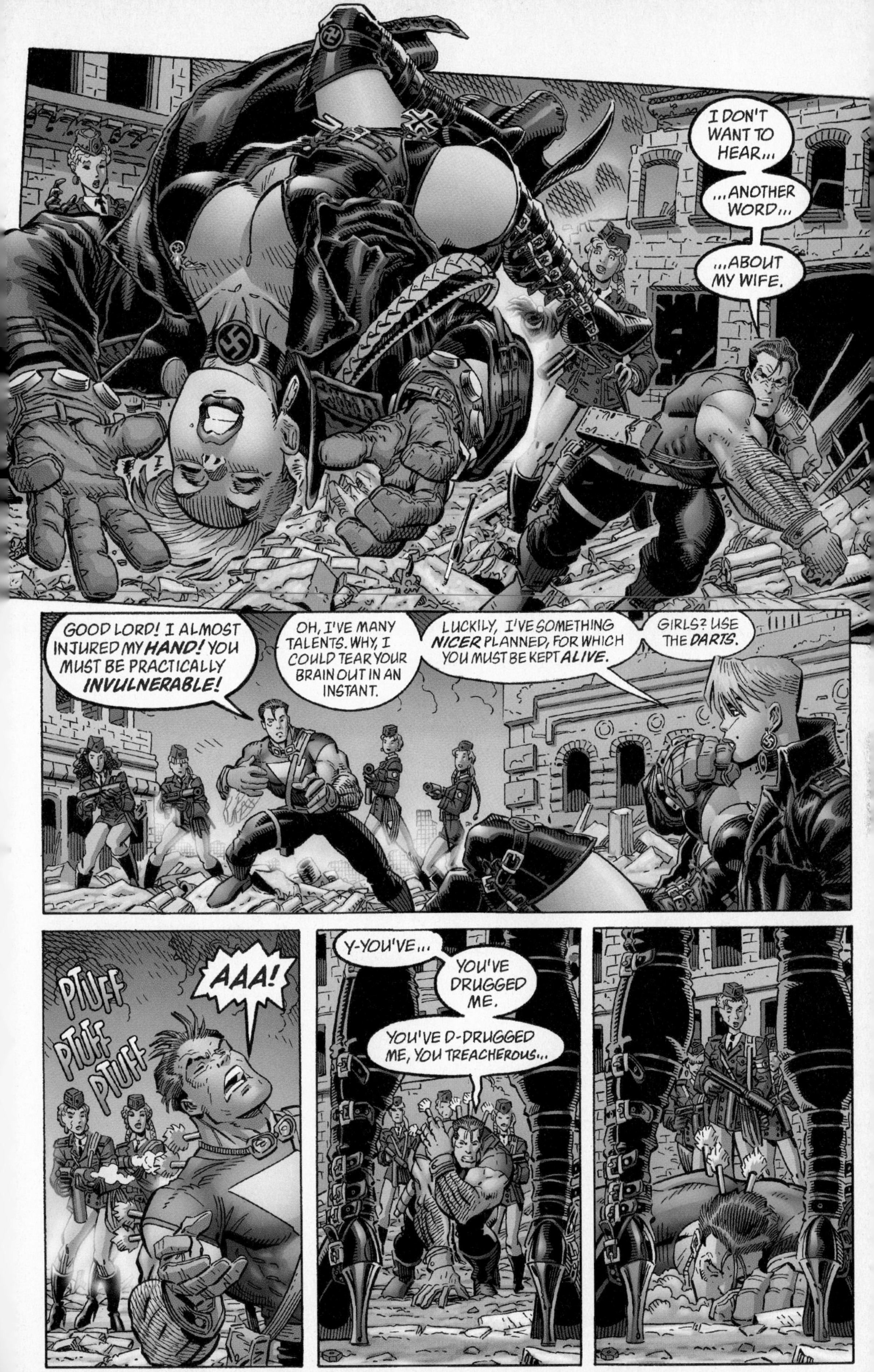

I DON'T WANT TO HEAR...
...ANOTHER WORD...
...ABOUT MY WIFE.
GOOD LORD! I ALMOST INJURED MY HAND! YOU MUST BE PRACTICALLY INVULNERABLE!
OH, I'VE MANY TALENTS. WHY, I COULD TEAR YOUR BRAIN OUT IN AN INSTANT.
LUCKILY, I'VE SOMETHING NICER PLANNED, FOR WHICH YOU MUST BE KEPT ALIVE.
GIRLS? USE THE DARTS.
PTUFF
PTUFF
PTUFF
AAA!
Y-YOU'VE...
YOU'VE DRUGGED ME.
YOU'VE D-DRUGGED ME, YOU TREACHEROUS...

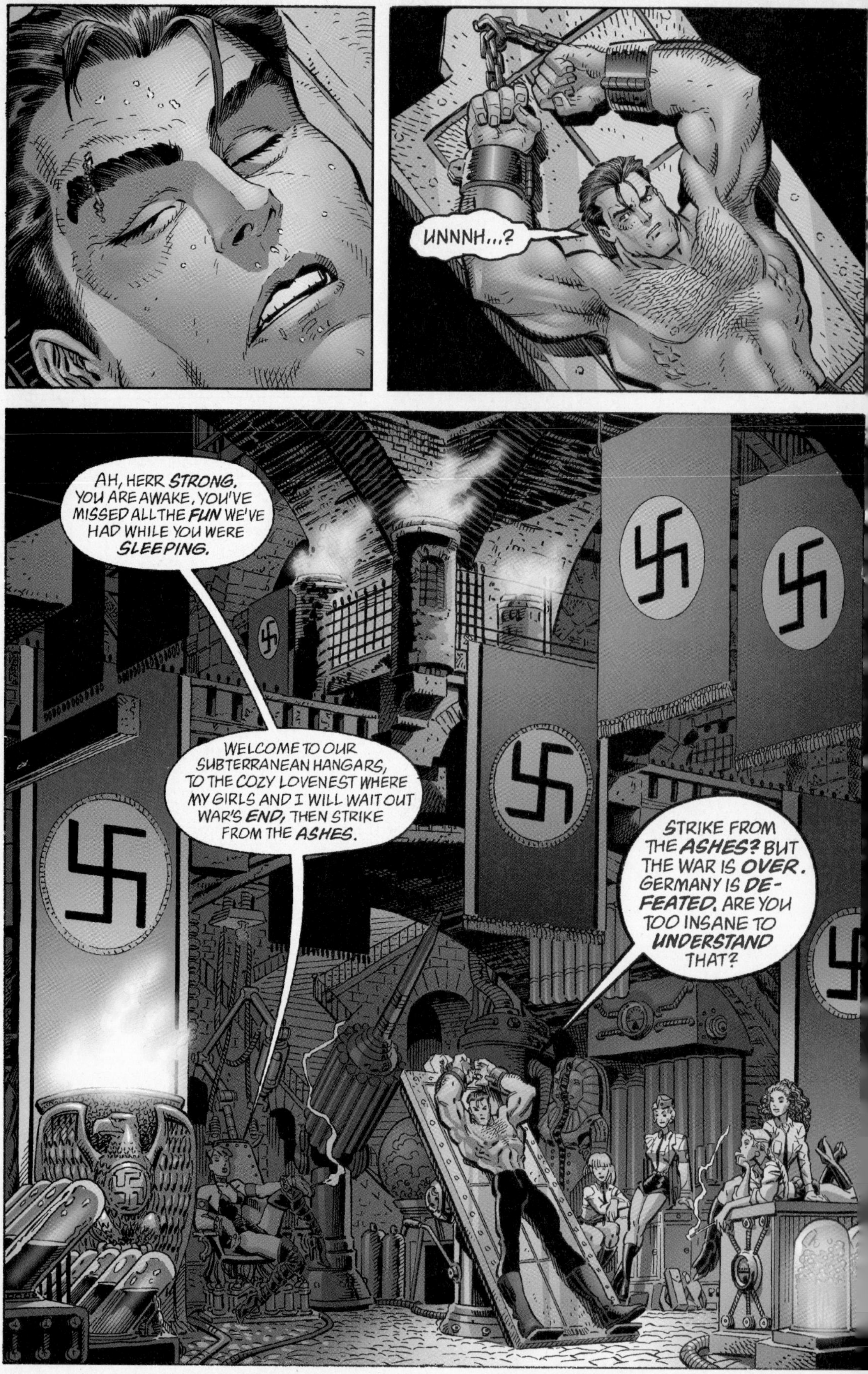
UNNNH...?
AH, HERR STRONG. YOU ARE AWAKE. YOU'VE MISSED ALL THE FUN WE'VE HAD WHILE YOU WERE SLEEPING.
WELCOME TO OUR SUBTERRANEAN HANGARS, TO THE COZY LOVENEST WHERE MY GIRLS AND I WILL WAIT OUT WAR'S END, THEN STRIKE FROM THE ASHES.
STRIKE FROM THE ASHES? BUT THE WAR IS OVER. GERMANY IS DE-FEATED. ARE YOU TOO INSANE TO UNDERSTAND THAT?

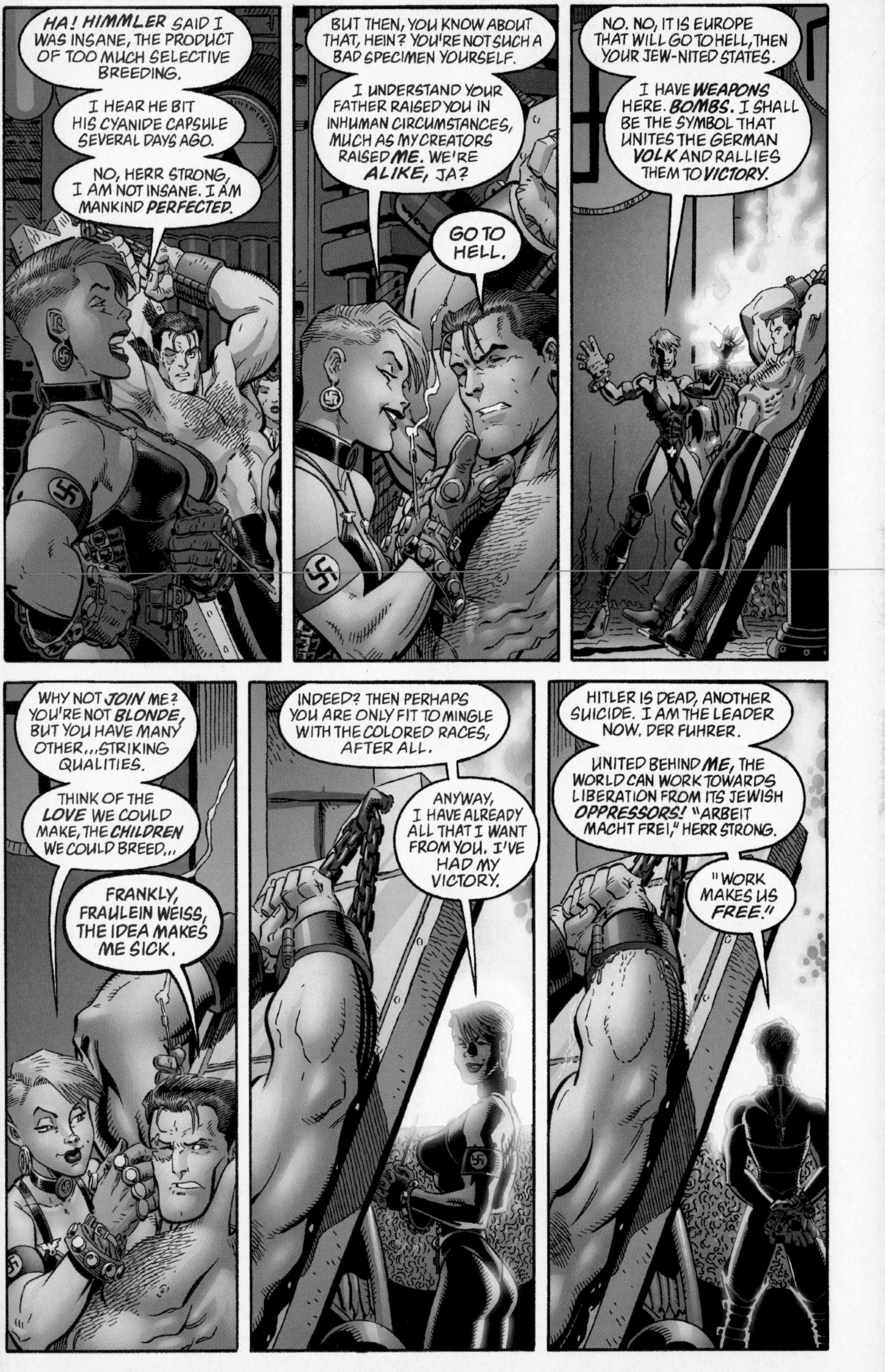
HA! HIMMLER SAID I WAS INSANE, THE PRODUCT OF TOO MUCH SELECTIVE BREEDING.
I HEAR HE BIT HIS CYANIDE CAPSULE SEVERAL DAYS AGO.
NO, HERR STRONG, I AM NOT INSANE. I AM MANKIND PERFECTED.
BUT THEN, YOU KNOW ABOUT THAT, HEIN? YOU'RE NOT SUCH A BAD SPECIMEN YOURSELF.
I UNDERSTAND YOUR FATHER RAISED YOU IN INHUMAN CIRCUMSTANCES, MUCH AS MY CREATORS RAISED ME. WE'RE ALIKE, JA?
GO TO HELL.
NO. NO, IT IS EUROPE THAT WILL GO TO HELL, THEN YOUR JEW-NITED STATES.
I HAVE WEAPONS HERE. BOMBS. I SHALL BE THE SYMBOL THAT UNITES THE GERMAN VOLK AND RALLIES THEM TO VICTORY.
WHY NOT JOIN ME? YOU'RE NOT BLONDE, BUT YOU HAVE MANY OTHER...STRIKING QUALITIES.
THINK OF THE LOVE WE COULD MAKE, THE CHILDREN WE COULD BREED...
FRANKLY, FRAULEIN WEISS, THE IDEA MAKES ME SICK.
INDEED? THEN PERHAPS YOU ARE ONLY FIT TO MINGLE WITH THE COLORED RACES, AFTER ALL.
ANYWAY, I HAVE ALREADY ALL THAT I WANT FROM YOU. I'VE HAD MY VICTORY.
HITLER IS DEAD, ANOTHER SUICIDE. I AM THE LEADER NOW. DER FUHRER.
UNITED BEHIND ME, THE WORLD CAN WORK TOWARDS LIBERATION FROM ITS JEWISH OPPRESSORS! "ARBEIT MACHT FREI," HERR STRONG.
"WORK MAKES US FREE!"

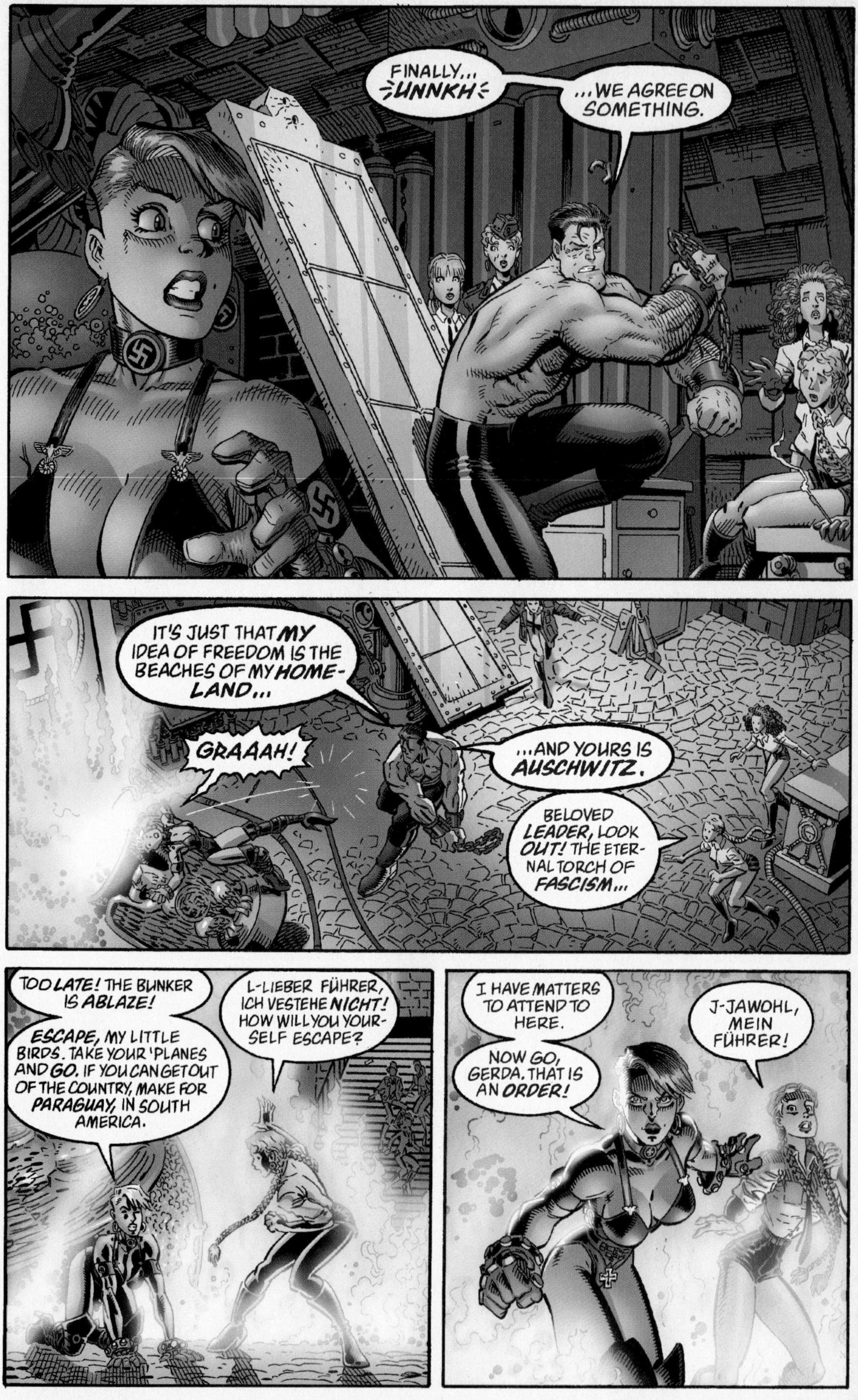
FINALLY... -UNNKH-
...WE AGREE ON SOMETHING.
IT'S JUST THAT MY IDEA OF FREEDOM IS THE BEACHES OF MY HOME-LAND...
GRAAAH!
...AND YOURS IS AUSCHWITZ.
BELOVED LEADER, LOOK OUT! THE ETERNAL TORCH OF FASCISM...
TOO LATE! THE BUNKER IS ABLAZE!
ESCAPE, MY LITTLE BIRDS. TAKE YOUR 'PLANES AND GO. IF YOU CAN GET OUT OF THE COUNTRY, MAKE FOR PARAGUAY, IN SOUTH AMERICA.
L-LIEBER FÜHRER, ICH VESTEHE NICHT! HOW WILL YOU YOURSELF ESCAPE?
I HAVE MATTERS TO ATTEND TO HERE.
NOW GO, GERDA. THAT IS AN ORDER!
J-JAWOHL, MEIN FÜHRER!

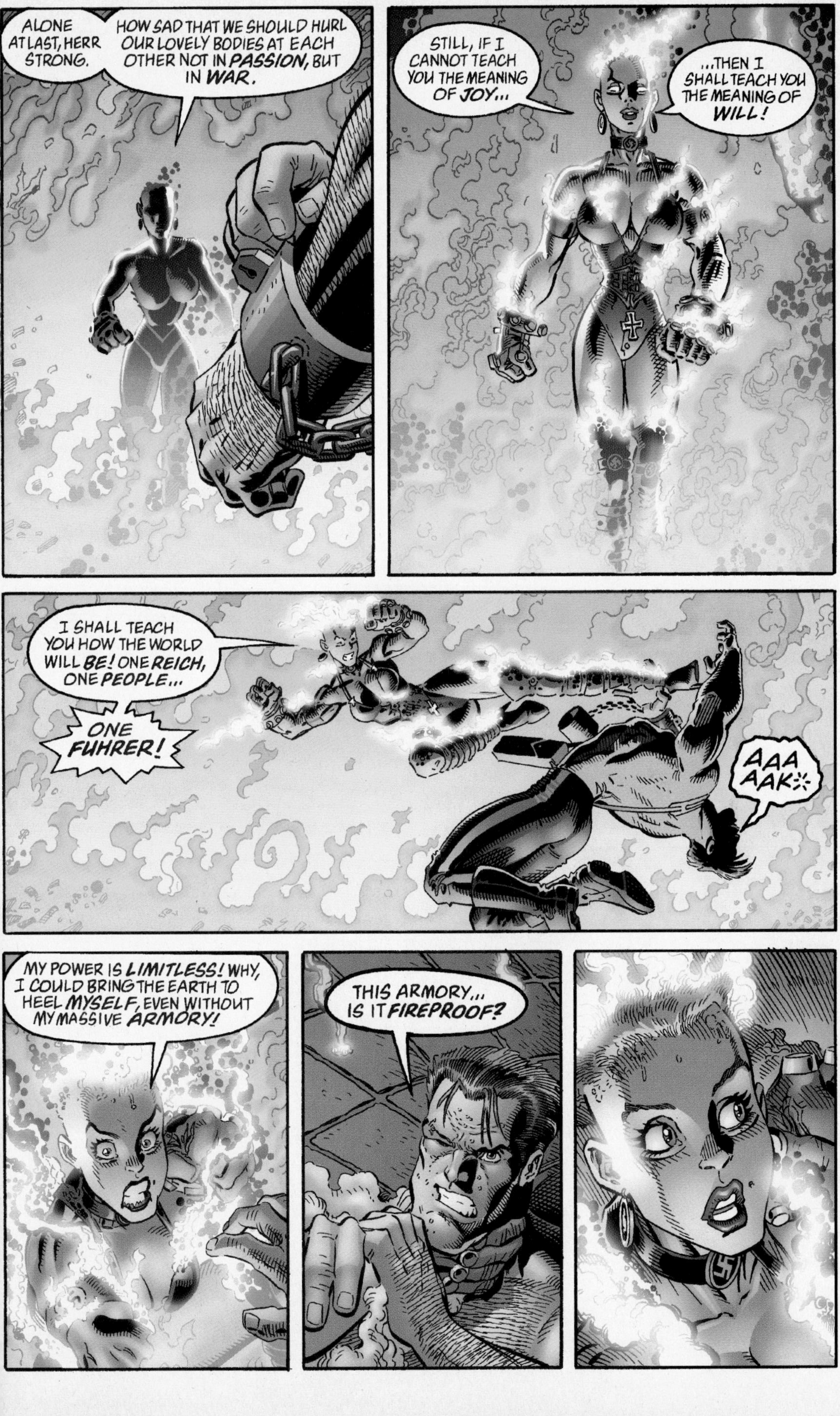

ALONE AT LAST, HERR STRONG.
HOW SAD THAT WE SHOULD HURL OUR LOVELY BODIES AT EACH OTHER NOT IN PASSION, BUT IN WAR.
STILL, IF I CANNOT TEACH YOU THE MEANING OF JOY...
...THEN I SHALL TEACH YOU THE MEANING OF WILL!
I SHALL TEACH YOU HOW THE WORLD WILL BE! ONE REICH, ONE PEOPLE...
ONE FUHRER!
AAA AAK!
MY POWER IS LIMITLESS! WHY, I COULD BRING THE EARTH TO HEEL MYSELF, EVEN WITHOUT MY MASSIVE ARMORY!
THIS ARMORY... IS IT FIREPROOF?

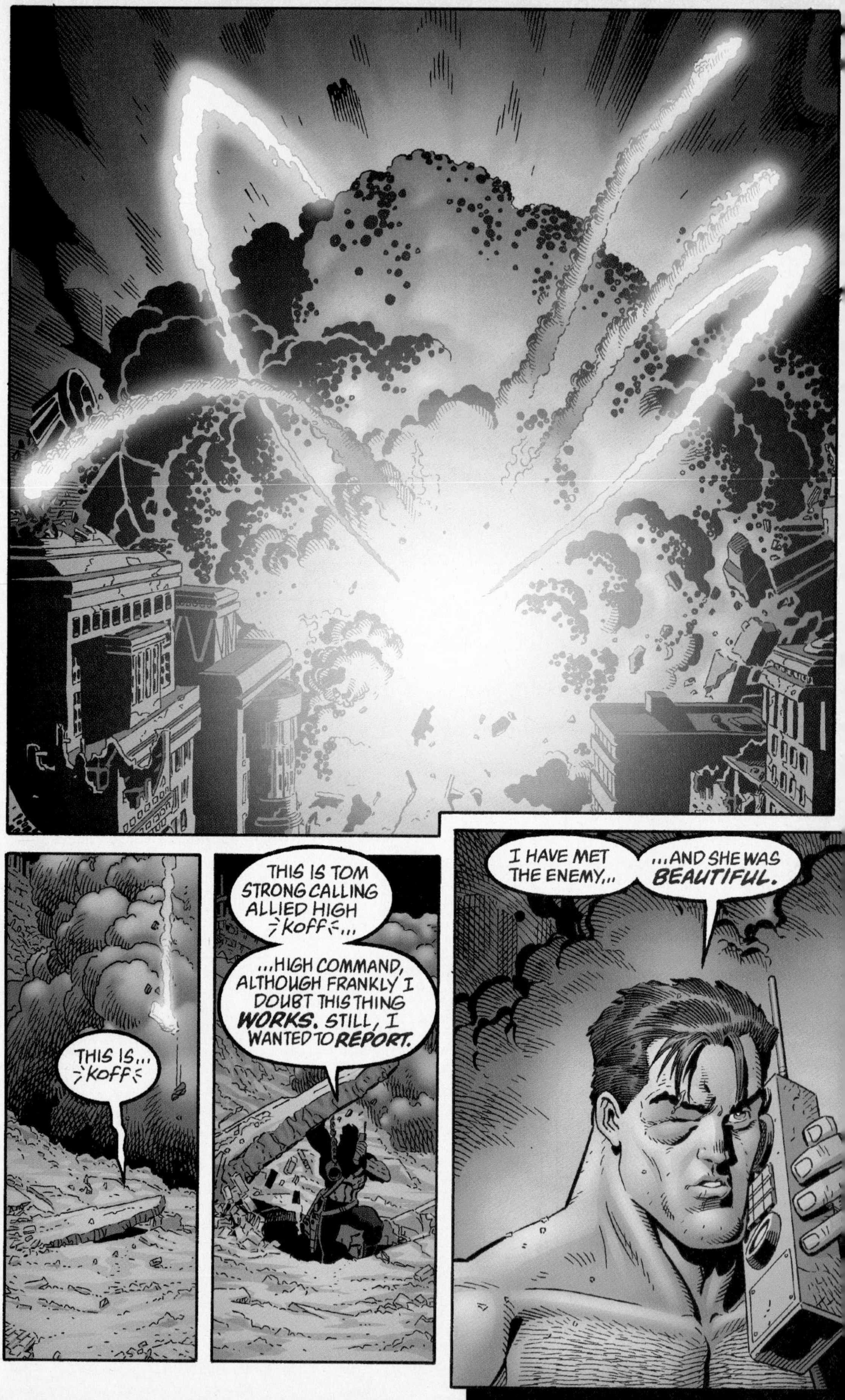
THIS IS... ≈KOFF≈
THIS IS TOM STRONG CALLING ALLIED HIGH ≈KOFF≈...
...HIGH COMMAND, ALTHOUGH FRANKLY I DOUBT THIS THING **WORKS.** STILL, I WANTED TO **REPORT.**
I HAVE MET THE ENEMY...
...AND SHE WAS **BEAUTIFUL.**

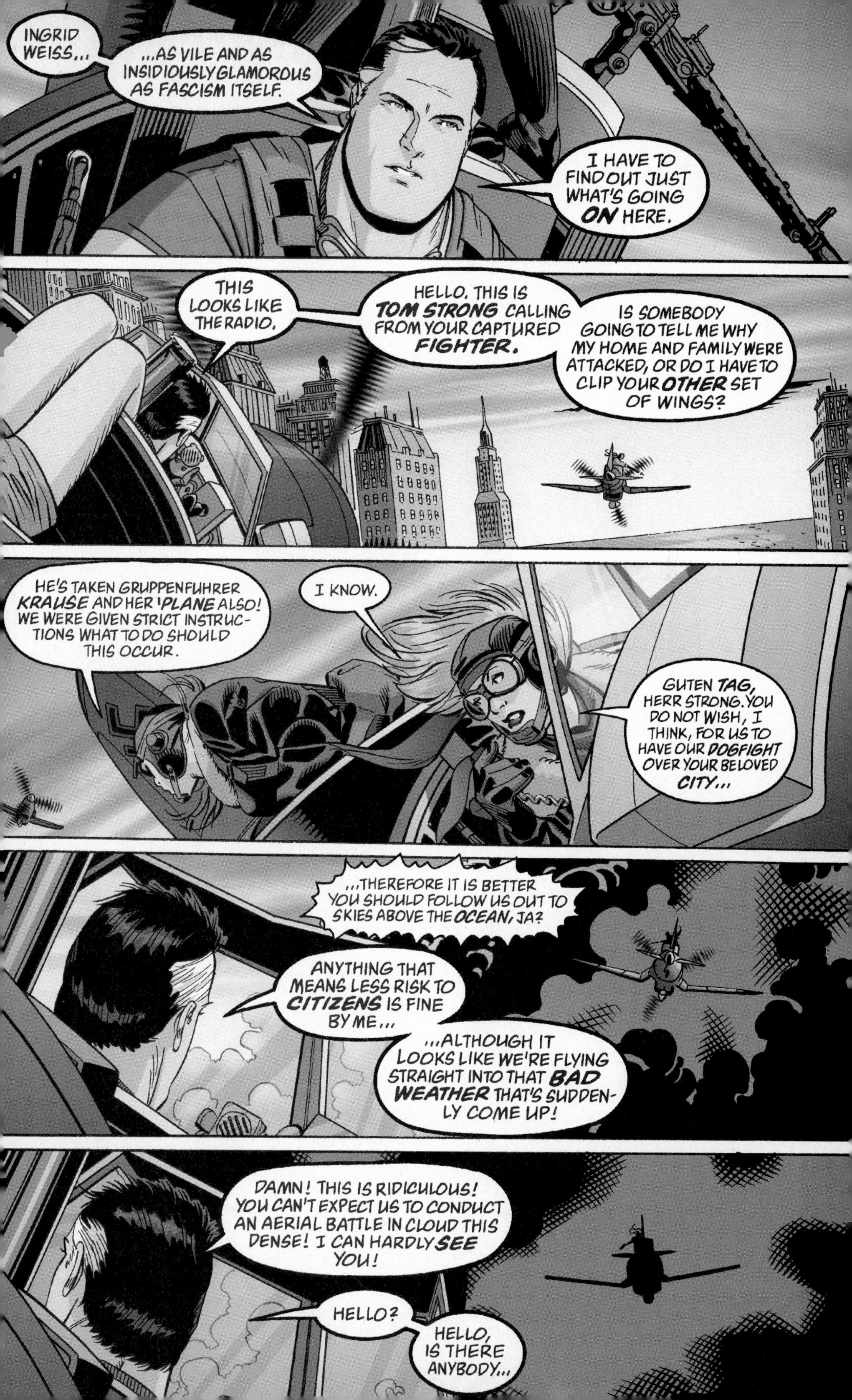
INGRID WEISS...
...AS VILE AND AS INSIDIOUSLY GLAMOROUS AS FASCISM ITSELF.
I HAVE TO FIND OUT JUST WHAT'S GOING ON HERE.
THIS LOOKS LIKE THE RADIO.
HELLO. THIS IS TOM STRONG CALLING FROM YOUR CAPTURED FIGHTER.
IS SOMEBODY GOING TO TELL ME WHY MY HOME AND FAMILY WERE ATTACKED, OR DO I HAVE TO CLIP YOUR OTHER SET OF WINGS?
HE'S TAKEN GRUPPENFUHRER KRAUSE AND HER 'PLANE ALSO! WE WERE GIVEN STRICT INSTRUCTIONS WHAT TO DO SHOULD THIS OCCUR.
I KNOW.
GUTEN TAG, HERR STRONG. YOU DO NOT WISH, I THINK, FOR US TO HAVE OUR DOGFIGHT OVER YOUR BELOVED CITY...
...THEREFORE IT IS BETTER YOU SHOULD FOLLOW US OUT TO SKIES ABOVE THE OCEAN, JA?
ANYTHING THAT MEANS LESS RISK TO CITIZENS IS FINE BY ME...
...ALTHOUGH IT LOOKS LIKE WE'RE FLYING STRAIGHT INTO THAT BAD WEATHER THAT'S SUDDENLY COME UP!
DAMN! THIS IS RIDICULOUS! YOU CAN'T EXPECT US TO CONDUCT AN AERIAL BATTLE IN CLOUD THIS DENSE! I CAN HARDLY SEE YOU!
HELLO?
HELLO, IS THERE ANYBODY...

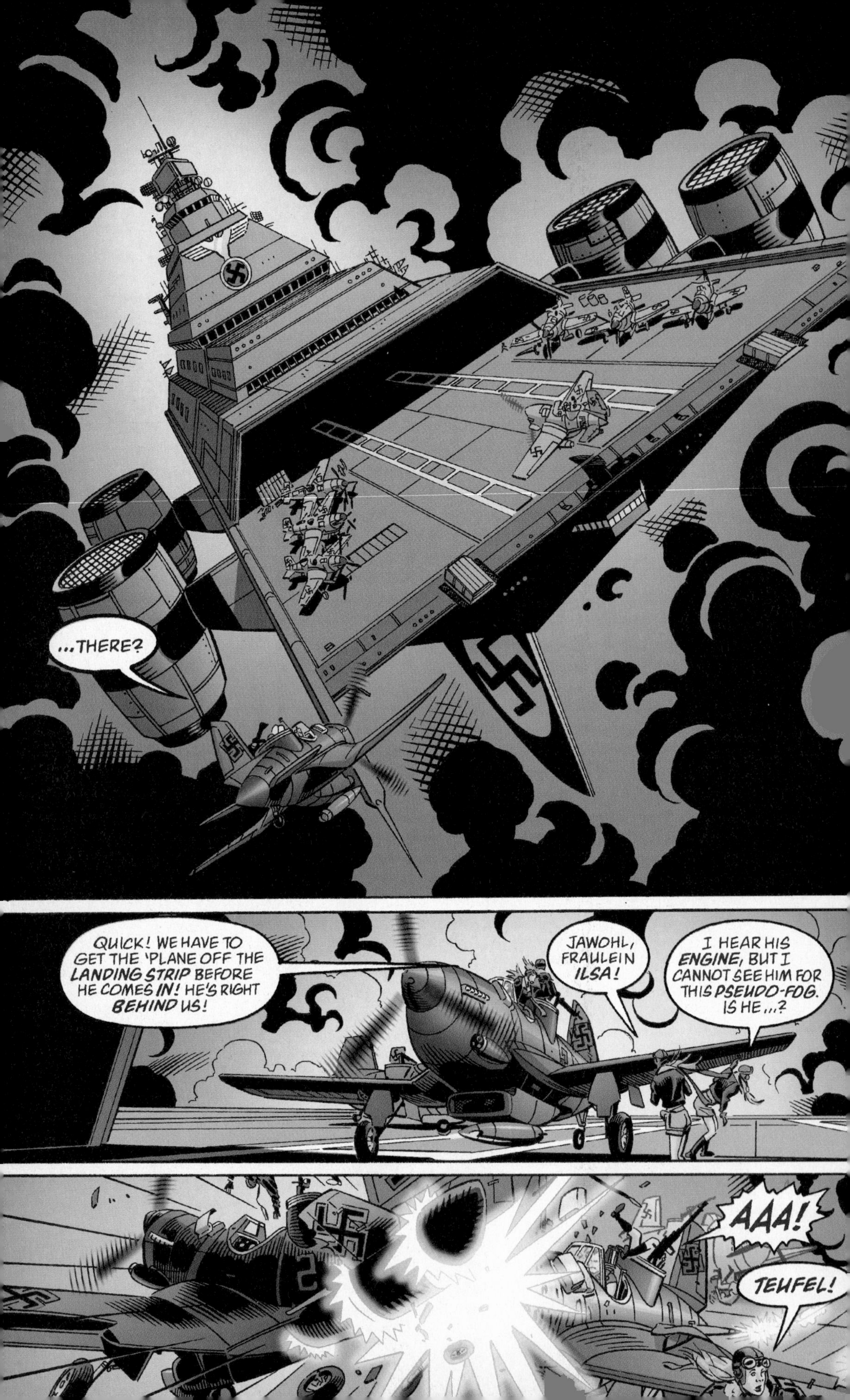
...THERE?
QUICK! WE HAVE TO GET THE 'PLANE OFF THE LANDING STRIP BEFORE HE COMES IN! HE'S RIGHT BEHIND US!
JAWOHL, FRAULEIN ILSA!
I HEAR HIS ENGINE, BUT I CANNOT SEE HIM FOR THIS PSEUDO-FOG. IS HE...?
AAA!
TEUFEL!

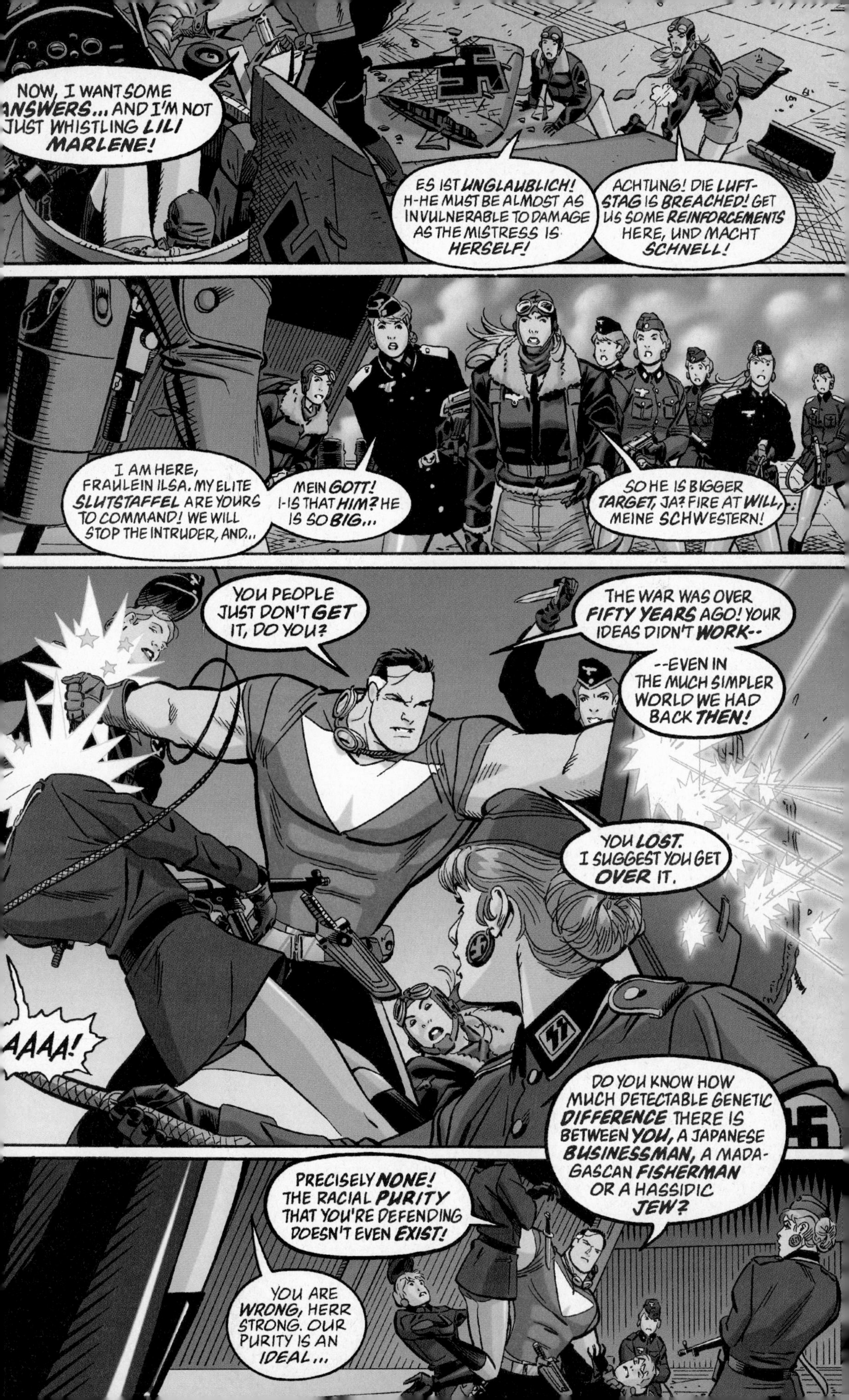
NOW, I WANT SOME ANSWERS... AND I'M NOT JUST WHISTLING LILI MARLENE!
ES IST UNGLAUBLICH! H-HE MUST BE ALMOST AS INVULNERABLE TO DAMAGE AS THE MISTRESS IS HERSELF!
ACHTUNG! DIE LUFT-STAG IS BREACHED! GET US SOME REINFORCEMENTS HERE, UND MACHT SCHNELL!
I AM HERE, FRAULEIN ILSA. MY ELITE SLUTSTAFFEL ARE YOURS TO COMMAND! WE WILL STOP THE INTRUDER, AND...
MEIN GOTT! I-IS THAT HIM? HE IS SO BIG...
SO HE IS BIGGER TARGET, JA? FIRE AT WILL, MEINE SCHWESTERN!
YOU PEOPLE JUST DON'T GET IT, DO YOU?
THE WAR WAS OVER FIFTY YEARS AGO! YOUR IDEAS DIDN'T WORK--
--EVEN IN THE MUCH SIMPLER WORLD WE HAD BACK THEN!
YOU LOST. I SUGGEST YOU GET OVER IT.
AAAA!
DO YOU KNOW HOW MUCH DETECTABLE GENETIC DIFFERENCE THERE IS BETWEEN YOU, A JAPANESE BUSINESSMAN, A MADA-GASCAN FISHERMAN OR A HASSIDIC JEW?
PRECISELY NONE! THE RACIAL PURITY THAT YOU'RE DEFENDING DOESN'T EVEN EXIST!
YOU ARE WRONG, HERR STRONG. OUR PURITY IS AN IDEAL...

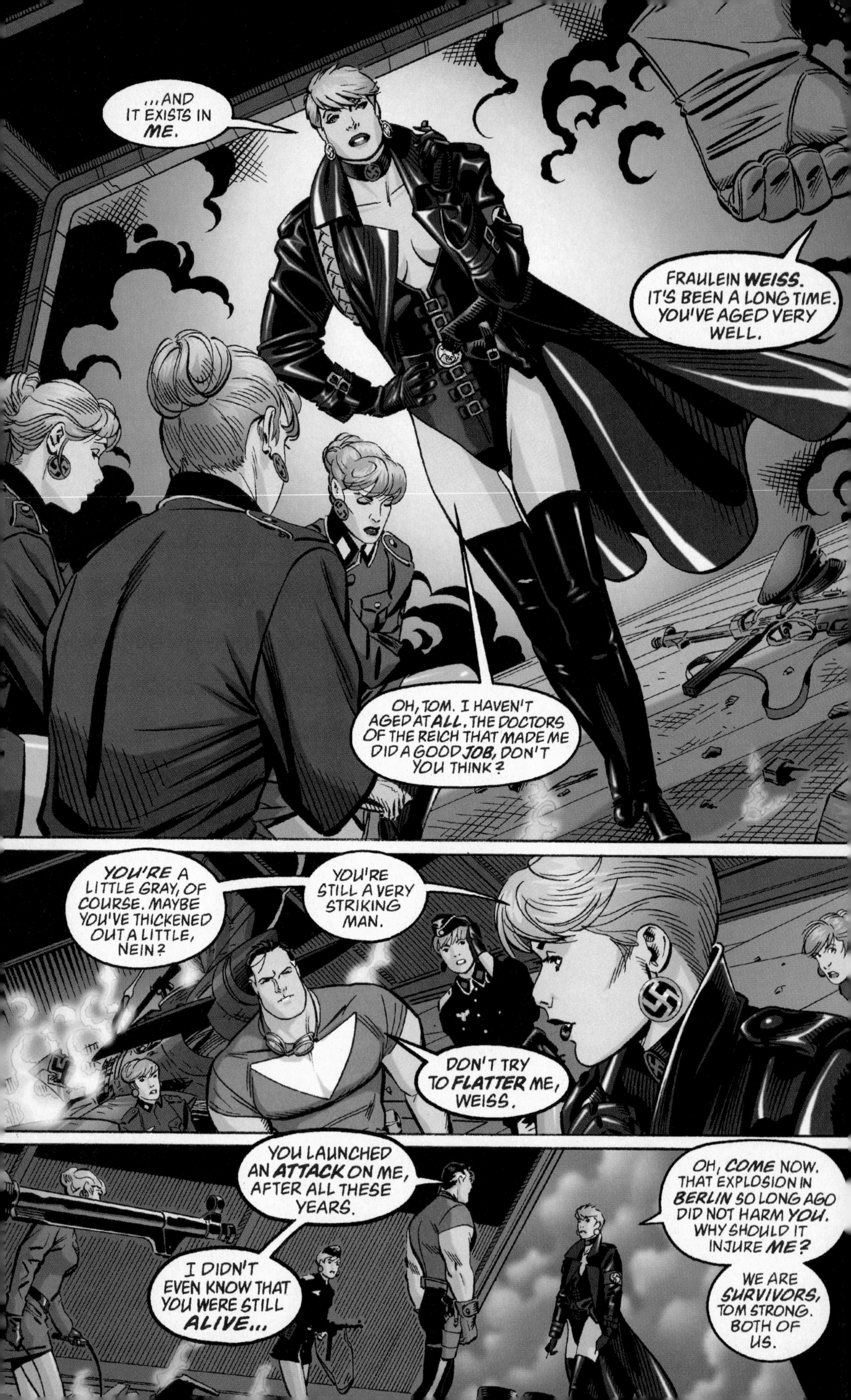
...AND IT EXISTS IN ME.
FRAULEIN WEISS. IT'S BEEN A LONG TIME. YOU'VE AGED VERY WELL.
OH, TOM. I HAVEN'T AGED AT ALL. THE DOCTORS OF THE REICH THAT MADE ME DID A GOOD JOB, DON'T YOU THINK?
YOU'RE A LITTLE GRAY, OF COURSE. MAYBE YOU'VE THICKENED OUT A LITTLE, NEIN?
YOU'RE STILL A VERY STRIKING MAN.
DON'T TRY TO FLATTER ME, WEISS.
YOU LAUNCHED AN ATTACK ON ME, AFTER ALL THESE YEARS.
I DIDN'T EVEN KNOW THAT YOU WERE STILL ALIVE...
OH, COME NOW. THAT EXPLOSION IN BERLIN SO LONG AGO DID NOT HARM YOU. WHY SHOULD IT INJURE ME?
WE ARE SURVIVORS, TOM STRONG. BOTH OF US.

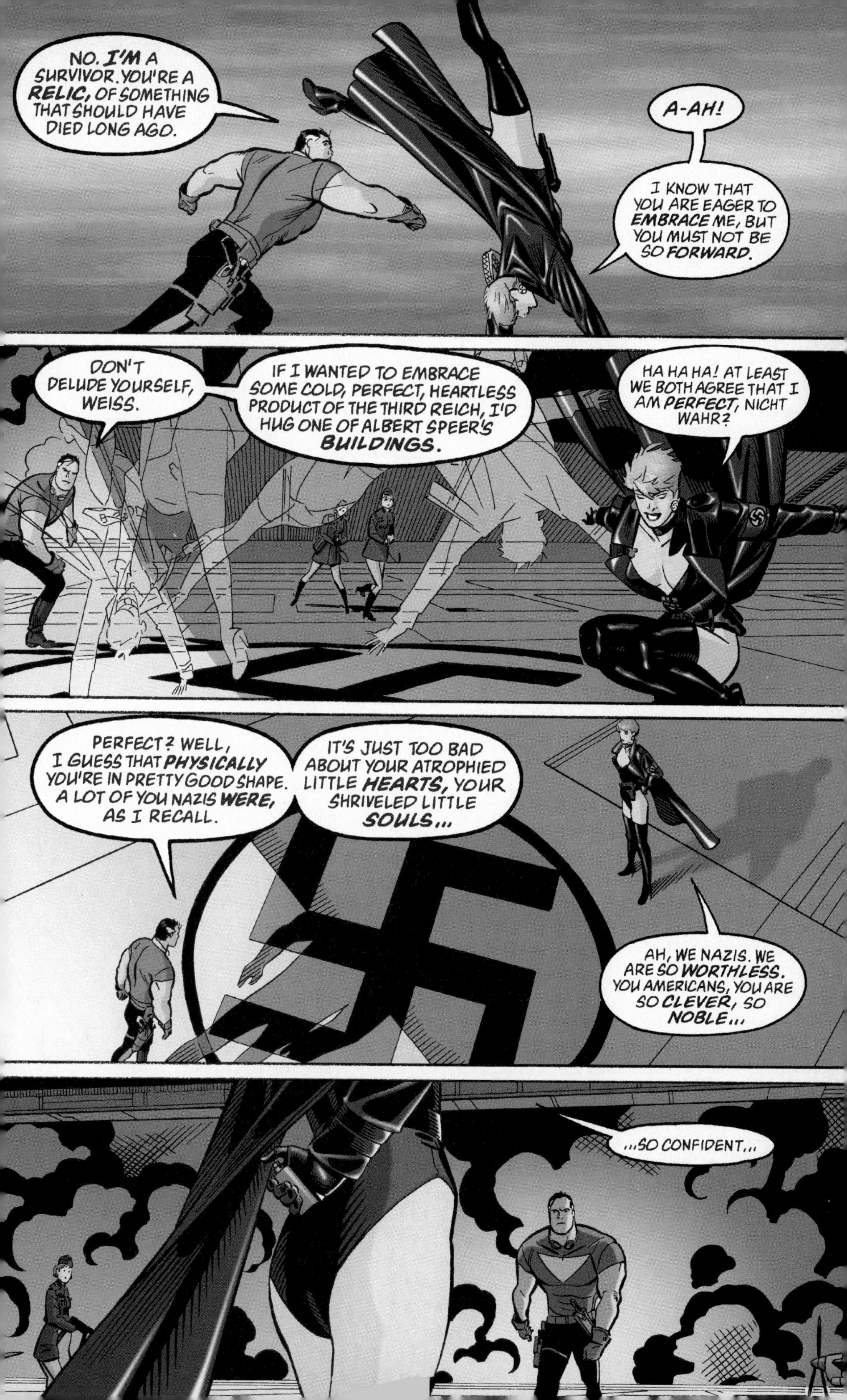

NO. I'M A SURVIVOR. YOU'RE A RELIC, OF SOMETHING THAT SHOULD HAVE DIED LONG AGO.
A-AH!
I KNOW THAT YOU ARE EAGER TO EMBRACE ME, BUT YOU MUST NOT BE SO FORWARD.
DON'T DELUDE YOURSELF, WEISS.
IF I WANTED TO EMBRACE SOME COLD, PERFECT, HEARTLESS PRODUCT OF THE THIRD REICH, I'D HUG ONE OF ALBERT SPEER'S BUILDINGS.
HA HA HA! AT LEAST WE BOTH AGREE THAT I AM PERFECT, NICHT WAHR?
PERFECT? WELL, I GUESS THAT PHYSICALLY YOU'RE IN PRETTY GOOD SHAPE. A LOT OF YOU NAZIS WERE, AS I RECALL.
IT'S JUST TOO BAD ABOUT YOUR ATROPHIED LITTLE HEARTS, YOUR SHRIVELED LITTLE SOULS...
AH, WE NAZIS. WE ARE SO WORTHLESS. YOU AMERICANS, YOU ARE SO CLEVER, SO NOBLE...
...SO CONFIDENT...

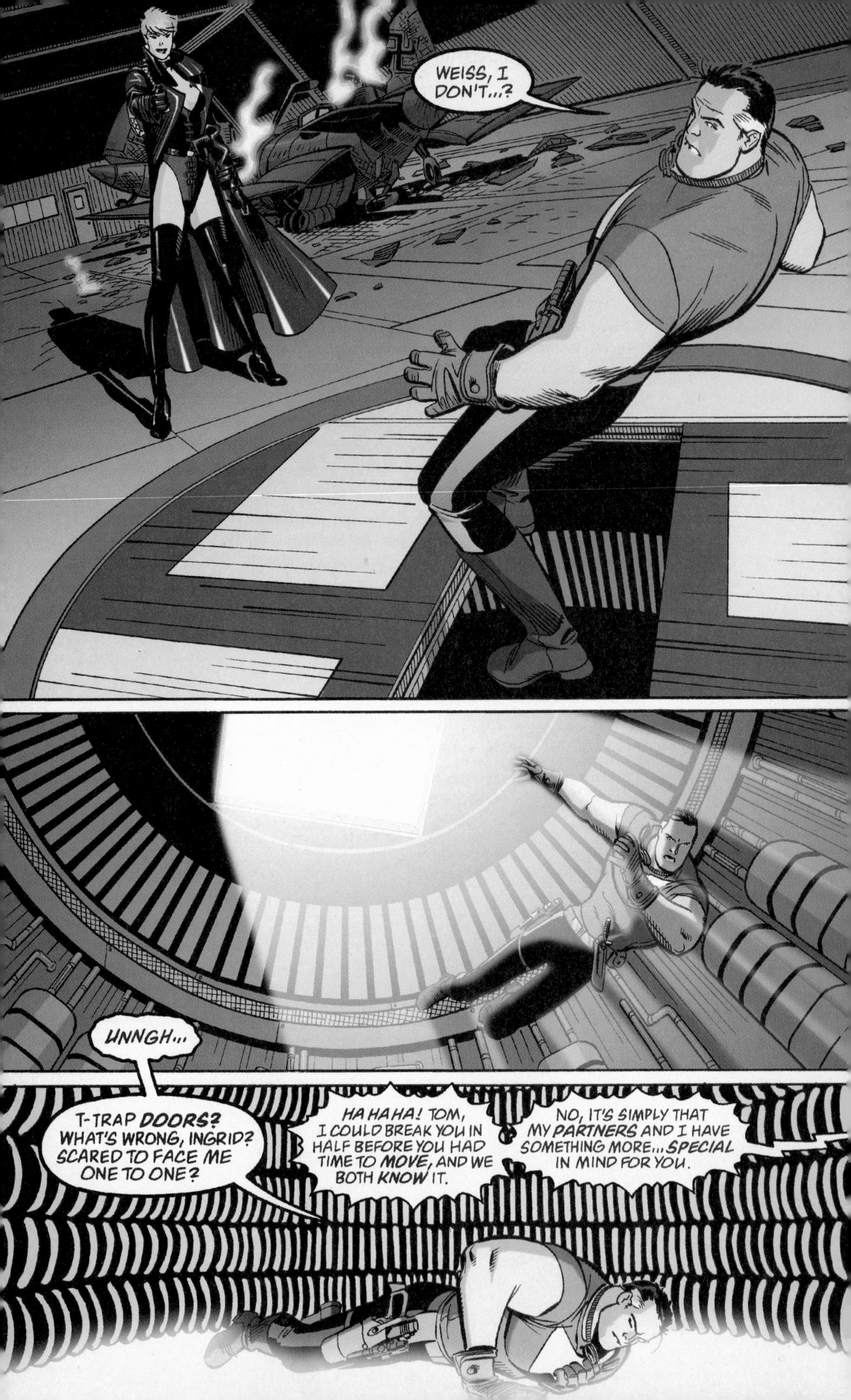

WEISS, I DON'T...?
UNNGH...
T-TRAP DOORS? WHAT'S WRONG, INGRID? SCARED TO FACE ME ONE TO ONE?
HA HA HA! TOM, I COULD BREAK YOU IN HALF BEFORE YOU HAD TIME TO MOVE, AND WE BOTH KNOW IT.
NO, IT'S SIMPLY THAT MY PARTNERS AND I HAVE SOMETHING MORE... SPECIAL IN MIND FOR YOU.

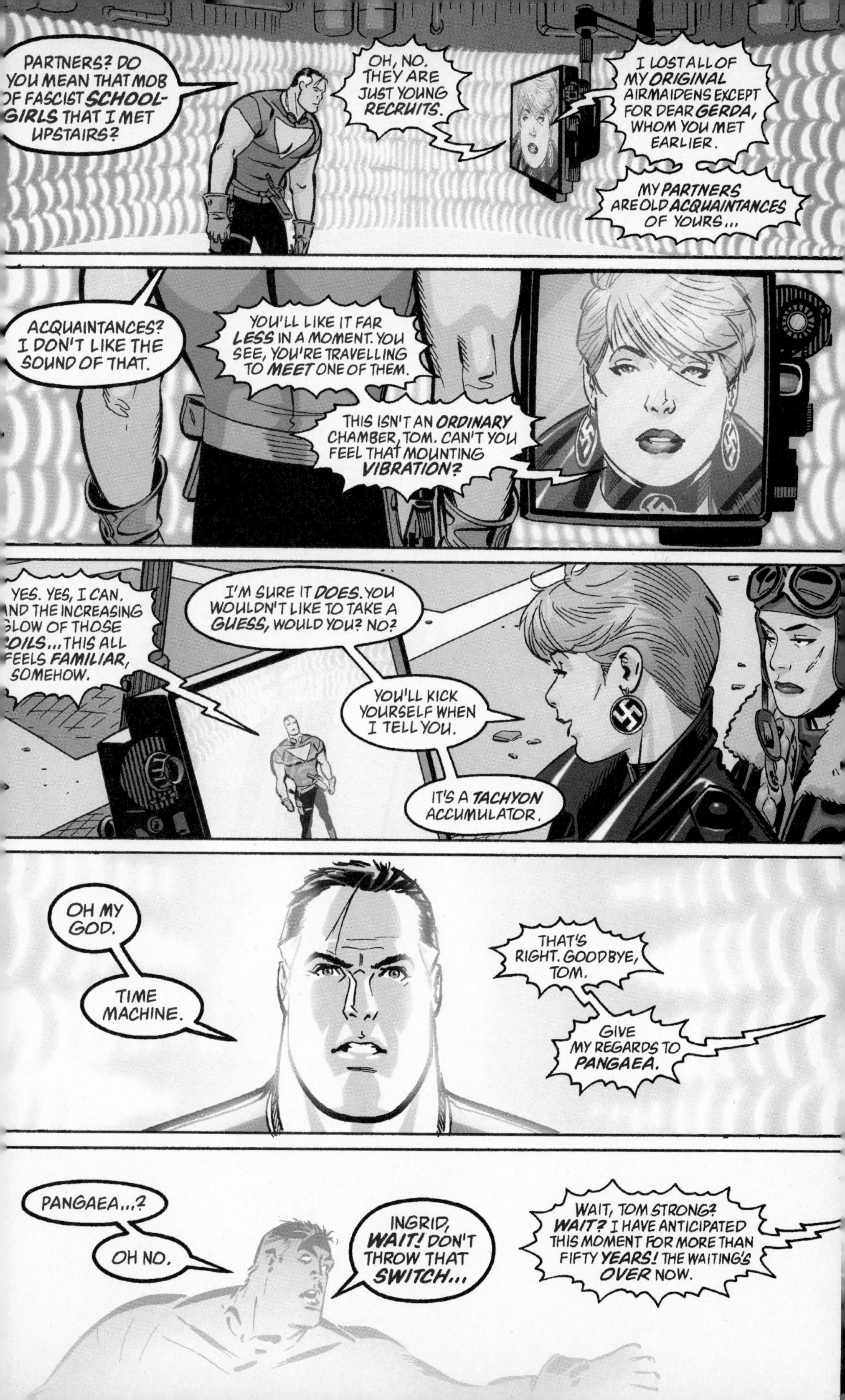
PARTNERS? DO YOU MEAN THAT MOB OF FASCIST SCHOOL-GIRLS THAT I MET UPSTAIRS?
OH, NO. THEY ARE JUST YOUNG RECRUITS.
I LOST ALL OF MY ORIGINAL AIRMAIDENS EXCEPT FOR DEAR GERDA, WHOM YOU MET EARLIER.
MY PARTNERS ARE OLD ACQUAINTANCES OF YOURS...
ACQUAINTANCES? I DON'T LIKE THE SOUND OF THAT.
YOU'LL LIKE IT FAR LESS IN A MOMENT. YOU SEE, YOU'RE TRAVELLING TO MEET ONE OF THEM.
THIS ISN'T AN ORDINARY CHAMBER, TOM. CAN'T YOU FEEL THAT MOUNTING VIBRATION?
YES. YES, I CAN. AND THE INCREASING GLOW OF THOSE COILS... THIS ALL FEELS FAMILIAR, SOMEHOW.
I'M SURE IT DOES. YOU WOULDN'T LIKE TO TAKE A GUESS, WOULD YOU? NO?
YOU'LL KICK YOURSELF WHEN I TELL YOU.
IT'S A TACHYON ACCUMULATOR.
OH MY GOD.
TIME MACHINE.
THAT'S RIGHT. GOODBYE, TOM.
GIVE MY REGARDS TO PANGAEA.
PANGAEA...?
OH NO.
INGRID, WAIT! DON'T THROW THAT SWITCH...
WAIT, TOM STRONG? WAIT? I HAVE ANTICIPATED THIS MOMENT FOR MORE THAN FIFTY YEARS! THE WAITING'S OVER NOW.

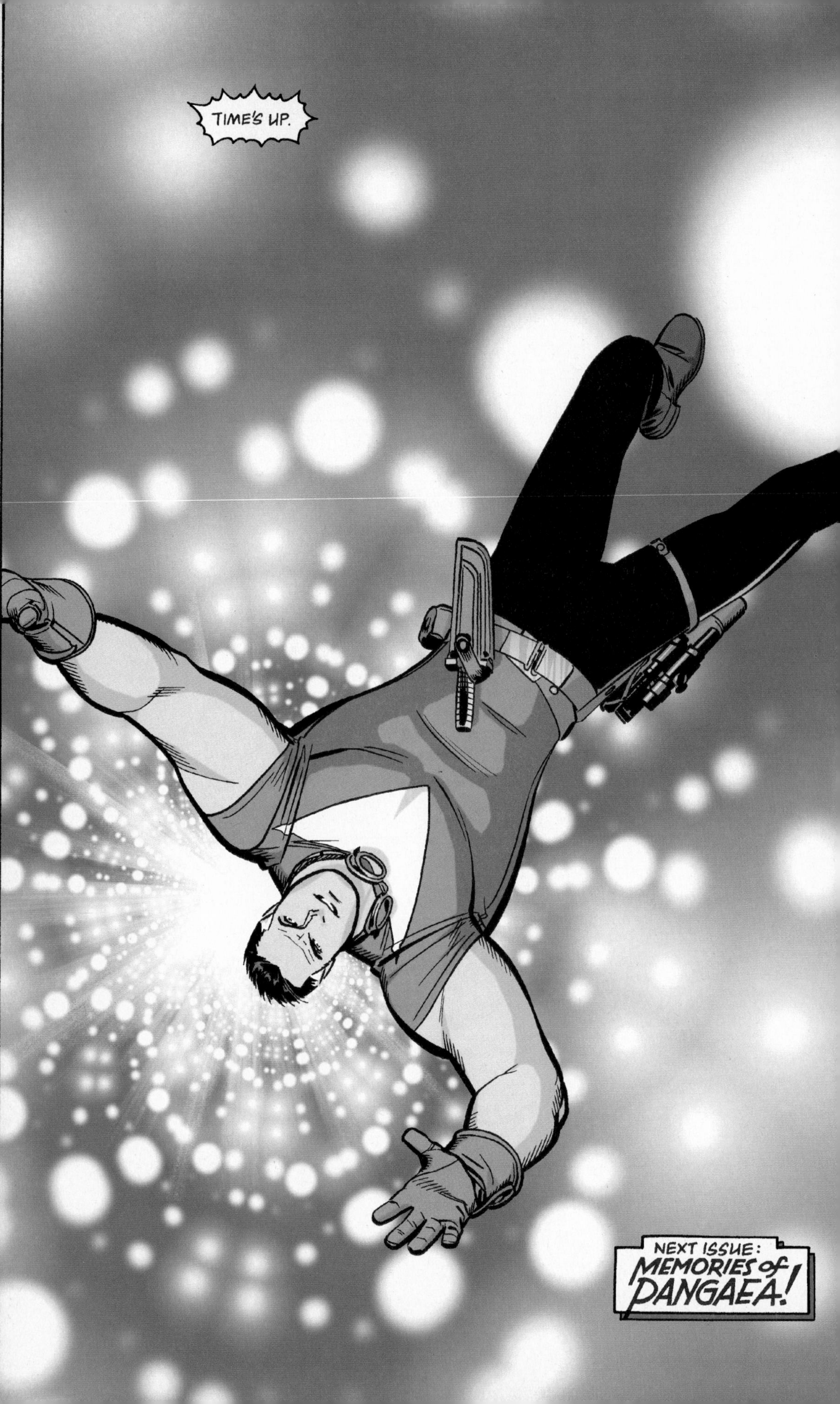
TIME'S UP.
NEXT ISSUE:
MEMORIES of PANGAEA!

CHAPTER FIVE

In which a Long Journey is begun,
a Daring Experiment is remembered,
and TOM uncovers a Deeper Ploy.

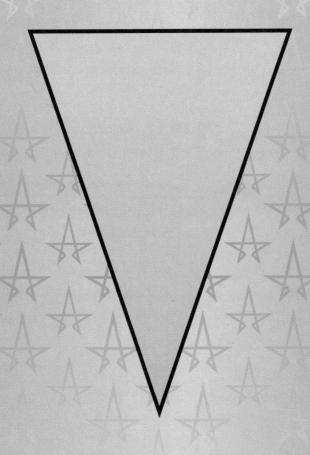

**Cover art:
Jerry Ordway**

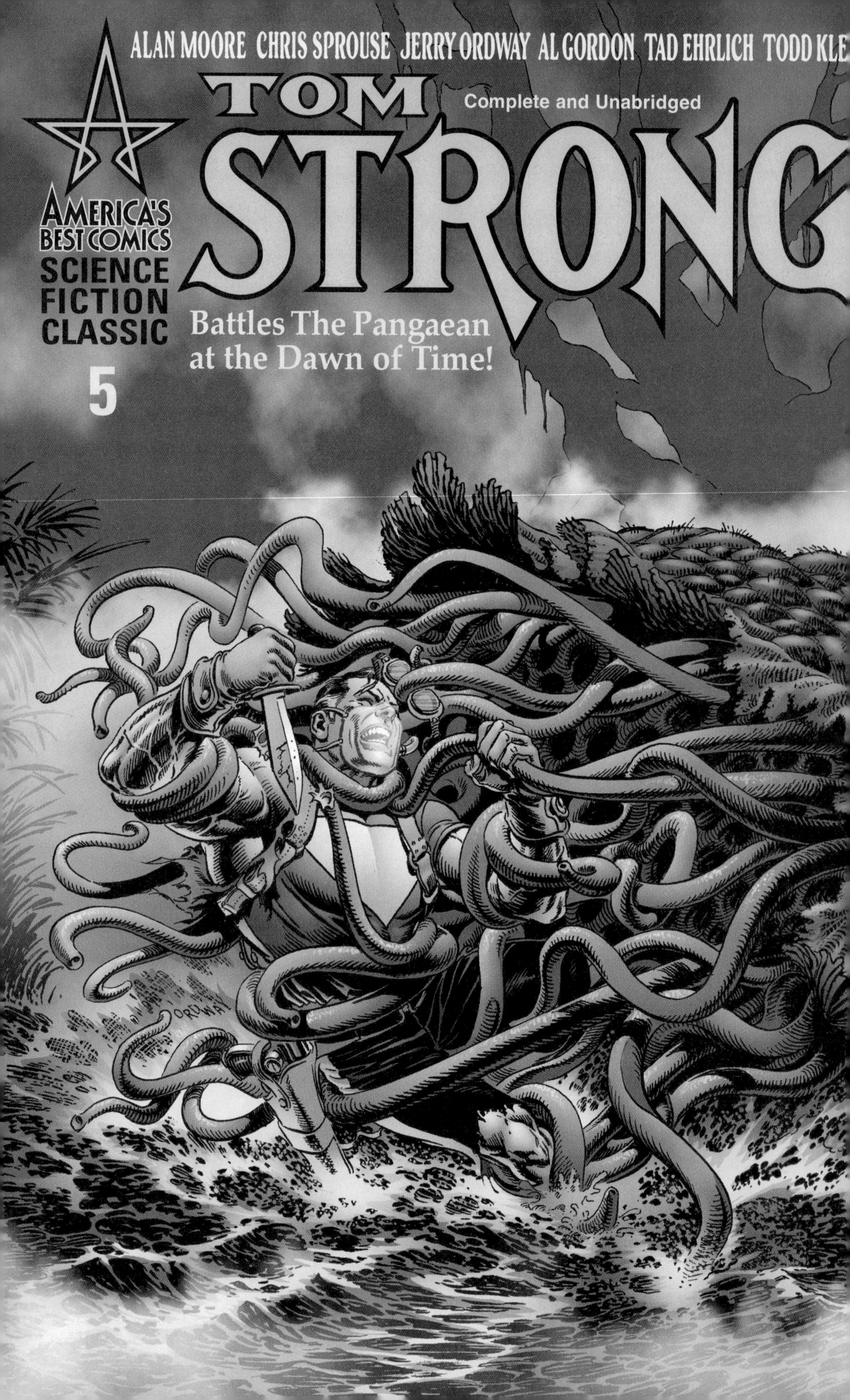

ALAN MOORE CHRIS SPROUSE JERRY ORDWAY AL GORDON TAD EHRLICH TODD KLE
TOM STRONG
Complete and Unabridged
AMERICA'S BEST COMICS
SCIENCE FICTION CLASSIC
5
Battles The Pangaean at the Dawn of Time!

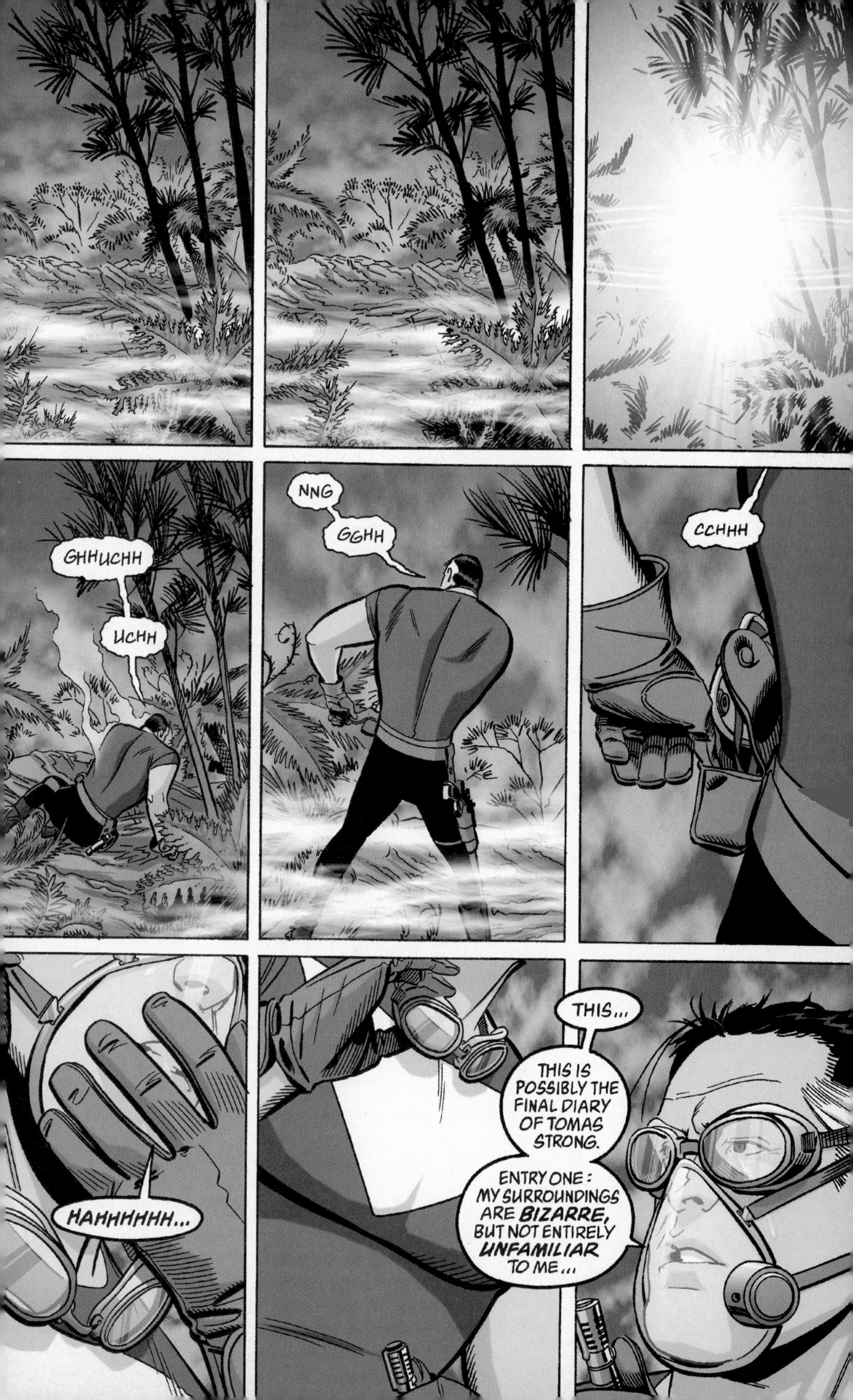
GHHUCHH
UCHH
NNG
GGHH
CCHHH
HAHHHHHH...
THIS...
THIS IS POSSIBLY THE FINAL DIARY OF TOMAS STRONG.
ENTRY ONE: MY SURROUNDINGS ARE **BIZARRE**, BUT NOT ENTIRELY **UNFAMILIAR** TO ME...

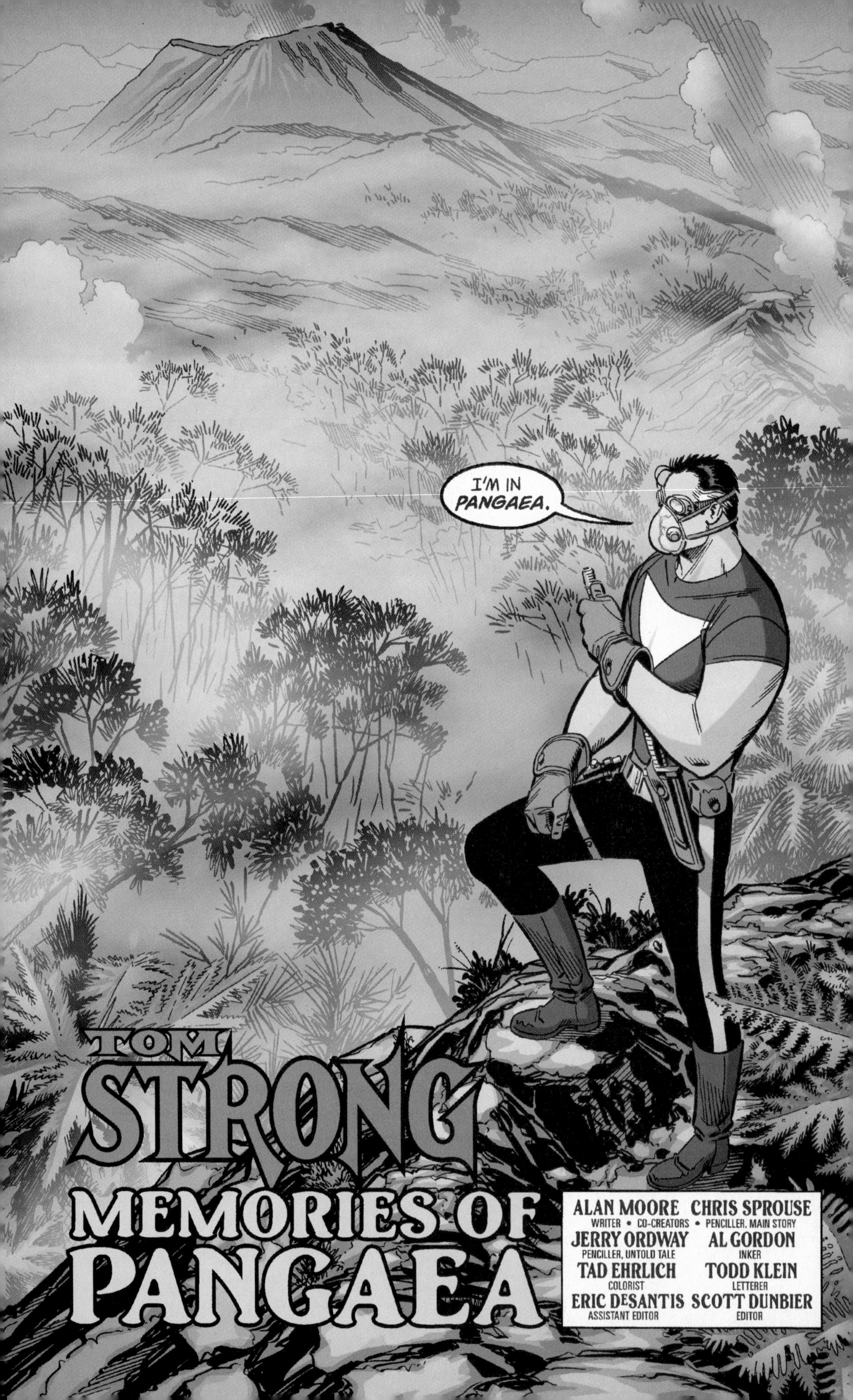
I'M IN PANGAEA.
TOM STRONG
MEMORIES OF PANGAEA
ALAN MOORE WRITER • CO-CREATORS • CHRIS SPROUSE PENCILLER, MAIN STORY
JERRY ORDWAY PENCILLER, UNTOLD TALE
AL GORDON INKER
TAD EHRLICH COLORIST
TODD KLEIN LETTERER
ERIC DESANTIS ASSISTANT EDITOR
SCOTT DUNBIER EDITOR

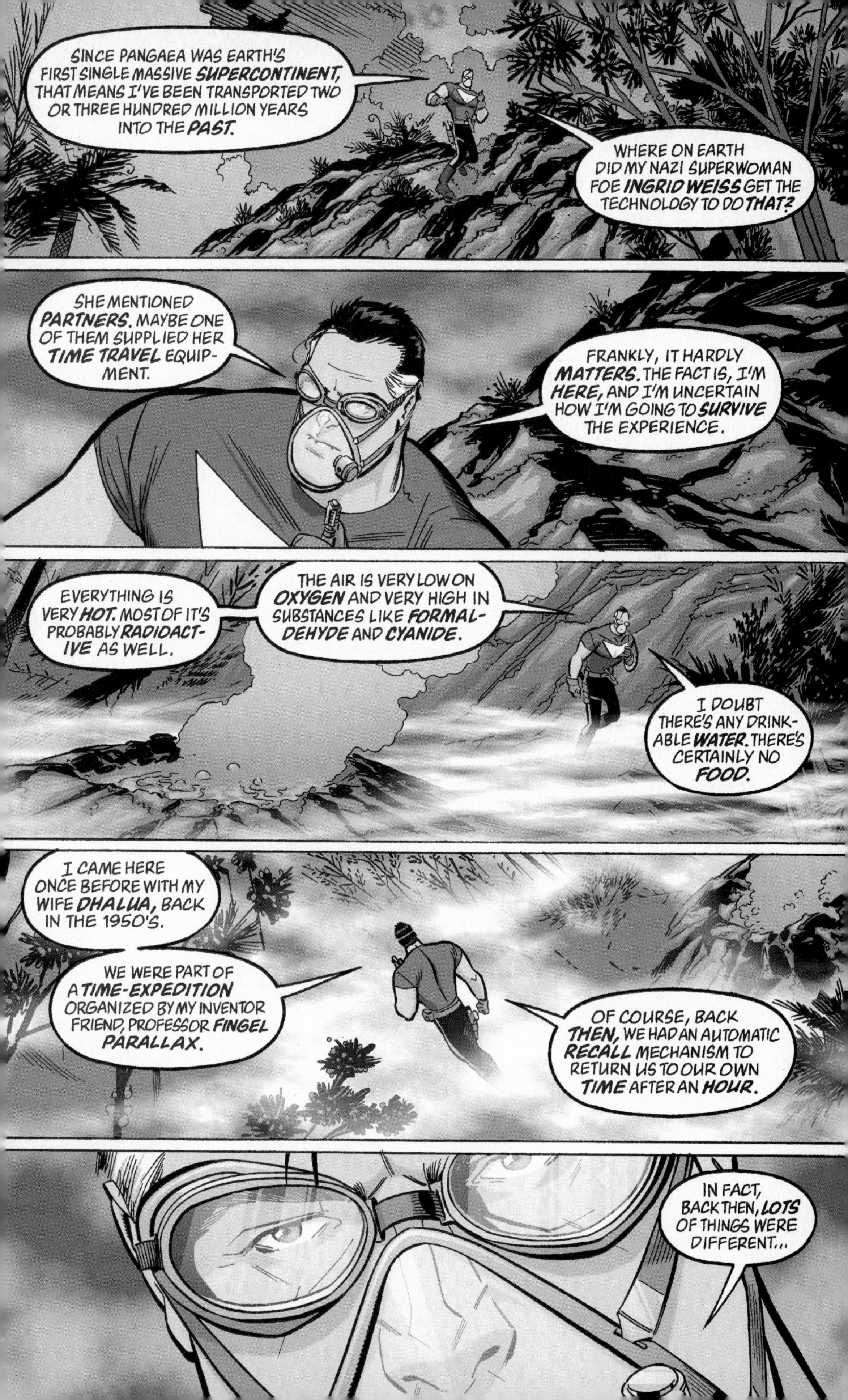
SINCE PANGAEA WAS EARTH'S FIRST SINGLE MASSIVE SUPERCONTINENT, THAT MEANS I'VE BEEN TRANSPORTED TWO OR THREE HUNDRED MILLION YEARS INTO THE PAST.
WHERE ON EARTH DID MY NAZI SUPERWOMAN FOE INGRID WEISS GET THE TECHNOLOGY TO DO THAT?
SHE MENTIONED PARTNERS. MAYBE ONE OF THEM SUPPLIED HER TIME TRAVEL EQUIP-MENT.
FRANKLY, IT HARDLY MATTERS. THE FACT IS, I'M HERE, AND I'M UNCERTAIN HOW I'M GOING TO SURVIVE THE EXPERIENCE.
EVERYTHING IS VERY HOT. MOST OF IT'S PROBABLY RADIOACT-IVE AS WELL.
THE AIR IS VERY LOW ON OXYGEN AND VERY HIGH IN SUBSTANCES LIKE FORMAL-DEHYDE AND CYANIDE.
I DOUBT THERE'S ANY DRINK-ABLE WATER. THERE'S CERTAINLY NO FOOD.
I CAME HERE ONCE BEFORE WITH MY WIFE DHALUA, BACK IN THE 1950'S.
WE WERE PART OF A TIME-EXPEDITION ORGANIZED BY MY INVENTOR FRIEND, PROFESSOR FINGEL PARALLAX.
OF COURSE, BACK THEN, WE HAD AN AUTOMATIC RECALL MECHANISM TO RETURN US TO OUR OWN TIME AFTER AN HOUR.
IN FACT, BACK THEN, LOTS OF THINGS WERE DIFFERENT...

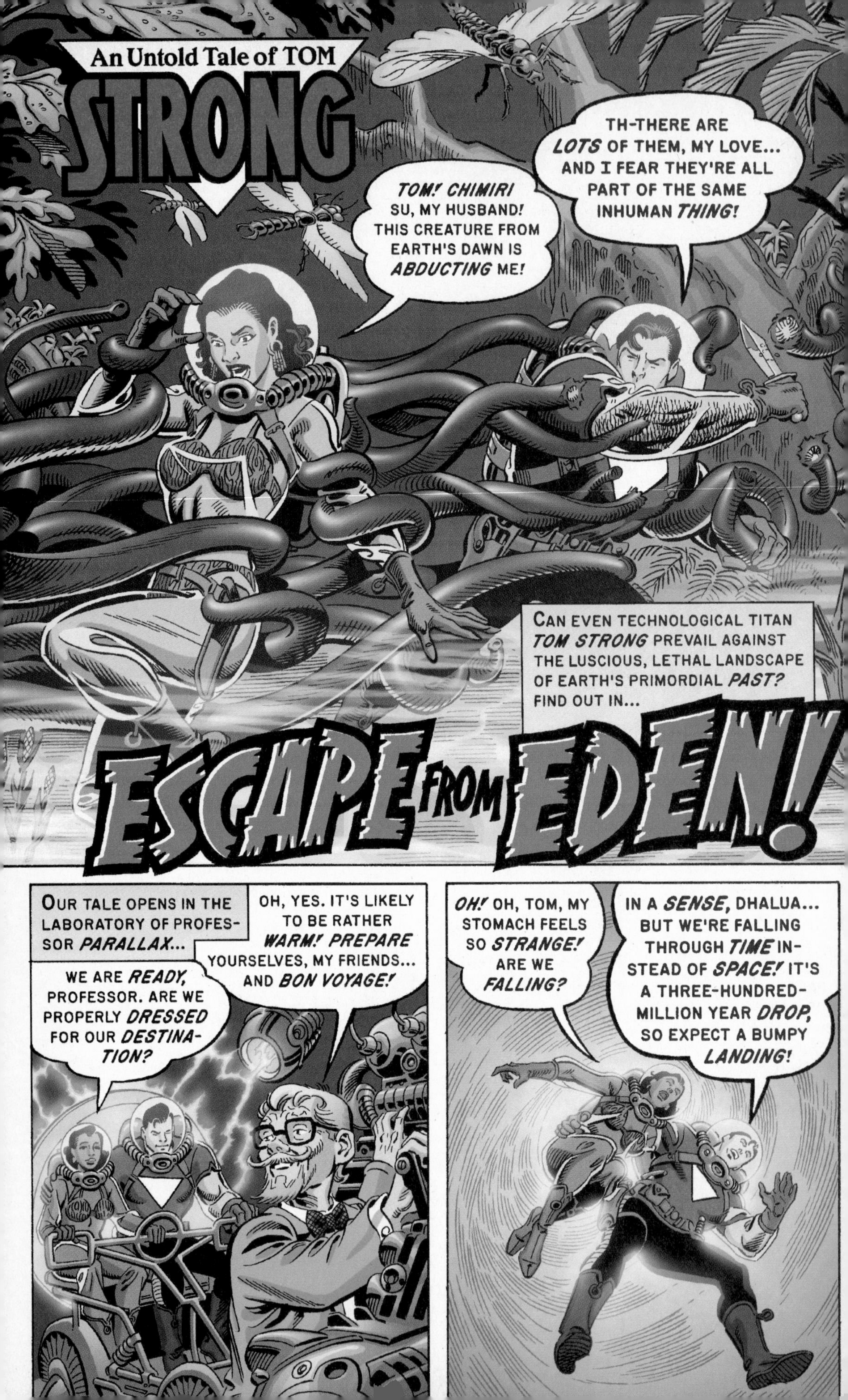

An Untold Tale of TOM
STRONG
TOM! CHIMIRI SU, MY HUSBAND! THIS CREATURE FROM EARTH'S DAWN IS ABDUCTING ME!
TH-THERE ARE LOTS OF THEM, MY LOVE... AND I FEAR THEY'RE ALL PART OF THE SAME INHUMAN THING!
CAN EVEN TECHNOLOGICAL TITAN TOM STRONG PREVAIL AGAINST THE LUSCIOUS, LETHAL LANDSCAPE OF EARTH'S PRIMORDIAL PAST? FIND OUT IN...
ESCAPE FROM EDEN!
OUR TALE OPENS IN THE LABORATORY OF PROFES-SOR PARALLAX...
WE ARE READY, PROFESSOR. ARE WE PROPERLY DRESSED FOR OUR DESTINA-TION?
OH, YES. IT'S LIKELY TO BE RATHER WARM! PREPARE YOURSELVES, MY FRIENDS... AND BON VOYAGE!
OH! OH, TOM, MY STOMACH FEELS SO STRANGE! ARE WE FALLING?
IN A SENSE, DHALUA... BUT WE'RE FALLING THROUGH TIME IN-STEAD OF SPACE! IT'S A THREE-HUNDRED-MILLION YEAR DROP, SO EXPECT A BUMPY LANDING!

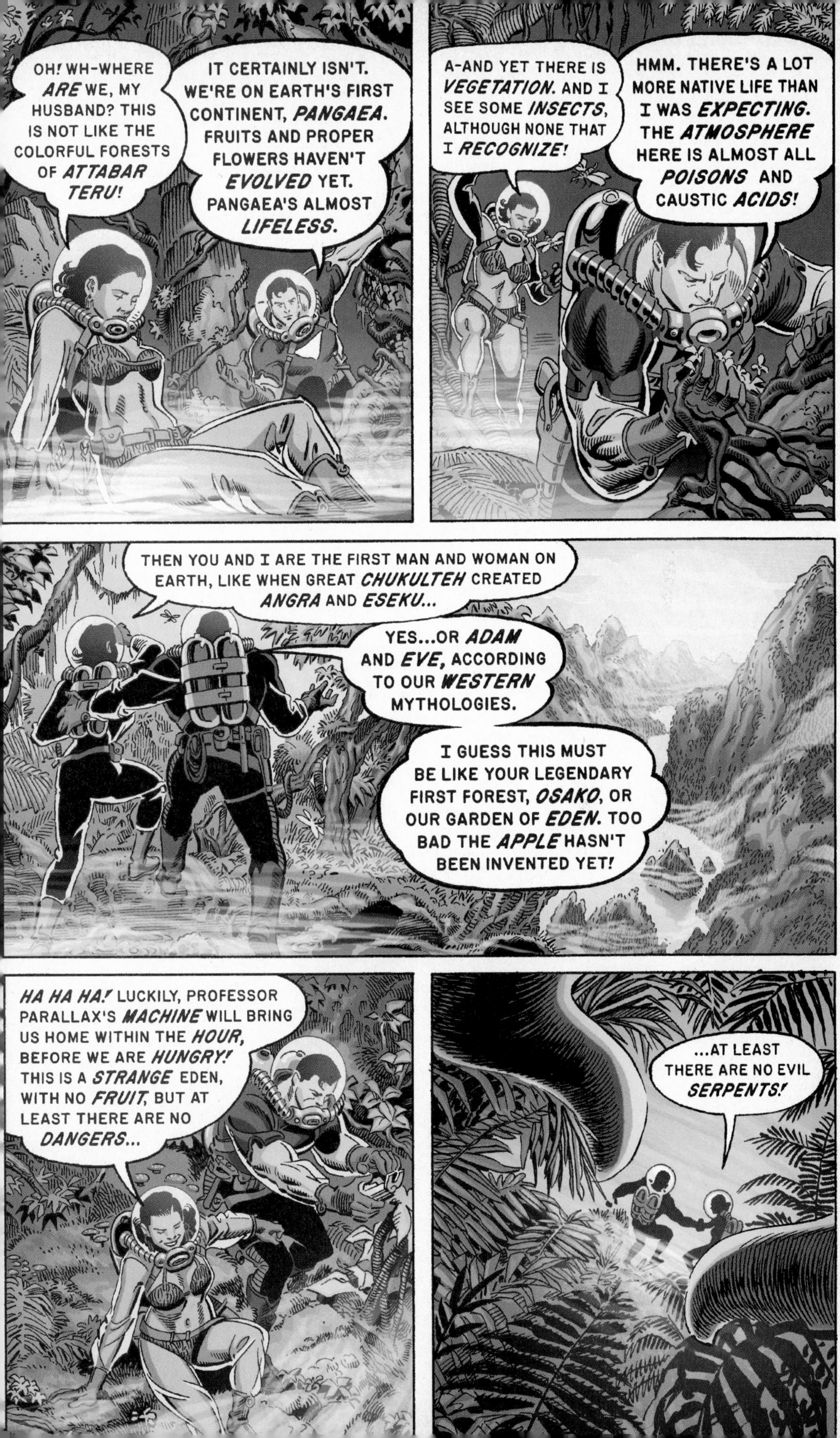
OH! WH-WHERE ARE WE, MY HUSBAND? THIS IS NOT LIKE THE COLORFUL FORESTS OF ATTABAR TERU!
IT CERTAINLY ISN'T. WE'RE ON EARTH'S FIRST CONTINENT, PANGAEA. FRUITS AND PROPER FLOWERS HAVEN'T EVOLVED YET. PANGAEA'S ALMOST LIFELESS.
A-AND YET THERE IS VEGETATION. AND I SEE SOME INSECTS, ALTHOUGH NONE THAT I RECOGNIZE!
HMM. THERE'S A LOT MORE NATIVE LIFE THAN I WAS EXPECTING. THE ATMOSPHERE HERE IS ALMOST ALL POISONS AND CAUSTIC ACIDS!
THEN YOU AND I ARE THE FIRST MAN AND WOMAN ON EARTH, LIKE WHEN GREAT CHUKULTEH CREATED ANGRA AND ESEKU...
YES...OR ADAM AND EVE, ACCORDING TO OUR WESTERN MYTHOLOGIES.
I GUESS THIS MUST BE LIKE YOUR LEGENDARY FIRST FOREST, OSAKO, OR OUR GARDEN OF EDEN. TOO BAD THE APPLE HASN'T BEEN INVENTED YET!
HA HA HA! LUCKILY, PROFESSOR PARALLAX'S MACHINE WILL BRING US HOME WITHIN THE HOUR, BEFORE WE ARE HUNGRY! THIS IS A STRANGE EDEN, WITH NO FRUIT, BUT AT LEAST THERE ARE NO DANGERS...
...AT LEAST THERE ARE NO EVIL SERPENTS!

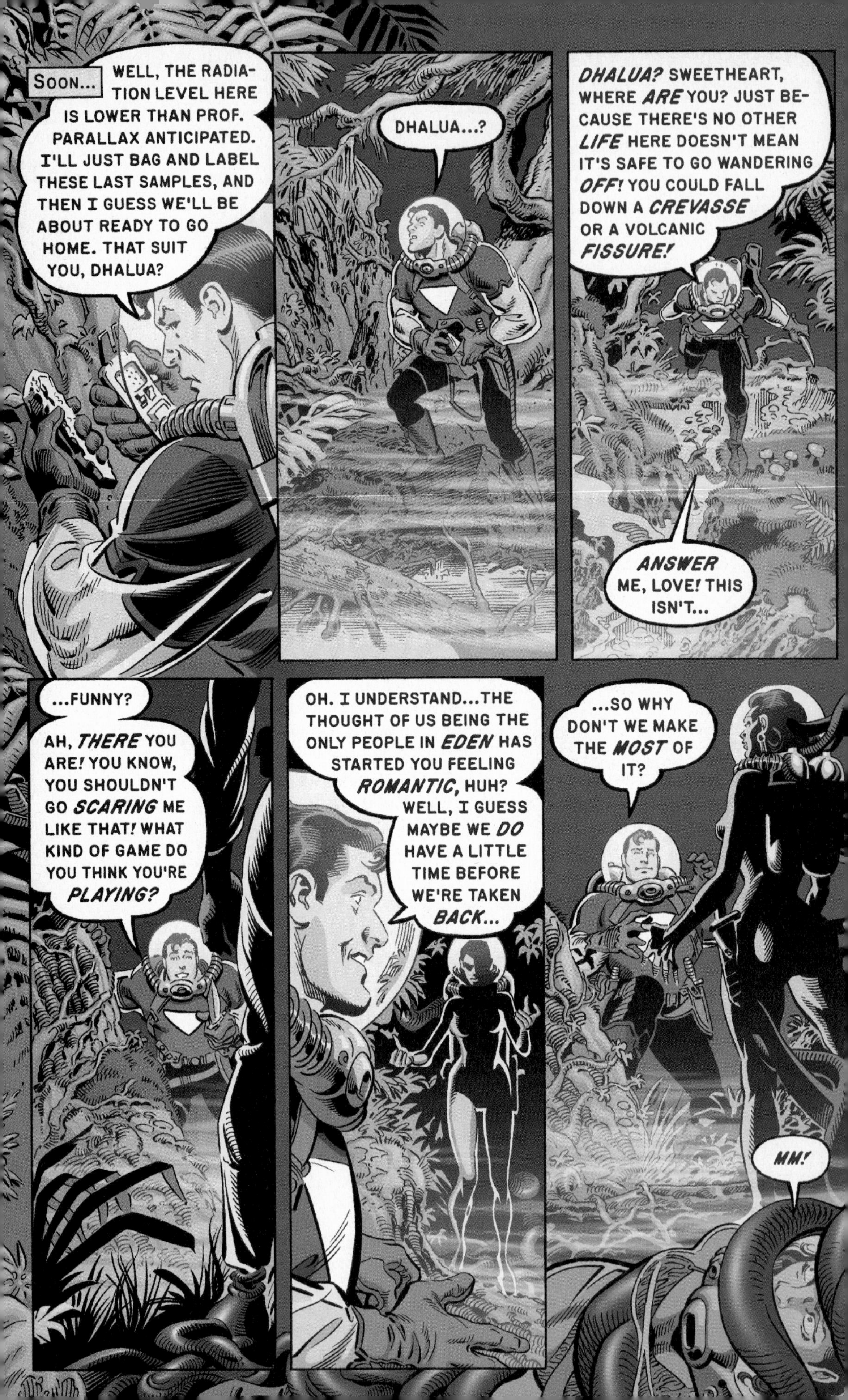

SOON...
WELL, THE RADIATION LEVEL HERE IS LOWER THAN PROF. PARALLAX ANTICIPATED. I'LL JUST BAG AND LABEL THESE LAST SAMPLES, AND THEN I GUESS WE'LL BE ABOUT READY TO GO HOME. THAT SUIT YOU, DHALUA?
DHALUA...?
DHALUA? SWEETHEART, WHERE ARE YOU? JUST BECAUSE THERE'S NO OTHER LIFE HERE DOESN'T MEAN IT'S SAFE TO GO WANDERING OFF! YOU COULD FALL DOWN A CREVASSE OR A VOLCANIC FISSURE!
ANSWER ME, LOVE! THIS ISN'T...
...FUNNY?
AH, THERE YOU ARE! YOU KNOW, YOU SHOULDN'T GO SCARING ME LIKE THAT! WHAT KIND OF GAME DO YOU THINK YOU'RE PLAYING?
OH. I UNDERSTAND...THE THOUGHT OF US BEING THE ONLY PEOPLE IN EDEN HAS STARTED YOU FEELING ROMANTIC, HUH? WELL, I GUESS MAYBE WE DO HAVE A LITTLE TIME BEFORE WE'RE TAKEN BACK...
...SO WHY DON'T WE MAKE THE MOST OF IT?
MM!

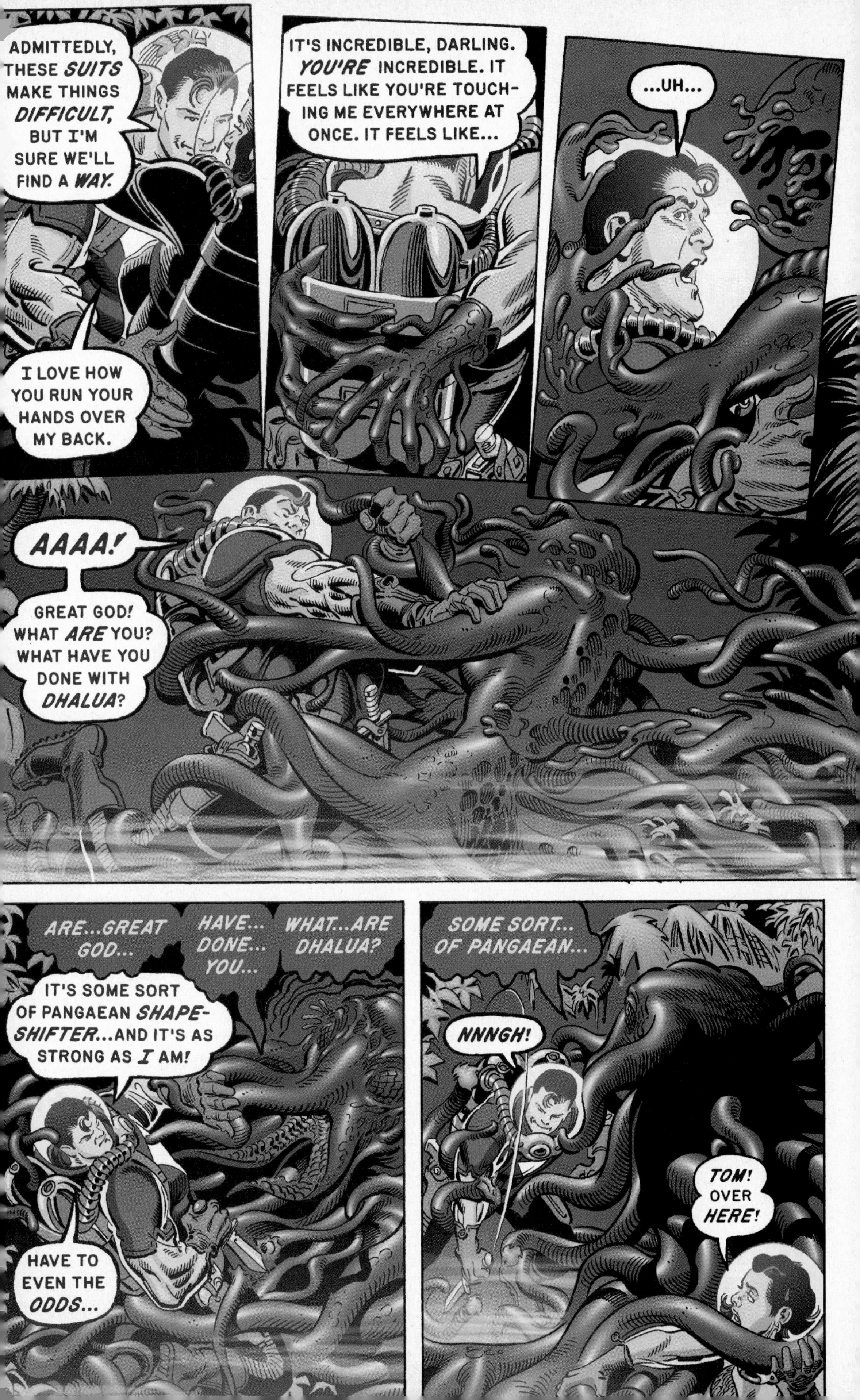
ADMITTEDLY, THESE SUITS MAKE THINGS DIFFICULT, BUT I'M SURE WE'LL FIND A WAY.
I LOVE HOW YOU RUN YOUR HANDS OVER MY BACK.
IT'S INCREDIBLE, DARLING. YOU'RE INCREDIBLE. IT FEELS LIKE YOU'RE TOUCHING ME EVERYWHERE AT ONCE. IT FEELS LIKE...
...UH...
AAAA!
GREAT GOD! WHAT ARE YOU? WHAT HAVE YOU DONE WITH DHALUA?
ARE...GREAT GOD...
HAVE... DONE... YOU...
WHAT...ARE DHALUA?
IT'S SOME SORT OF PANGAEAN SHAPE-SHIFTER...AND IT'S AS STRONG AS I AM!
HAVE TO EVEN THE ODDS...
SOME SORT... OF PANGAEAN...
NNNGH!
TOM! OVER HERE!

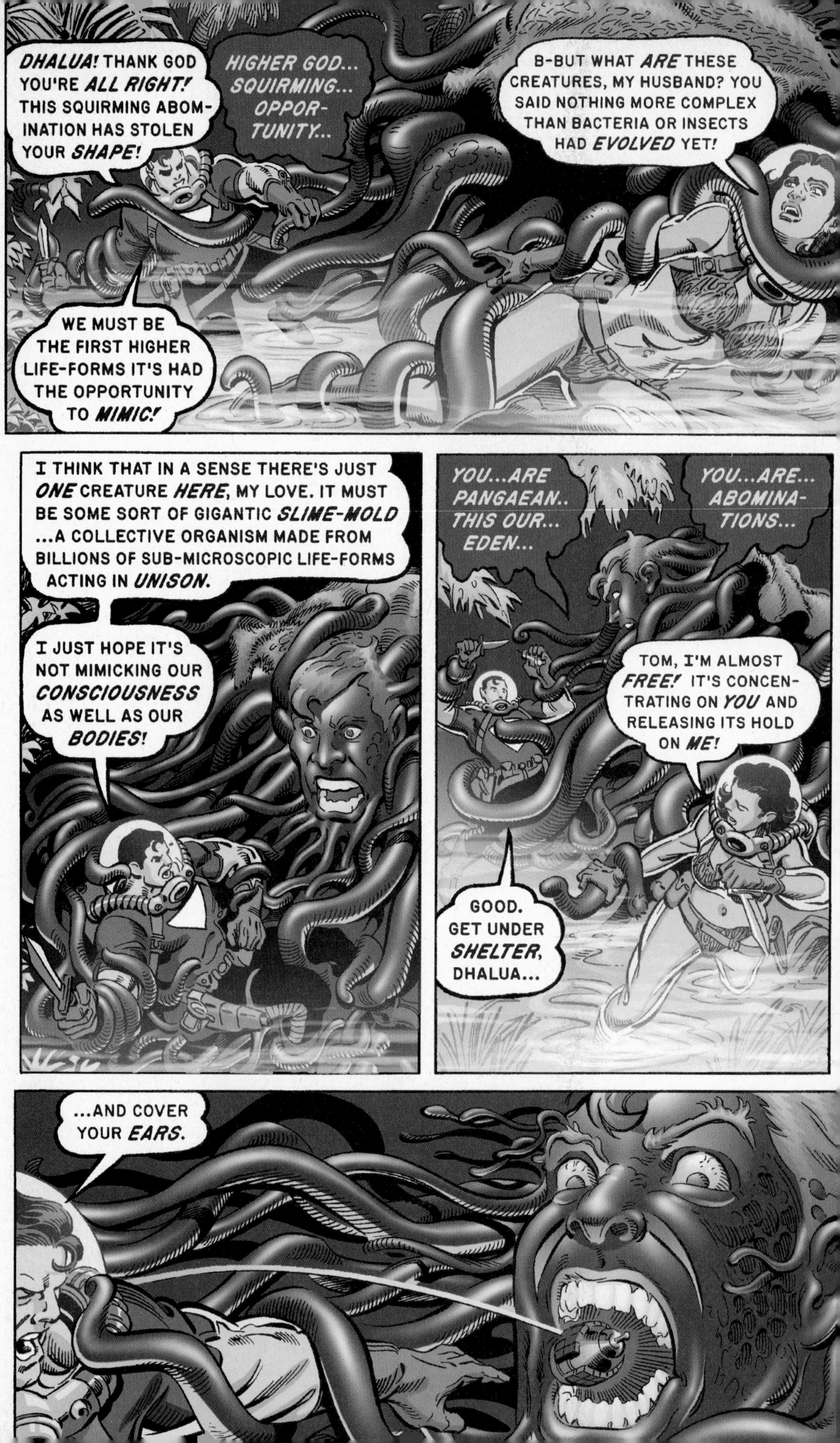

DHALUA! THANK GOD YOU'RE ALL RIGHT! THIS SQUIRMING ABOMINATION HAS STOLEN YOUR SHAPE!
HIGHER GOD... SQUIRMING... OPPORTUNITY...
B-BUT WHAT ARE THESE CREATURES, MY HUSBAND? YOU SAID NOTHING MORE COMPLEX THAN BACTERIA OR INSECTS HAD EVOLVED YET!
WE MUST BE THE FIRST HIGHER LIFE-FORMS IT'S HAD THE OPPORTUNITY TO MIMIC!
I THINK THAT IN A SENSE THERE'S JUST ONE CREATURE HERE, MY LOVE. IT MUST BE SOME SORT OF GIGANTIC SLIME-MOLD ...A COLLECTIVE ORGANISM MADE FROM BILLIONS OF SUB-MICROSCOPIC LIFE-FORMS ACTING IN UNISON.
I JUST HOPE IT'S NOT MIMICKING OUR CONSCIOUSNESS AS WELL AS OUR BODIES!
YOU...ARE PANGAEAN.. THIS OUR... EDEN...
YOU...ARE... ABOMINATIONS...
TOM, I'M ALMOST FREE! IT'S CONCENTRATING ON YOU AND RELEASING ITS HOLD ON ME!
GOOD. GET UNDER SHELTER, DHALUA...
...AND COVER YOUR EARS.

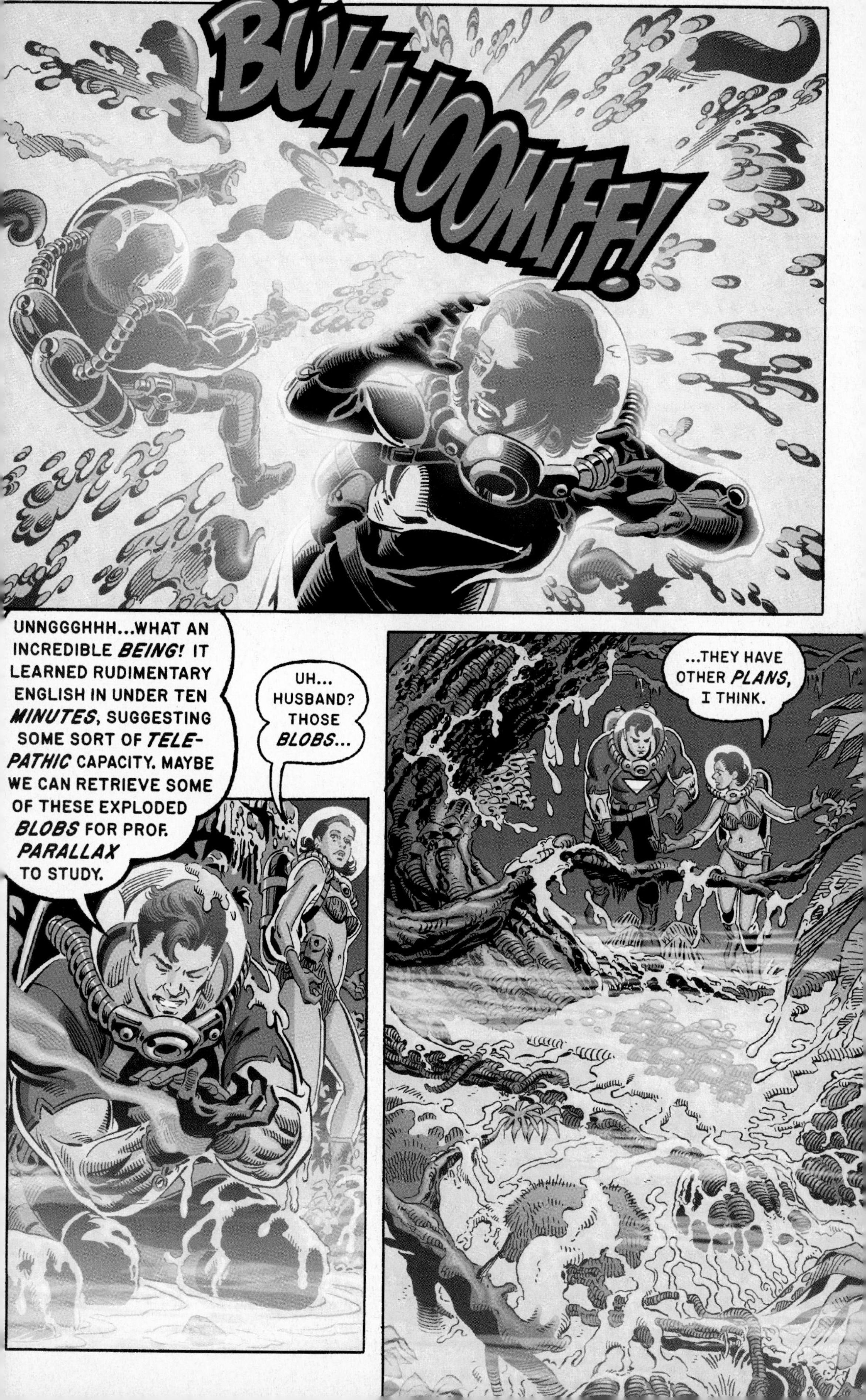
BUHWOOMFF!
UNNGGGHHH...WHAT AN INCREDIBLE BEING! IT LEARNED RUDIMENTARY ENGLISH IN UNDER TEN MINUTES, SUGGESTING SOME SORT OF TELE-PATHIC CAPACITY. MAYBE WE CAN RETRIEVE SOME OF THESE EXPLODED BLOBS FOR PROF. PARALLAX TO STUDY.
UH... HUSBAND? THOSE BLOBS...
...THEY HAVE OTHER PLANS, I THINK.

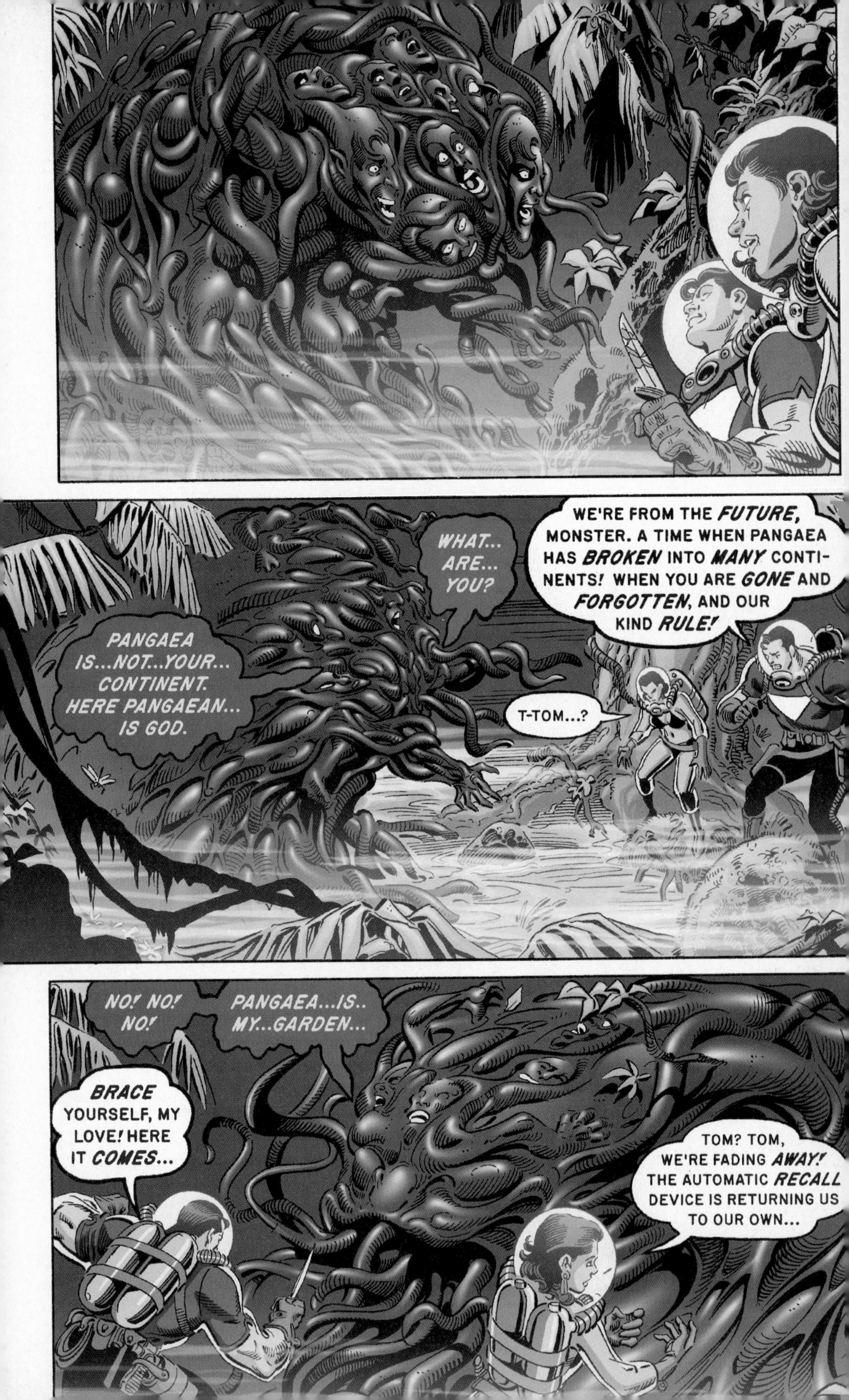
WHAT... ARE... YOU?
WE'RE FROM THE FUTURE, MONSTER. A TIME WHEN PANGAEA HAS BROKEN INTO MANY CONTINENTS! WHEN YOU ARE GONE AND FORGOTTEN, AND OUR KIND RULE!
PANGAEA IS...NOT...YOUR... CONTINENT. HERE PANGAEAN... IS GOD.
T-TOM...?
NO! NO! NO!
PANGAEA...IS.. MY...GARDEN...
BRACE YOURSELF, MY LOVE! HERE IT COMES...
TOM? TOM, WE'RE FADING AWAY! THE AUTOMATIC RECALL DEVICE IS RETURNING US TO OUR OWN...

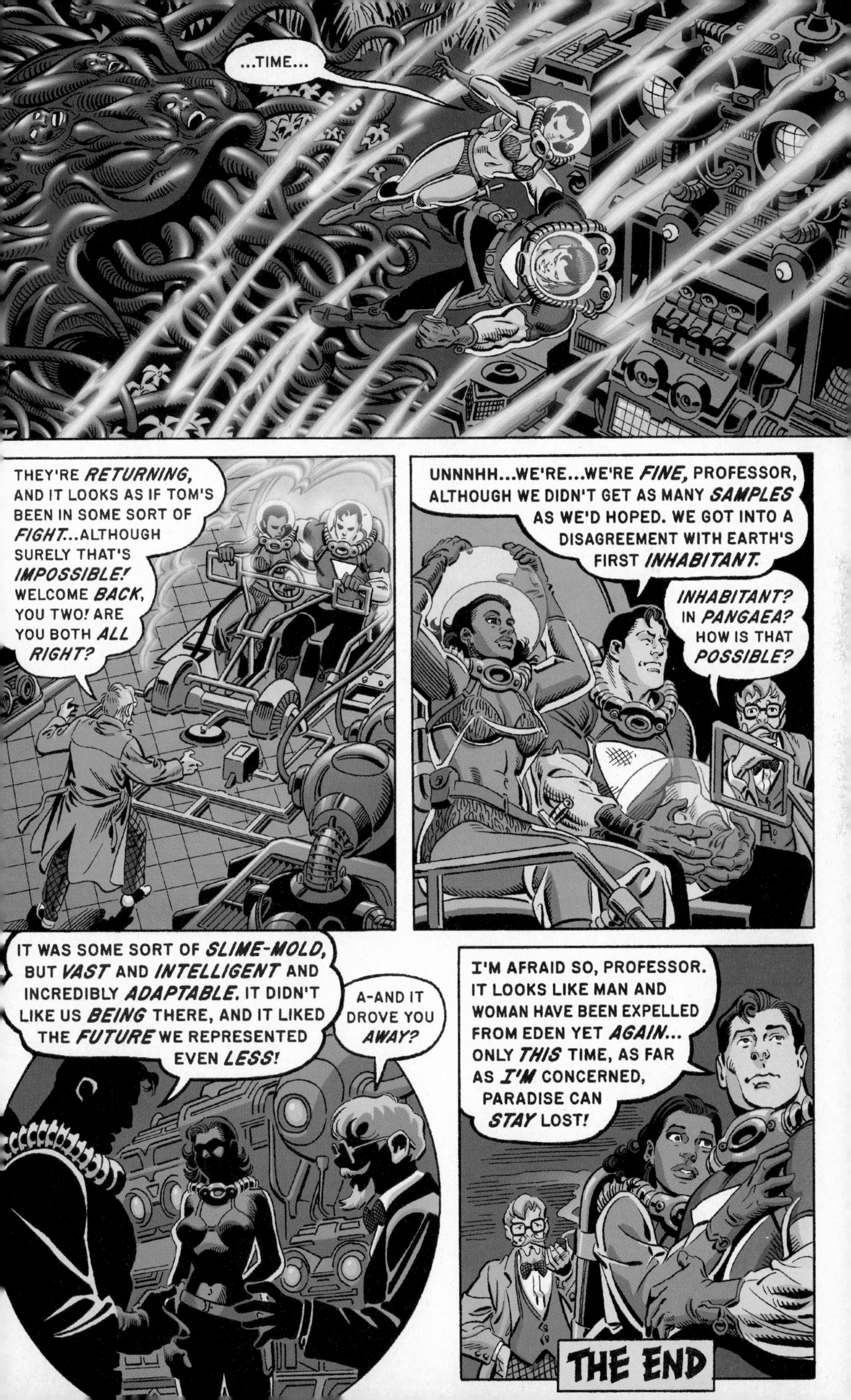
...TIME...
THEY'RE RETURNING, AND IT LOOKS AS IF TOM'S BEEN IN SOME SORT OF FIGHT... ALTHOUGH SURELY THAT'S IMPOSSIBLE! WELCOME BACK, YOU TWO! ARE YOU BOTH ALL RIGHT?
UNNNHH...WE'RE...WE'RE FINE, PROFESSOR, ALTHOUGH WE DIDN'T GET AS MANY SAMPLES AS WE'D HOPED. WE GOT INTO A DISAGREEMENT WITH EARTH'S FIRST INHABITANT.
INHABITANT? IN PANGAEA? HOW IS THAT POSSIBLE?
IT WAS SOME SORT OF SLIME-MOLD, BUT VAST AND INTELLIGENT AND INCREDIBLY ADAPTABLE. IT DIDN'T LIKE US BEING THERE, AND IT LIKED THE FUTURE WE REPRESENTED EVEN LESS!
A-AND IT DROVE YOU AWAY?
I'M AFRAID SO, PROFESSOR. IT LOOKS LIKE MAN AND WOMAN HAVE BEEN EXPELLED FROM EDEN YET AGAIN... ONLY THIS TIME, AS FAR AS I'M CONCERNED, PARADISE CAN STAY LOST!
THE END

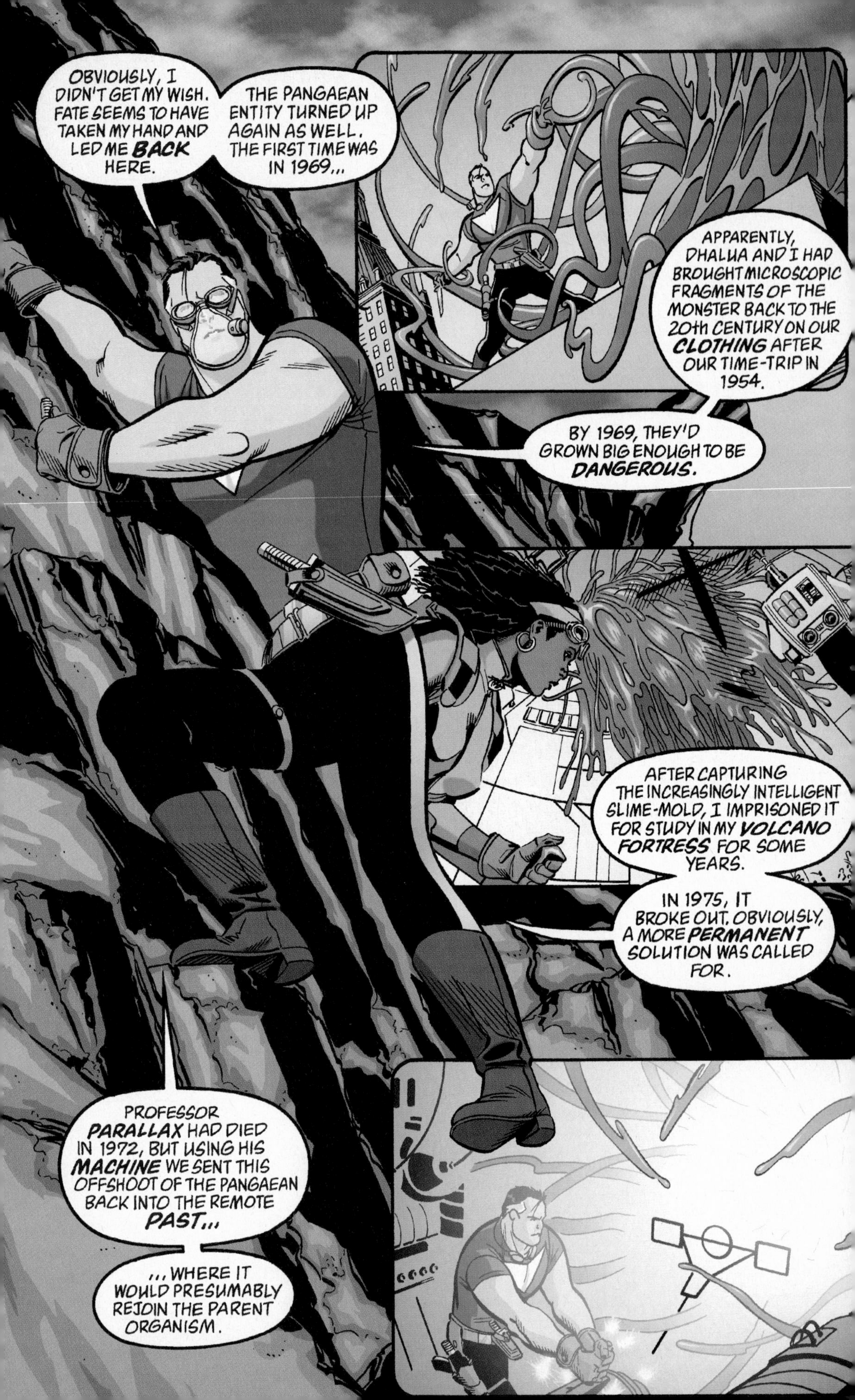
OBVIOUSLY, I DIDN'T GET MY WISH. FATE SEEMS TO HAVE TAKEN MY HAND AND LED ME BACK HERE.
THE PANGAEAN ENTITY TURNED UP AGAIN AS WELL. THE FIRST TIME WAS IN 1969...
APPARENTLY, DHALUA AND I HAD BROUGHT MICROSCOPIC FRAGMENTS OF THE MONSTER BACK TO THE 20th CENTURY ON OUR CLOTHING AFTER OUR TIME-TRIP IN 1954.
BY 1969, THEY'D GROWN BIG ENOUGH TO BE DANGEROUS.
AFTER CAPTURING THE INCREASINGLY INTELLIGENT SLIME-MOLD, I IMPRISONED IT FOR STUDY IN MY VOLCANO FORTRESS FOR SOME YEARS.
IN 1975, IT BROKE OUT. OBVIOUSLY, A MORE PERMANENT SOLUTION WAS CALLED FOR.
PROFESSOR PARALLAX HAD DIED IN 1972, BUT USING HIS MACHINE WE SENT THIS OFFSHOOT OF THE PANGAEAN BACK INTO THE REMOTE PAST...
...WHERE IT WOULD PRESUMABLY REJOIN THE PARENT ORGANISM.

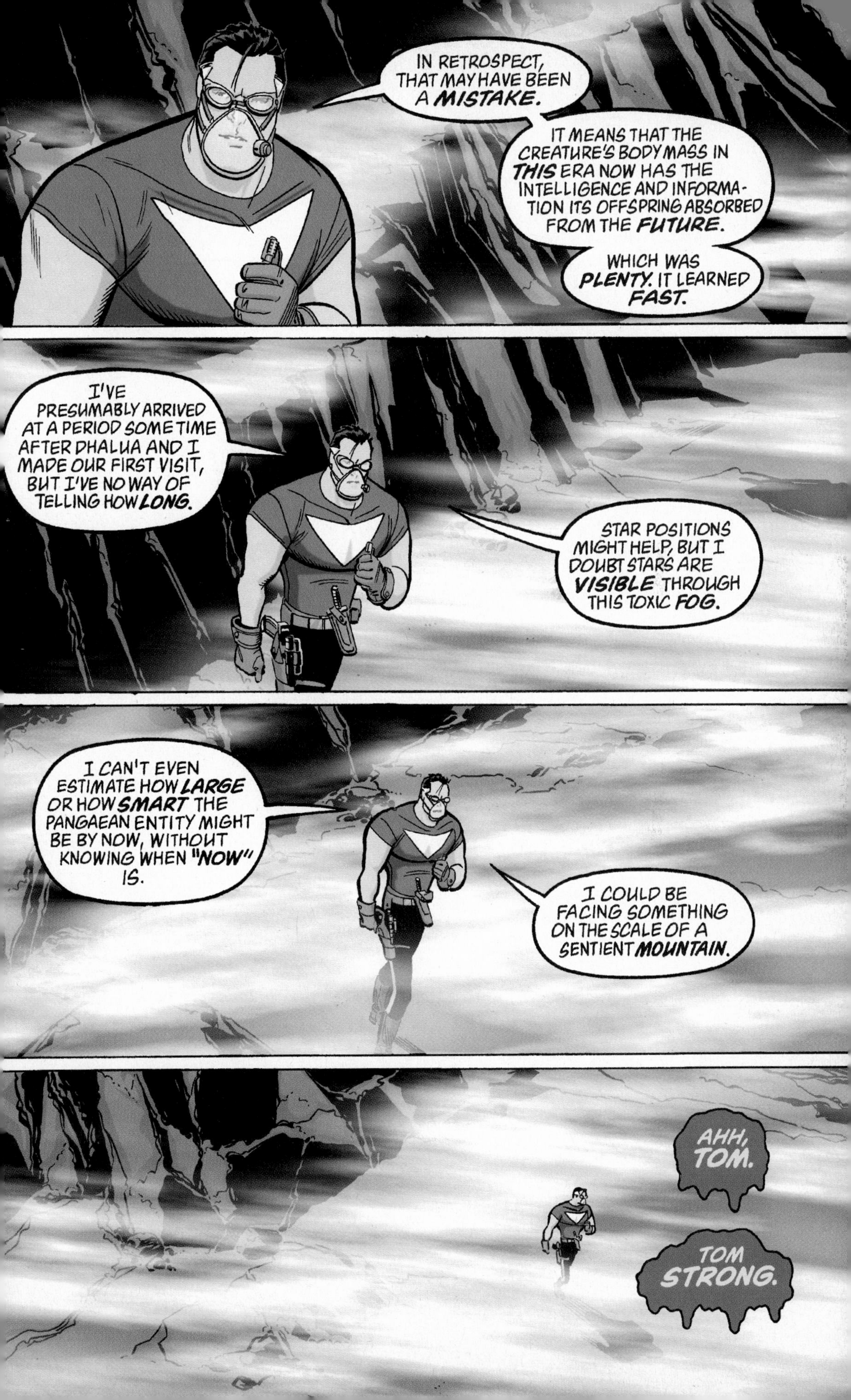
IN RETROSPECT, THAT MAY HAVE BEEN A MISTAKE.
IT MEANS THAT THE CREATURE'S BODY MASS IN THIS ERA NOW HAS THE INTELLIGENCE AND INFORMATION ITS OFFSPRING ABSORBED FROM THE FUTURE.
WHICH WAS PLENTY. IT LEARNED FAST.
I'VE PRESUMABLY ARRIVED AT A PERIOD SOME TIME AFTER DHALUA AND I MADE OUR FIRST VISIT, BUT I'VE NO WAY OF TELLING HOW LONG.
STAR POSITIONS MIGHT HELP, BUT I DOUBT STARS ARE VISIBLE THROUGH THIS TOXIC FOG.
I CAN'T EVEN ESTIMATE HOW LARGE OR HOW SMART THE PANGAEAN ENTITY MIGHT BE BY NOW, WITHOUT KNOWING WHEN "NOW" IS.
I COULD BE FACING SOMETHING ON THE SCALE OF A SENTIENT MOUNTAIN.
AHH, TOM.
TOM STRONG.

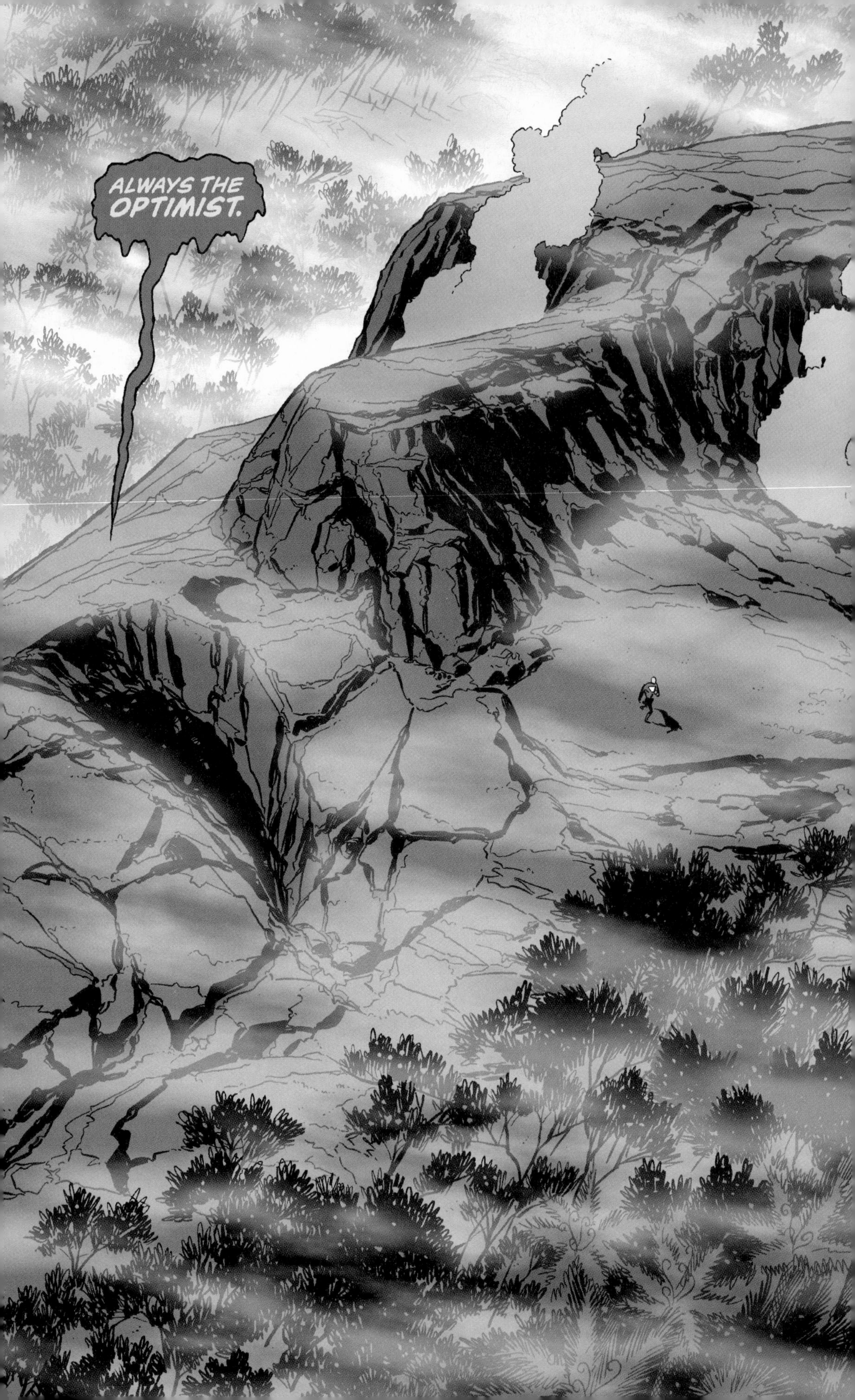
ALWAYS THE OPTIMIST.

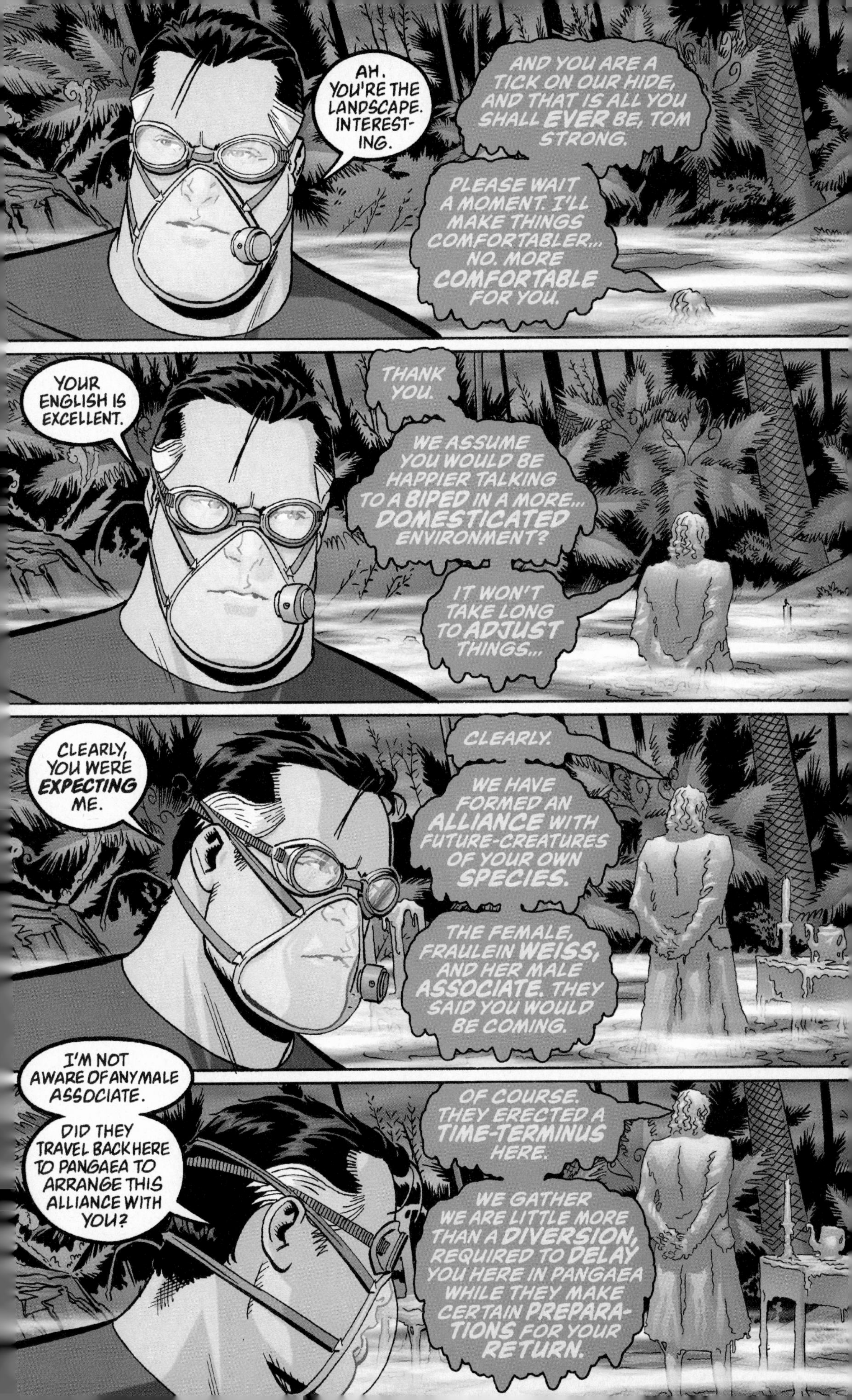
AH. YOU'RE THE LANDSCAPE. INTERESTING.
AND YOU ARE A TICK ON OUR HIDE, AND THAT IS ALL YOU SHALL EVER BE, TOM STRONG.
PLEASE WAIT A MOMENT. I'LL MAKE THINGS COMFORTABLER... NO. MORE COMFORTABLE FOR YOU.
YOUR ENGLISH IS EXCELLENT.
THANK YOU.
WE ASSUME YOU WOULD BE HAPPIER TALKING TO A BIPED IN A MORE... DOMESTICATED ENVIRONMENT?
IT WON'T TAKE LONG TO ADJUST THINGS...
CLEARLY, YOU WERE EXPECTING ME.
CLEARLY.
WE HAVE FORMED AN ALLIANCE WITH FUTURE-CREATURES OF YOUR OWN SPECIES.
THE FEMALE, FRAULEIN WEISS, AND HER MALE ASSOCIATE. THEY SAID YOU WOULD BE COMING.
I'M NOT AWARE OF ANY MALE ASSOCIATE.
DID THEY TRAVEL BACK HERE TO PANGAEA TO ARRANGE THIS ALLIANCE WITH YOU?
OF COURSE. THEY ERECTED A TIME-TERMINUS HERE.
WE GATHER WE ARE LITTLE MORE THAN A DIVERSION, REQUIRED TO DELAY YOU HERE IN PANGAEA WHILE THEY MAKE CERTAIN PREPARATIONS FOR YOUR RETURN.

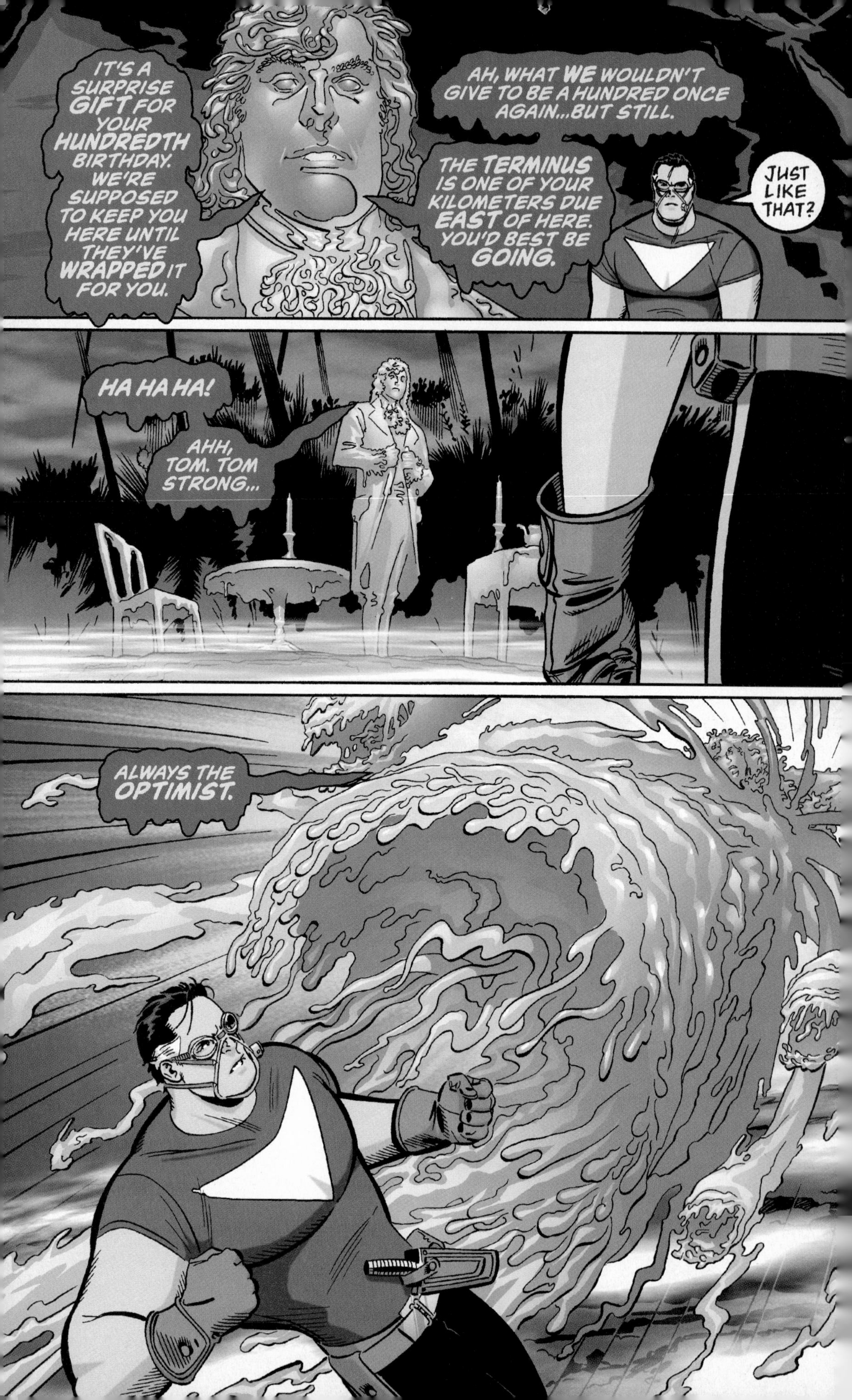
IT'S A SURPRISE GIFT FOR YOUR HUNDREDTH BIRTHDAY. WE'RE SUPPOSED TO KEEP YOU HERE UNTIL THEY'VE WRAPPED IT FOR YOU.
AH, WHAT WE WOULDN'T GIVE TO BE A HUNDRED ONCE AGAIN...BUT STILL.
THE TERMINUS IS ONE OF YOUR KILOMETERS DUE EAST OF HERE. YOU'D BEST BE GOING.
JUST LIKE THAT?
HA HA HA!
AHH, TOM. TOM STRONG...
ALWAYS THE OPTIMIST.

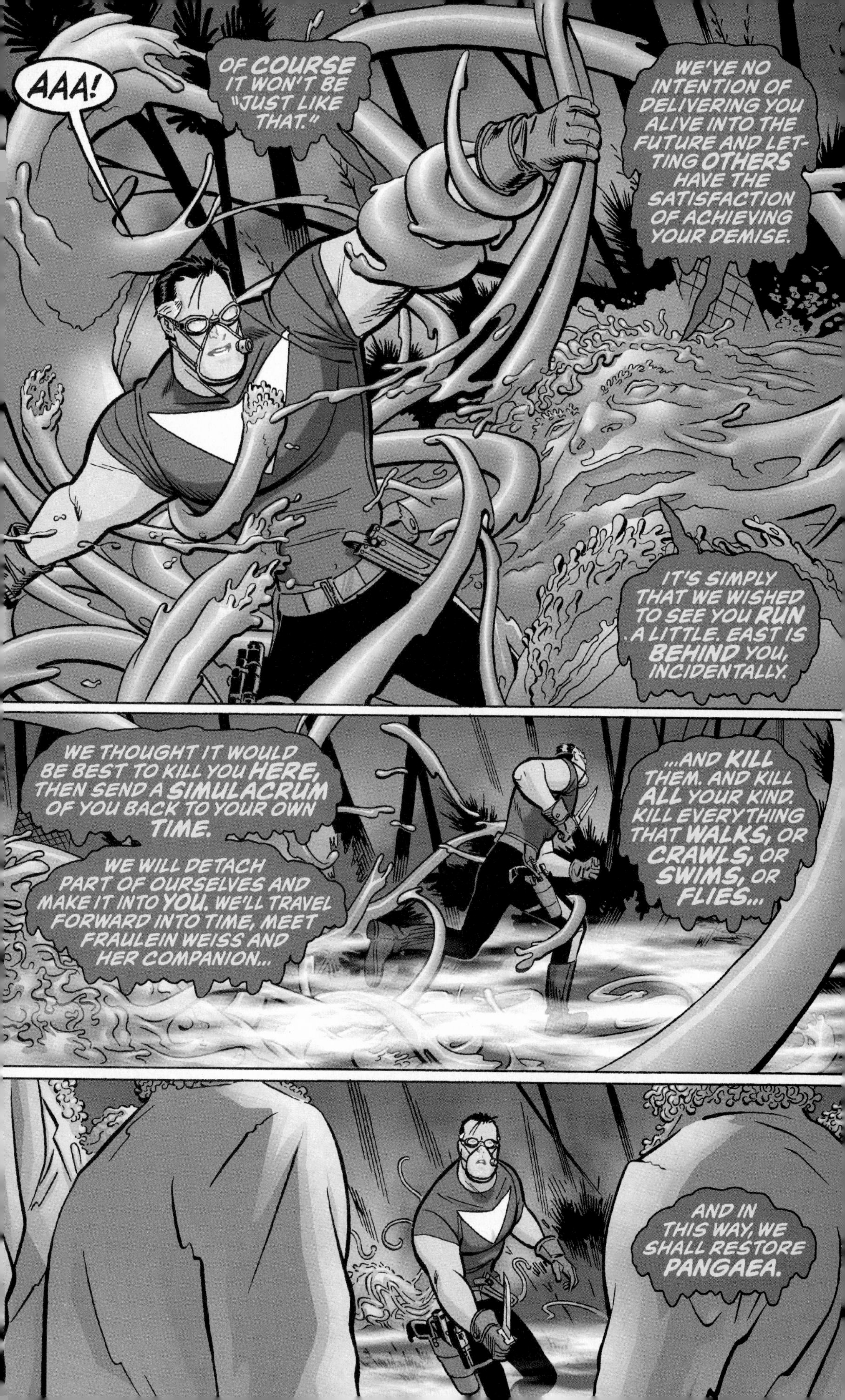
AAA!
OF COURSE IT WON'T BE "JUST LIKE THAT."
WE'VE NO INTENTION OF DELIVERING YOU ALIVE INTO THE FUTURE AND LETTING OTHERS HAVE THE SATISFACTION OF ACHIEVING YOUR DEMISE.
IT'S SIMPLY THAT WE WISHED TO SEE YOU RUN A LITTLE. EAST IS BEHIND YOU, INCIDENTALLY.
WE THOUGHT IT WOULD BE BEST TO KILL YOU HERE, THEN SEND A SIMULACRUM OF YOU BACK TO YOUR OWN TIME.
WE WILL DETACH PART OF OURSELVES AND MAKE IT INTO YOU. WE'LL TRAVEL FORWARD INTO TIME, MEET FRAULEIN WEISS AND HER COMPANION...
...AND KILL THEM. AND KILL ALL YOUR KIND. KILL EVERYTHING THAT WALKS, OR CRAWLS, OR SWIMS, OR FLIES...
AND IN THIS WAY, WE SHALL RESTORE PANGAEA.

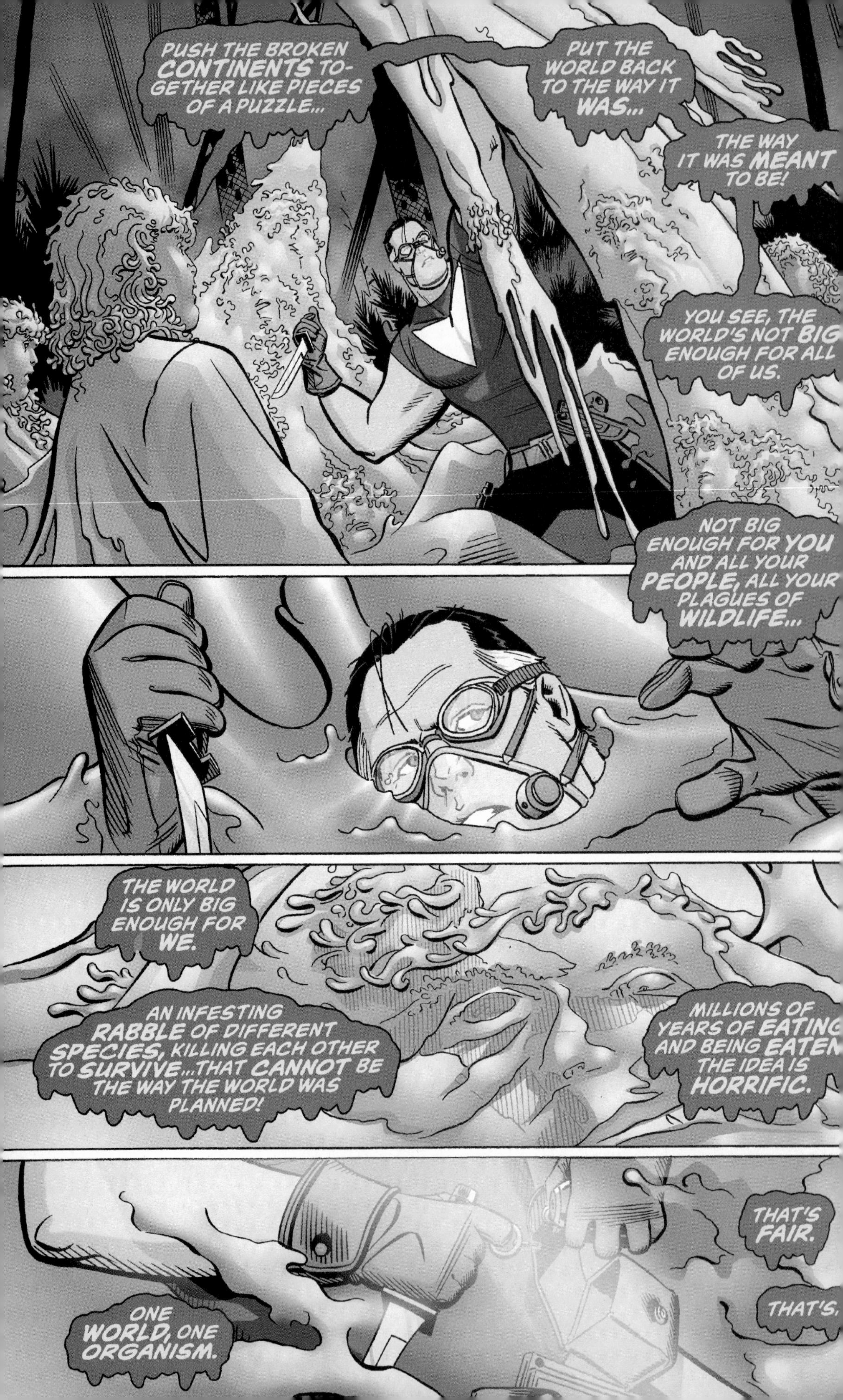
PUSH THE BROKEN CONTINENTS TOGETHER LIKE PIECES OF A PUZZLE...
PUT THE WORLD BACK TO THE WAY IT WAS...
THE WAY IT WAS MEANT TO BE!
YOU SEE, THE WORLD'S NOT BIG ENOUGH FOR ALL OF US.
NOT BIG ENOUGH FOR YOU AND ALL YOUR PEOPLE, ALL YOUR PLAGUES OF WILDLIFE...
THE WORLD IS ONLY BIG ENOUGH FOR WE.
AN INFESTING RABBLE OF DIFFERENT SPECIES, KILLING EACH OTHER TO SURVIVE...THAT CANNOT BE THE WAY THE WORLD WAS PLANNED!
MILLIONS OF YEARS OF EATING AND BEING EATEN THE IDEA IS HORRIFIC.
THAT'S FAIR.
THAT'S...
ONE WORLD, ONE ORGANISM.

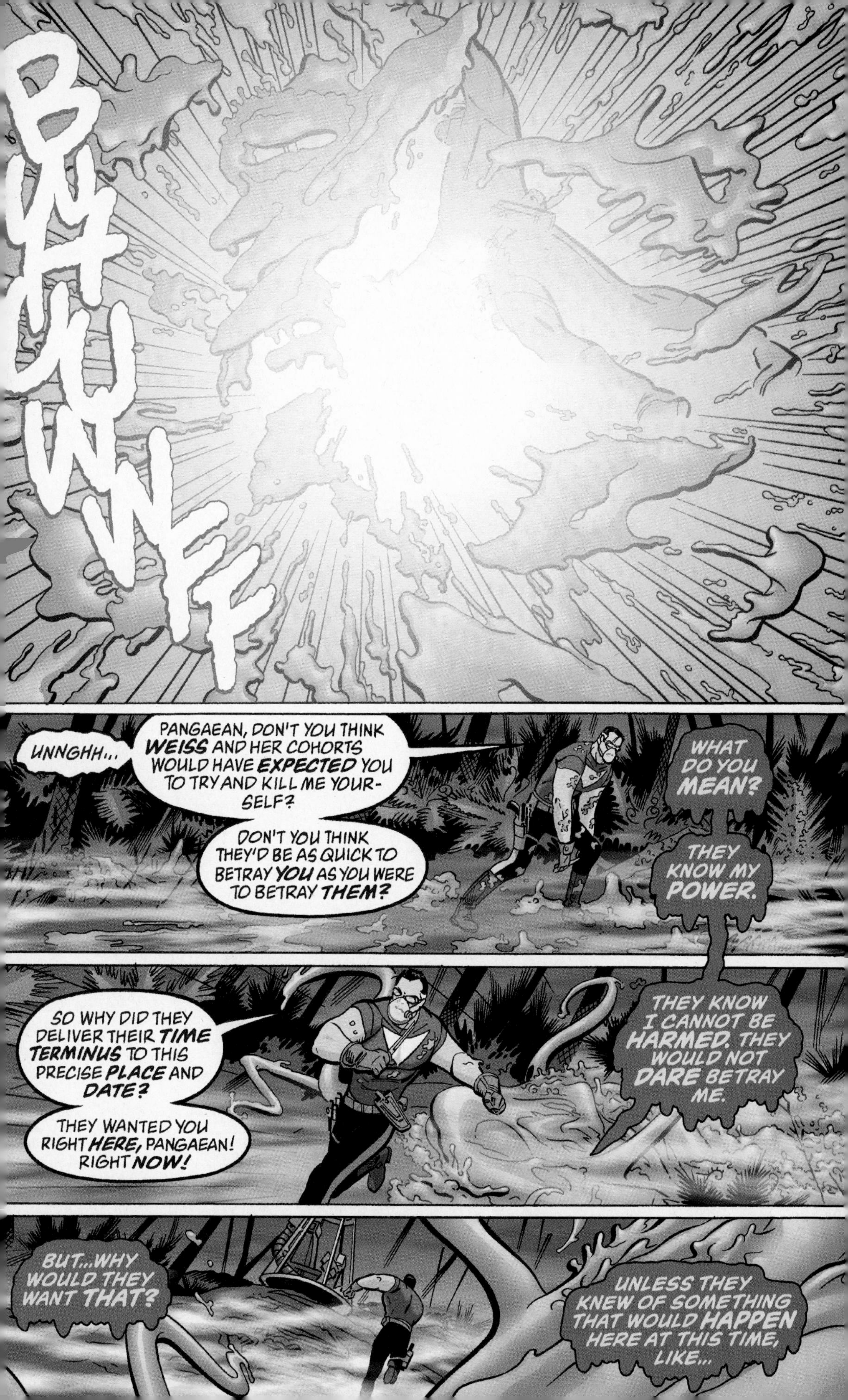
BUHWFF
UNNGHH...
PANGAEAN, DON'T YOU THINK WEISS AND HER COHORTS WOULD HAVE EXPECTED YOU TO TRY AND KILL ME YOURSELF?
DON'T YOU THINK THEY'D BE AS QUICK TO BETRAY YOU AS YOU WERE TO BETRAY THEM?
WHAT DO YOU MEAN?
THEY KNOW MY POWER.
SO WHY DID THEY DELIVER THEIR TIME TERMINUS TO THIS PRECISE PLACE AND DATE?
THEY WANTED YOU RIGHT HERE, PANGAEAN! RIGHT NOW!
THEY KNOW I CANNOT BE HARMED. THEY WOULD NOT DARE BETRAY ME.
BUT...WHY WOULD THEY WANT THAT?
UNLESS THEY KNEW OF SOMETHING THAT WOULD HAPPEN HERE AT THIS TIME, LIKE...

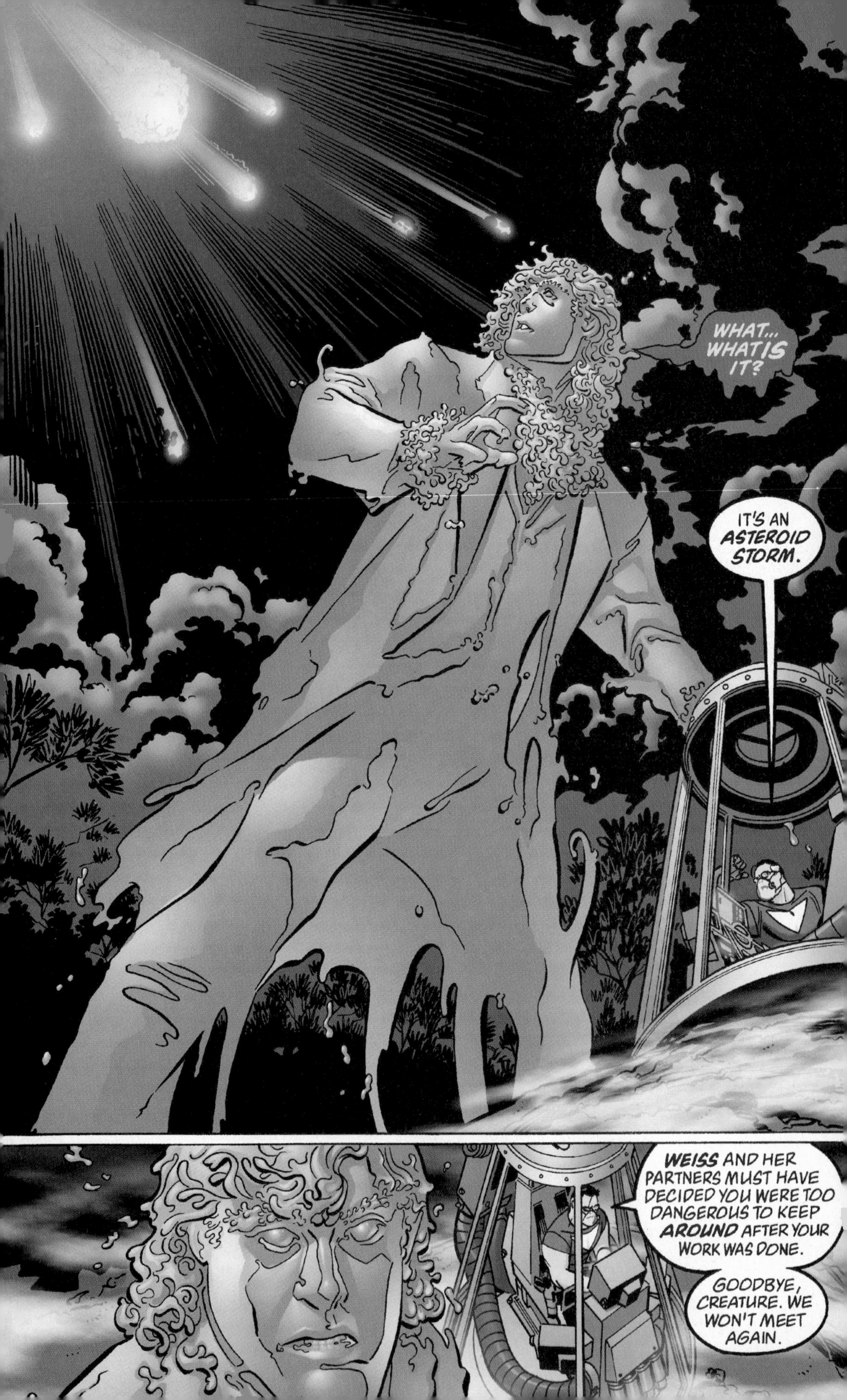
WHAT... WHAT IS IT?
IT'S AN ASTEROID STORM.
WEISS AND HER PARTNERS MUST HAVE DECIDED YOU WERE TOO DANGEROUS TO KEEP AROUND AFTER YOUR WORK WAS DONE.
GOODBYE, CREATURE. WE WON'T MEET AGAIN.

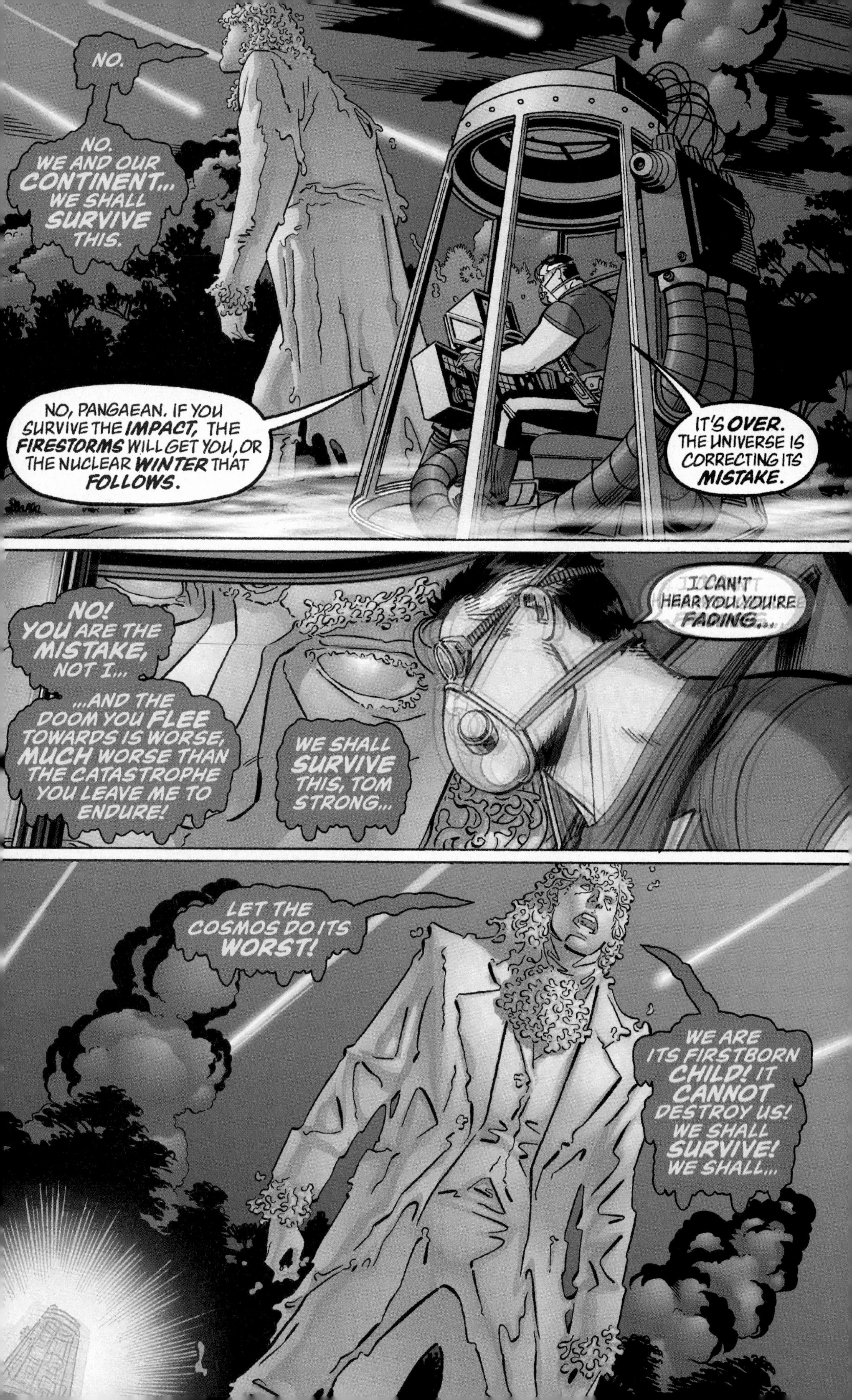
NO.
NO. WE AND OUR CONTINENT... WE SHALL SURVIVE THIS.
NO, PANGAEAN. IF YOU SURVIVE THE IMPACT, THE FIRESTORMS WILL GET YOU, OR THE NUCLEAR WINTER THAT FOLLOWS.
IT'S OVER. THE UNIVERSE IS CORRECTING ITS MISTAKE.
NO! YOU ARE THE MISTAKE, NOT I...
...AND THE DOOM YOU FLEE TOWARDS IS WORSE, MUCH WORSE THAN THE CATASTROPHE YOU LEAVE ME TO ENDURE!
I CAN'T HEAR YOU. YOU'RE FADING...
WE SHALL SURVIVE THIS, TOM STRONG...
LET THE COSMOS DO ITS WORST!
WE ARE ITS FIRSTBORN CHILD! IT CANNOT DESTROY US! WE SHALL SURVIVE! WE SHALL...

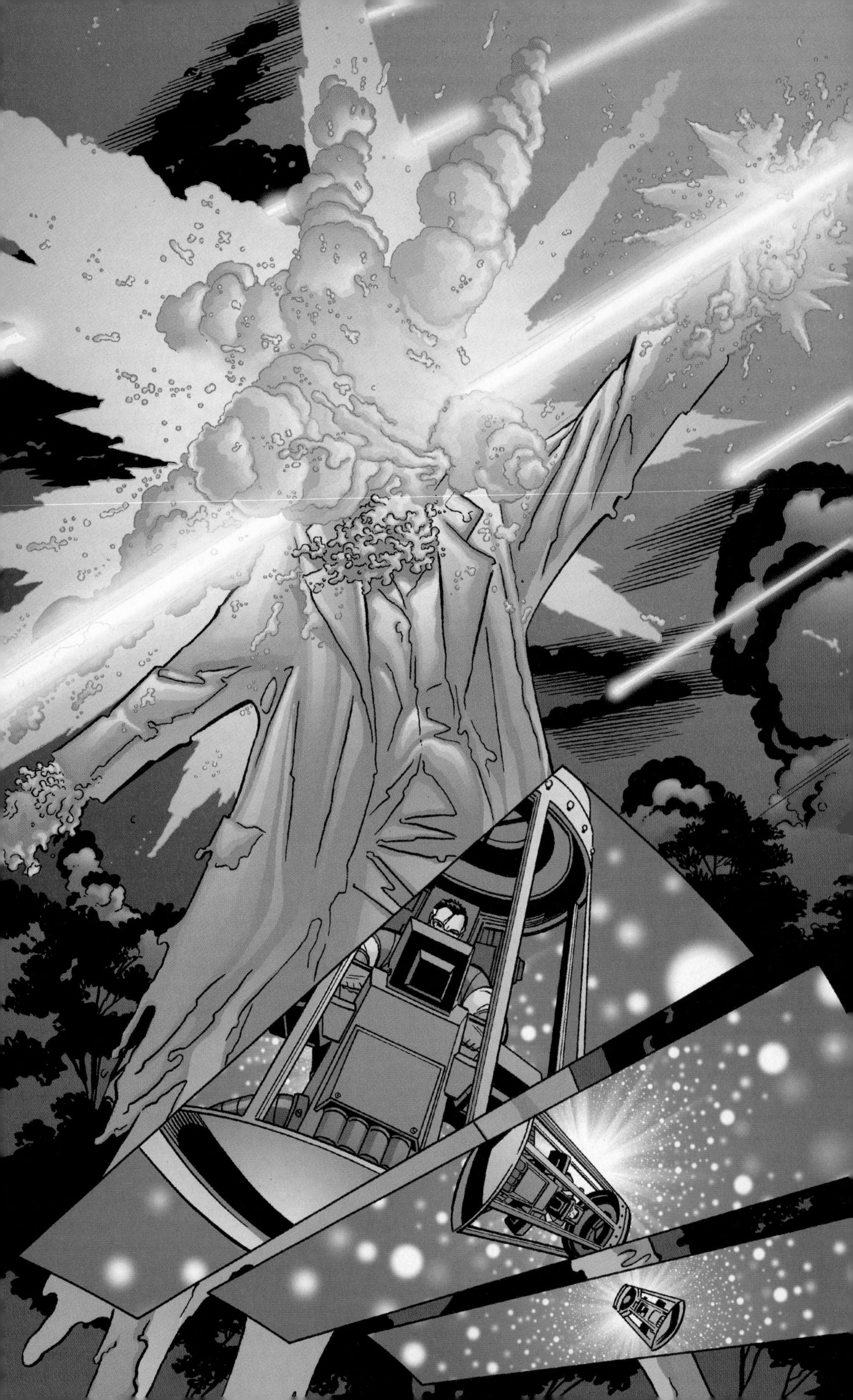

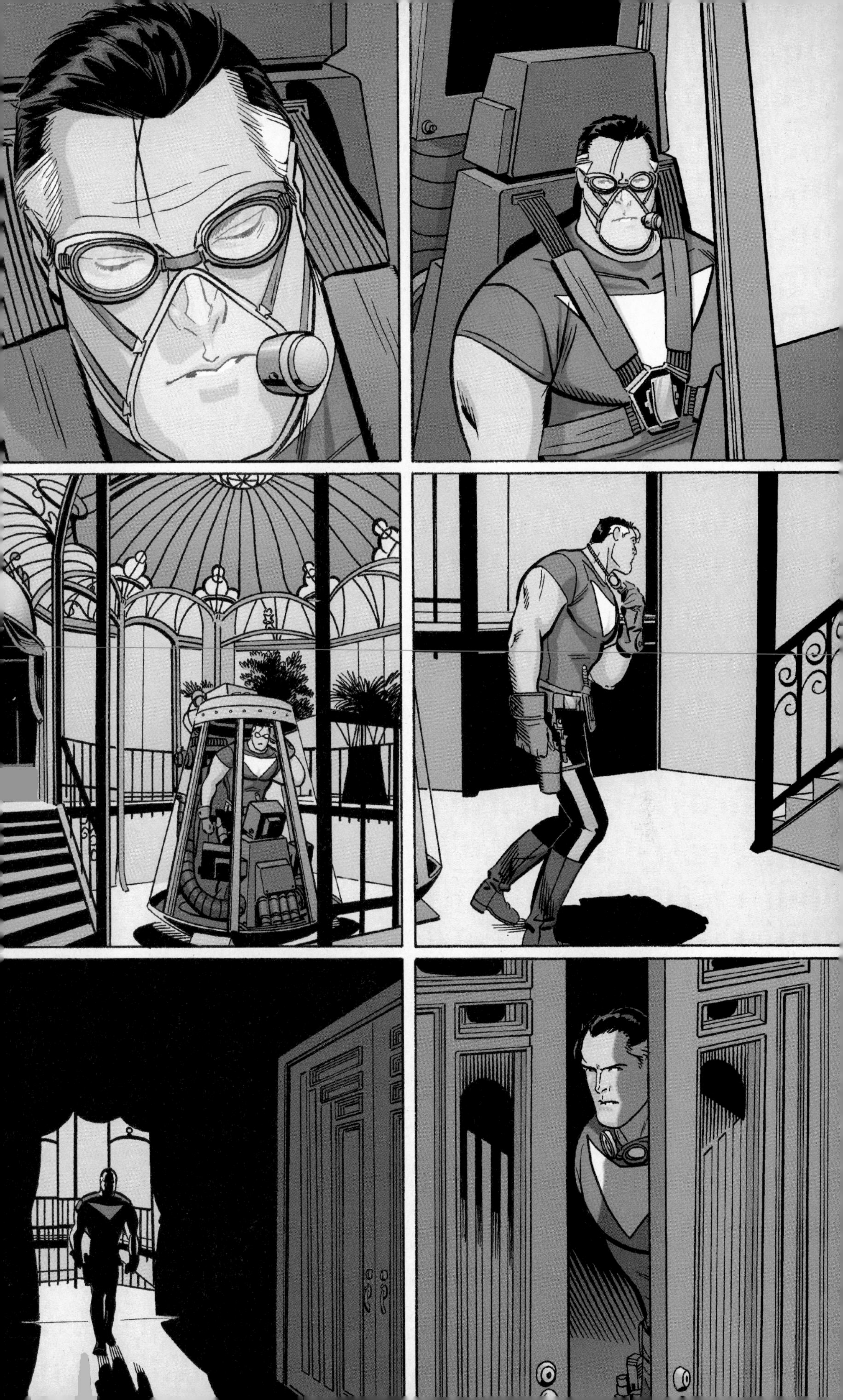

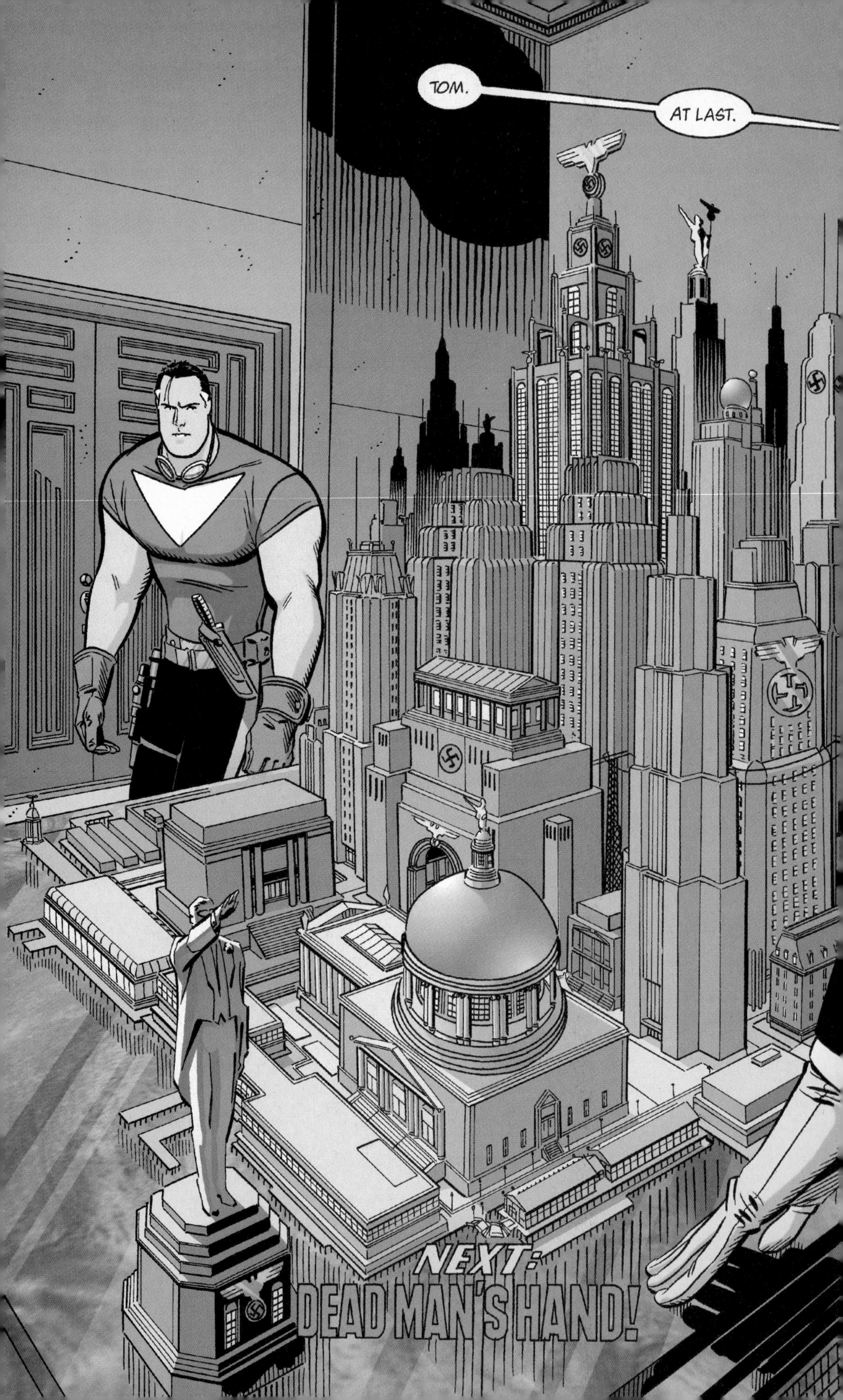
TOM.
AT LAST.
NEXT:
DEAD MAN'S HAND!

CHAPTER SIX

In which a Firm Hand is revealed,
a Fiery Trap is revisited, and
TOM learns a Family Secret.

Cover art:
Dave Gibbons

Alan Moore Chris Sprouse
Dave Gibbons Al Gorde
Todd Klein
AMERICA'S BEST COMICS
6
Tom Strong
MONTHLY
DEAD MAN'S HAND

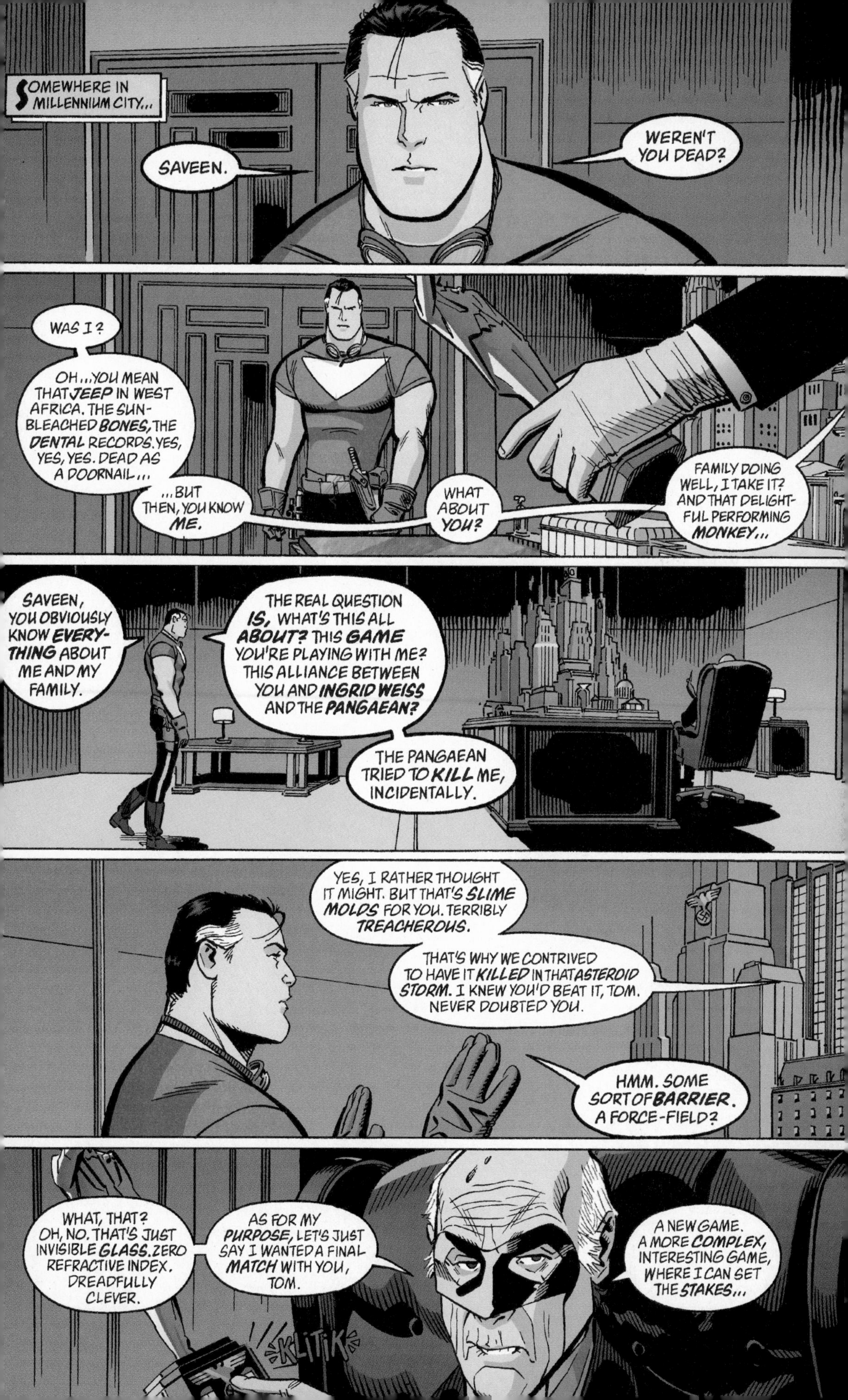
SOMEWHERE IN MILLENNIUM CITY...
SAVEEN.
WEREN'T YOU DEAD?
WAS I?
OH...YOU MEAN THAT JEEP IN WEST AFRICA. THE SUN-BLEACHED BONES, THE DENTAL RECORDS. YES, YES, YES. DEAD AS A DOORNAIL...
...BUT THEN, YOU KNOW ME.
WHAT ABOUT YOU?
FAMILY DOING WELL, I TAKE IT? AND THAT DELIGHTFUL PERFORMING MONKEY...
SAVEEN, YOU OBVIOUSLY KNOW EVERYTHING ABOUT ME AND MY FAMILY.
THE REAL QUESTION IS, WHAT'S THIS ALL ABOUT? THIS GAME YOU'RE PLAYING WITH ME? THIS ALLIANCE BETWEEN YOU AND INGRID WEISS AND THE PANGAEAN?
THE PANGAEAN TRIED TO KILL ME, INCIDENTALLY.
YES, I RATHER THOUGHT IT MIGHT. BUT THAT'S SLIME MOLDS FOR YOU. TERRIBLY TREACHEROUS.
THAT'S WHY WE CONTRIVED TO HAVE IT KILLED IN THAT ASTEROID STORM. I KNEW YOU'D BEAT IT, TOM. NEVER DOUBTED YOU.
HMM. SOME SORT OF BARRIER. A FORCE-FIELD?
WHAT, THAT? OH, NO. THAT'S JUST INVISIBLE GLASS. ZERO REFRACTIVE INDEX. DREADFULLY CLEVER.
AS FOR MY PURPOSE, LET'S JUST SAY I WANTED A FINAL MATCH WITH YOU, TOM.
A NEW GAME. A MORE COMPLEX, INTERESTING GAME, WHERE I CAN SET THE STAKES...
KLITIK

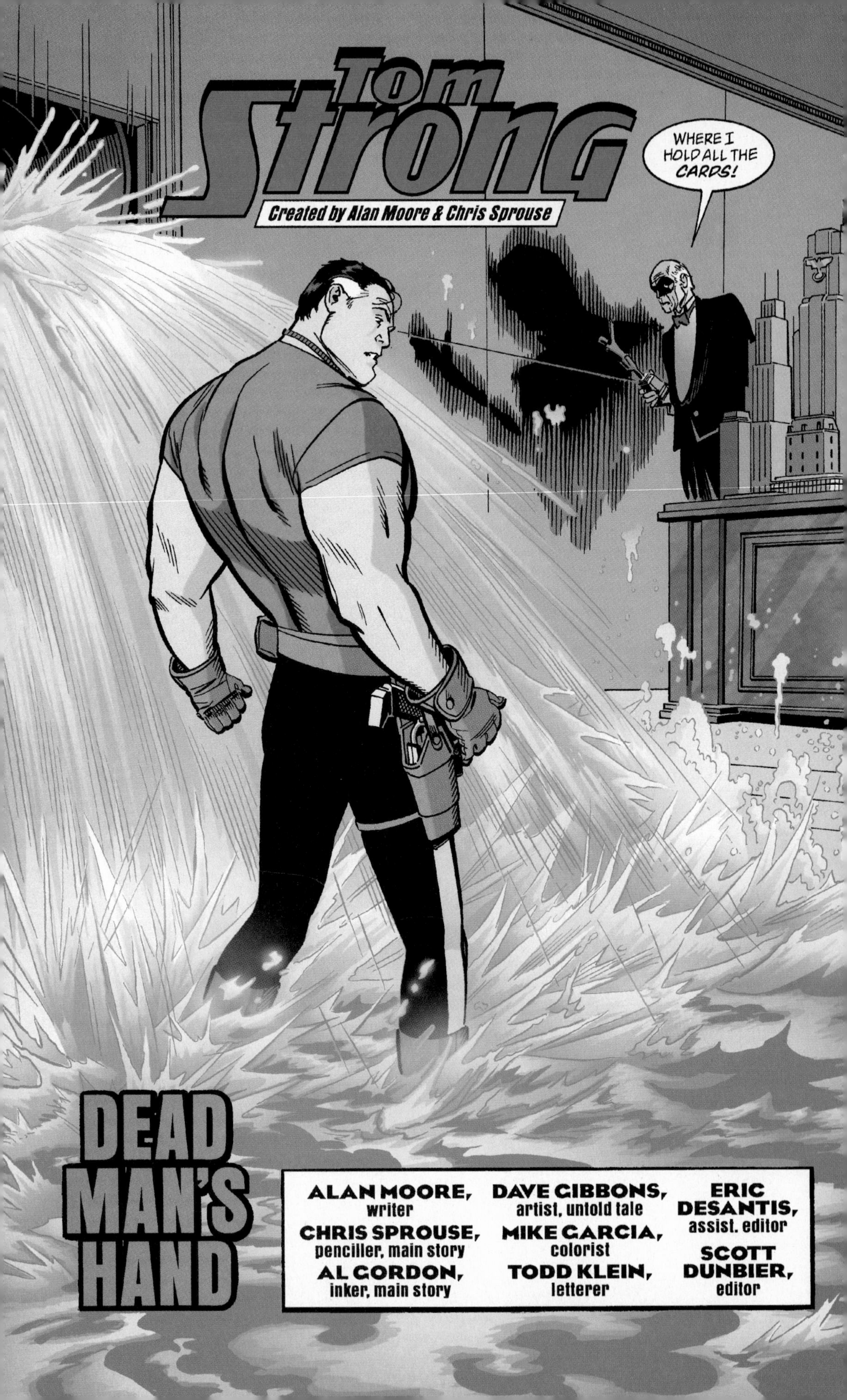
Tom Strong
Created by Alan Moore & Chris Sprouse
WHERE I HOLD ALL THE CARDS!
DEAD MAN'S HAND
ALAN MOORE, writer
CHRIS SPROUSE, penciller, main story
AL GORDON, inker, main story
DAVE GIBBONS, artist, untold tale
MIKE GARCIA, colorist
TODD KLEIN, letterer
ERIC DESANTIS, assist. editor
SCOTT DUNBIER, editor

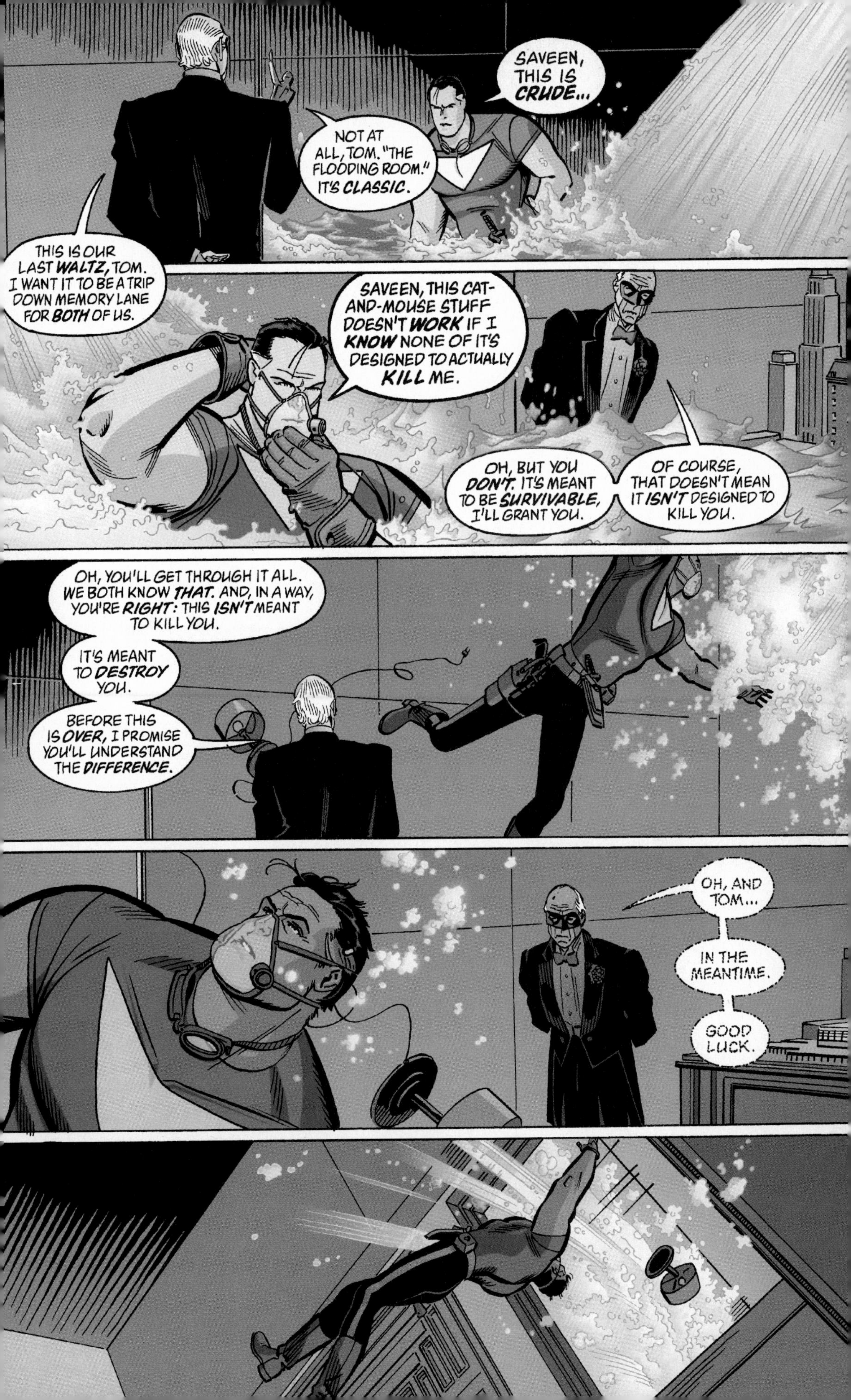
SAVEEN, THIS IS CRUDE...
NOT AT ALL, TOM. "THE FLOODING ROOM." IT'S CLASSIC.
THIS IS OUR LAST WALTZ, TOM. I WANT IT TO BE A TRIP DOWN MEMORY LANE FOR BOTH OF US.
SAVEEN, THIS CAT-AND-MOUSE STUFF DOESN'T WORK IF I KNOW NONE OF IT'S DESIGNED TO ACTUALLY KILL ME.
OH, BUT YOU DON'T. IT'S MEANT TO BE SURVIVABLE, I'LL GRANT YOU.
OF COURSE, THAT DOESN'T MEAN IT ISN'T DESIGNED TO KILL YOU.
OH, YOU'LL GET THROUGH IT ALL. WE BOTH KNOW THAT. AND, IN A WAY, YOU'RE RIGHT: THIS ISN'T MEANT TO KILL YOU.
IT'S MEANT TO DESTROY YOU.
BEFORE THIS IS OVER, I PROMISE YOU'LL UNDERSTAND THE DIFFERENCE.
OH, AND TOM...
IN THE MEANTIME.
GOOD LUCK.

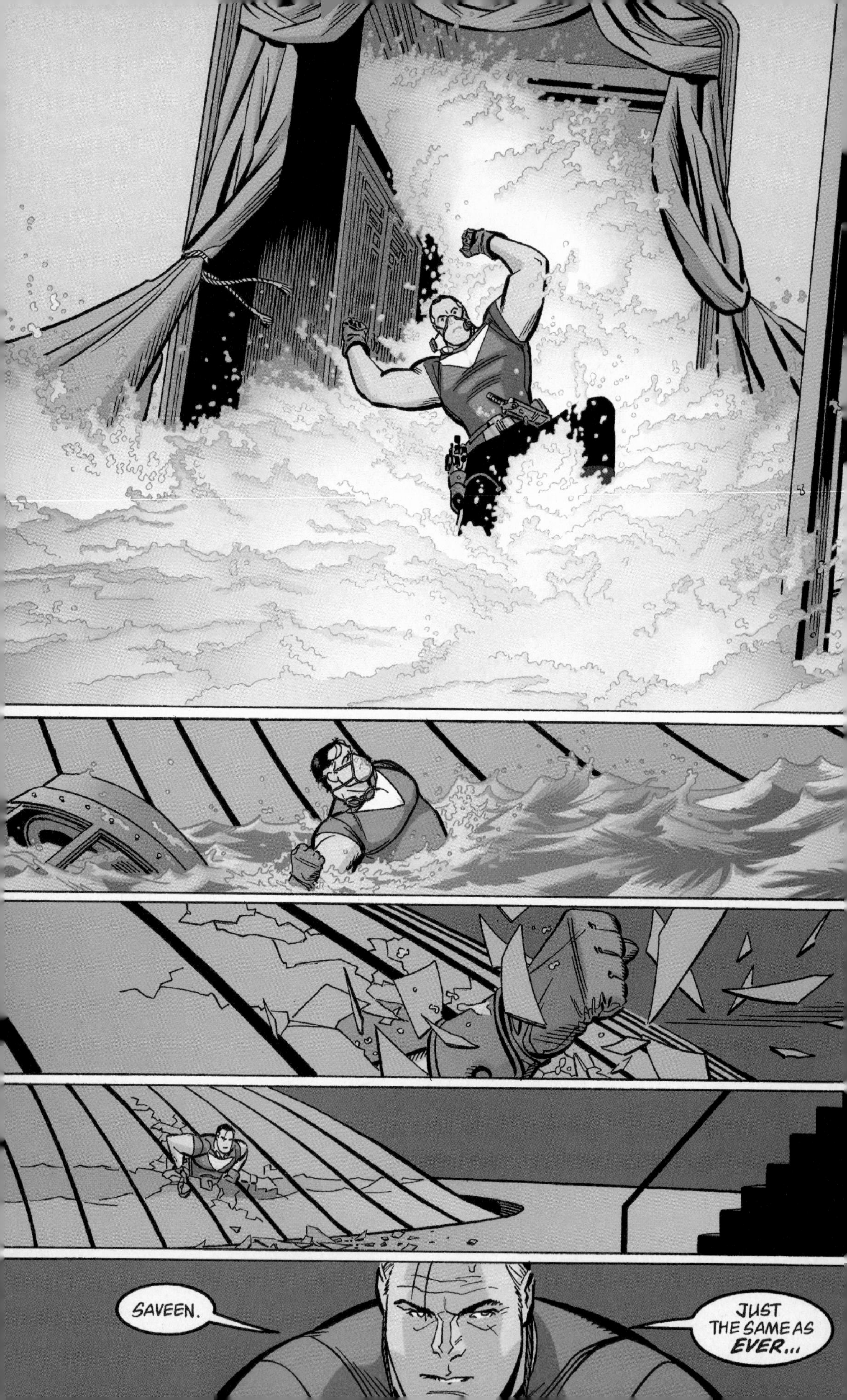
SAVEEN.
JUST THE SAME AS EVER...

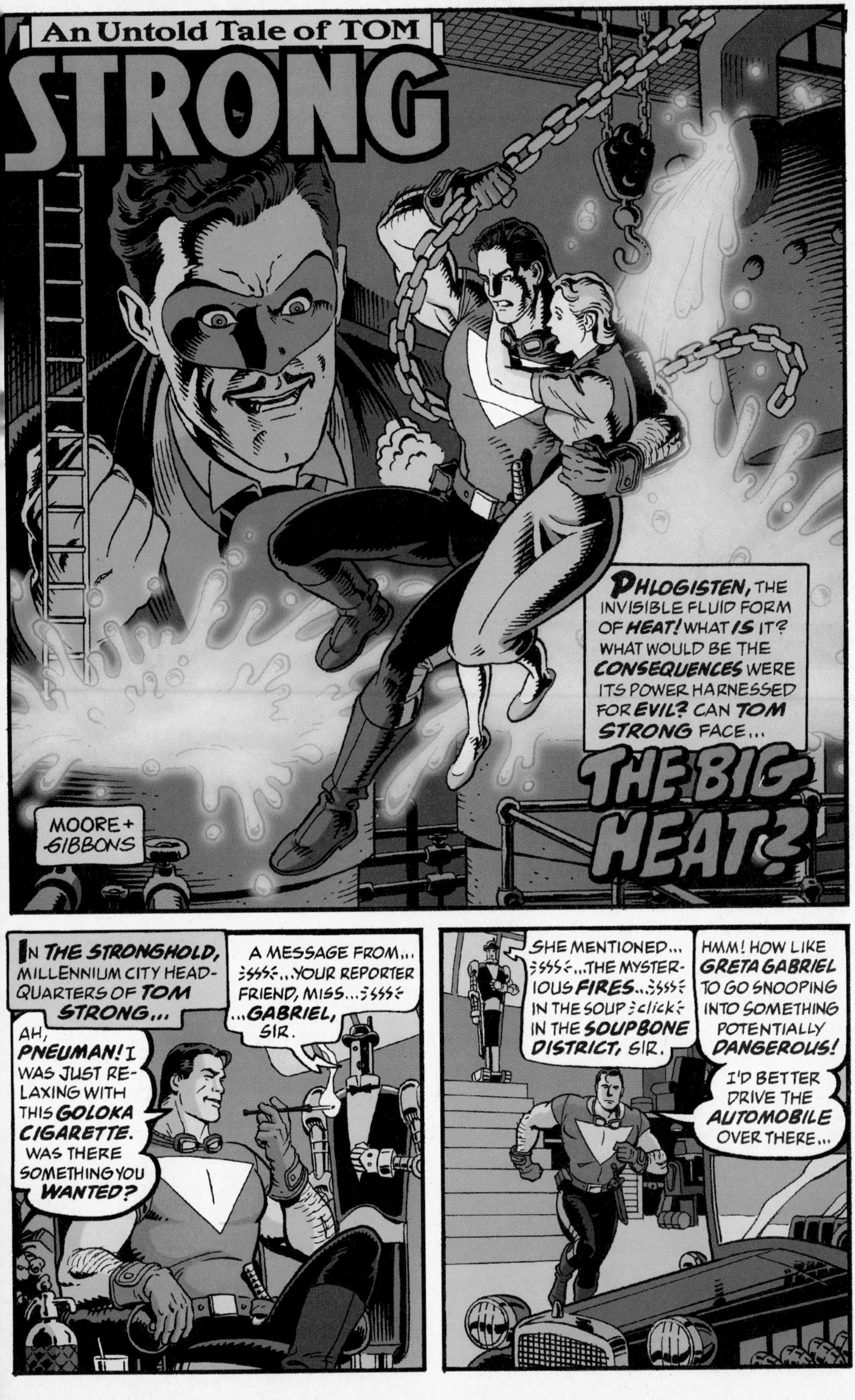
An Untold Tale of TOM
STRONG
PHLOGISTEN, THE INVISIBLE FLUID FORM OF HEAT! WHAT IS IT? WHAT WOULD BE THE CONSEQUENCES WERE ITS POWER HARNESSED FOR EVIL? CAN TOM STRONG FACE...
THE BIG HEAT?
MOORE + GIBBONS
IN THE STRONGHOLD, MILLENNIUM CITY HEADQUARTERS OF TOM STRONG...
AH, PNEUMAN! I WAS JUST RELAXING WITH THIS GOLOKA CIGARETTE. WAS THERE SOMETHING YOU WANTED?
A MESSAGE FROM... ssss ...YOUR REPORTER FRIEND, MISS... ssss ...GABRIEL, SIR.
SHE MENTIONED... ssss ...THE MYSTERIOUS FIRES... ssss IN THE SOUP click IN THE SOUPBONE DISTRICT, SIR.
HMM! HOW LIKE GRETA GABRIEL TO GO SNOOPING INTO SOMETHING POTENTIALLY DANGEROUS!
I'D BETTER DRIVE THE AUTOMOBILE OVER THERE...

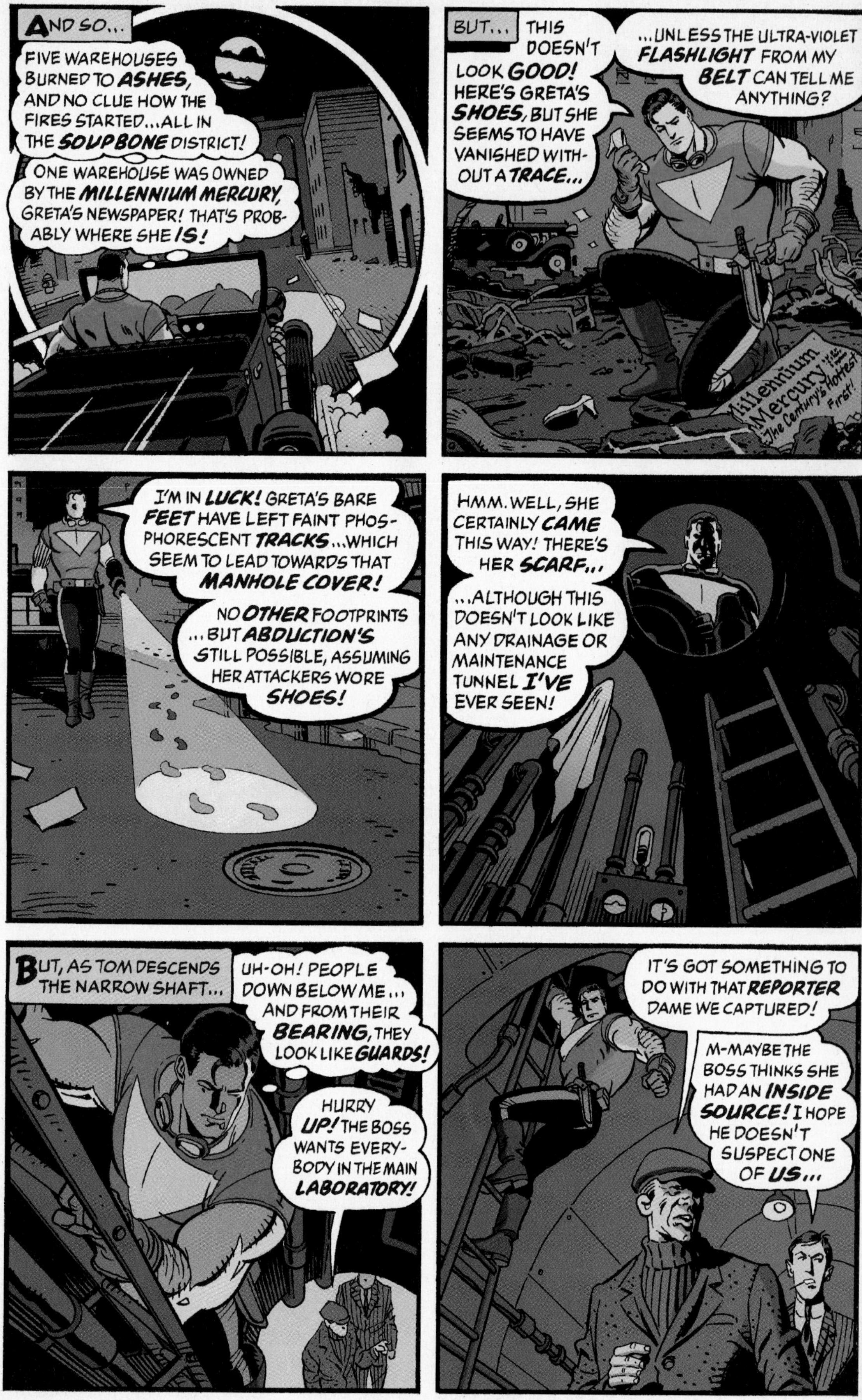
AND SO...
FIVE WAREHOUSES BURNED TO ASHES, AND NO CLUE HOW THE FIRES STARTED...ALL IN THE SOUPBONE DISTRICT!
ONE WAREHOUSE WAS OWNED BY THE MILLENNIUM MERCURY, GRETA'S NEWSPAPER! THAT'S PROBABLY WHERE SHE IS!
BUT...
THIS DOESN'T LOOK GOOD! HERE'S GRETA'S SHOES, BUT SHE SEEMS TO HAVE VANISHED WITHOUT A TRACE...
...UNLESS THE ULTRA-VIOLET FLASHLIGHT FROM MY BELT CAN TELL ME ANYTHING?
Millennium Mercury The Century's Hottest First!
I'M IN LUCK! GRETA'S BARE FEET HAVE LEFT FAINT PHOSPHORESCENT TRACKS...WHICH SEEM TO LEAD TOWARDS THAT MANHOLE COVER!
NO OTHER FOOTPRINTS ...BUT ABDUCTION'S STILL POSSIBLE, ASSUMING HER ATTACKERS WORE SHOES!
HMM. WELL, SHE CERTAINLY CAME THIS WAY! THERE'S HER SCARF...
...ALTHOUGH THIS DOESN'T LOOK LIKE ANY DRAINAGE OR MAINTENANCE TUNNEL I'VE EVER SEEN!
BUT, AS TOM DESCENDS THE NARROW SHAFT...
UH-OH! PEOPLE DOWN BELOW ME... AND FROM THEIR BEARING, THEY LOOK LIKE GUARDS!
HURRY UP! THE BOSS WANTS EVERYBODY IN THE MAIN LABORATORY!
IT'S GOT SOMETHING TO DO WITH THAT REPORTER DAME WE CAPTURED!
M-MAYBE THE BOSS THINKS SHE HAD AN INSIDE SOURCE! I HOPE HE DOESN'T SUSPECT ONE OF US...

OH, I THINK YOU BOYS HAVE MORE **PRESSING** THINGS TO WORRY ABOUT...

...LIKE **ME**, FOR INSTANCE!

IT'S **HIM**! IT'S THAT **"JUNGLE GENIUS"** GUY THAT'S BEEN IN ALL THE **PAPERS**!

UUGHHH!

THE NAME'S **TOM STRONG**...

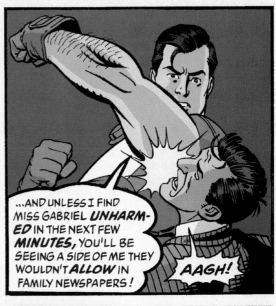

...AND UNLESS I FIND MISS GABRIEL **UNHARMED** IN THE NEXT FEW **MINUTES**, YOU'LL BE SEEING A SIDE OF ME THEY WOULDN'T **ALLOW** IN FAMILY NEWSPAPERS!

AAGH!

OH, I HOPE THAT WON'T BE **NECESSARY**, MR. STRONG. YOU SEE, I'VE BEEN **SO** LOOKING FORWARD TO MEETING YOU.

HUH? WHO THE DEVIL ARE **YOU**?

WHO THE DEVIL **INDEED**? MY NAME IS PAUL DORIAN **SAVEEN**...

...AND BESIDE **ME**, THE DEVIL IS A SUNDAY-AFTERNOON **AMATEUR**.

T-TOM, I'M **SORRY**! I'VE LED YOU INTO TERRIBLE **DANGER**!

SILENCE, WOMAN! THERE'LL BE TIME FOR APOLOGIES **LATER**. I WANT TO SHOW MR. STRONG MY **WORK**.

I'M SURE AS A FELLOW **SCIENTIST**, HE'LL BE IM-**PRESSED**.

MY FATHER CREATED MECHANICAL **INTELLIGENCE**, MR. SAVEEN. **FEW** THINGS IMPRESS ME.

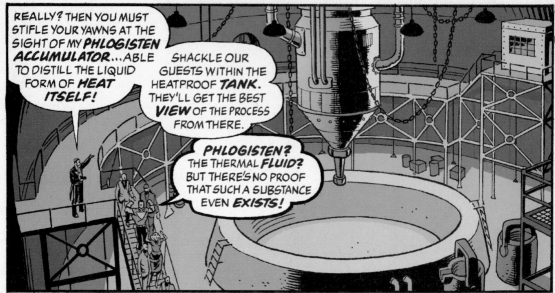

REALLY? THEN YOU MUST STIFLE YOUR YAWNS AT THE SIGHT OF MY *PHLOGISTEN ACCUMULATOR*...ABLE TO DISTILL THE LIQUID FORM OF *HEAT ITSELF!*

SHACKLE OUR GUESTS WITHIN THE HEATPROOF *TANK*. THEY'LL GET THE BEST *VIEW* OF THE PROCESS FROM THERE.

PHLOGISTEN? THE THERMAL *FLUID?* BUT THERE'S NO PROOF THAT SUCH A SUBSTANCE EVEN *EXISTS!*

AH. THEN YOU HAVE NOTHING TO FEAR, AND NOTHING SHALL POUR FROM THAT SPIGOT ABOVE YOU SAVE PURE *SCIENTIFIC CONJECTURE.*

FAREWELL, MR. STRONG. IT'S BEEN *BRIEF,* BUT MOST *INTERESTING.*

SAVEEN, *WAIT!* WHAT ABOUT THOSE *WAREHOUSE FIRES?*

A SINGLE DROPLET OF PHLOGISTEN *EACH*...MERE *TEST RUNS,* OBVIOUSLY. I'LL SOON HAVE ENOUGH TO BURN MILLENNIUM CITY OFF THE *MAP!*

NOW, COME, MEN... TO THE *CONTROL CHAMBER!*

TOM, I'M S-SCARED. PAUL SAVEEN'S AN INFAMOUS *SCIENCE-RENEGADE* FROM NEW YORK. THAT *PHLOGISTEN'S* PROBABLY AS DANGEROUS AS HE *SAYS* IT IS!

WELL, THAT WOULD EXPLAIN WHY HE MADE THIS TANK *HEATPROOF*...

...ALTHOUGH IT REMAINS TO BE SEEN WHETHER HE THOUGHT TO MAKE IT *STRONG-PROOF!*

OH, TOM! BE *CAREFUL!*

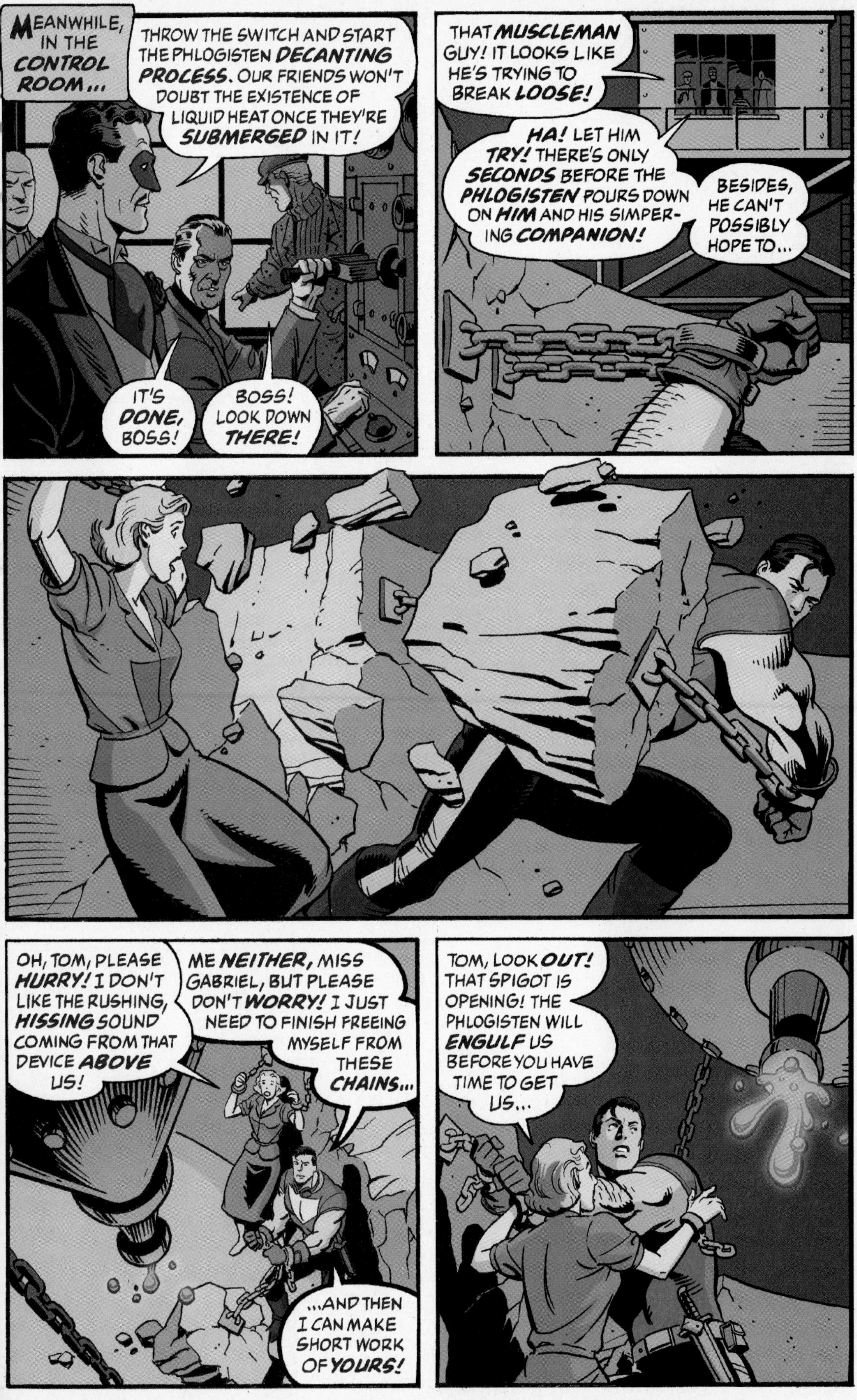
MEANWHILE, IN THE CONTROL ROOM...
THROW THE SWITCH AND START THE PHLOGISTEN DECANTING PROCESS. OUR FRIENDS WON'T DOUBT THE EXISTENCE OF LIQUID HEAT ONCE THEY'RE SUBMERGED IN IT!
IT'S DONE, BOSS!
BOSS! LOOK DOWN THERE!
THAT MUSCLEMAN GUY! IT LOOKS LIKE HE'S TRYING TO BREAK LOOSE!
HA! LET HIM TRY! THERE'S ONLY SECONDS BEFORE THE PHLOGISTEN POURS DOWN ON HIM AND HIS SIMPERING COMPANION!
BESIDES, HE CAN'T POSSIBLY HOPE TO...
OH, TOM, PLEASE HURRY! I DON'T LIKE THE RUSHING, HISSING SOUND COMING FROM THAT DEVICE ABOVE US!
ME NEITHER, MISS GABRIEL, BUT PLEASE DON'T WORRY! I JUST NEED TO FINISH FREEING MYSELF FROM THESE CHAINS...
...AND THEN I CAN MAKE SHORT WORK OF YOURS!
TOM, LOOK OUT! THAT SPIGOT IS OPENING! THE PHLOGISTEN WILL ENGULF US BEFORE YOU HAVE TIME TO GET US...

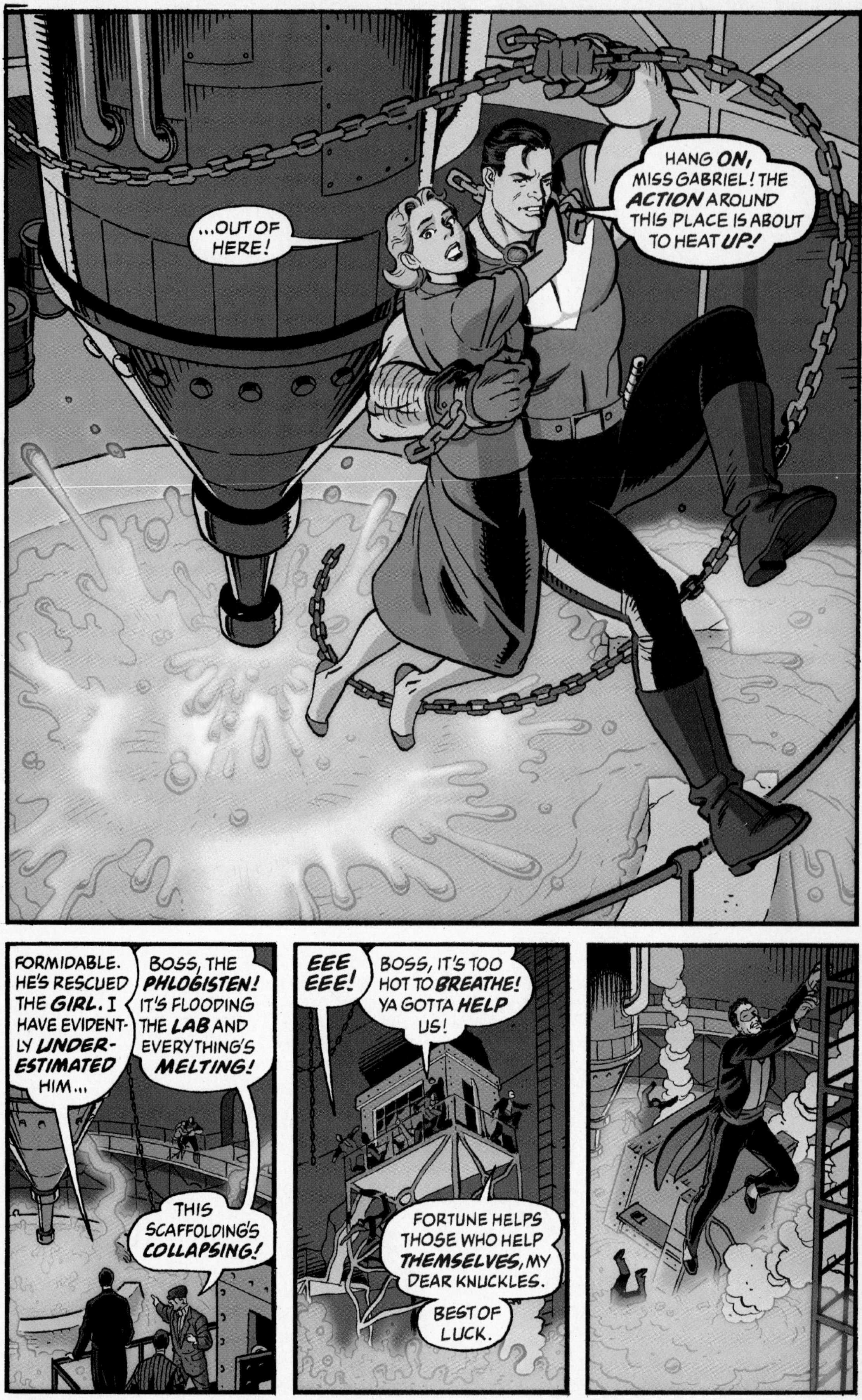
...OUT OF HERE!
HANG ON, MISS GABRIEL! THE ACTION AROUND THIS PLACE IS ABOUT TO HEAT UP!
FORMIDABLE. HE'S RESCUED THE GIRL. I HAVE EVIDENTLY UNDERESTIMATED HIM...
BOSS, THE PHLOGISTEN! IT'S FLOODING THE LAB AND EVERYTHING'S MELTING!
THIS SCAFFOLDING'S COLLAPSING!
EEE EEE!
BOSS, IT'S TOO HOT TO BREATHE! YA GOTTA HELP US!
FORTUNE HELPS THOSE WHO HELP THEMSELVES, MY DEAR KNUCKLES.
BEST OF LUCK.

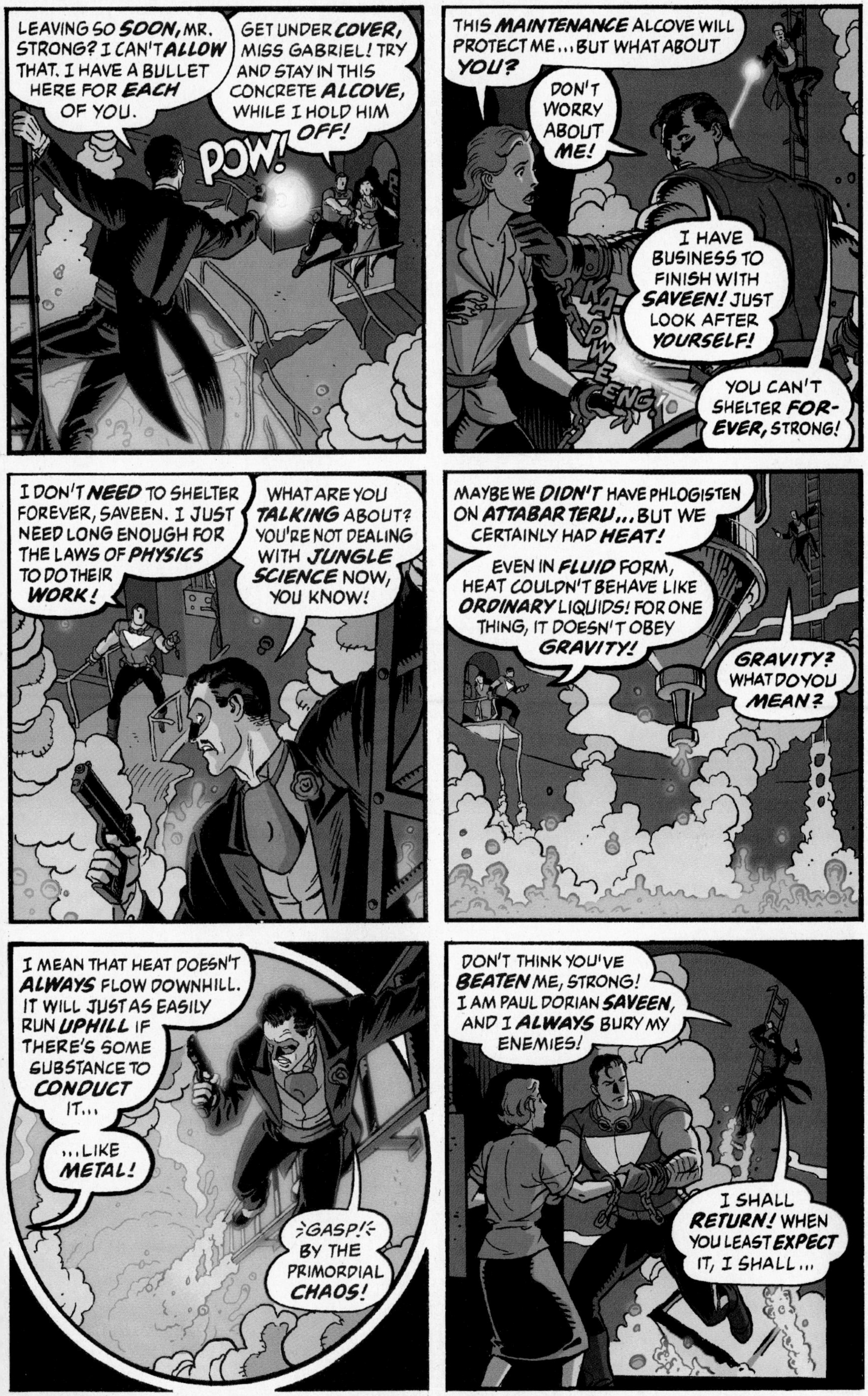
LEAVING SO SOON, MR. STRONG? I CAN'T ALLOW THAT. I HAVE A BULLET HERE FOR EACH OF YOU.
GET UNDER COVER, MISS GABRIEL! TRY AND STAY IN THIS CONCRETE ALCOVE, WHILE I HOLD HIM OFF!
POW!
THIS MAINTENANCE ALCOVE WILL PROTECT ME... BUT WHAT ABOUT YOU?
DON'T WORRY ABOUT ME!
I HAVE BUSINESS TO FINISH WITH SAVEEN! JUST LOOK AFTER YOURSELF!
KA-PWEEENG!
YOU CAN'T SHELTER FOR-EVER, STRONG!
I DON'T NEED TO SHELTER FOREVER, SAVEEN. I JUST NEED LONG ENOUGH FOR THE LAWS OF PHYSICS TO DO THEIR WORK!
WHAT ARE YOU TALKING ABOUT? YOU'RE NOT DEALING WITH JUNGLE SCIENCE NOW, YOU KNOW!
MAYBE WE DIDN'T HAVE PHLOGISTEN ON ATTABAR TERU... BUT WE CERTAINLY HAD HEAT!
EVEN IN FLUID FORM, HEAT COULDN'T BEHAVE LIKE ORDINARY LIQUIDS! FOR ONE THING, IT DOESN'T OBEY GRAVITY!
GRAVITY? WHAT DO YOU MEAN?
I MEAN THAT HEAT DOESN'T ALWAYS FLOW DOWNHILL. IT WILL JUST AS EASILY RUN UPHILL IF THERE'S SOME SUBSTANCE TO CONDUCT IT...
...LIKE METAL!
GASP! BY THE PRIMORDIAL CHAOS!
DON'T THINK YOU'VE BEATEN ME, STRONG! I AM PAUL DORIAN SAVEEN, AND I ALWAYS BURY MY ENEMIES!
I SHALL RETURN! WHEN YOU LEAST EXPECT IT, I SHALL...

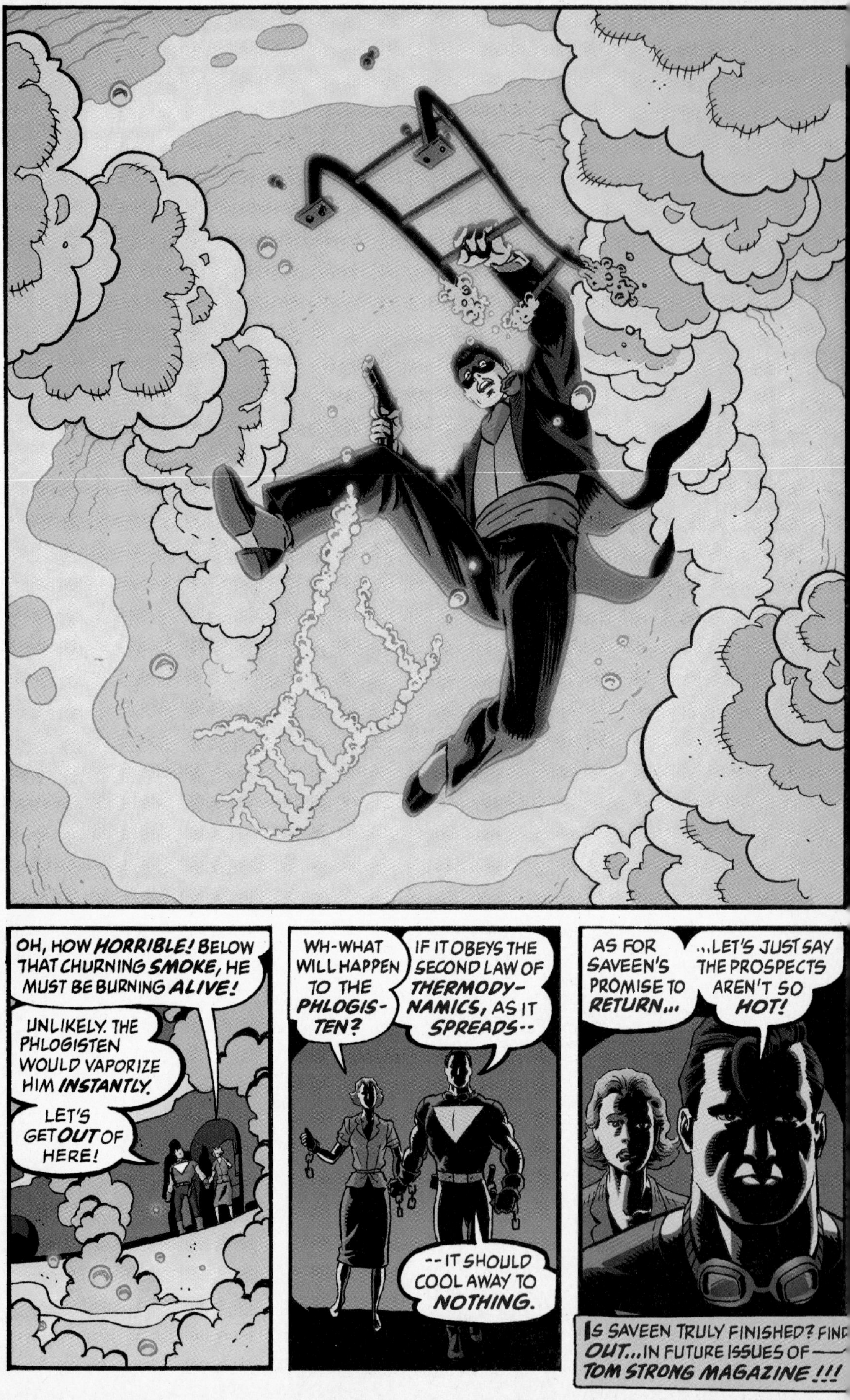

OH, HOW HORRIBLE! BELOW THAT CHURNING SMOKE, HE MUST BE BURNING ALIVE!
UNLIKELY. THE PHLOGISTEN WOULD VAPORIZE HIM INSTANTLY.
LET'S GET OUT OF HERE!
WH-WHAT WILL HAPPEN TO THE PHLOGIS-TEN?
IF IT OBEYS THE SECOND LAW OF THERMODY-NAMICS, AS IT SPREADS--
--IT SHOULD COOL AWAY TO NOTHING.
AS FOR SAVEEN'S PROMISE TO RETURN...
...LET'S JUST SAY THE PROSPECTS AREN'T SO HOT!
IS SAVEEN TRULY FINISHED? FIND OUT... IN FUTURE ISSUES OF — TOM STRONG MAGAZINE!!!

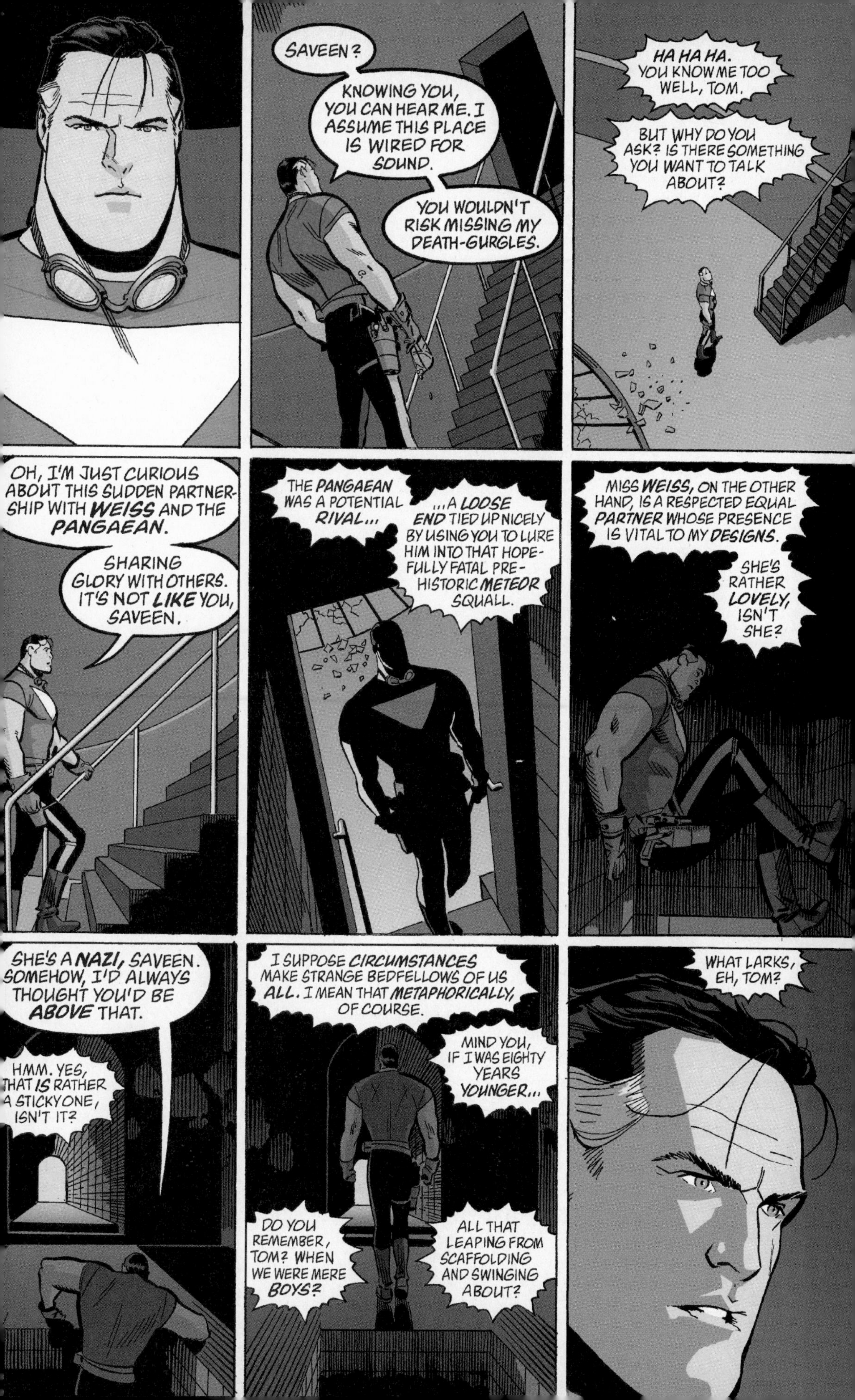
SAVEEN?
KNOWING YOU, YOU CAN HEAR ME. I ASSUME THIS PLACE IS WIRED FOR SOUND.
YOU WOULDN'T RISK MISSING MY DEATH-GURGLES.
HA HA HA. YOU KNOW ME TOO WELL, TOM.
BUT WHY DO YOU ASK? IS THERE SOMETHING YOU WANT TO TALK ABOUT?
OH, I'M JUST CURIOUS ABOUT THIS SUDDEN PARTNERSHIP WITH WEISS AND THE PANGAEAN.
SHARING GLORY WITH OTHERS. IT'S NOT LIKE YOU, SAVEEN.
THE PANGAEAN WAS A POTENTIAL RIVAL...
...A LOOSE END TIED UP NICELY BY USING YOU TO LURE HIM INTO THAT HOPEFULLY FATAL PREHISTORIC METEOR SQUALL.
MISS WEISS, ON THE OTHER HAND, IS A RESPECTED EQUAL PARTNER WHOSE PRESENCE IS VITAL TO MY DESIGNS.
SHE'S RATHER LOVELY, ISN'T SHE?
SHE'S A NAZI, SAVEEN. SOMEHOW, I'D ALWAYS THOUGHT YOU'D BE ABOVE THAT.
HMM. YES, THAT IS RATHER A STICKY ONE, ISN'T IT?
I SUPPOSE CIRCUMSTANCES MAKE STRANGE BEDFELLOWS OF US ALL. I MEAN THAT METAPHORICALLY, OF COURSE.
MIND YOU, IF I WAS EIGHTY YEARS YOUNGER...
DO YOU REMEMBER, TOM? WHEN WE WERE MERE BOYS?
ALL THAT LEAPING FROM SCAFFOLDING AND SWINGING ABOUT?
WHAT LARKS, EH, TOM?

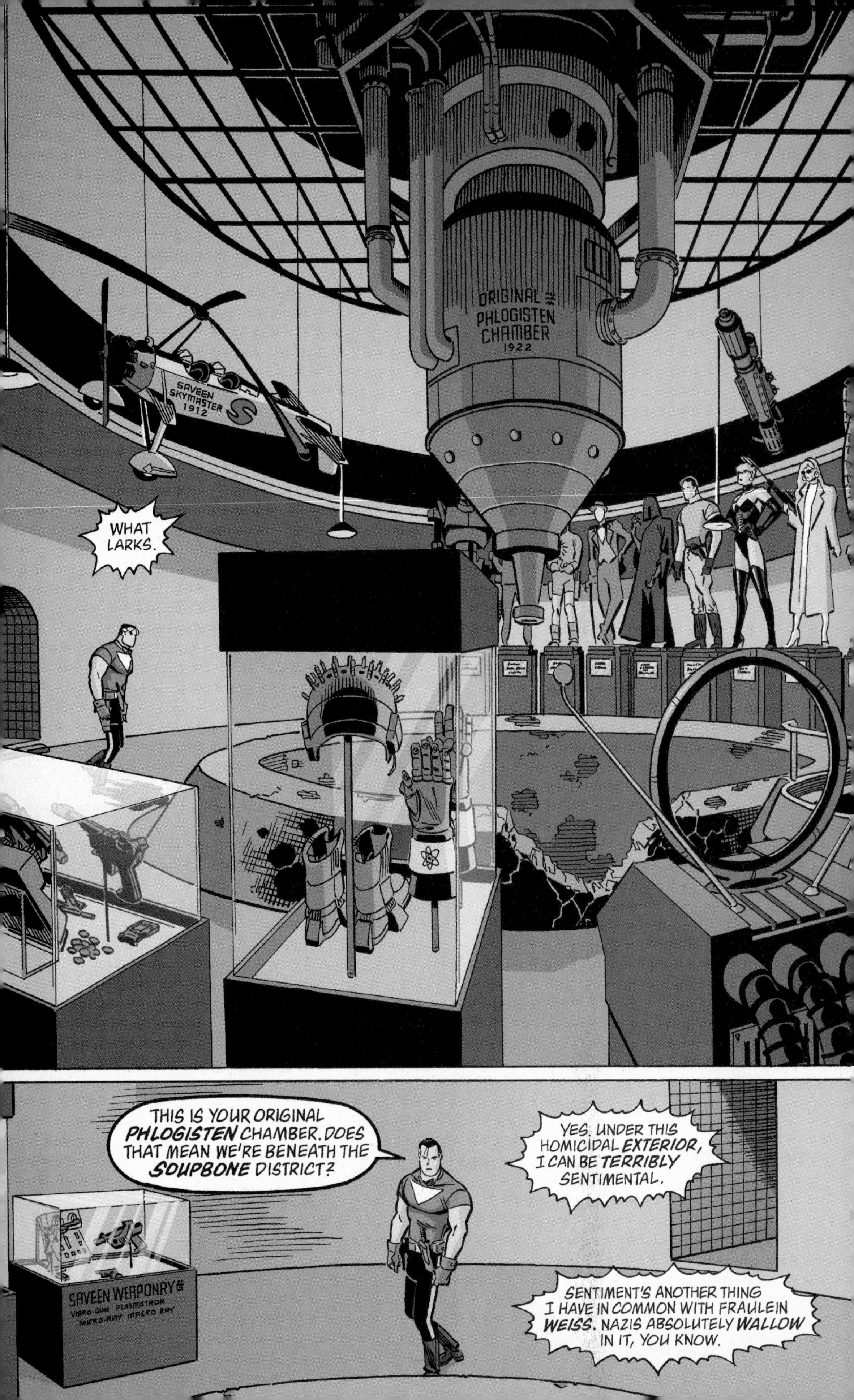

ORIGINAL PHLOGISTEN CHAMBER 1922
SAVEEN SKYMASTER 1912
WHAT LARKS.
THIS IS YOUR ORIGINAL PHLOGISTEN CHAMBER. DOES THAT MEAN WE'RE BENEATH THE SOUPBONE DISTRICT?
YES. UNDER THIS HOMICIDAL EXTERIOR, I CAN BE TERRIBLY SENTIMENTAL.
SENTIMENT'S ANOTHER THING I HAVE IN COMMON WITH FRAULEIN WEISS. NAZIS ABSOLUTELY WALLOW IN IT, YOU KNOW.
SAVEEN WEAPONRY
VIBRO-GUN PLASMATRON
MICRO-RAY MACRO RAY

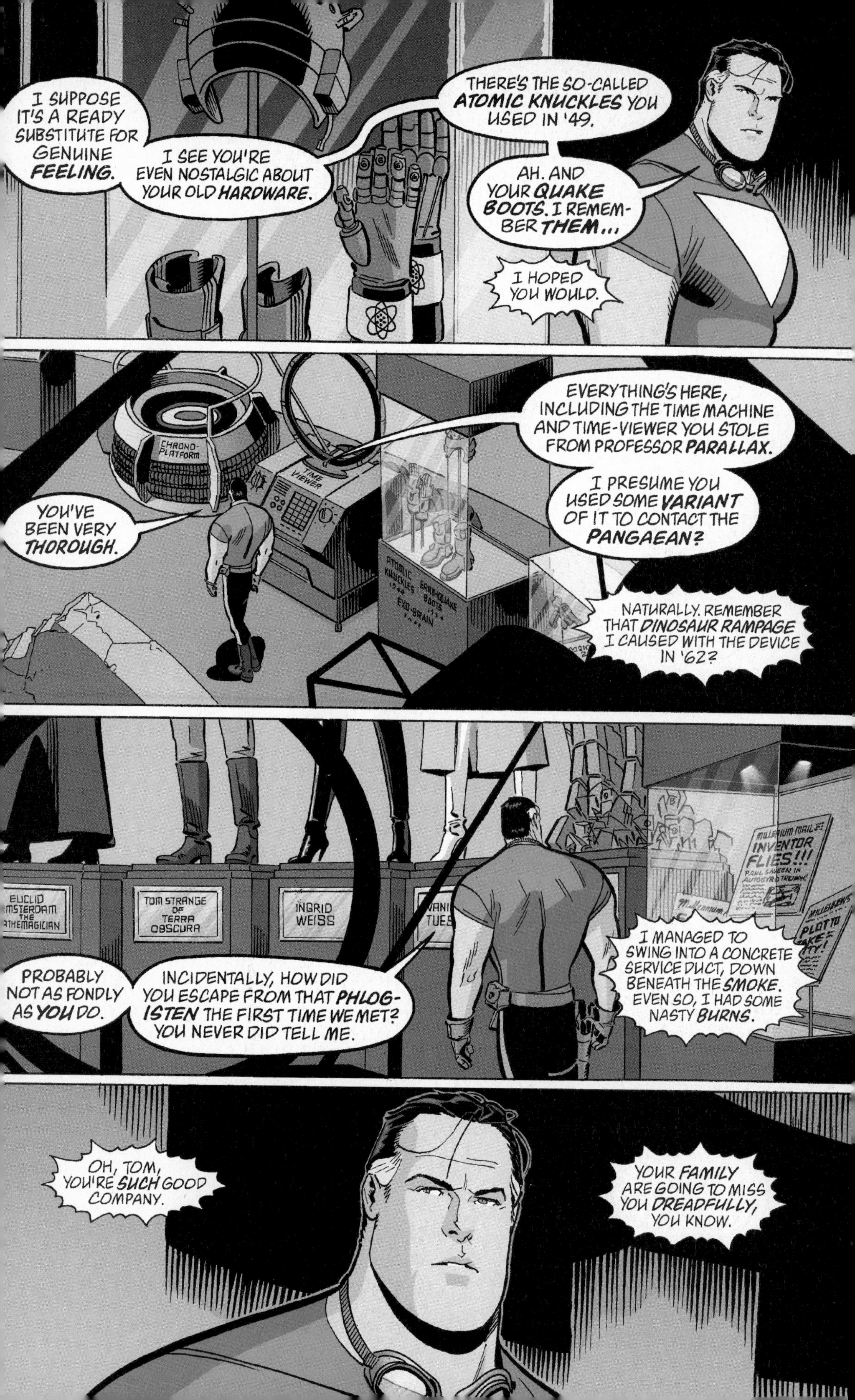
I SEE YOU'RE EVEN NOSTALGIC ABOUT YOUR OLD **HARDWARE**.
I SUPPOSE IT'S A READY SUBSTITUTE FOR GENUINE **FEELING**.
THERE'S THE SO-CALLED **ATOMIC KNUCKLES** YOU USED IN '49.
AH. AND YOUR **QUAKE BOOTS**. I REMEMBER **THEM**...
I HOPED YOU WOULD.
CHRONO-PLATFORM
TIME VIEWER
EVERYTHING'S HERE, INCLUDING THE TIME MACHINE AND TIME-VIEWER YOU STOLE FROM PROFESSOR **PARALLAX**.
YOU'VE BEEN VERY **THOROUGH**.
I PRESUME YOU USED SOME **VARIANT** OF IT TO CONTACT THE **PANGAEAN**?
ATOMIC KNUCKLES 1949
EARTHQUAKE BOOTS
EXO-BRAIN
NATURALLY. REMEMBER THAT **DINOSAUR RAMPAGE** I CAUSED WITH THE DEVICE IN '62?
TOM STRANGE OF TERRA OBSCURA
INGRID WEISS
INVENTOR FLIES!!!
INCIDENTALLY, HOW DID YOU ESCAPE FROM THAT **PHLOGISTEN** THE FIRST TIME WE MET? YOU NEVER DID TELL ME.
PROBABLY NOT AS FONDLY AS **YOU** DO.
I MANAGED TO SWING INTO A CONCRETE SERVICE DUCT, DOWN BENEATH THE **SMOKE**. EVEN SO, I HAD SOME NASTY **BURNS**.
OH, TOM, YOU'RE **SUCH** GOOD COMPANY.
YOUR **FAMILY** ARE GOING TO MISS YOU **DREADFULLY**, YOU KNOW.

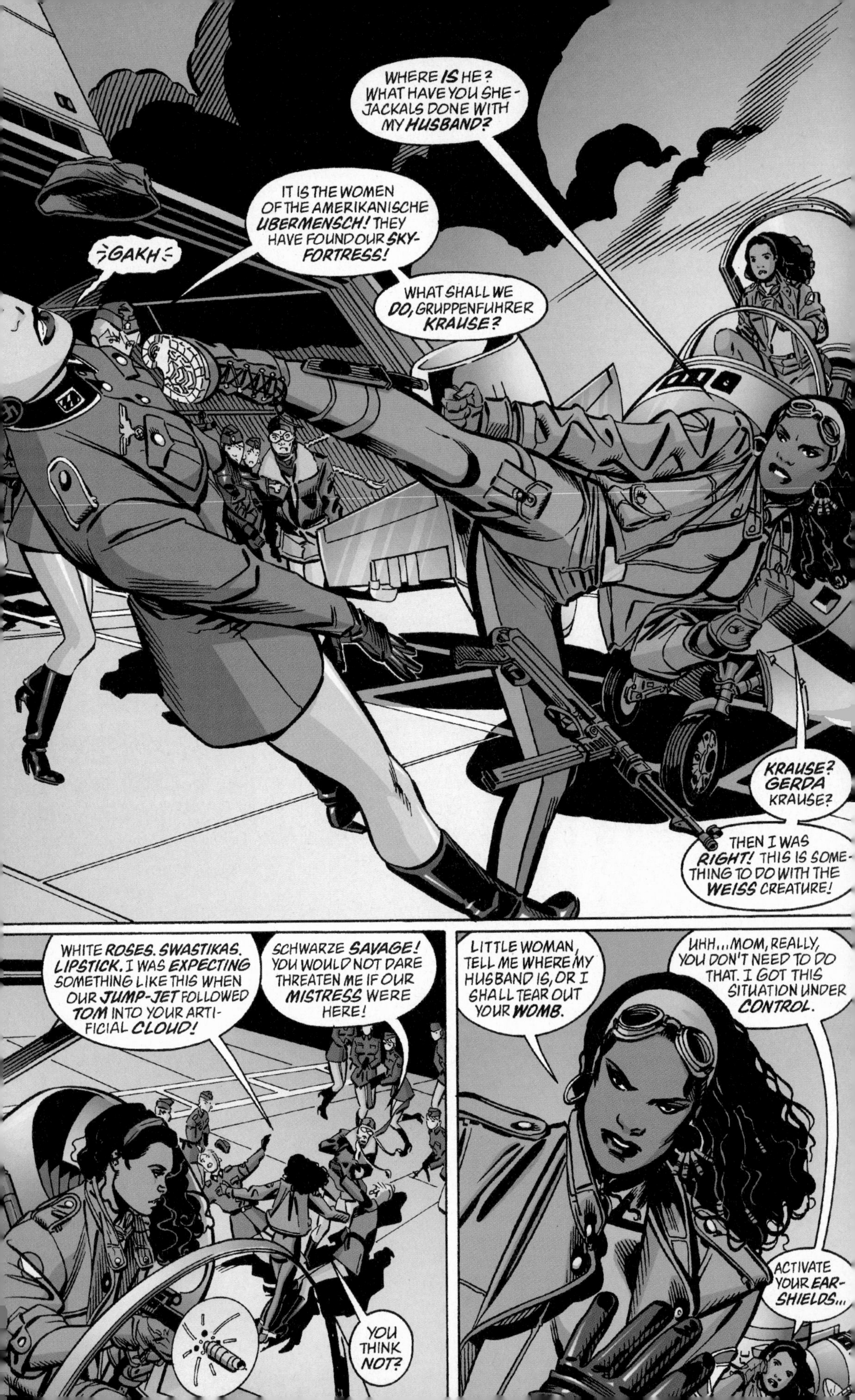
WHERE IS HE? WHAT HAVE YOU SHE-JACKALS DONE WITH MY HUSBAND?
IT IS THE WOMEN OF THE AMERIKANISCHE UBERMENSCH! THEY HAVE FOUND OUR SKY-FORTRESS!
GAKH
WHAT SHALL WE DO, GRUPPENFUHRER KRAUSE?
KRAUSE? GERDA KRAUSE?
THEN I WAS RIGHT! THIS IS SOMETHING TO DO WITH THE WEISS CREATURE!
WHITE ROSES. SWASTIKAS. LIPSTICK. I WAS EXPECTING SOMETHING LIKE THIS WHEN OUR JUMP-JET FOLLOWED TOM INTO YOUR ARTIFICIAL CLOUD!
SCHWARZE SAVAGE! YOU WOULD NOT DARE THREATEN ME IF OUR MISTRESS WERE HERE!
YOU THINK NOT?
LITTLE WOMAN, TELL ME WHERE MY HUSBAND IS, OR I SHALL TEAR OUT YOUR WOMB.
UHH... MOM, REALLY, YOU DON'T NEED TO DO THAT. I GOT THIS SITUATION UNDER CONTROL.
ACTIVATE YOUR EAR-SHIELDS...

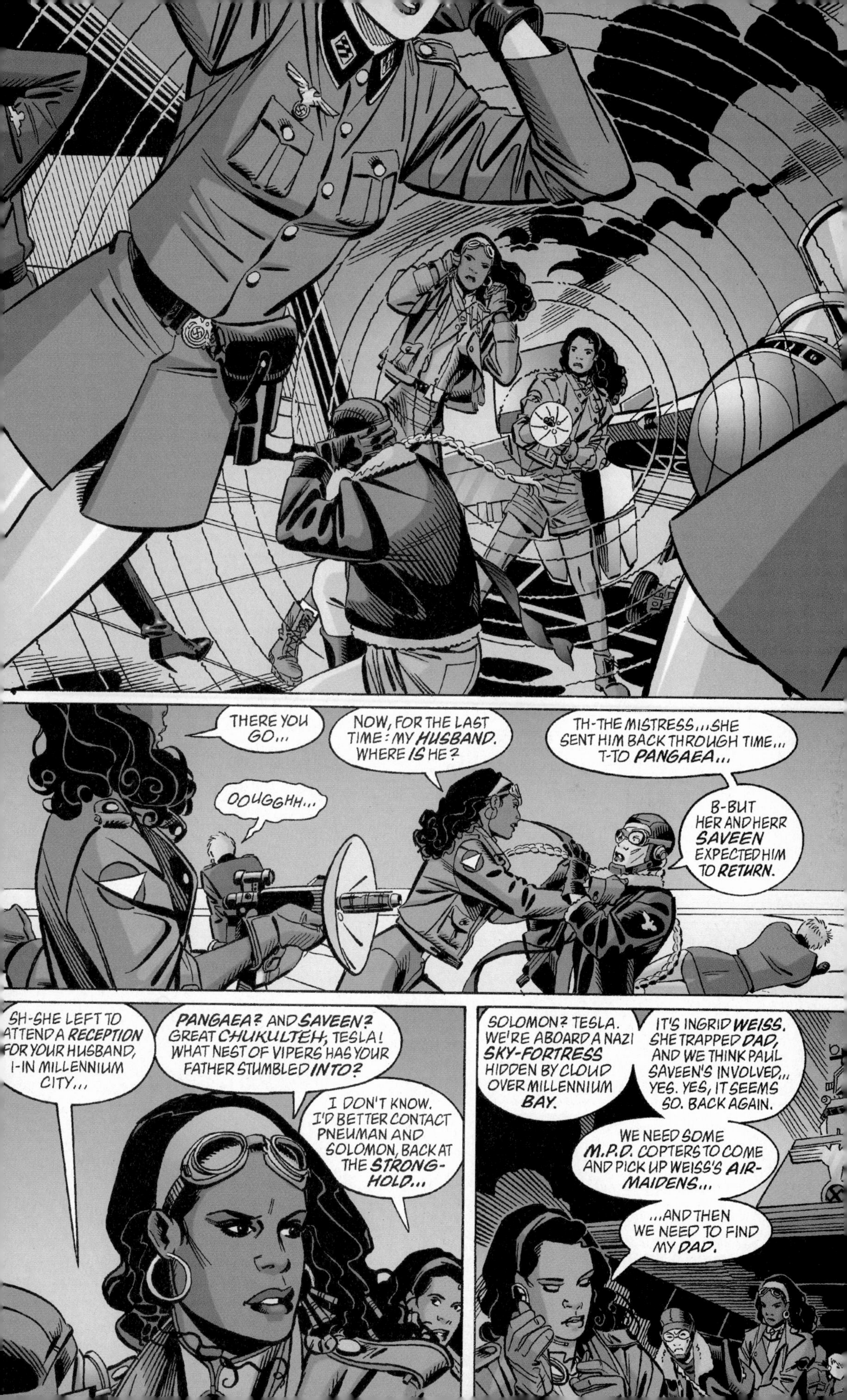
THERE YOU GO...
NOW, FOR THE LAST TIME: MY HUSBAND. WHERE IS HE?
TH-THE MISTRESS... SHE SENT HIM BACK THROUGH TIME... T-TO PANGAEA...
OOUGGHH...
B-BUT HER AND HERR SAVEEN EXPECTED HIM TO RETURN.
SH-SHE LEFT TO ATTEND A RECEPTION FOR YOUR HUSBAND, I-IN MILLENNIUM CITY...
PANGAEA? AND SAVEEN? GREAT CHUKULTEH, TESLA! WHAT NEST OF VIPERS HAS YOUR FATHER STUMBLED INTO?
I DON'T KNOW. I'D BETTER CONTACT PNEUMAN AND SOLOMON, BACK AT THE STRONGHOLD...
SOLOMON? TESLA. WE'RE ABOARD A NAZI SKY-FORTRESS HIDDEN BY CLOUD OVER MILLENNIUM BAY.
IT'S INGRID WEISS. SHE TRAPPED DAD, AND WE THINK PAUL SAVEEN'S INVOLVED... YES. YES, IT SEEMS SO. BACK AGAIN.
WE NEED SOME M.P.D. COPTERS TO COME AND PICK UP WEISS'S AIR-MAIDENS...
...AND THEN WE NEED TO FIND MY DAD.

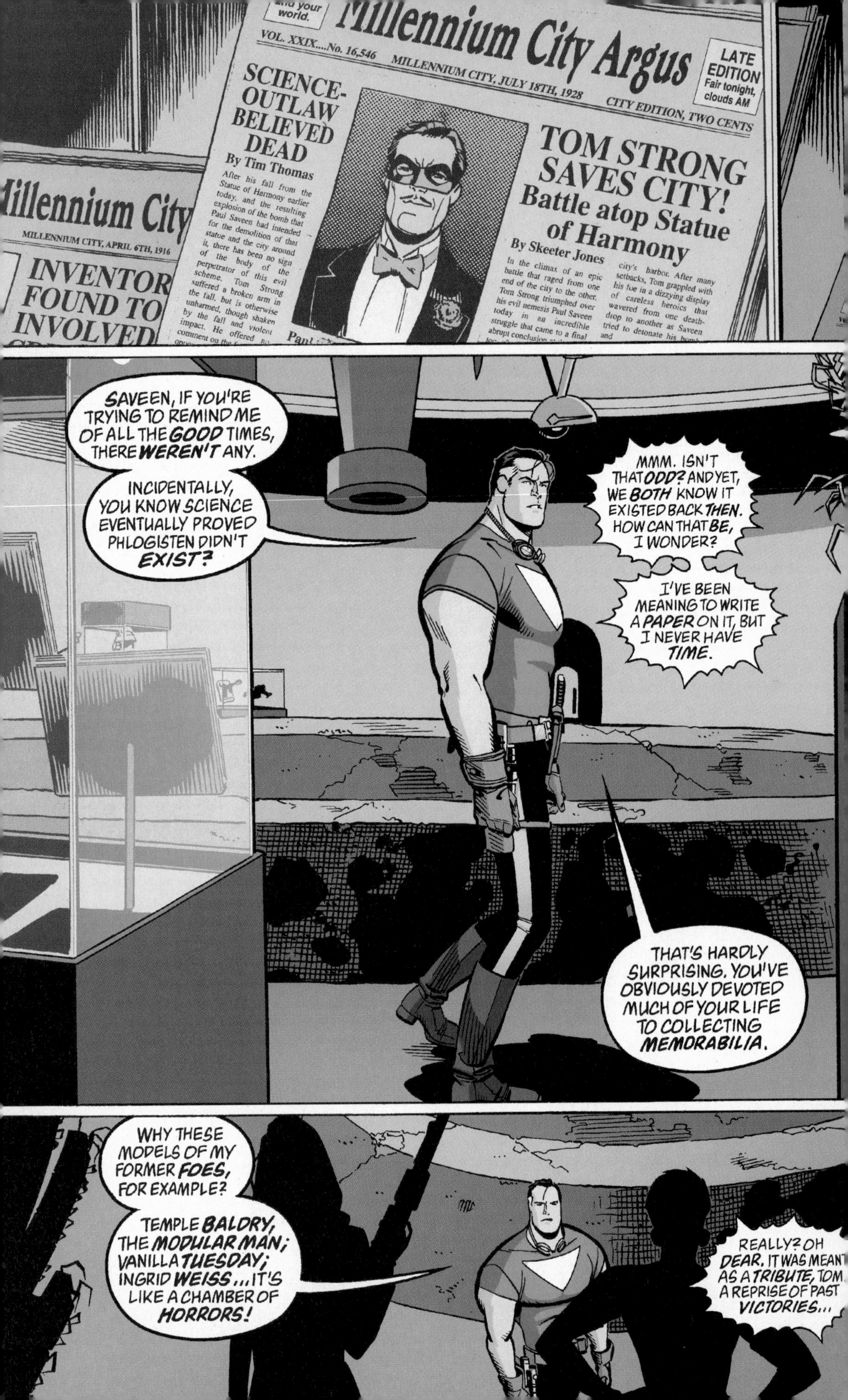
and your world.
Millennium City Argus
VOL. XXIX....No. 16,546
MILLENNIUM CITY, JULY 18TH, 1928
LATE EDITION
Fair tonight, clouds AM
CITY EDITION, TWO CENTS
SCIENCE-OUTLAW BELIEVED DEAD
By Tim Thomas
After his fall from the Statue of Harmony earlier today, and the resulting explosion of the bomb that Paul Saveen had intended for the demolition of that statue and the city around it, there has been no sign of the body of the perpetrator of this evil scheme. Tom Strong suffered a broken arm in the fall, but is otherwise unharmed, though shaken by the fall and violent impact. He offered
TOM STRONG SAVES CITY!
Battle atop Statue of Harmony
By Skeeter Jones
In the climax of an epic battle that raged from one end of the city to the other, Tom Strong triumphed over his evil nemesis Paul Saveen today in an incredible struggle that came to a final
city's harbor. After many setbacks, Tom grappled with his foe in a dizzying display of careless heroics that wavered from one death-drop to another as Saveen tried to detonate his bomb and
Millennium City
MILLENNIUM CITY, APRIL 6TH, 1916
INVENTOR FOUND TO INVOLVED
SAVEEN, IF YOU'RE TRYING TO REMIND ME OF ALL THE GOOD TIMES, THERE WEREN'T ANY.
INCIDENTALLY, YOU KNOW SCIENCE EVENTUALLY PROVED PHLOGISTEN DIDN'T EXIST?
MMM. ISN'T THAT ODD? AND YET, WE BOTH KNOW IT EXISTED BACK THEN. HOW CAN THAT BE, I WONDER?
I'VE BEEN MEANING TO WRITE A PAPER ON IT, BUT I NEVER HAVE TIME.
THAT'S HARDLY SURPRISING. YOU'VE OBVIOUSLY DEVOTED MUCH OF YOUR LIFE TO COLLECTING MEMORABILIA.
WHY THESE MODELS OF MY FORMER FOES, FOR EXAMPLE?
TEMPLE BALDRY, THE MODULAR MAN; VANILLA TUESDAY; INGRID WEISS... IT'S LIKE A CHAMBER OF HORRORS!
REALLY? OH DEAR. IT WAS MEANT AS A TRIBUTE, TOM. A REPRISE OF PAST VICTORIES...

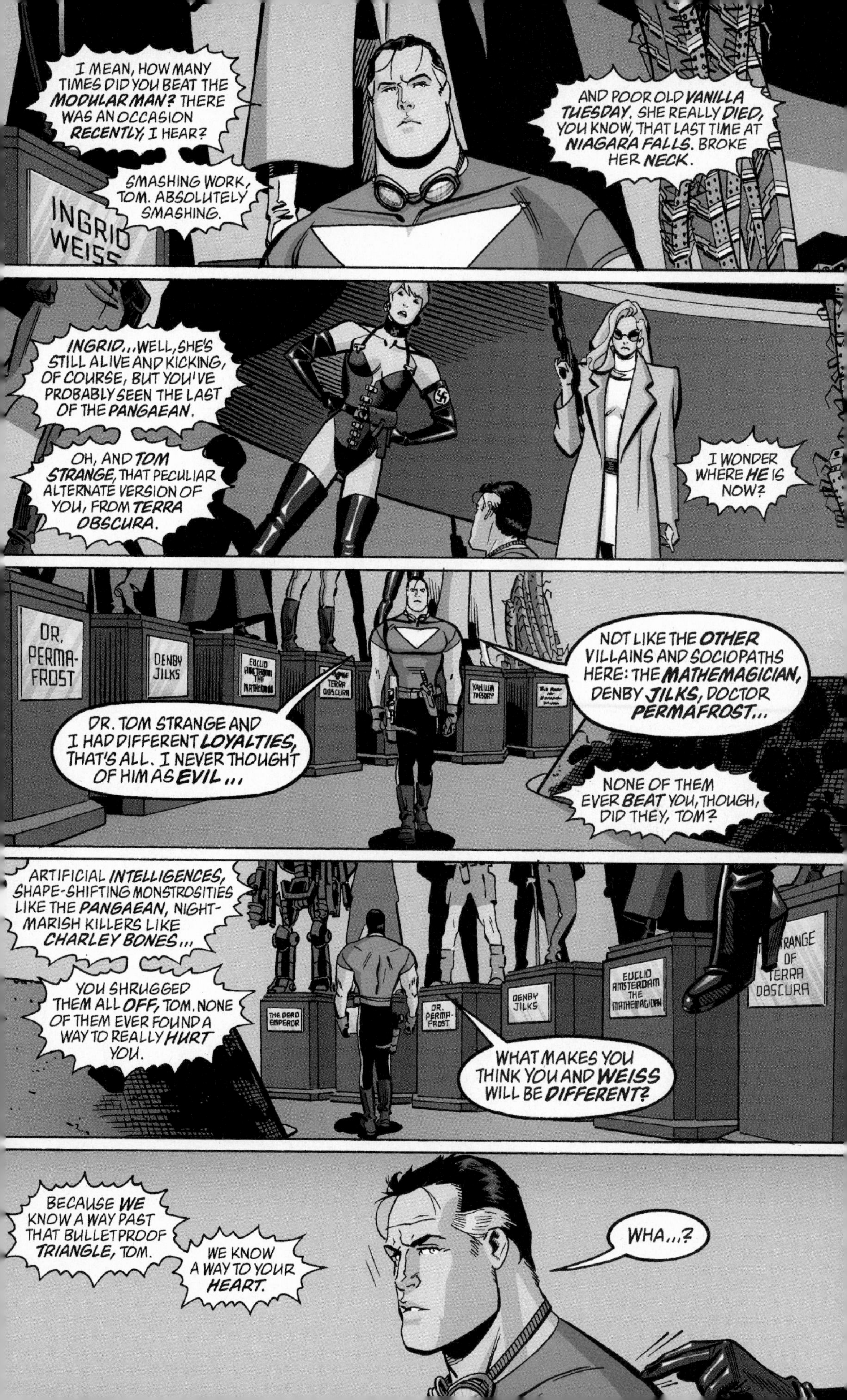
I MEAN, HOW MANY TIMES DID YOU BEAT THE MODULAR MAN? THERE WAS AN OCCASION RECENTLY, I HEAR?
AND POOR OLD VANILLA TUESDAY. SHE REALLY DIED, YOU KNOW, THAT LAST TIME AT NIAGARA FALLS. BROKE HER NECK.
SMASHING WORK, TOM. ABSOLUTELY SMASHING.
INGRID WEISS
INGRID... WELL, SHE'S STILL ALIVE AND KICKING, OF COURSE, BUT YOU'VE PROBABLY SEEN THE LAST OF THE PANGAEAN.
OH, AND TOM STRANGE, THAT PECULIAR ALTERNATE VERSION OF YOU, FROM TERRA OBSCURA.
I WONDER WHERE HE IS NOW?
DR. PERMA-FROST
DENBY JILKS
VANILLA TUESDAY
DR. TOM STRANGE AND I HAD DIFFERENT LOYALTIES, THAT'S ALL. I NEVER THOUGHT OF HIM AS EVIL...
NOT LIKE THE OTHER VILLAINS AND SOCIOPATHS HERE: THE MATHEMAGICIAN, DENBY JILKS, DOCTOR PERMAFROST...
NONE OF THEM EVER BEAT YOU, THOUGH, DID THEY, TOM?
ARTIFICIAL INTELLIGENCES, SHAPE-SHIFTING MONSTROSITIES LIKE THE PANGAEAN, NIGHT-MARISH KILLERS LIKE CHARLEY BONES...
YOU SHRUGGED THEM ALL OFF, TOM. NONE OF THEM EVER FOUND A WAY TO REALLY HURT YOU.
DR. PERMA-FROST
DENBY JILKS
EUCLID AMSTERDAM THE MATHEMAGICIAN
WHAT MAKES YOU THINK YOU AND WEISS WILL BE DIFFERENT?
BECAUSE WE KNOW A WAY PAST THAT BULLETPROOF TRIANGLE, TOM.
WE KNOW A WAY TO YOUR HEART.
WHA...?

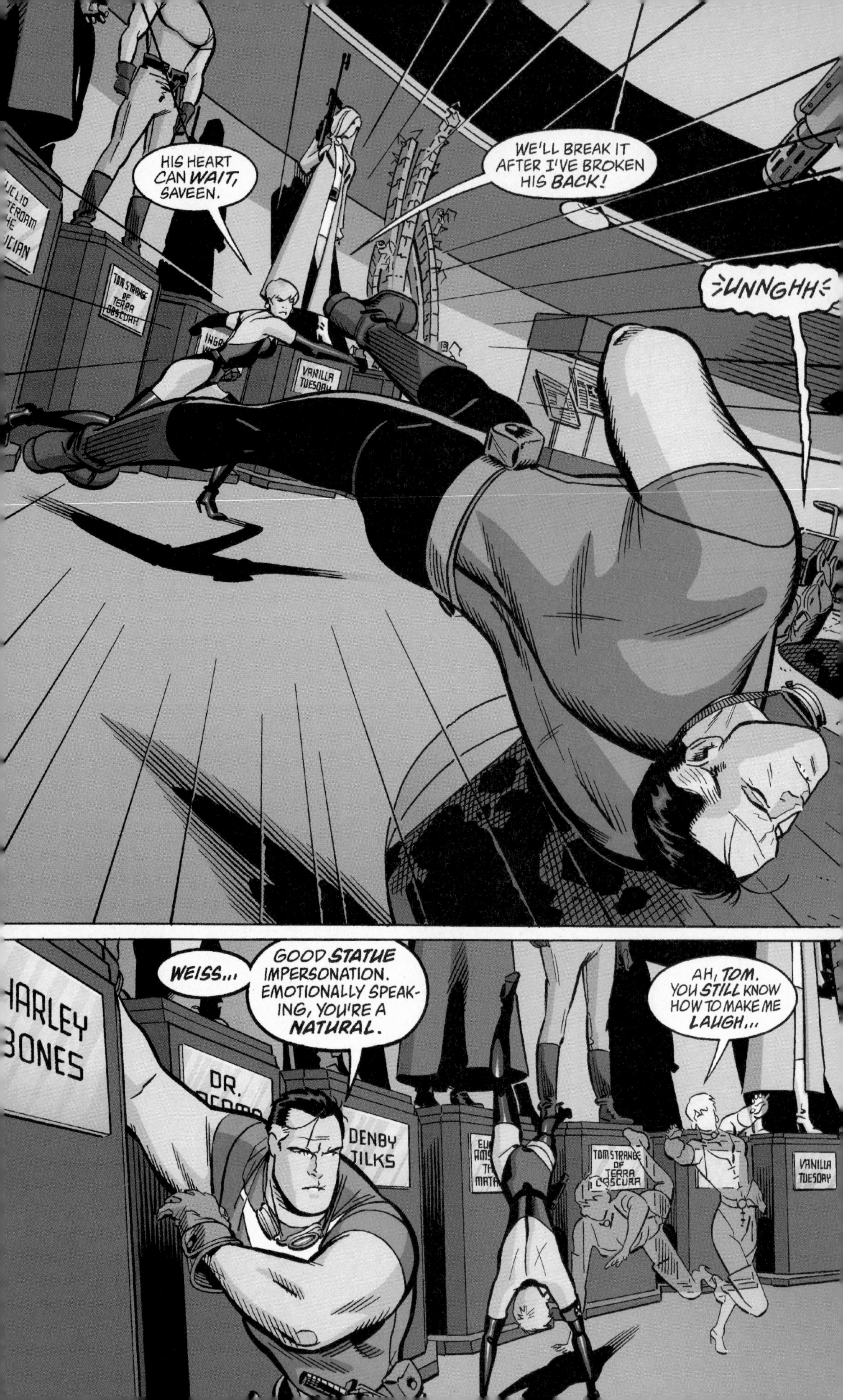
HIS HEART CAN WAIT, SAVEEN.
WE'LL BREAK IT AFTER I'VE BROKEN HIS BACK!
UNNGHH
EUCLID ...TERDAM THE ...ICIAN
TOM STRANGE OF TERRA OBSCURA
VANILLA TUESDAY
WEISS...
GOOD STATUE IMPERSONATION. EMOTIONALLY SPEAK-ING, YOU'RE A NATURAL.
AH, TOM. YOU STILL KNOW HOW TO MAKE ME LAUGH...
HARLEY BONES
DR.
DENBY JILKS
TOM STRANGE OF TERRA OBSCURA
VANILLA TUESDAY

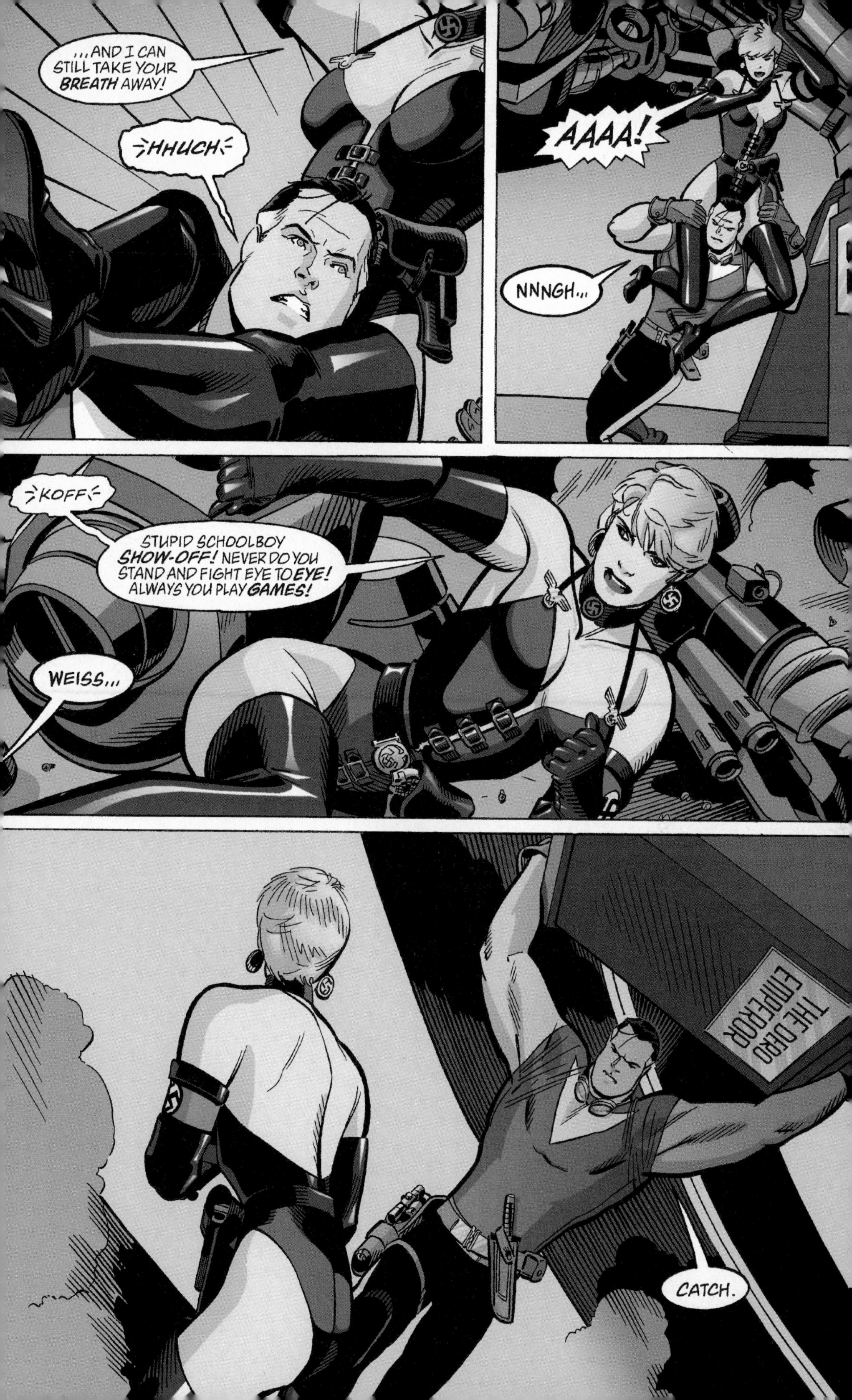
...AND I CAN STILL TAKE YOUR BREATH AWAY!
HHUCH
AAAA!
NNNGH...
KOFF
STUPID SCHOOLBOY SHOW-OFF! NEVER DO YOU STAND AND FIGHT EYE TO EYE! ALWAYS YOU PLAY GAMES!
WEISS...
THE DERO EMPEROR
CATCH.

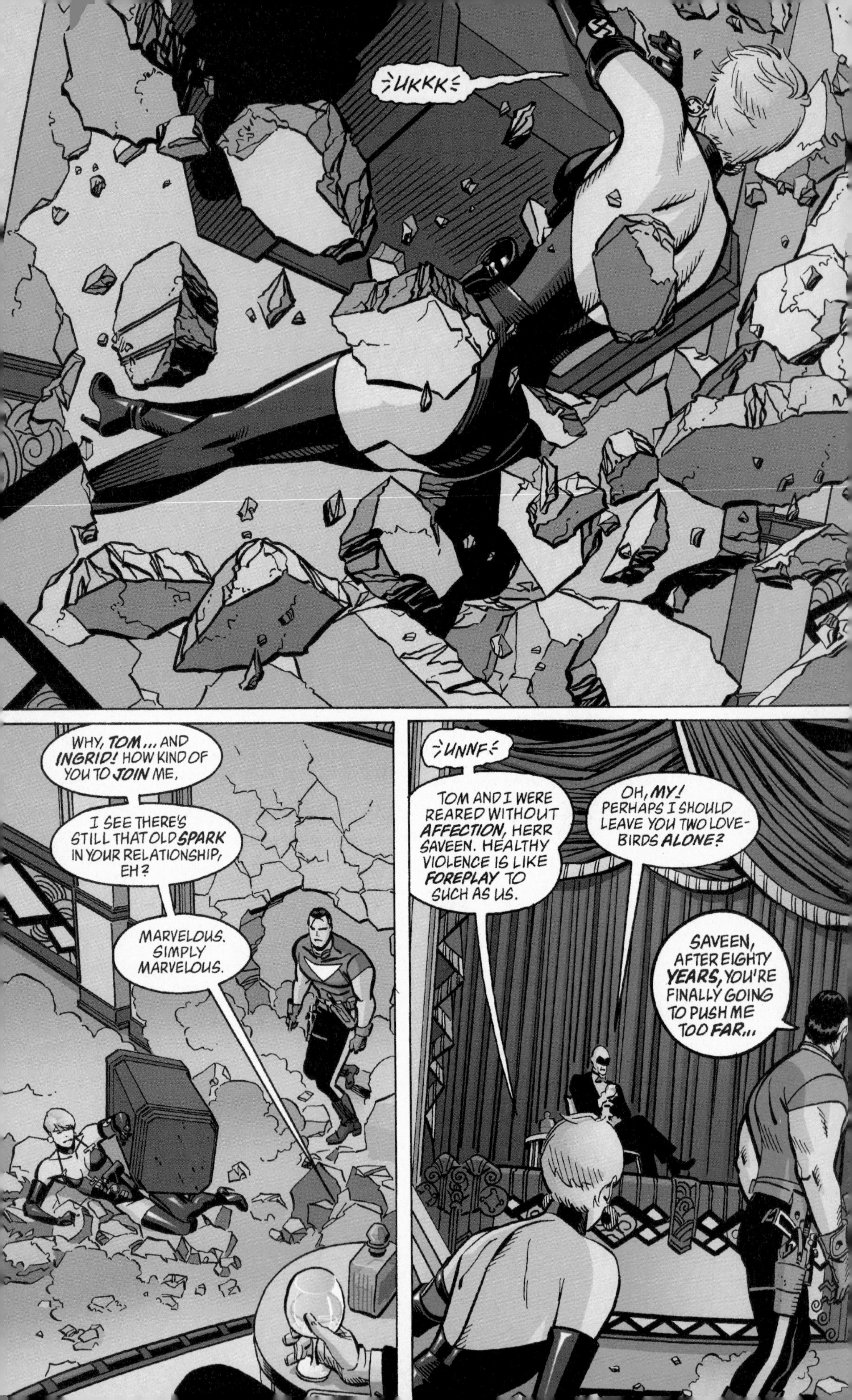
UKKK
WHY, TOM... AND INGRID! HOW KIND OF YOU TO JOIN ME.
I SEE THERE'S STILL THAT OLD SPARK IN YOUR RELATIONSHIP, EH?
MARVELOUS. SIMPLY MARVELOUS.
UNNF
TOM AND I WERE REARED WITHOUT AFFECTION, HERR SAVEEN. HEALTHY VIOLENCE IS LIKE FOREPLAY TO SUCH AS US.
OH, MY! PERHAPS I SHOULD LEAVE YOU TWO LOVE-BIRDS ALONE?
SAVEEN, AFTER EIGHTY YEARS, YOU'RE FINALLY GOING TO PUSH ME TOO FAR...

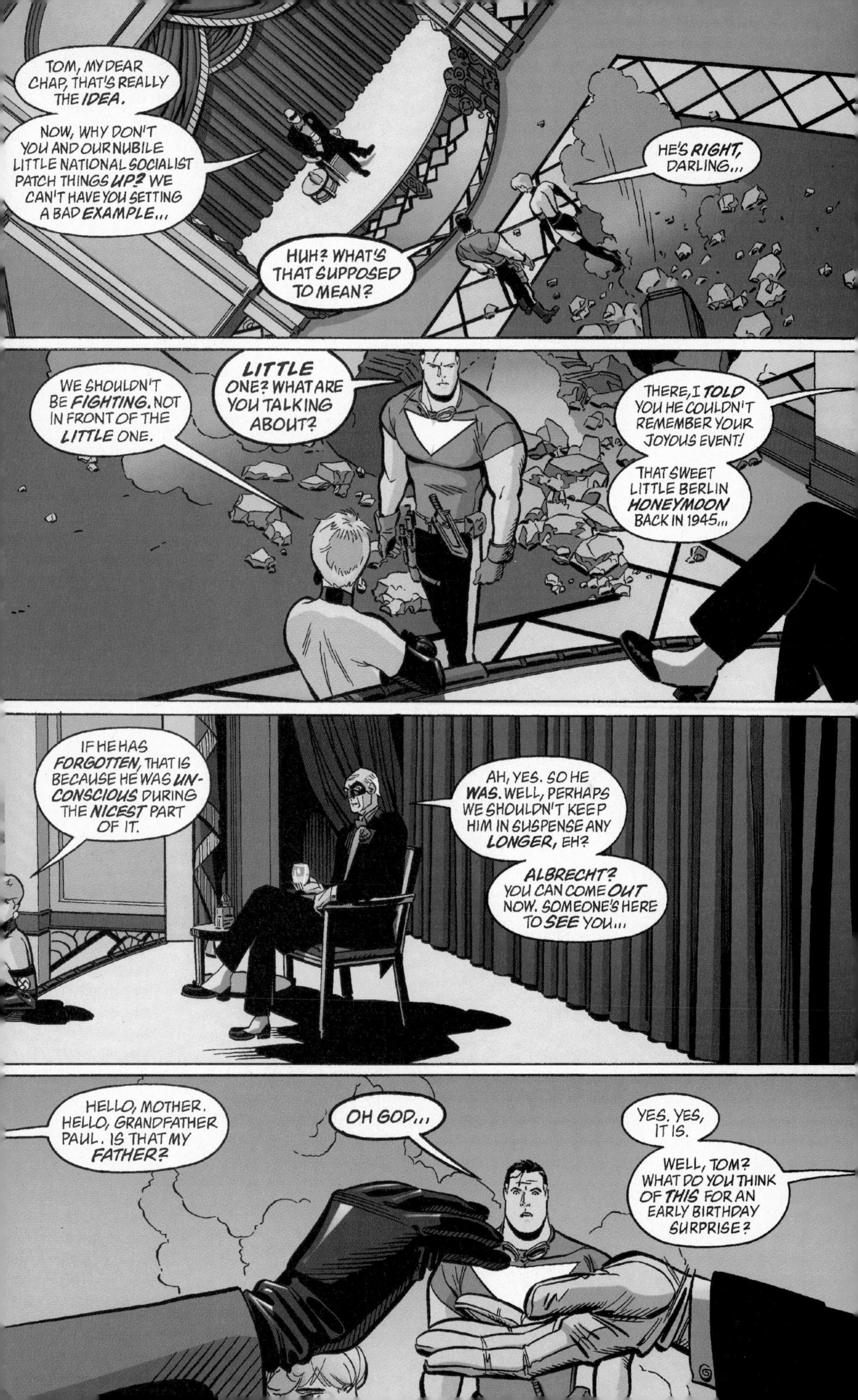

TOM, MY DEAR CHAP, THAT'S REALLY THE *IDEA*.
NOW, WHY DON'T YOU AND OUR NUBILE LITTLE NATIONAL *SOCIALIST* PATCH THINGS *UP?* WE CAN'T HAVE YOU SETTING A BAD *EXAMPLE*...
HE'S *RIGHT,* DARLING...
HUH? WHAT'S THAT SUPPOSED TO MEAN?
WE SHOULDN'T BE *FIGHTING.* NOT IN FRONT OF THE *LITTLE* ONE.
LITTLE ONE? WHAT ARE YOU TALKING ABOUT?
THERE, I *TOLD* YOU HE COULDN'T REMEMBER YOUR JOYOUS EVENT!
THAT SWEET LITTLE BERLIN *HONEYMOON* BACK IN 1945...
IF HE HAS *FORGOTTEN,* THAT IS BECAUSE HE WAS *UN-CONSCIOUS* DURING THE *NICEST* PART OF IT.
AH, YES. SO HE *WAS.* WELL, PERHAPS WE SHOULDN'T KEEP HIM IN SUSPENSE ANY *LONGER,* EH?
ALBRECHT? YOU CAN COME *OUT* NOW. SOMEONE'S HERE TO *SEE* YOU...
HELLO, MOTHER. HELLO, GRANDFATHER PAUL. IS THAT MY *FATHER?*
OH GOD...
YES. YES, IT IS.
WELL, TOM? WHAT DO YOU THINK OF *THIS* FOR AN EARLY BIRTHDAY SURPRISE?

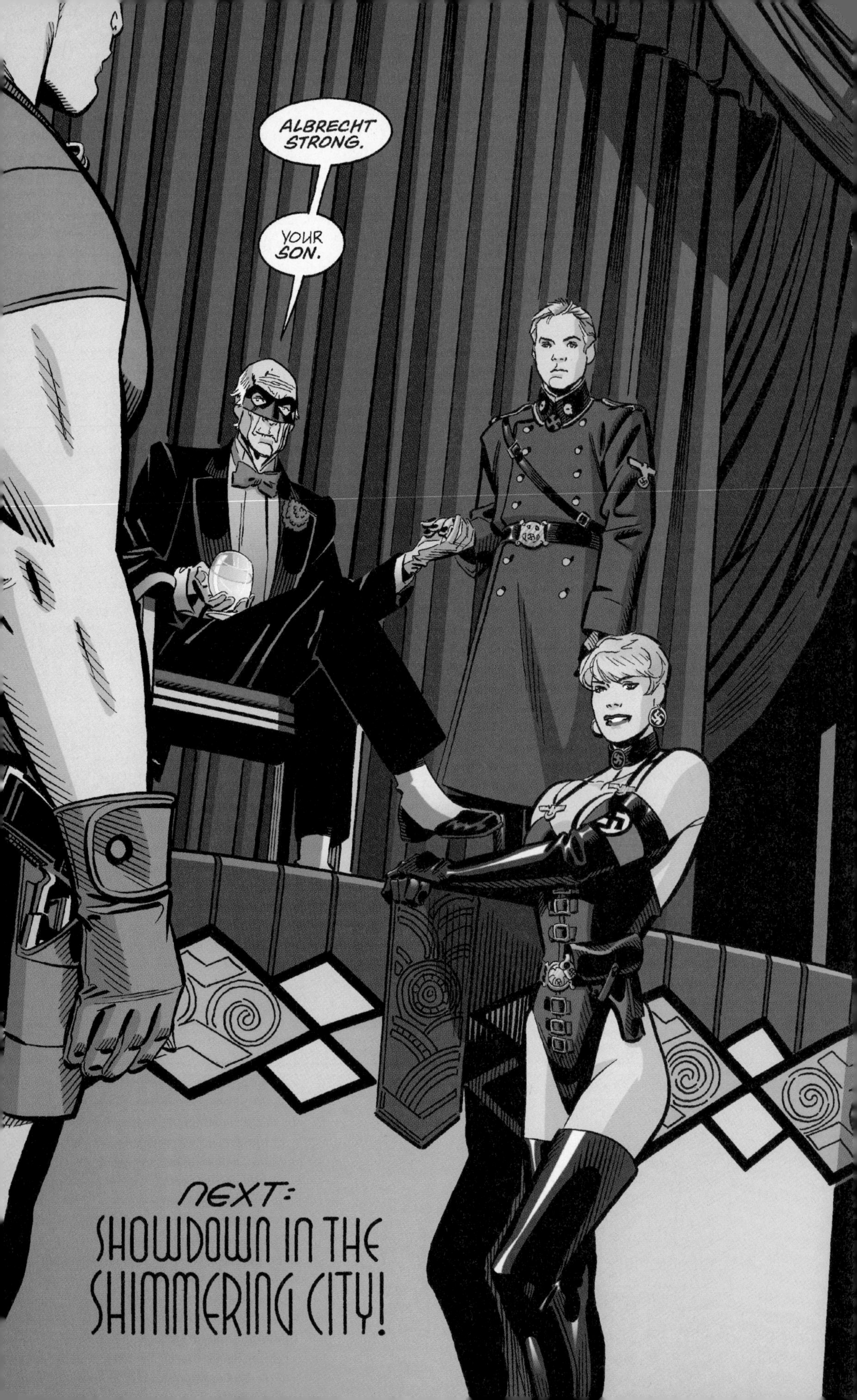
ALBRECHT STRONG.
YOUR SON.
NEXT:
SHOWDOWN IN THE SHIMMERING CITY!

CHAPTER SEVEN

In which TOM considers the Future,
his Enemies glory in the Past, and
DHALUA tackles the Present.

Cover art:
Gary Frank &
Cam Smith

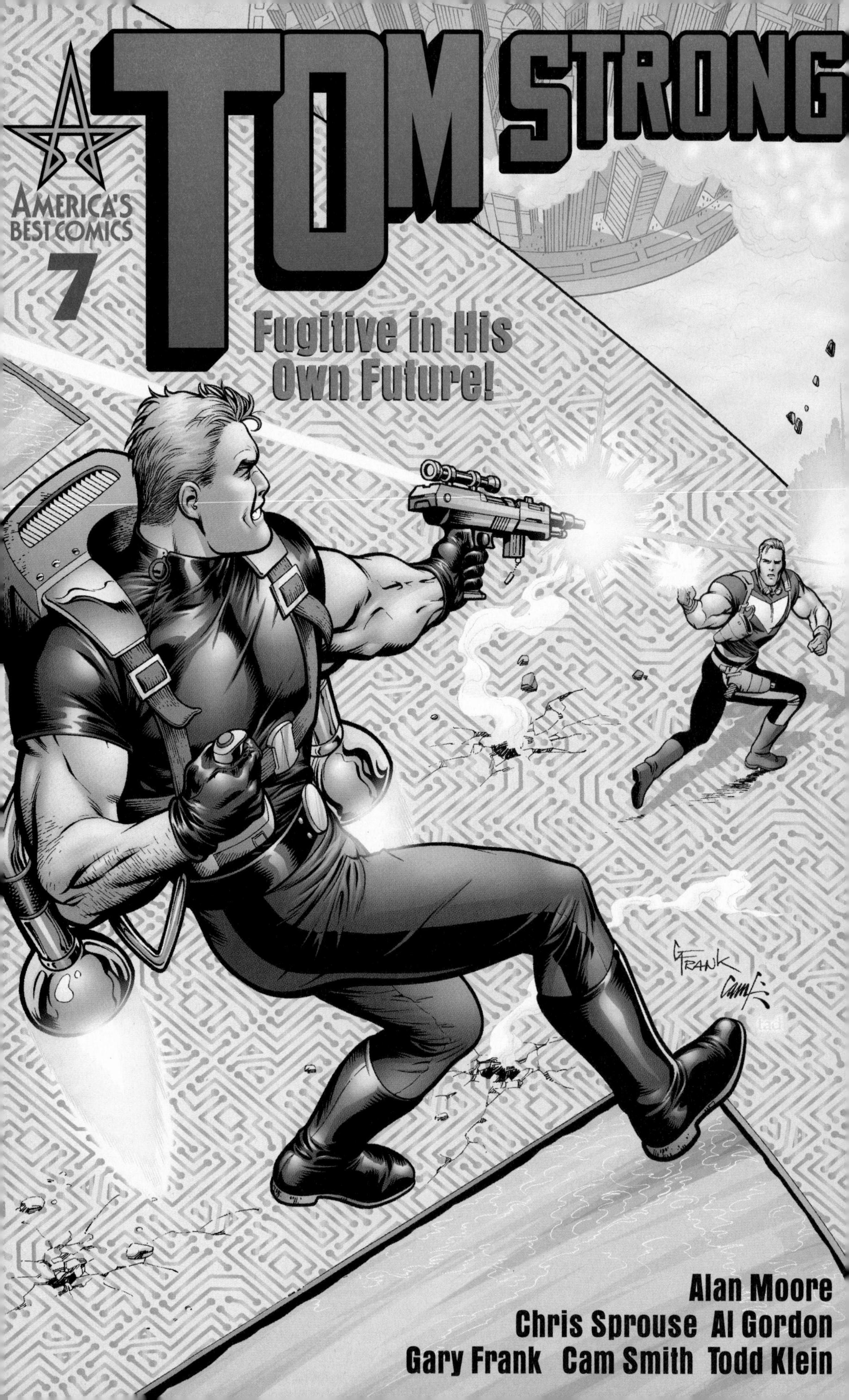
AMERICA'S BEST COMICS
7
TOM STRONG
Fugitive in His Own Future!
Alan Moore
Chris Sprouse Al Gordon
Gary Frank Cam Smith Todd Klein

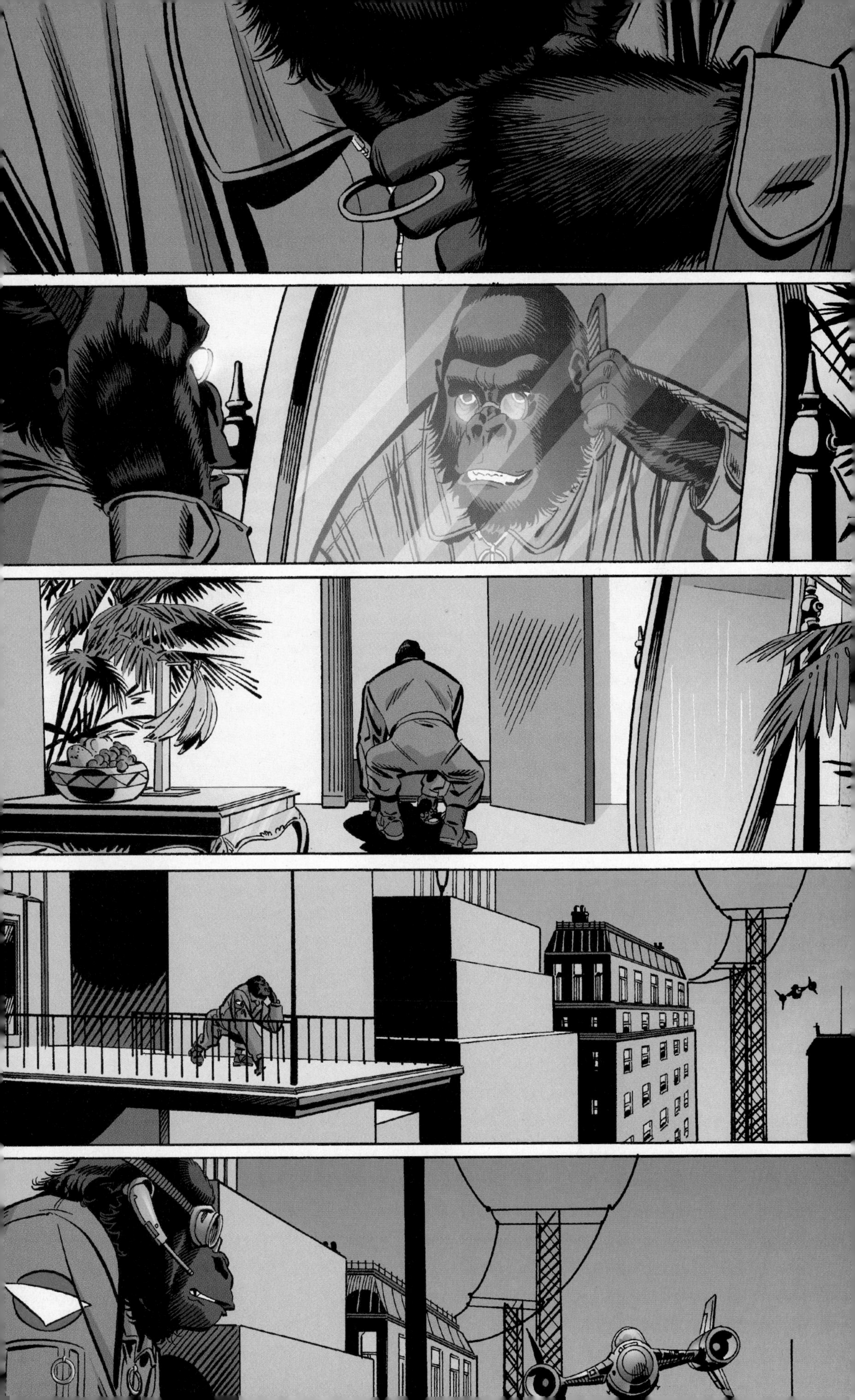

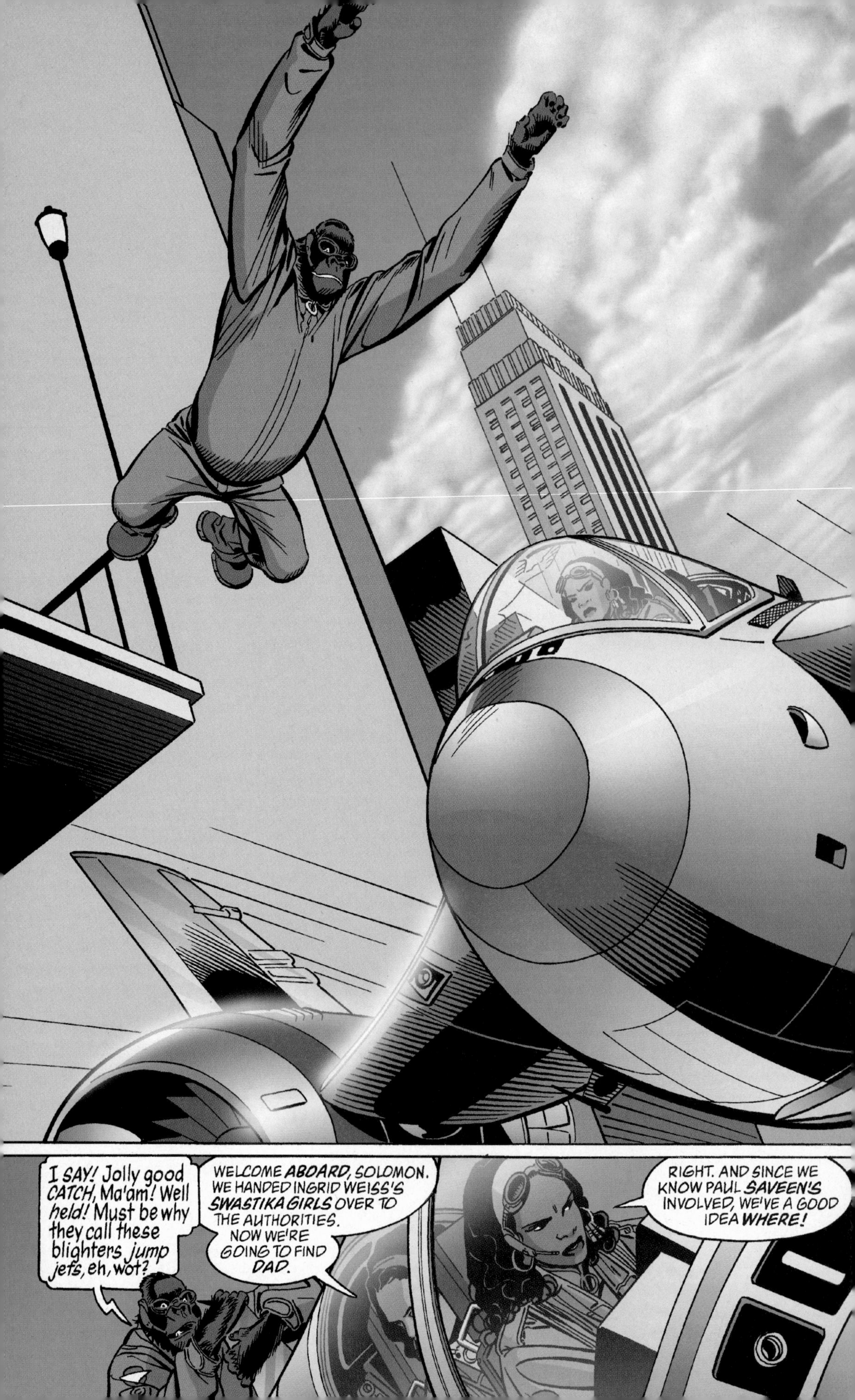

I SAY! Jolly good CATCH, Ma'am! Well held! Must be why they call these blighters jump jets, eh, wot?
WELCOME ABOARD, SOLOMON. WE HANDED INGRID WEISS'S SWASTIKA GIRLS OVER TO THE AUTHORITIES. NOW WE'RE GOING TO FIND DAD.
RIGHT. AND SINCE WE KNOW PAUL SAVEEN'S INVOLVED, WE'VE A GOOD IDEA WHERE!

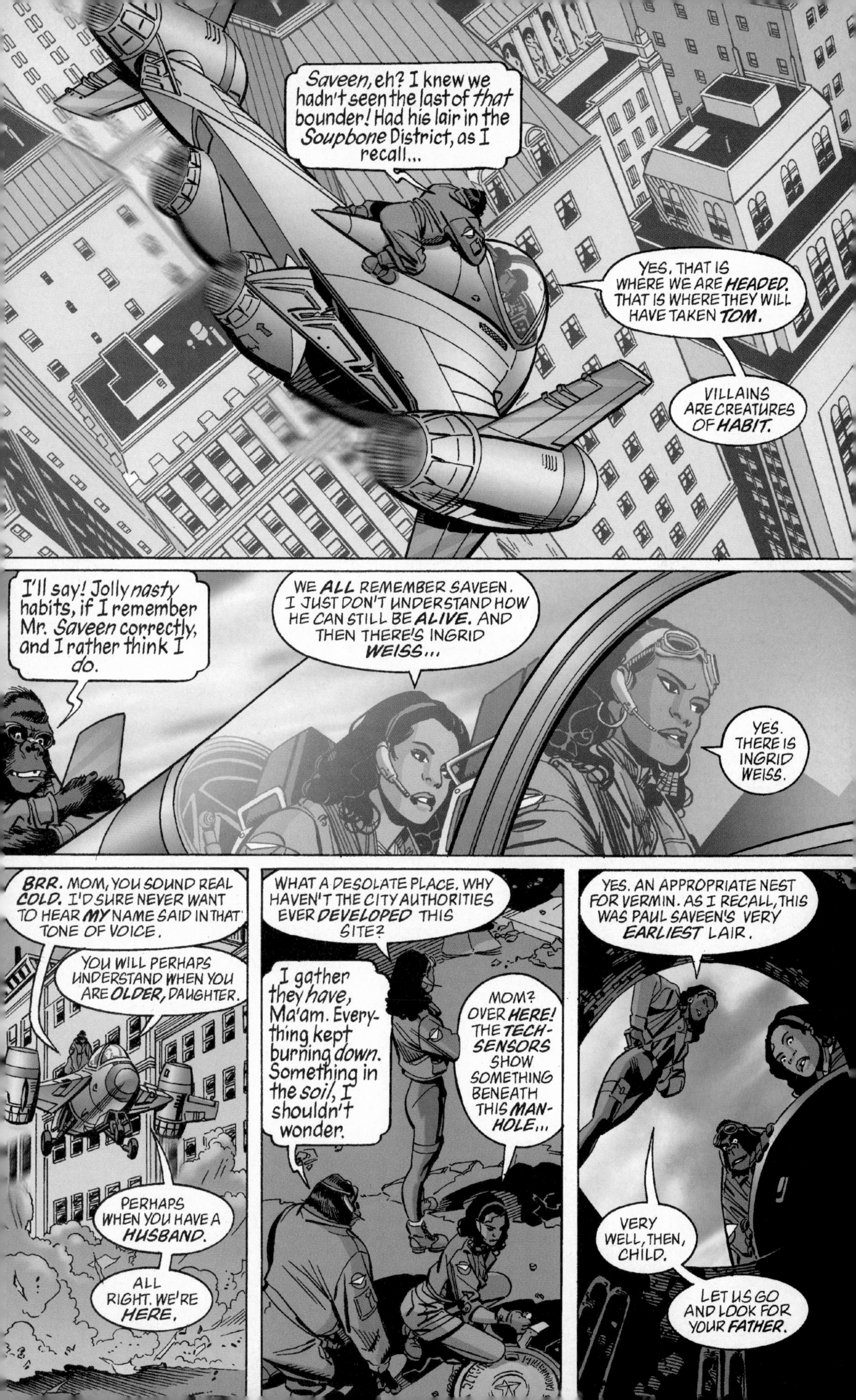
Saveen, eh? I knew we hadn't seen the last of that bounder! Had his lair in the Soupbone District, as I recall...
YES. THAT IS WHERE WE ARE HEADED. THAT IS WHERE THEY WILL HAVE TAKEN TOM.
VILLAINS ARE CREATURES OF HABIT.
I'll say! Jolly nasty habits, if I remember Mr. Saveen correctly, and I rather think I do.
WE ALL REMEMBER SAVEEN. I JUST DON'T UNDERSTAND HOW HE CAN STILL BE ALIVE. AND THEN THERE'S INGRID WEISS...
YES. THERE IS INGRID WEISS.
BRR. MOM, YOU SOUND REAL COLD. I'D SURE NEVER WANT TO HEAR MY NAME SAID IN THAT TONE OF VOICE.
YOU WILL PERHAPS UNDERSTAND WHEN YOU ARE OLDER, DAUGHTER.
PERHAPS WHEN YOU HAVE A HUSBAND.
ALL RIGHT. WE'RE HERE.
WHAT A DESOLATE PLACE. WHY HAVEN'T THE CITY AUTHORITIES EVER DEVELOPED THIS SITE?
I gather they have, Ma'am. Everything kept burning down. Something in the soil, I shouldn't wonder.
MOM? OVER HERE! THE TECH-SENSORS SHOW SOMETHING BENEATH THIS MAN-HOLE...
YES. AN APPROPRIATE NEST FOR VERMIN. AS I RECALL, THIS WAS PAUL SAVEEN'S VERY EARLIEST LAIR.
VERY WELL, THEN, CHILD.
LET US GO AND LOOK FOR YOUR FATHER.

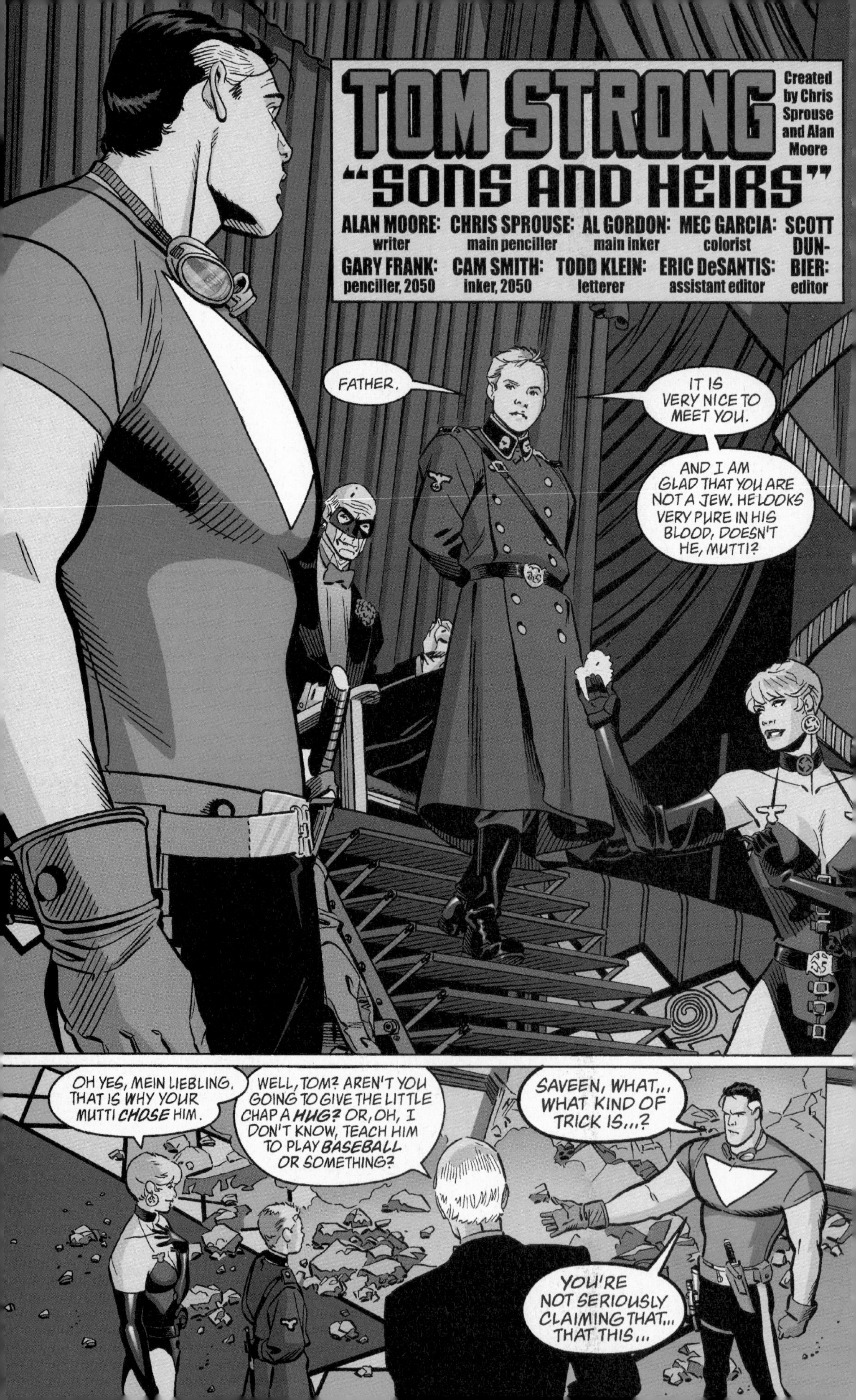
TOM STRONG
Created by Chris Sprouse and Alan Moore
"SONS AND HEIRS"
ALAN MOORE: writer
CHRIS SPROUSE: main penciller
AL GORDON: main inker
MEC GARCIA: colorist
SCOTT DUNBIER: editor
GARY FRANK: penciller, 2050
CAM SMITH: inker, 2050
TODD KLEIN: letterer
ERIC DeSANTIS: assistant editor
FATHER.
IT IS VERY NICE TO MEET YOU.
AND I AM GLAD THAT YOU ARE NOT A JEW. HE LOOKS VERY PURE IN HIS BLOOD, DOESN'T HE, MUTTI?
OH YES, MEIN LIEBLING. THAT IS WHY YOUR MUTTI CHOSE HIM.
WELL, TOM? AREN'T YOU GOING TO GIVE THE LITTLE CHAP A HUG? OR, OH, I DON'T KNOW, TEACH HIM TO PLAY BASEBALL OR SOMETHING?
SAVEEN, WHAT... WHAT KIND OF TRICK IS...?
YOU'RE NOT SERIOUSLY CLAIMING THAT... THAT THIS...

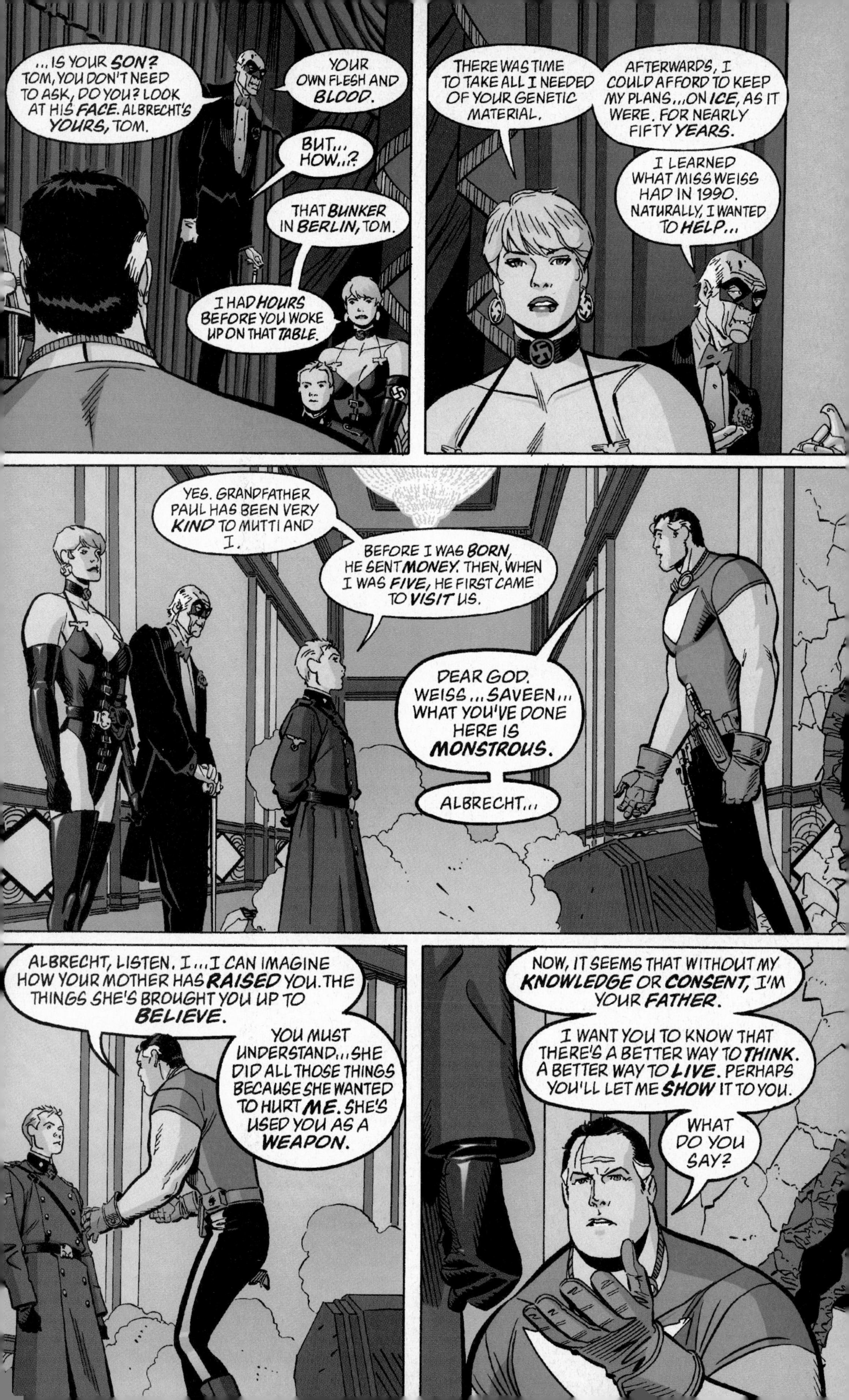
...IS YOUR SON? TOM, YOU DON'T NEED TO ASK, DO YOU? LOOK AT HIS FACE. ALBRECHT'S YOURS, TOM.
YOUR OWN FLESH AND BLOOD.
BUT... HOW...?
THAT BUNKER IN BERLIN, TOM.
I HAD HOURS BEFORE YOU WOKE UP ON THAT TABLE.
THERE WAS TIME TO TAKE ALL I NEEDED OF YOUR GENETIC MATERIAL.
AFTERWARDS, I COULD AFFORD TO KEEP MY PLANS...ON ICE, AS IT WERE. FOR NEARLY FIFTY YEARS.
I LEARNED WHAT MISS WEISS HAD IN 1990. NATURALLY, I WANTED TO HELP...
YES. GRANDFATHER PAUL HAS BEEN VERY KIND TO MUTTI AND I.
BEFORE I WAS BORN, HE SENT MONEY. THEN, WHEN I WAS FIVE, HE FIRST CAME TO VISIT US.
DEAR GOD. WEISS... SAVEEN... WHAT YOU'VE DONE HERE IS MONSTROUS.
ALBRECHT...
ALBRECHT, LISTEN. I...I CAN IMAGINE HOW YOUR MOTHER HAS RAISED YOU. THE THINGS SHE'S BROUGHT YOU UP TO BELIEVE.
YOU MUST UNDERSTAND...SHE DID ALL THOSE THINGS BECAUSE SHE WANTED TO HURT ME. SHE'S USED YOU AS A WEAPON.
NOW, IT SEEMS THAT WITHOUT MY KNOWLEDGE OR CONSENT, I'M YOUR FATHER.
I WANT YOU TO KNOW THAT THERE'S A BETTER WAY TO THINK. A BETTER WAY TO LIVE. PERHAPS YOU'LL LET ME SHOW IT TO YOU.
WHAT DO YOU SAY?

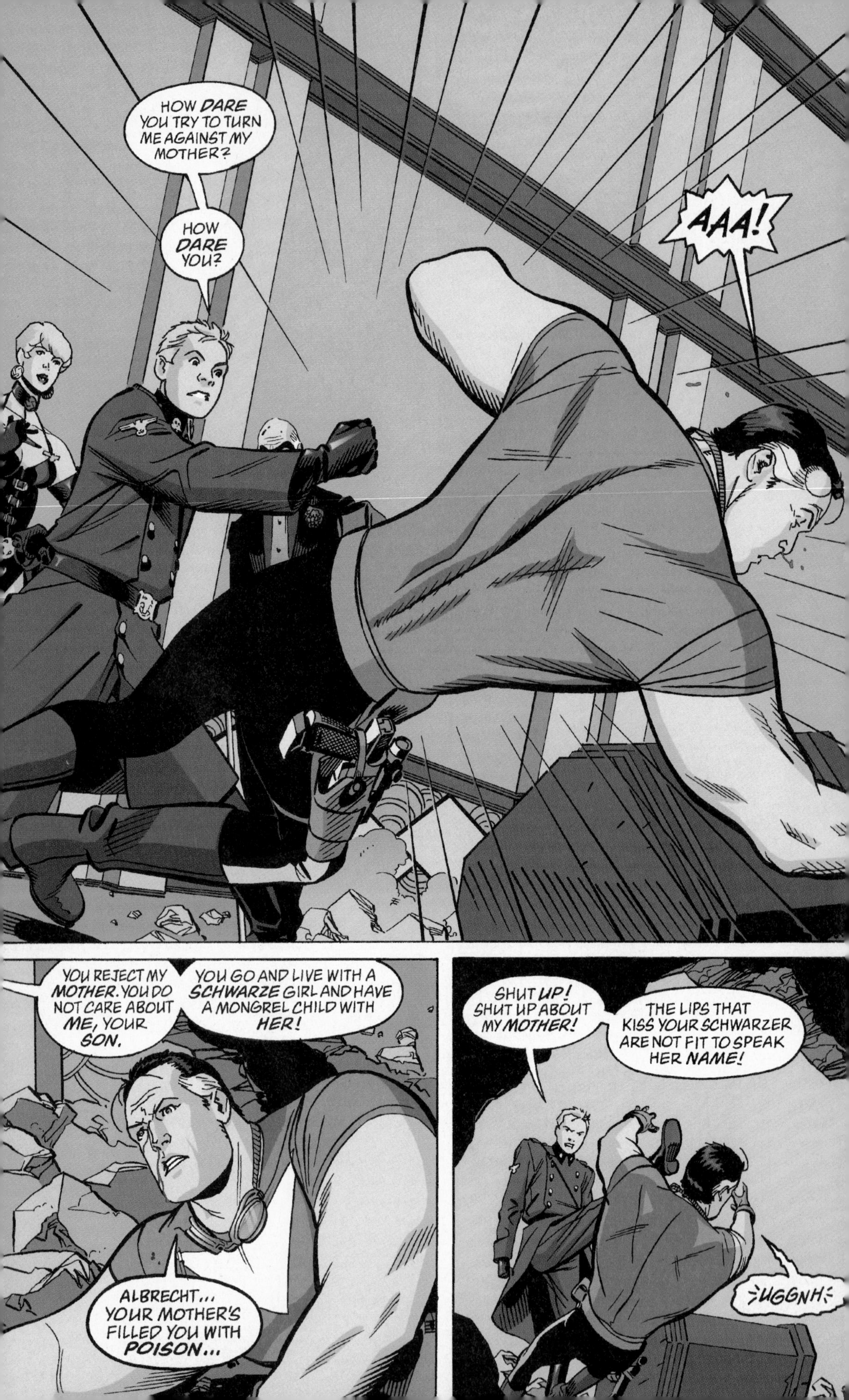
HOW DARE YOU TRY TO TURN ME AGAINST MY MOTHER?
HOW DARE YOU?
AAA!
YOU REJECT MY MOTHER. YOU DO NOT CARE ABOUT ME, YOUR SON.
YOU GO AND LIVE WITH A SCHWARZE GIRL AND HAVE A MONGREL CHILD WITH HER!
ALBRECHT... YOUR MOTHER'S FILLED YOU WITH POISON...
SHUT UP! SHUT UP ABOUT MY MOTHER!
THE LIPS THAT KISS YOUR SCHWARZER ARE NOT FIT TO SPEAK HER NAME!
UGGNH

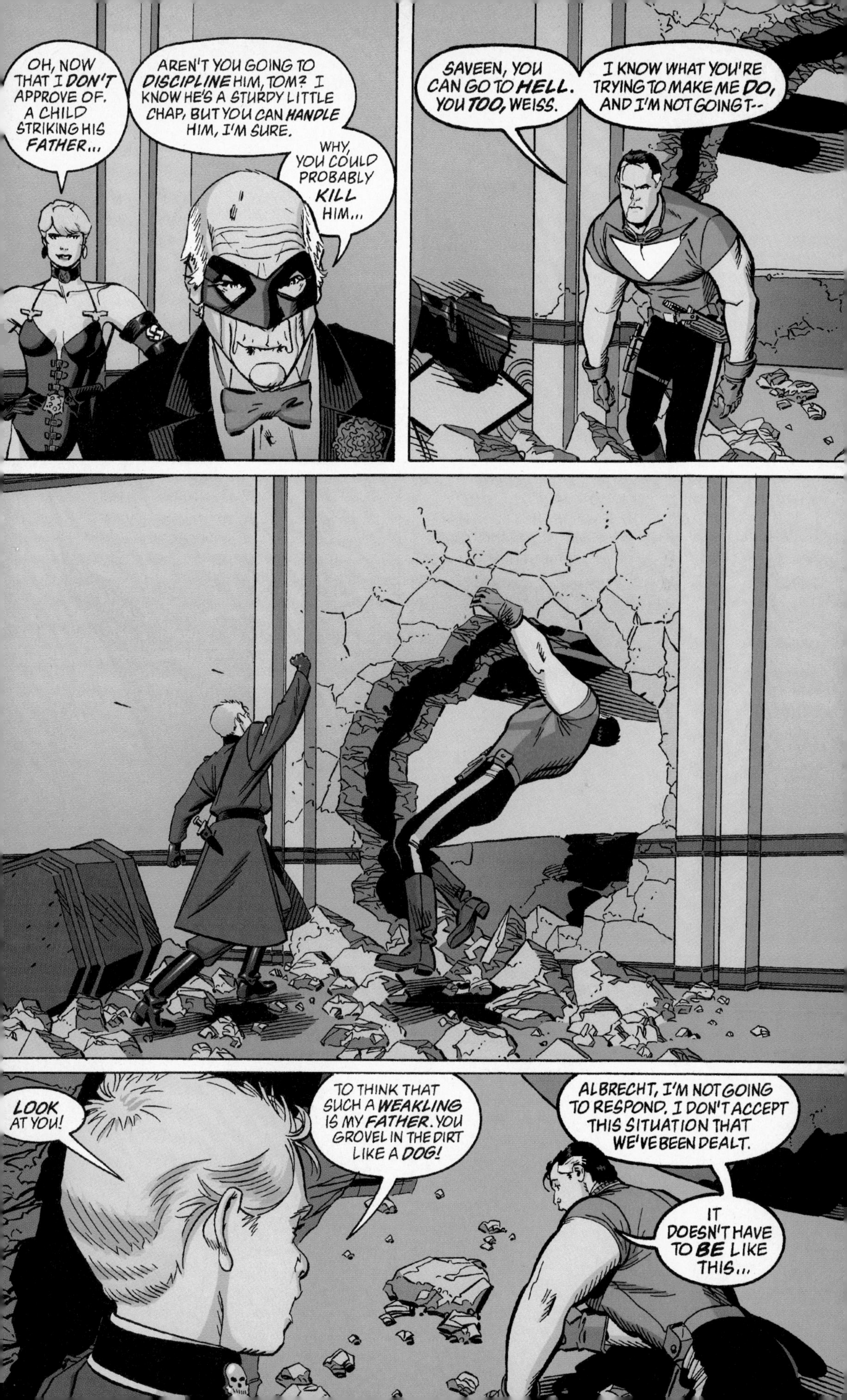
OH, NOW THAT I DON'T APPROVE OF. A CHILD STRIKING HIS FATHER...
AREN'T YOU GOING TO DISCIPLINE HIM, TOM? I KNOW HE'S A STURDY LITTLE CHAP, BUT YOU CAN HANDLE HIM, I'M SURE.
WHY, YOU COULD PROBABLY KILL HIM...
SAVEEN, YOU CAN GO TO HELL. YOU TOO, WEISS.
I KNOW WHAT YOU'RE TRYING TO MAKE ME DO, AND I'M NOT GOING T--
LOOK AT YOU!
TO THINK THAT SUCH A WEAKLING IS MY FATHER. YOU GROVEL IN THE DIRT LIKE A DOG!
ALBRECHT, I'M NOT GOING TO RESPOND. I DON'T ACCEPT THIS SITUATION THAT WE'VE BEEN DEALT.
IT DOESN'T HAVE TO BE LIKE THIS...

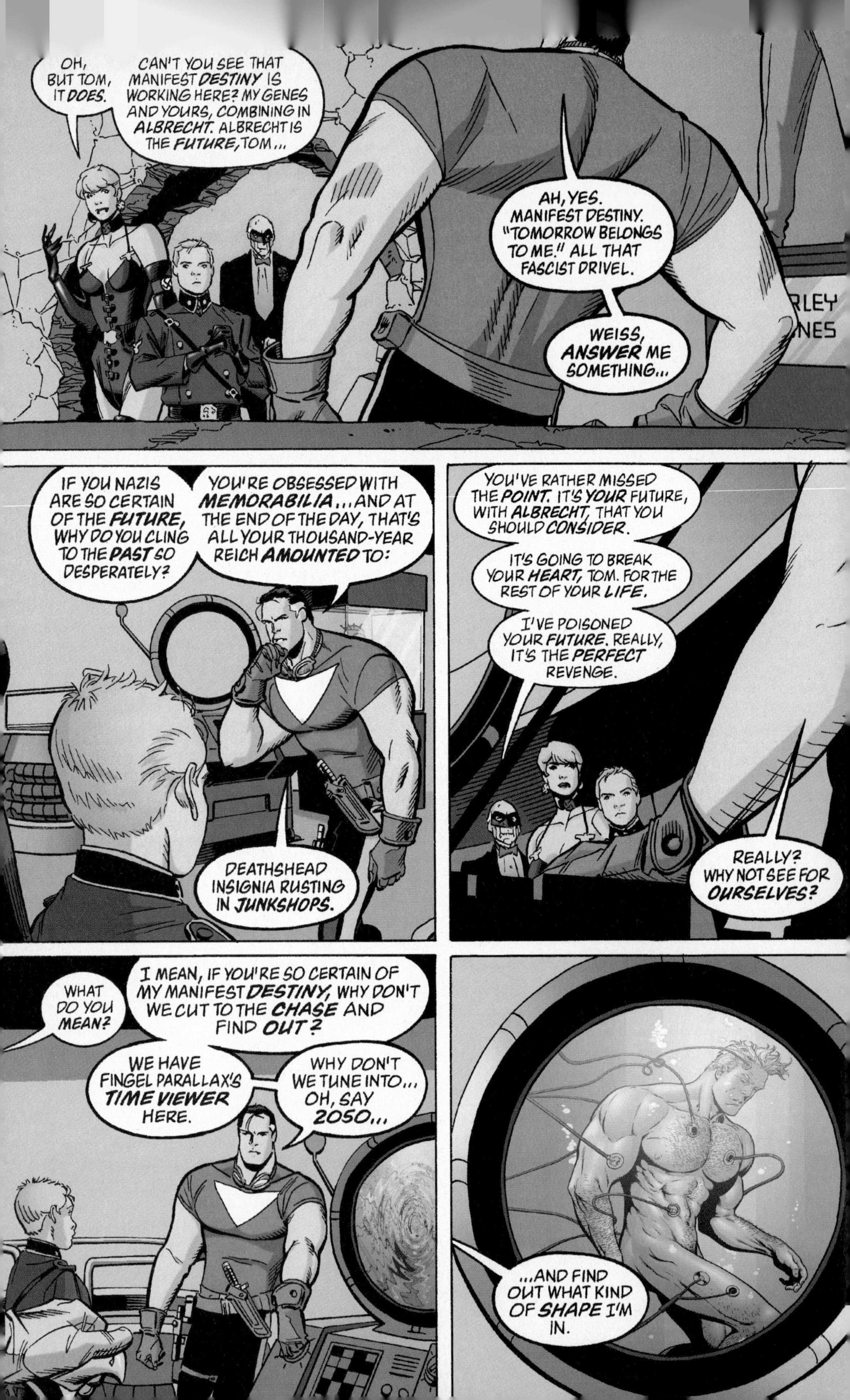
OH, BUT TOM, IT DOES.
CAN'T YOU SEE THAT MANIFEST DESTINY IS WORKING HERE? MY GENES AND YOURS, COMBINING IN ALBRECHT. ALBRECHT IS THE FUTURE, TOM...
AH, YES. MANIFEST DESTINY. "TOMORROW BELONGS TO ME." ALL THAT FASCIST DRIVEL.
WEISS, ANSWER ME SOMETHING...
IF YOU NAZIS ARE SO CERTAIN OF THE FUTURE, WHY DO YOU CLING TO THE PAST SO DESPERATELY?
YOU'RE OBSESSED WITH MEMORABILIA... AND AT THE END OF THE DAY, THAT'S ALL YOUR THOUSAND-YEAR REICH AMOUNTED TO:
DEATHSHEAD INSIGNIA RUSTING IN JUNKSHOPS.
YOU'VE RATHER MISSED THE POINT. IT'S YOUR FUTURE, WITH ALBRECHT, THAT YOU SHOULD CONSIDER.
IT'S GOING TO BREAK YOUR HEART, TOM. FOR THE REST OF YOUR LIFE.
I'VE POISONED YOUR FUTURE. REALLY, IT'S THE PERFECT REVENGE.
REALLY? WHY NOT SEE FOR OURSELVES?
WHAT DO YOU MEAN?
I MEAN, IF YOU'RE SO CERTAIN OF MY MANIFEST DESTINY, WHY DON'T WE CUT TO THE CHASE AND FIND OUT?
WE HAVE FINGEL PARALLAX'S TIME VIEWER HERE.
WHY DON'T WE TUNE INTO... OH, SAY 2050...
...AND FIND OUT WHAT KIND OF SHAPE I'M IN.

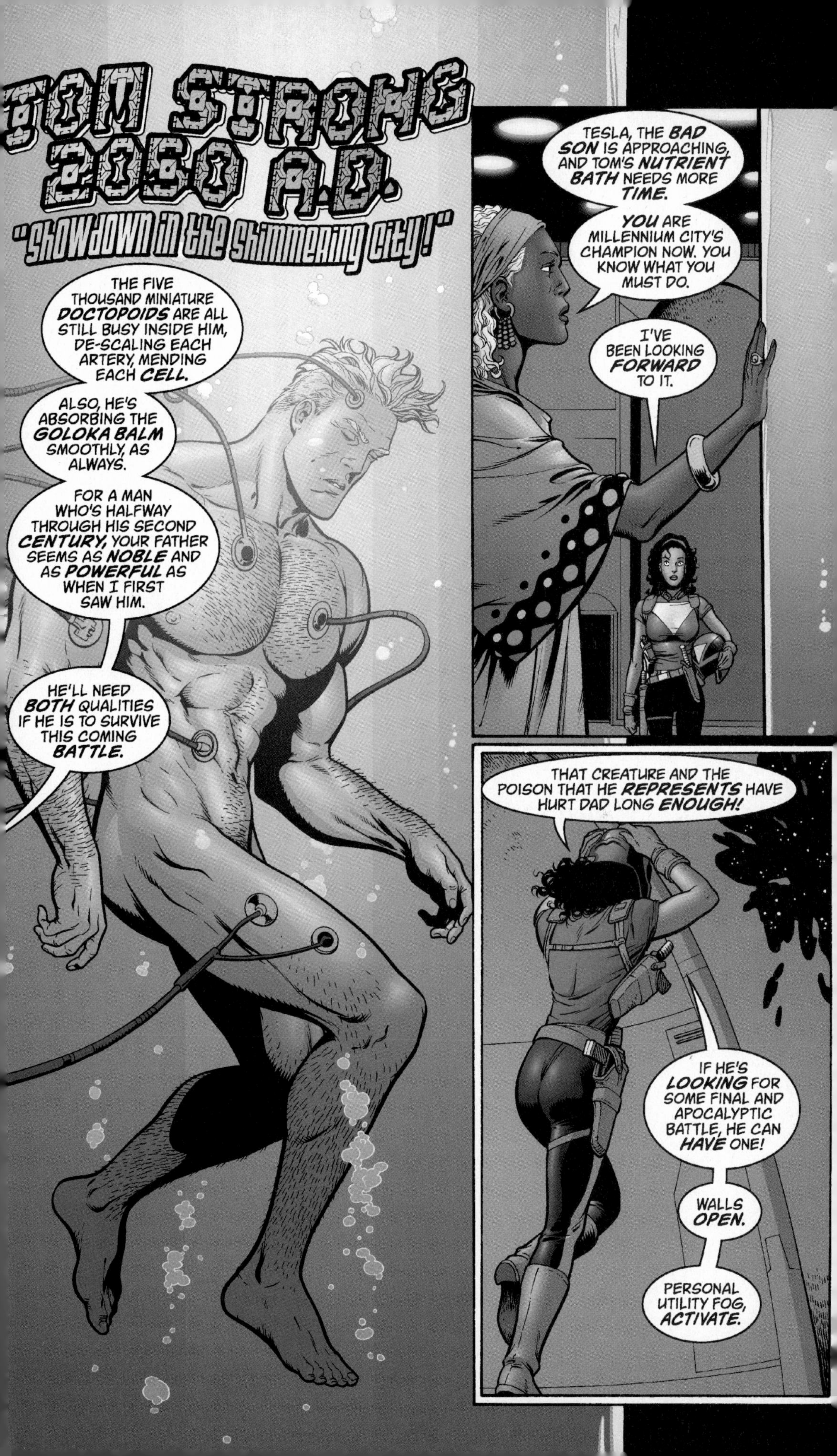

TOM STRONG 2050 A.D.
"SHOWDOWN IN THE SHIMMERING CITY!"
THE FIVE THOUSAND MINIATURE DOCTOPOIDS ARE ALL STILL BUSY INSIDE HIM, DE-SCALING EACH ARTERY, MENDING EACH CELL.
ALSO, HE'S ABSORBING THE GOLOKA BALM SMOOTHLY, AS ALWAYS.
FOR A MAN WHO'S HALFWAY THROUGH HIS SECOND CENTURY, YOUR FATHER SEEMS AS NOBLE AND AS POWERFUL AS WHEN I FIRST SAW HIM.
HE'LL NEED BOTH QUALITIES IF HE IS TO SURVIVE THIS COMING BATTLE.
TESLA, THE BAD SON IS APPROACHING, AND TOM'S NUTRIENT BATH NEEDS MORE TIME.
YOU ARE MILLENNIUM CITY'S CHAMPION NOW. YOU KNOW WHAT YOU MUST DO.
I'VE BEEN LOOKING FORWARD TO IT.
THAT CREATURE AND THE POISON THAT HE REPRESENTS HAVE HURT DAD LONG ENOUGH!
IF HE'S LOOKING FOR SOME FINAL AND APOCALYPTIC BATTLE, HE CAN HAVE ONE!
WALLS OPEN.
PERSONAL UTILITY FOG, ACTIVATE.

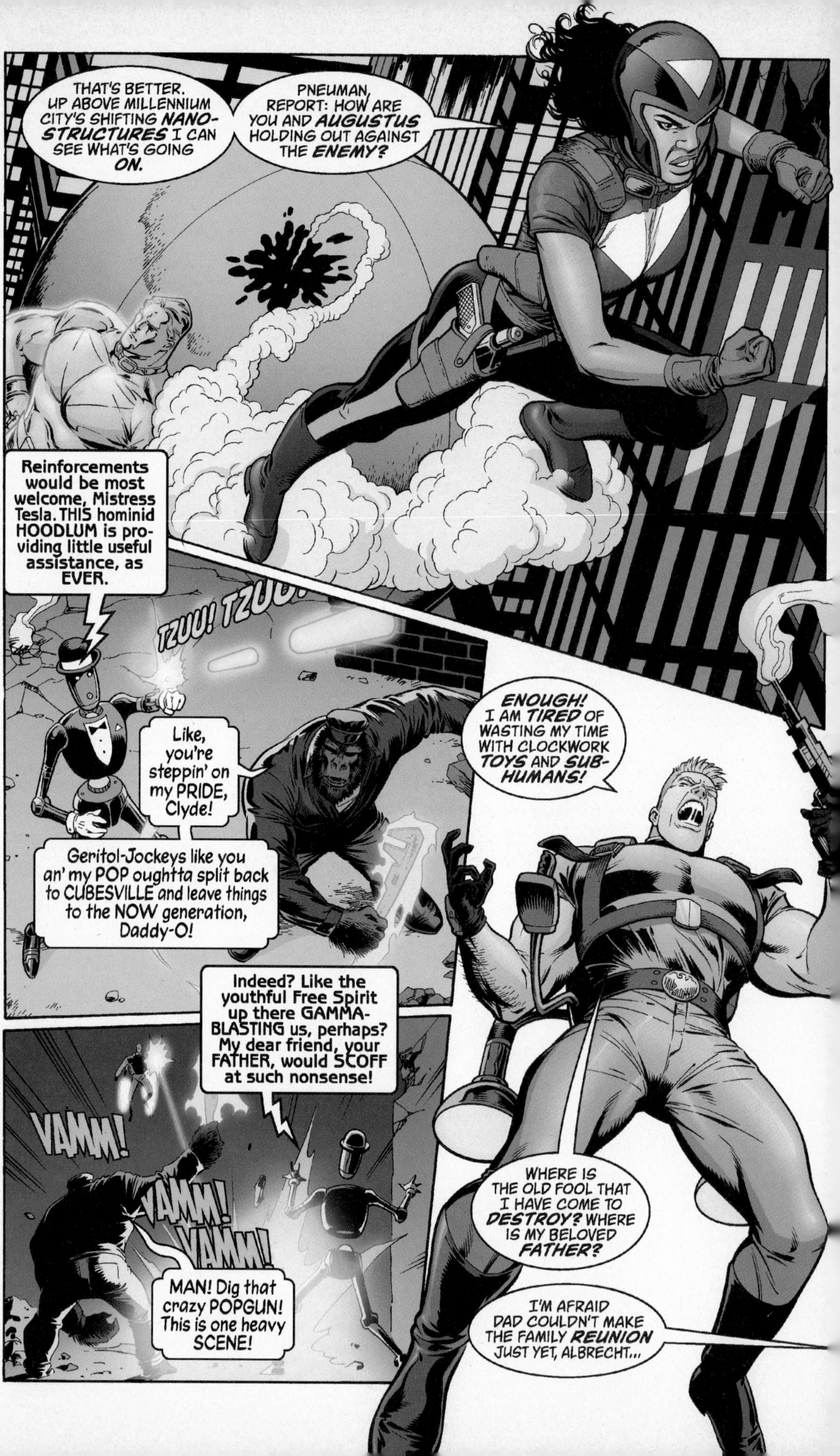
THAT'S BETTER. UP ABOVE MILLENNIUM CITY'S SHIFTING NANO-STRUCTURES I CAN SEE WHAT'S GOING ON.
PNEUMAN, REPORT: HOW ARE YOU AND AUGUSTUS HOLDING OUT AGAINST THE ENEMY?
Reinforcements would be most welcome, Mistress Tesla. THIS hominid HOODLUM is providing little useful assistance, as EVER.
TZUU! TZUU!
Like, you're steppin' on my PRIDE, Clyde!
Geritol-Jockeys like you an' my POP oughtta split back to CUBESVILLE and leave things to the NOW generation, Daddy-O!
ENOUGH! I AM TIRED OF WASTING MY TIME WITH CLOCKWORK TOYS AND SUB-HUMANS!
Indeed? Like the youthful Free Spirit up there GAMMA-BLASTING us, perhaps? My dear friend, your FATHER, would SCOFF at such nonsense!
VAMM!
VAMM!
VAMM!
MAN! Dig that crazy POPGUN! This is one heavy SCENE!
WHERE IS THE OLD FOOL THAT I HAVE COME TO DESTROY? WHERE IS MY BELOVED FATHER?
I'M AFRAID DAD COULDN'T MAKE THE FAMILY REUNION JUST YET, ALBRECHT...

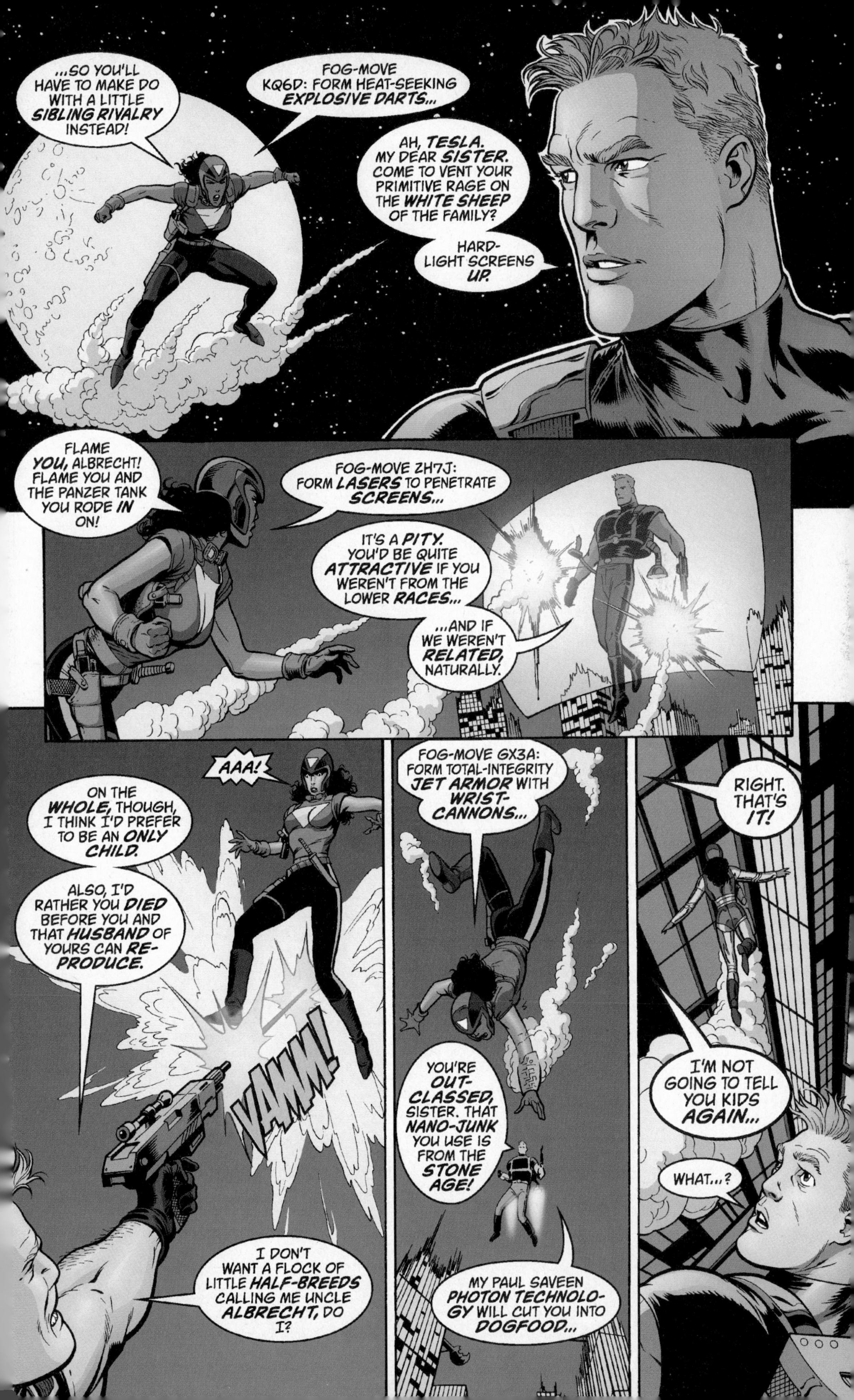
...SO YOU'LL HAVE TO MAKE DO WITH A LITTLE SIBLING RIVALRY INSTEAD!
FOG-MOVE KQ6D: FORM HEAT-SEEKING EXPLOSIVE DARTS...
AH, TESLA. MY DEAR SISTER. COME TO VENT YOUR PRIMITIVE RAGE ON THE WHITE SHEEP OF THE FAMILY?
HARD-LIGHT SCREENS UP.
FLAME YOU, ALBRECHT! FLAME YOU AND THE PANZER TANK YOU RODE IN ON!
FOG-MOVE ZH7J: FORM LASERS TO PENETRATE SCREENS...
IT'S A PITY. YOU'D BE QUITE ATTRACTIVE IF YOU WEREN'T FROM THE LOWER RACES...
...AND IF WE WEREN'T RELATED, NATURALLY.
AAA!
ON THE WHOLE, THOUGH, I THINK I'D PREFER TO BE AN ONLY CHILD.
ALSO, I'D RATHER YOU DIED BEFORE YOU AND THAT HUSBAND OF YOURS CAN RE-PRODUCE.
VAMM!
I DON'T WANT A FLOCK OF LITTLE HALF-BREEDS CALLING ME UNCLE ALBRECHT, DO I?
FOG-MOVE GX3A: FORM TOTAL-INTEGRITY JET ARMOR WITH WRIST-CANNONS...
YOU'RE OUT-CLASSED, SISTER. THAT NANO-JUNK YOU USE IS FROM THE STONE AGE!
MY PAUL SAVEEN PHOTON TECHNOLOGY WILL CUT YOU INTO DOGFOOD...
RIGHT. THAT'S IT!
I'M NOT GOING TO TELL YOU KIDS AGAIN...
WHAT...?

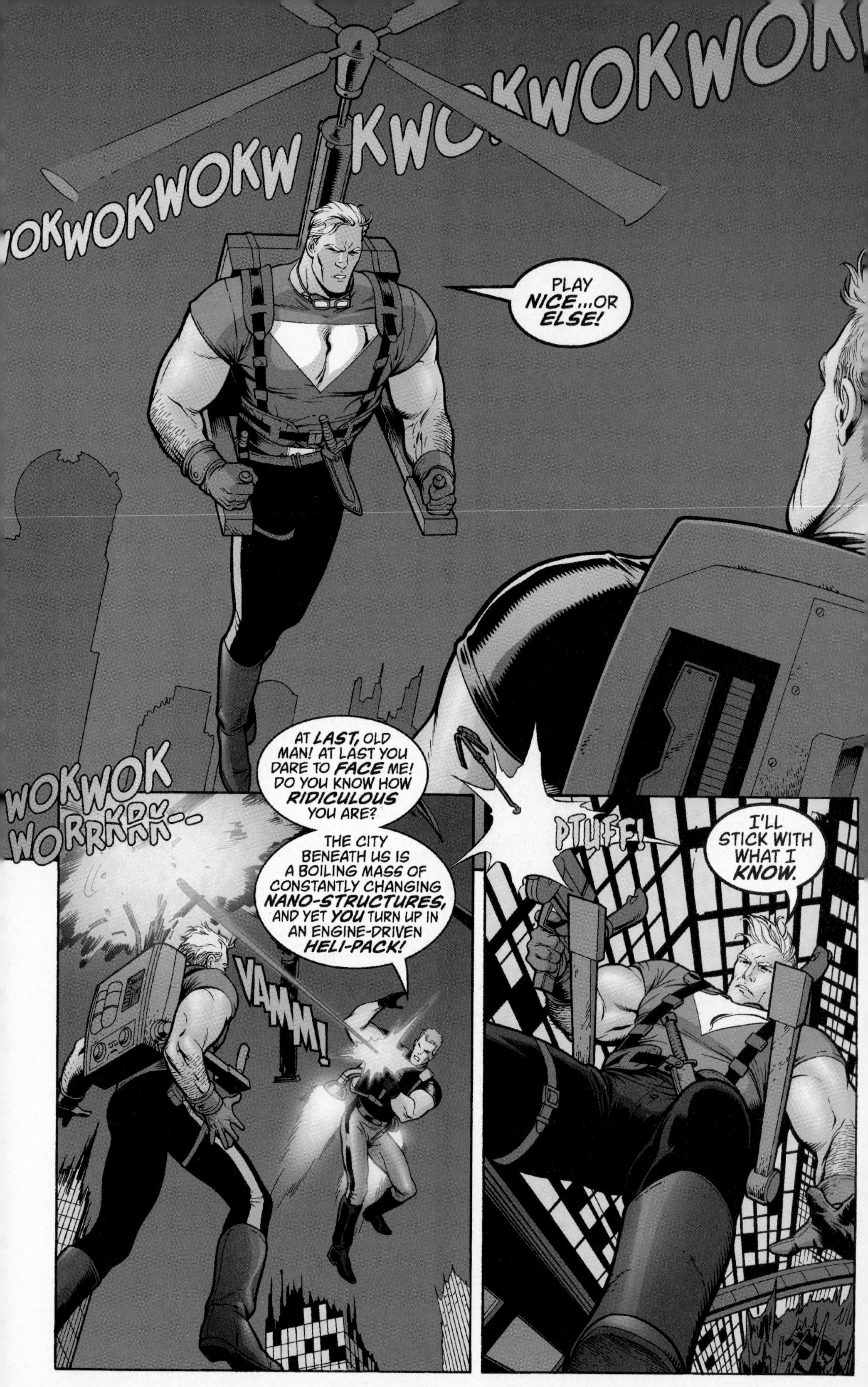
WOKWOKWOKW KWOKWOKWOK
PLAY NICE...OR ELSE!
WOKWOK WORRRKRK--
AT LAST, OLD MAN! AT LAST YOU DARE TO FACE ME! DO YOU KNOW HOW RIDICULOUS YOU ARE?
THE CITY BENEATH US IS A BOILING MASS OF CONSTANTLY CHANGING NANO-STRUCTURES, AND YET YOU TURN UP IN AN ENGINE-DRIVEN HELI-PACK!
VAMM!
PTUFF!
I'LL STICK WITH WHAT I KNOW.

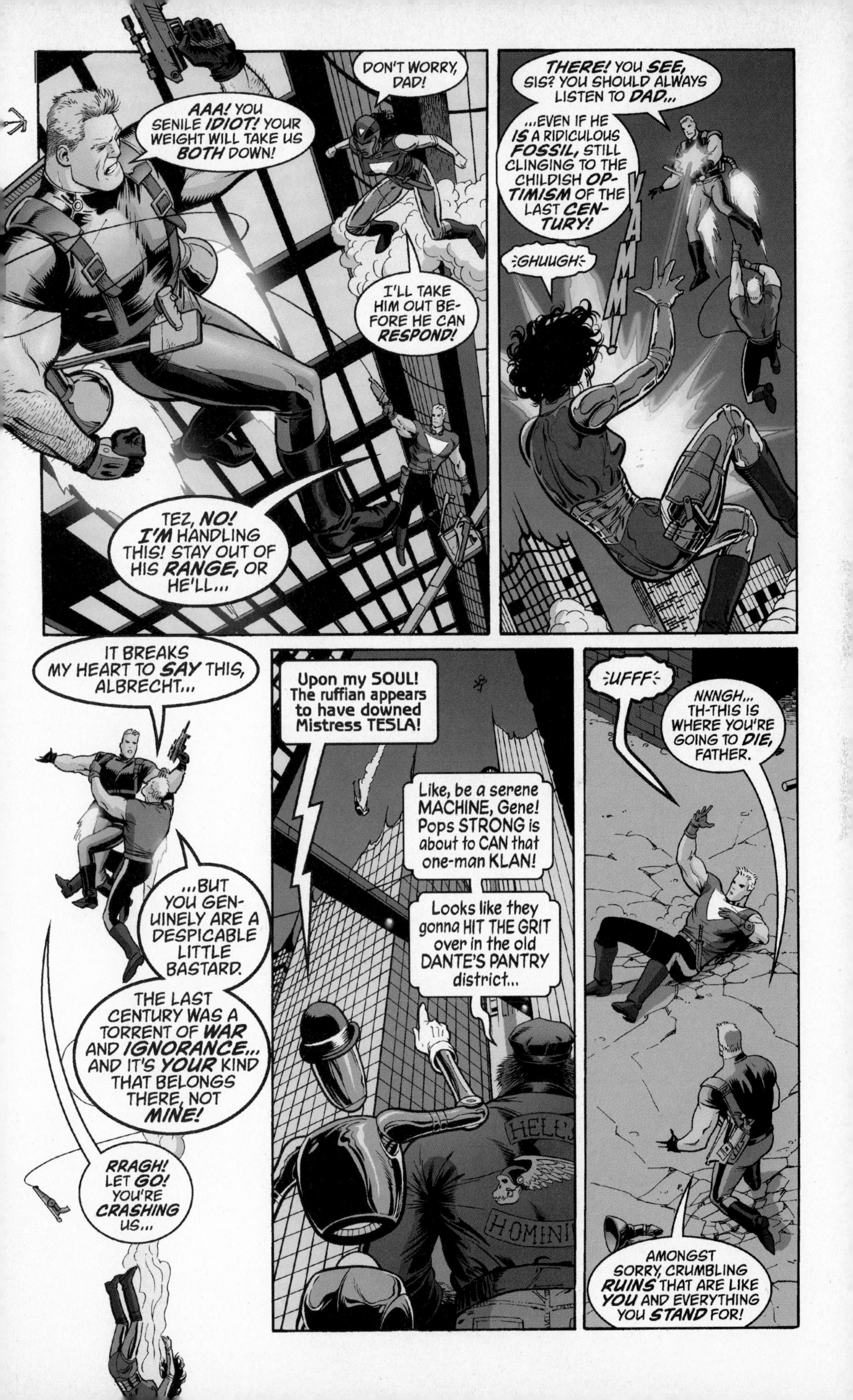
DON'T WORRY, DAD!
AAA! YOU SENILE IDIOT! YOUR WEIGHT WILL TAKE US BOTH DOWN!
I'LL TAKE HIM OUT BEFORE HE CAN RESPOND!
TEZ, NO! I'M HANDLING THIS! STAY OUT OF HIS RANGE, OR HE'LL...
THERE! YOU SEE, SIS? YOU SHOULD ALWAYS LISTEN TO DAD...
...EVEN IF HE IS A RIDICULOUS FOSSIL, STILL CLINGING TO THE CHILDISH OPTIMISM OF THE LAST CENTURY!
VLAMM
GHUUGH
IT BREAKS MY HEART TO SAY THIS, ALBRECHT...
...BUT YOU GENUINELY ARE A DESPICABLE LITTLE BASTARD.
THE LAST CENTURY WAS A TORRENT OF WAR AND IGNORANCE... AND IT'S YOUR KIND THAT BELONGS THERE, NOT MINE!
RRAGH! LET GO! YOU'RE CRASHING US...
Upon my SOUL! The ruffian appears to have downed Mistress TESLA!
Like, be a serene MACHINE, Gene! Pops STRONG is about to CAN that one-man KLAN!
Looks like they gonna HIT THE GRIT over in the old DANTE'S PANTRY district...
HELL'S
HOMINI
UFFF
NNNGH... TH-THIS IS WHERE YOU'RE GOING TO DIE, FATHER.
AMONGST SORRY, CRUMBLING RUINS THAT ARE LIKE YOU AND EVERYTHING YOU STAND FOR!

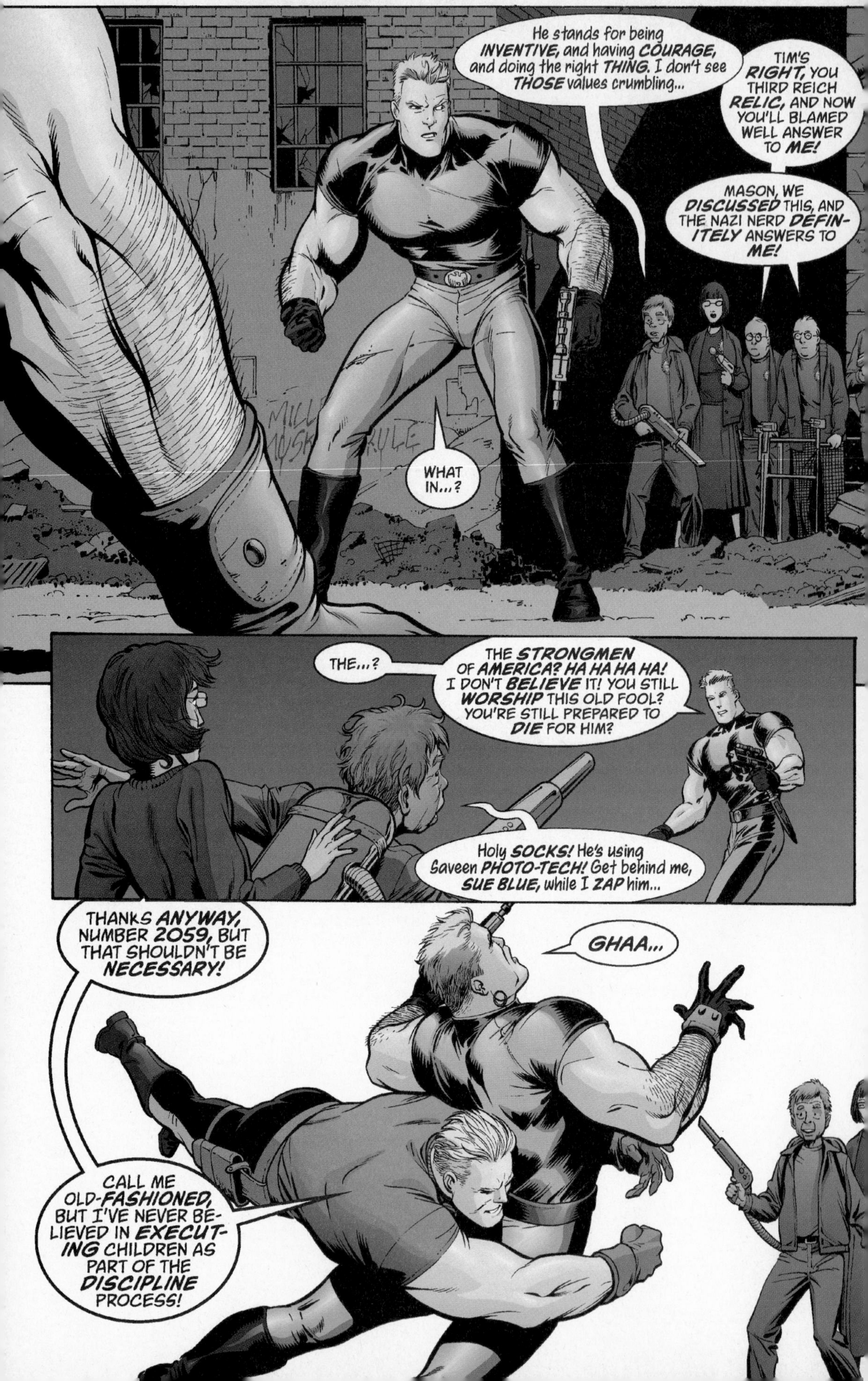
He stands for being INVENTIVE, and having COURAGE, and doing the right THING. I don't see THOSE values crumbling...
TIM'S RIGHT, YOU THIRD REICH RELIC, AND NOW YOU'LL BLAMED WELL ANSWER TO ME!
MASON, WE DISCUSSED THIS, AND THE NAZI NERD DEFIN-ITELY ANSWERS TO ME!
MILL MUSK RULE
WHAT IN...?
THE...?
THE STRONGMEN OF AMERICA? HA HA HA HA! I DON'T BELIEVE IT! YOU STILL WORSHIP THIS OLD FOOL? YOU'RE STILL PREPARED TO DIE FOR HIM?
Holy SOCKS! He's using Saveen PHOTO-TECH! Get behind me, SUE BLUE, while I ZAP him...
THANKS ANYWAY, NUMBER 2059, BUT THAT SHOULDN'T BE NECESSARY!
GHAA...
CALL ME OLD-FASHIONED, BUT I'VE NEVER BE-LIEVED IN EXECUT-ING CHILDREN AS PART OF THE DISCIPLINE PROCESS!

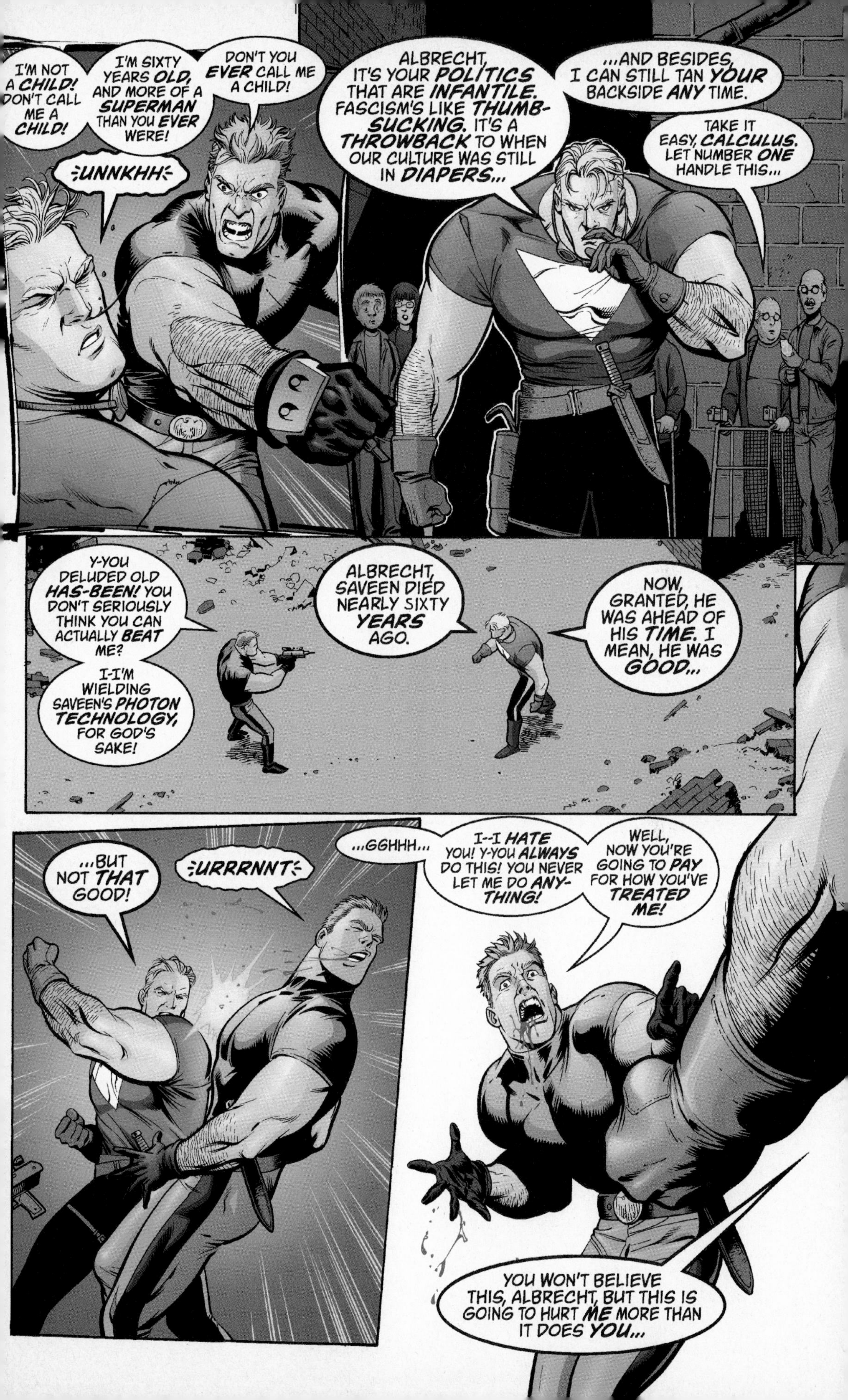
I'M NOT A CHILD! DON'T CALL ME A CHILD!
I'M SIXTY YEARS OLD, AND MORE OF A SUPERMAN THAN YOU EVER WERE!
DON'T YOU EVER CALL ME A CHILD!
UNNKHH
ALBRECHT, IT'S YOUR POLITICS THAT ARE INFANTILE. FASCISM'S LIKE THUMB-SUCKING. IT'S A THROWBACK TO WHEN OUR CULTURE WAS STILL IN DIAPERS...
...AND BESIDES, I CAN STILL TAN YOUR BACKSIDE ANY TIME.
TAKE IT EASY, CALCULUS. LET NUMBER ONE HANDLE THIS...
Y-YOU DELUDED OLD HAS-BEEN! YOU DON'T SERIOUSLY THINK YOU CAN ACTUALLY BEAT ME?
I-I'M WIELDING SAVEEN'S PHOTON TECHNOLOGY, FOR GOD'S SAKE!
ALBRECHT, SAVEEN DIED NEARLY SIXTY YEARS AGO.
NOW, GRANTED, HE WAS AHEAD OF HIS TIME. I MEAN, HE WAS GOOD...
...BUT NOT THAT GOOD!
URRRNNT
...GGHHH...
I--I HATE YOU! Y-YOU ALWAYS DO THIS! YOU NEVER LET ME DO ANY-THING!
WELL, NOW YOU'RE GOING TO PAY FOR HOW YOU'VE TREATED ME!
YOU WON'T BELIEVE THIS, ALBRECHT, BUT THIS IS GOING TO HURT ME MORE THAN IT DOES YOU...

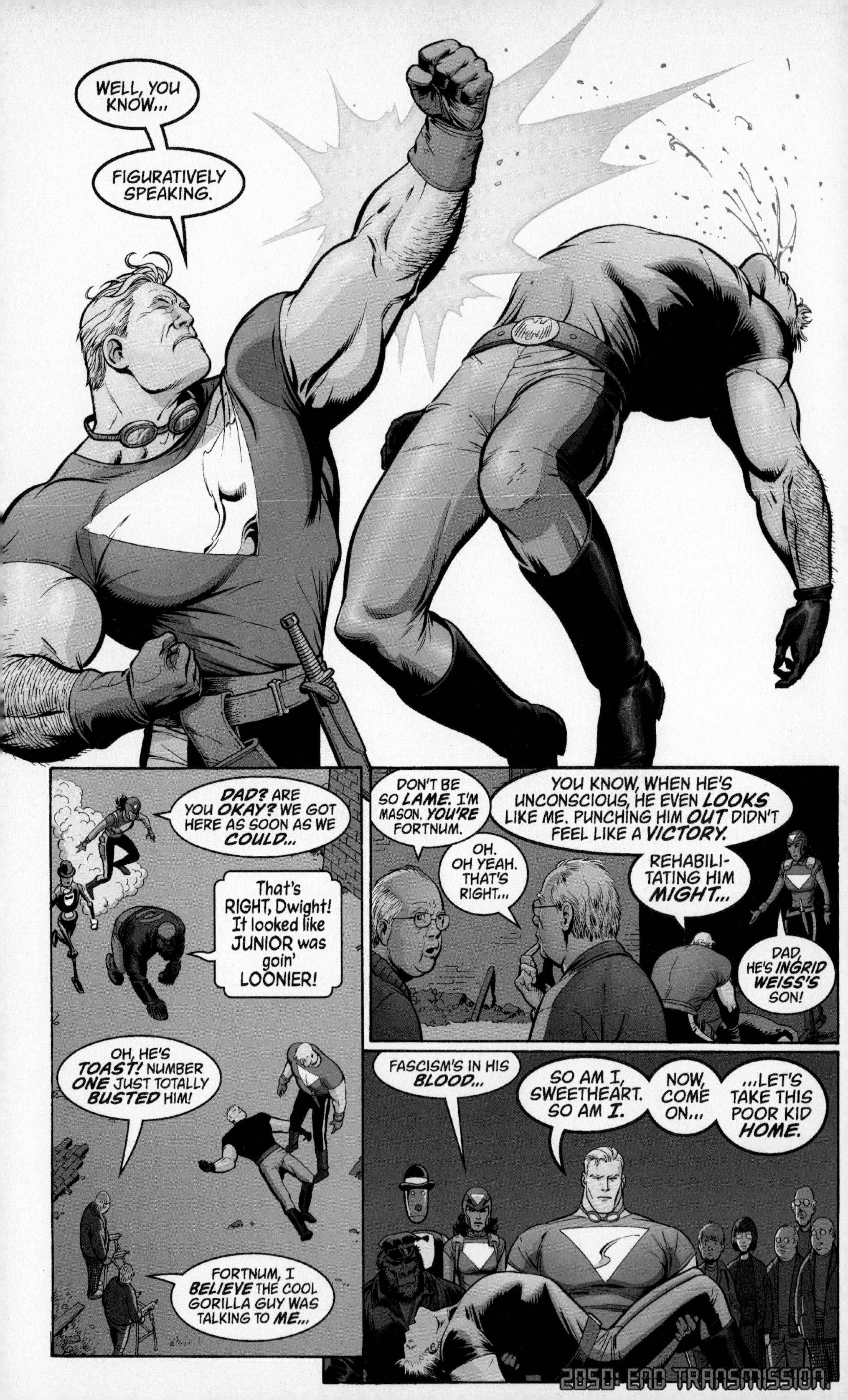

WELL, YOU KNOW...
FIGURATIVELY SPEAKING.
DAD? ARE YOU OKAY? WE GOT HERE AS SOON AS WE COULD...
That's RIGHT, Dwight! It looked like JUNIOR was goin' LOONIER!
DON'T BE SO LAME. I'M MASON. YOU'RE FORTNUM.
OH. OH YEAH. THAT'S RIGHT...
YOU KNOW, WHEN HE'S UNCONSCIOUS, HE EVEN LOOKS LIKE ME. PUNCHING HIM OUT DIDN'T FEEL LIKE A VICTORY.
REHABILITATING HIM MIGHT...
DAD, HE'S INGRID WEISS'S SON!
OH, HE'S TOAST! NUMBER ONE JUST TOTALLY BUSTED HIM!
FORTNUM, I BELIEVE THE COOL GORILLA GUY WAS TALKING TO ME...
FASCISM'S IN HIS BLOOD...
SO AM I, SWEETHEART. SO AM I.
NOW, COME ON...
...LET'S TAKE THIS POOR KID HOME.
2050: END TRANSMISSION.

NO! I WILL NOT STAND FOR IT!

I WILL NOT BE PITIED BY YOU!

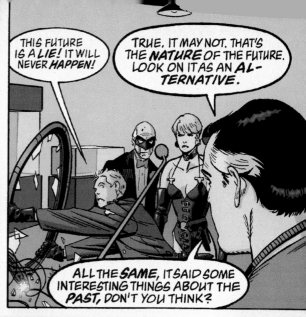

THIS FUTURE IS A LIE! IT WILL NEVER HAPPEN!

TRUE, IT MAY NOT. THAT'S THE NATURE OF THE FUTURE. LOOK ON IT AS AN ALTERNATIVE.

ALL THE SAME, IT SAID SOME INTERESTING THINGS ABOUT THE PAST, DON'T YOU THINK?

WH-WHAT ARE YOU SAYING?

I'M SAYING THAT THE FUTURE OF 2050 SEEMS TO THINK THAT SAVEEN HAS BEEN DEAD FOR NEARLY SIXTY YEARS.

THAT WOULD MAKE THE DATE OF DEATH... LET'S SEE. SOMEWHERE AROUND 1992? CORRECT ME IF I'M WRONG, SAVEEN.

I MEAN, YOU NEVER DID EXPLAIN THE FAKED DEATH IN AFRICA; THE SKELETON IDENTIFIED BY DENTAL RECORDS...

UHH...

EARTHQUAKE BOOTS

HERR SAVEEN? WH-WHAT DOES HE MEAN?

NOTHING. IGNORE HIM.

TOM, MY DEAR CHAP, THAT BODY WAS A CLONE. OTHERWISE I COULDN'T BE HERE, COULD I?

GOOD POINT. I'LL BE GETTING TO THAT IN A MOMENT.

SO, SAVEEN, THIS CLONE; IT SOUNDS INGENIOUS, EVEN FOR YOU. HOW DID YOU CLONE EVERY CHIPPED TOOTH? EVERY EXACT FILLING?

I..., UH...

LOOK, YOU CAN'T EXPECT ME TO REMEMBER EVERY DETAIL...

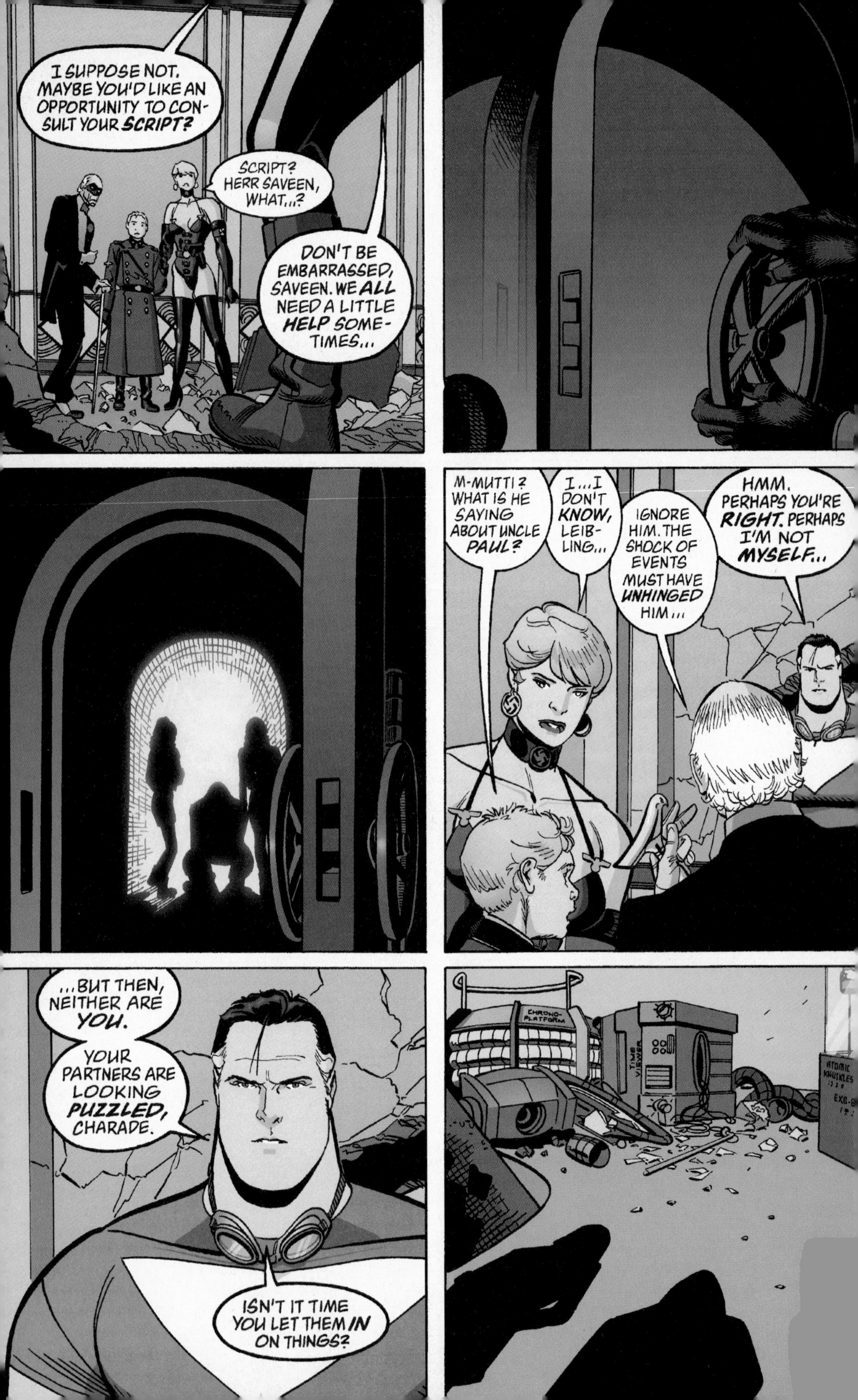
I SUPPOSE NOT. MAYBE YOU'D LIKE AN OPPORTUNITY TO CONSULT YOUR SCRIPT?
SCRIPT? HERR SAVEEN, WHAT...?
DON'T BE EMBARRASSED, SAVEEN. WE ALL NEED A LITTLE HELP SOMETIMES...
M-MUTTI? WHAT IS HE SAYING ABOUT UNCLE PAUL?
I...I DON'T KNOW, LEIBLING...
IGNORE HIM. THE SHOCK OF EVENTS MUST HAVE UNHINGED HIM...
HMM. PERHAPS YOU'RE RIGHT. PERHAPS I'M NOT MYSELF...
...BUT THEN, NEITHER ARE YOU.
YOUR PARTNERS ARE LOOKING PUZZLED, CHARADE.
ISN'T IT TIME YOU LET THEM IN ON THINGS?
CHRONO-PLATFORM
TIME VIEWER
ATOMIC KNUCKLES

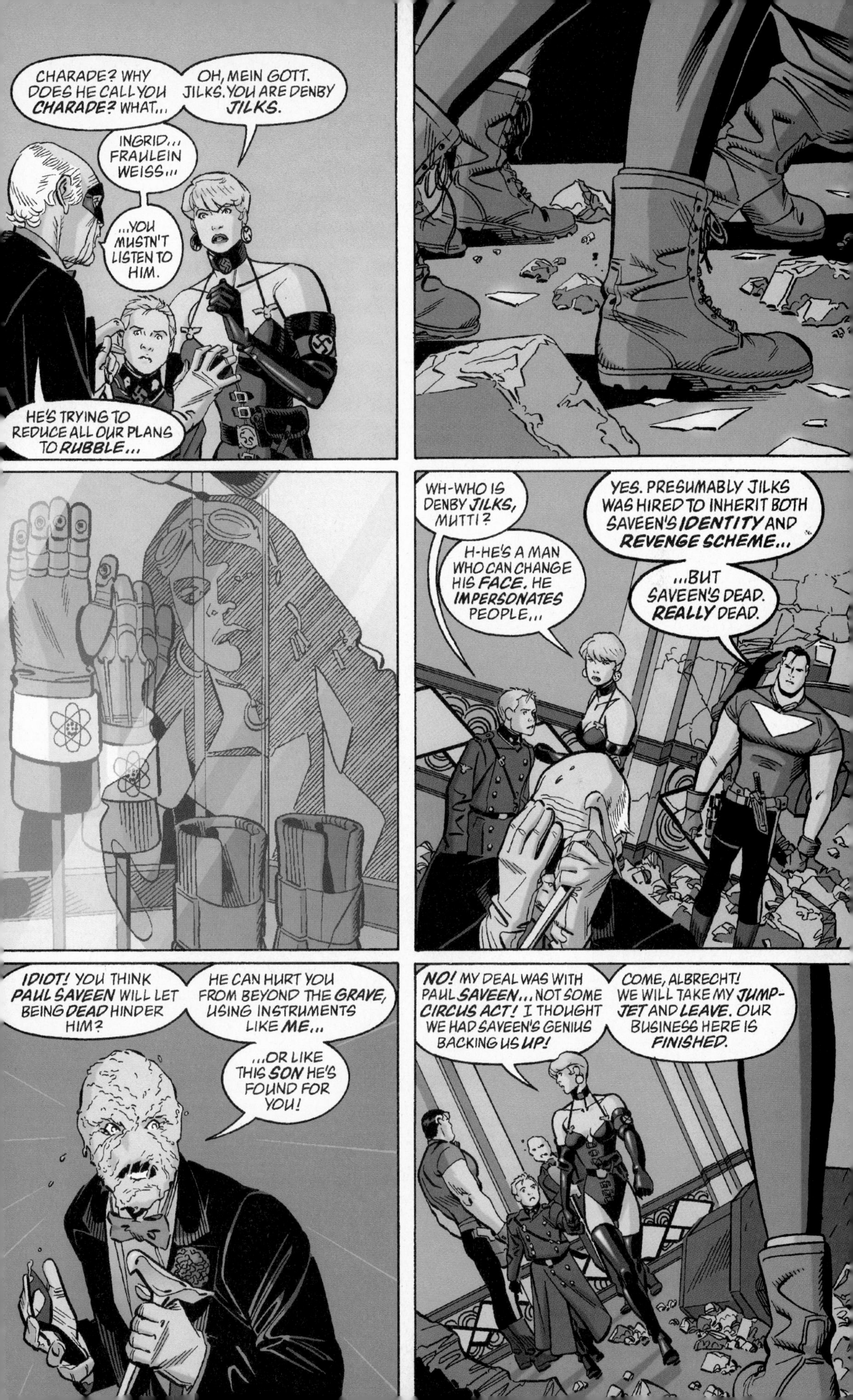
CHARADE? WHY DOES HE CALL YOU CHARADE? WHAT...
OH, MEIN GOTT. JILKS. YOU ARE DENBY JILKS.
INGRID... FRAULEIN WEISS...
...YOU MUSTN'T LISTEN TO HIM.
HE'S TRYING TO REDUCE ALL OUR PLANS TO RUBBLE...
WH-WHO IS DENBY JILKS, MUTTI?
H-HE'S A MAN WHO CAN CHANGE HIS FACE. HE IMPERSONATES PEOPLE...
YES. PRESUMABLY JILKS WAS HIRED TO INHERIT BOTH SAVEEN'S IDENTITY AND REVENGE SCHEME...
...BUT SAVEEN'S DEAD. REALLY DEAD.
IDIOT! YOU THINK PAUL SAVEEN WILL LET BEING DEAD HINDER HIM?
HE CAN HURT YOU FROM BEYOND THE GRAVE, USING INSTRUMENTS LIKE ME...
...OR LIKE THIS SON HE'S FOUND FOR YOU!
NO! MY DEAL WAS WITH PAUL SAVEEN... NOT SOME CIRCUS ACT! I THOUGHT WE HAD SAVEEN'S GENIUS BACKING US UP!
COME, ALBRECHT! WE WILL TAKE MY JUMP-JET AND LEAVE. OUR BUSINESS HERE IS FINISHED.

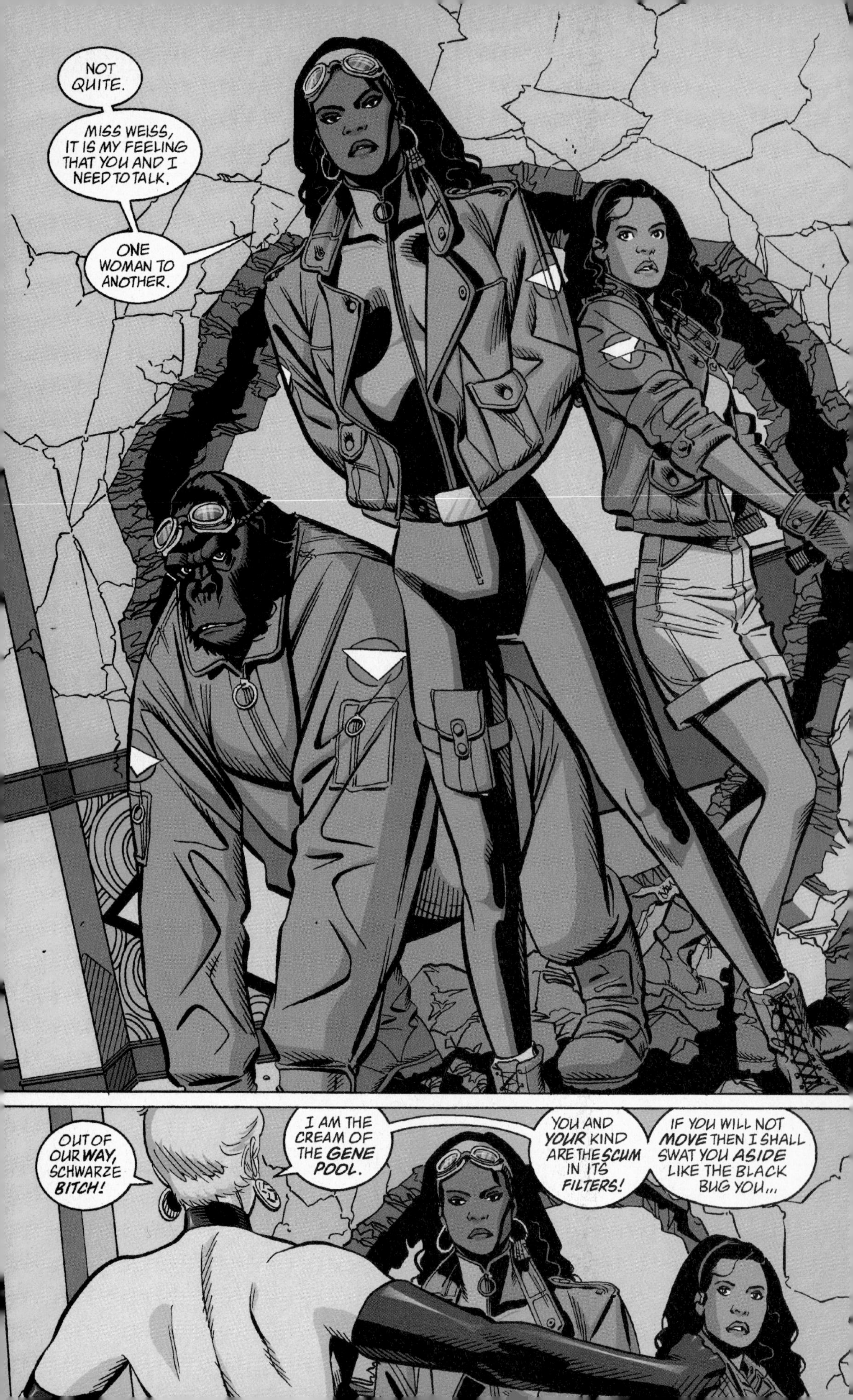
NOT QUITE.
MISS WEISS, IT IS MY FEELING THAT YOU AND I NEED TO TALK.
ONE WOMAN TO ANOTHER.
OUT OF OUR WAY, SCHWARZE BITCH!
I AM THE CREAM OF THE GENE POOL.
YOU AND YOUR KIND ARE THE SCUM IN ITS FILTERS!
IF YOU WILL NOT MOVE THEN I SHALL SWAT YOU ASIDE LIKE THE BLACK BUG YOU...

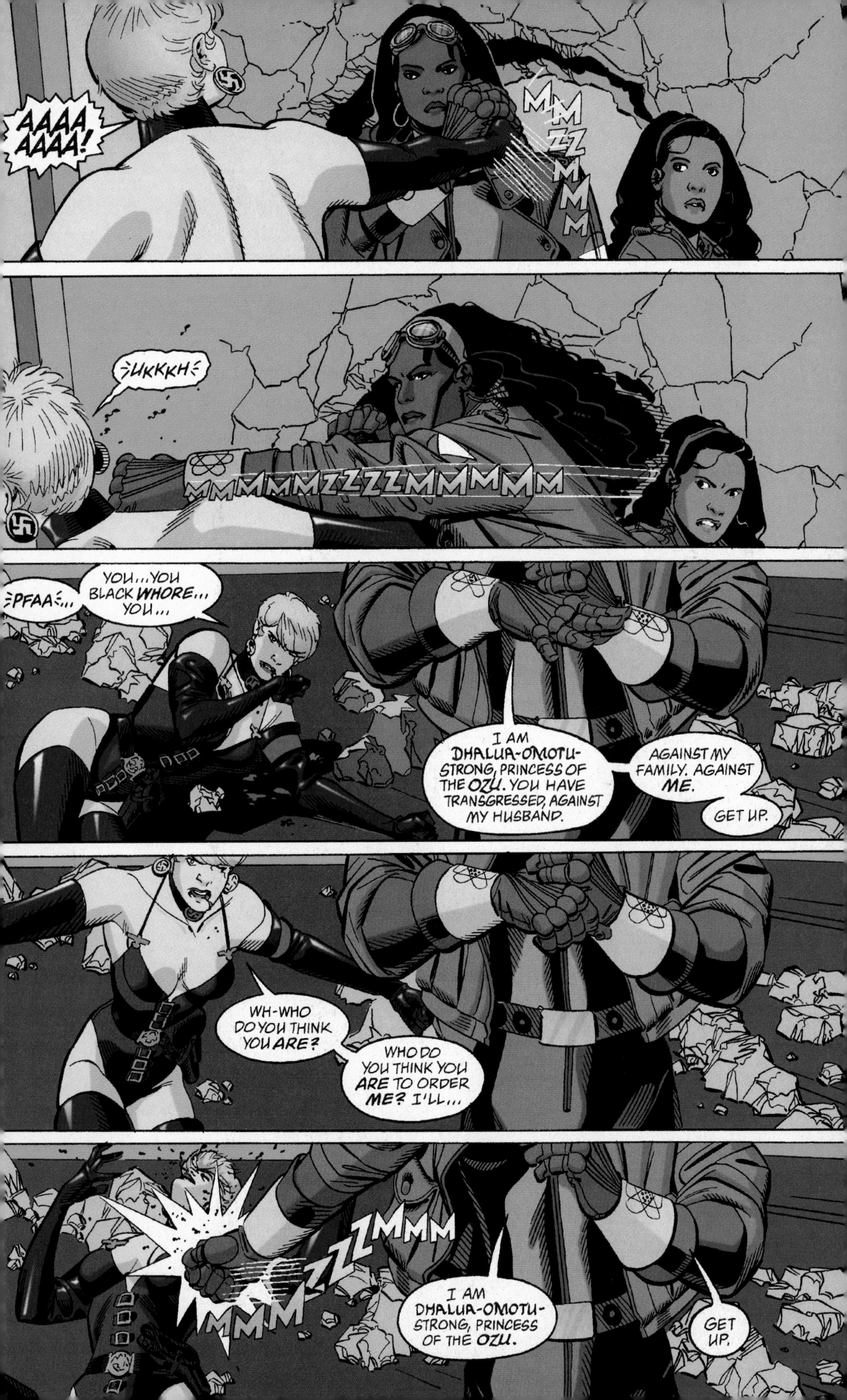

AAAA AAAA!
MMMZZMMM
UKKKH
MMMMMZZZZMMMMMM
PFAA...
YOU...YOU BLACK WHORE... YOU...
I AM DHALUA-OMOTU-STRONG, PRINCESS OF THE OZU. YOU HAVE TRANSGRESSED, AGAINST MY HUSBAND.
AGAINST MY FAMILY. AGAINST ME.
GET UP.
WH-WHO DO YOU THINK YOU ARE?
WHO DO YOU THINK YOU ARE TO ORDER ME? I'LL...
MMMZZZMMM
I AM DHALUA-OMOTU-STRONG, PRINCESS OF THE OZU.
GET UP.

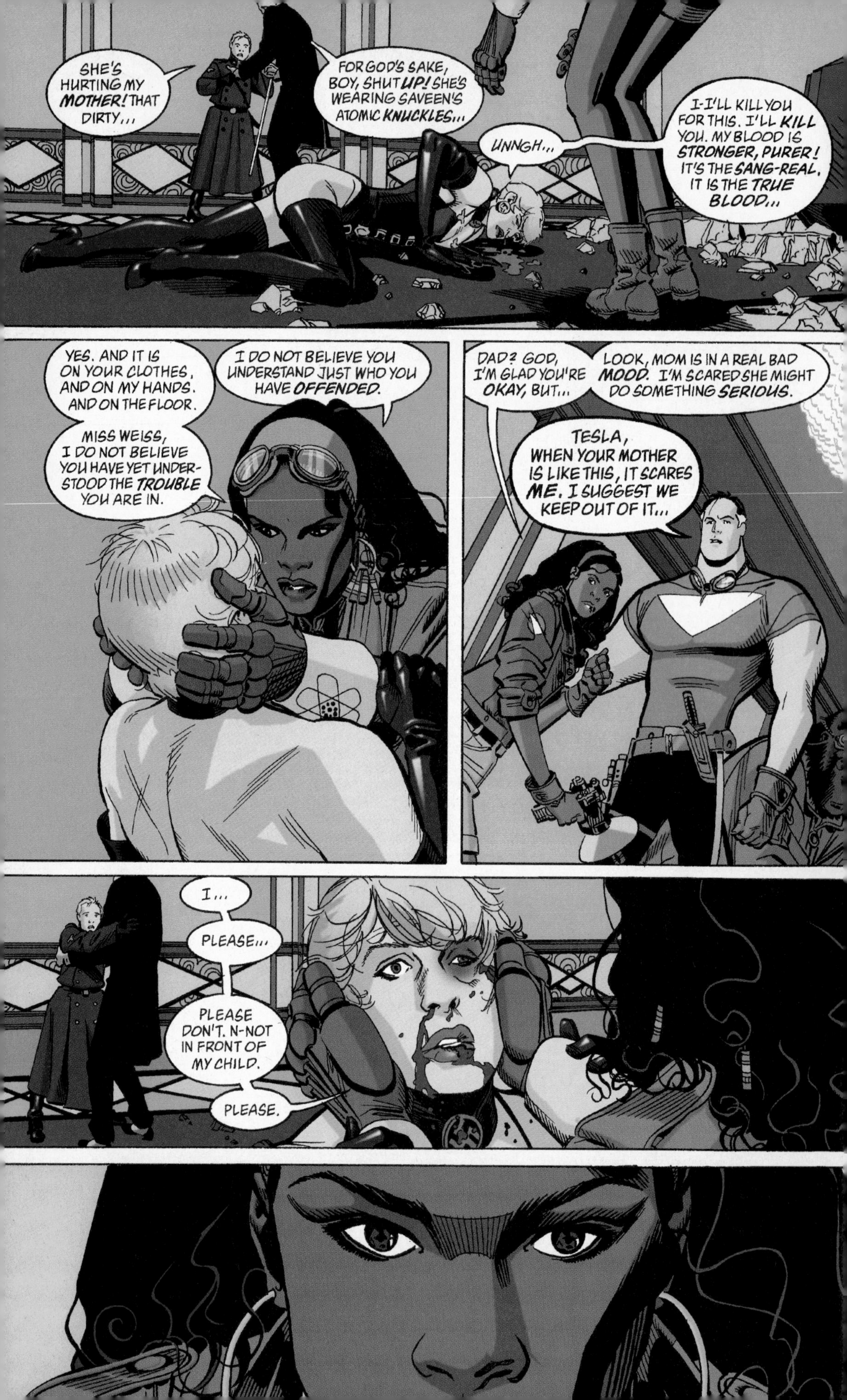
SHE'S HURTING MY MOTHER! THAT DIRTY...
FOR GOD'S SAKE, BOY, SHUT UP! SHE'S WEARING SAVEEN'S ATOMIC KNUCKLES...
UNNGH...
I-I'LL KILL YOU FOR THIS. I'LL KILL YOU. MY BLOOD IS STRONGER, PURER! IT'S THE SANG-REAL. IT IS THE TRUE BLOOD...
YES. AND IT IS ON YOUR CLOTHES, AND ON MY HANDS. AND ON THE FLOOR.
I DO NOT BELIEVE YOU UNDERSTAND JUST WHO YOU HAVE OFFENDED.
MISS WEISS, I DO NOT BELIEVE YOU HAVE YET UNDERSTOOD THE TROUBLE YOU ARE IN.
DAD? GOD, I'M GLAD YOU'RE OKAY, BUT...
LOOK, MOM IS IN A REAL BAD MOOD. I'M SCARED SHE MIGHT DO SOMETHING SERIOUS.
TESLA, WHEN YOUR MOTHER IS LIKE THIS, IT SCARES ME. I SUGGEST WE KEEP OUT OF IT...
I...
PLEASE...
PLEASE DON'T. N-NOT IN FRONT OF MY CHILD.
PLEASE.

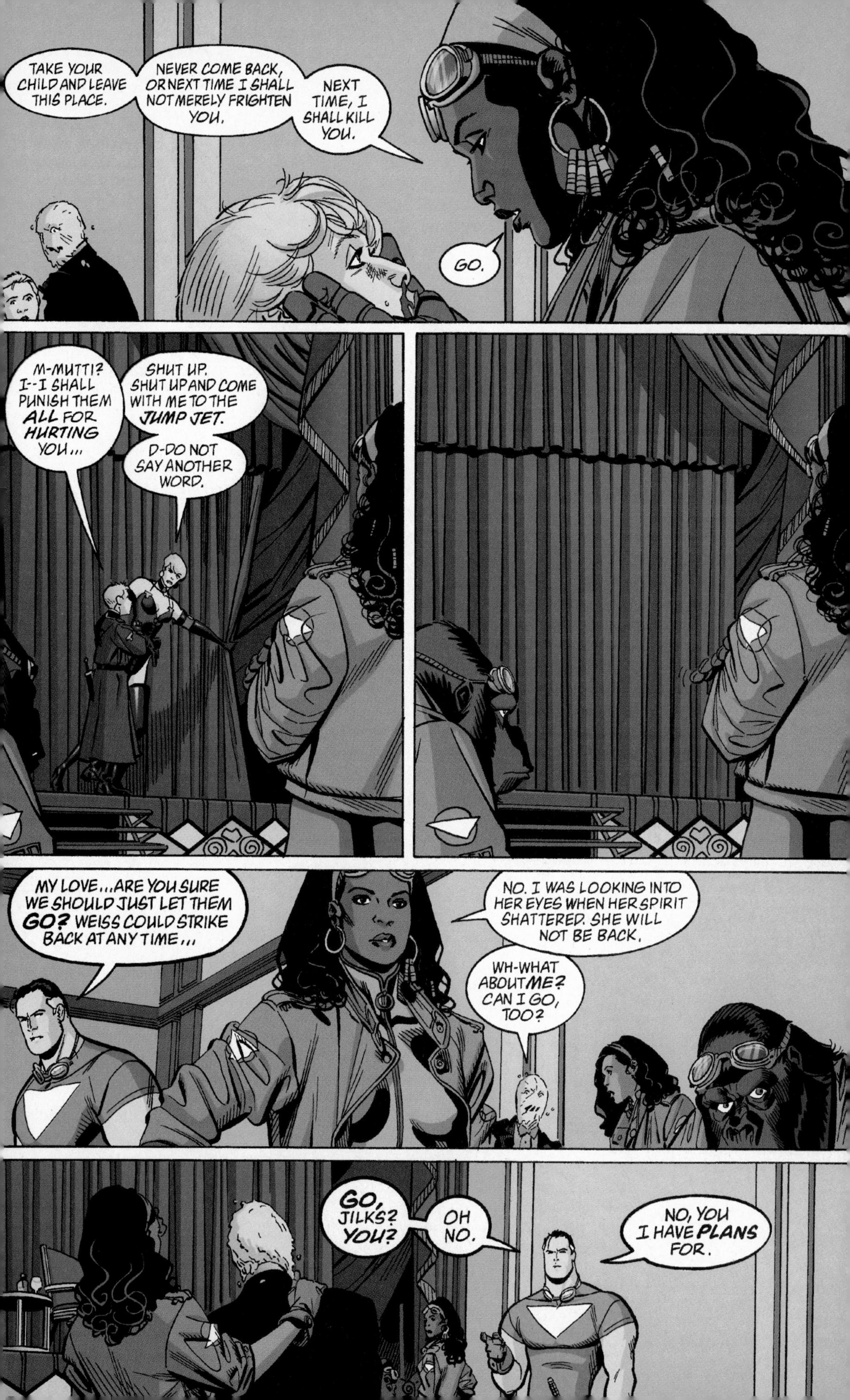
TAKE YOUR CHILD AND LEAVE THIS PLACE.
NEVER COME BACK, OR NEXT TIME I SHALL NOT MERELY FRIGHTEN YOU.
NEXT TIME, I SHALL KILL YOU.
GO.
M-MUTTI? I--I SHALL PUNISH THEM ALL FOR HURTING YOU...
SHUT UP. SHUT UP AND COME WITH ME TO THE JUMP JET.
D-DO NOT SAY ANOTHER WORD.
MY LOVE...ARE YOU SURE WE SHOULD JUST LET THEM GO? WEISS COULD STRIKE BACK AT ANY TIME...
NO. I WAS LOOKING INTO HER EYES WHEN HER SPIRIT SHATTERED. SHE WILL NOT BE BACK.
WH-WHAT ABOUT ME? CAN I GO, TOO?
GO, JILKS? YOU?
OH NO.
NO, YOU I HAVE PLANS FOR.

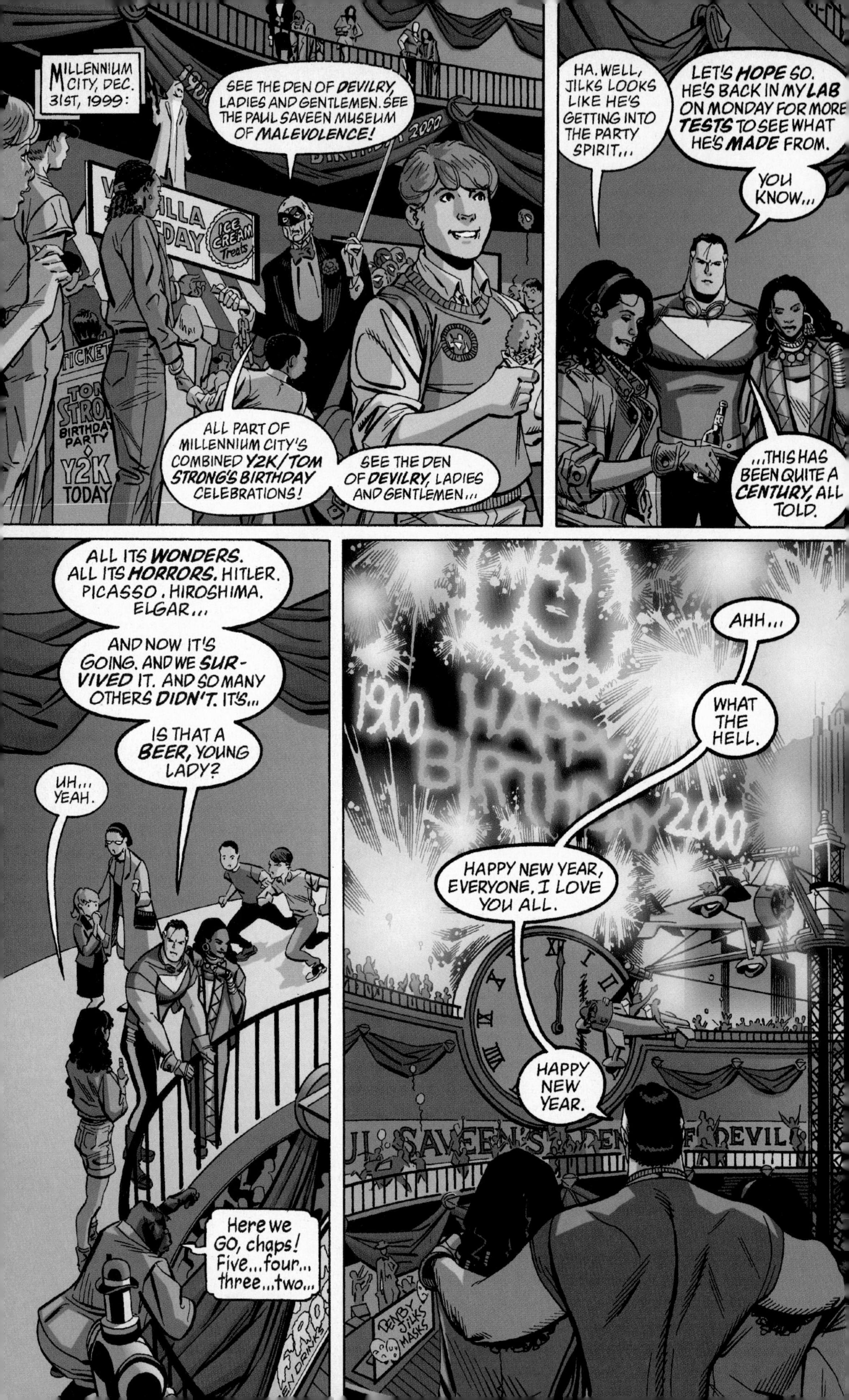
MILLENNIUM CITY, DEC. 31ST, 1999:
SEE THE DEN OF DEVILRY, LADIES AND GENTLEMEN. SEE THE PAUL SAVEEN MUSEUM OF MALEVOLENCE!
ALL PART OF MILLENNIUM CITY'S COMBINED Y2K/TOM STRONG'S BIRTHDAY CELEBRATIONS!
SEE THE DEN OF DEVILRY, LADIES AND GENTLEMEN...
TICKETS
TOM STRONG BIRTHDAY PARTY
Y2K TODAY
ICE CREAM Treats
HA. WELL, JILKS LOOKS LIKE HE'S GETTING INTO THE PARTY SPIRIT...
LET'S HOPE SO. HE'S BACK IN MY LAB ON MONDAY FOR MORE TESTS TO SEE WHAT HE'S MADE FROM.
YOU KNOW...
...THIS HAS BEEN QUITE A CENTURY, ALL TOLD.
ALL ITS WONDERS. ALL ITS HORRORS. HITLER. PICASSO. HIROSHIMA. ELGAR...
AND NOW IT'S GOING. AND WE SURVIVED IT. AND SO MANY OTHERS DIDN'T. IT'S...
IS THAT A BEER, YOUNG LADY?
UH... YEAH.
Here we GO, chaps! Five...four... three...two...
AHH...
WHAT THE HELL.
HAPPY NEW YEAR, EVERYONE. I LOVE YOU ALL.
HAPPY NEW YEAR.
1900
2000
DENBY JILKS MASKS

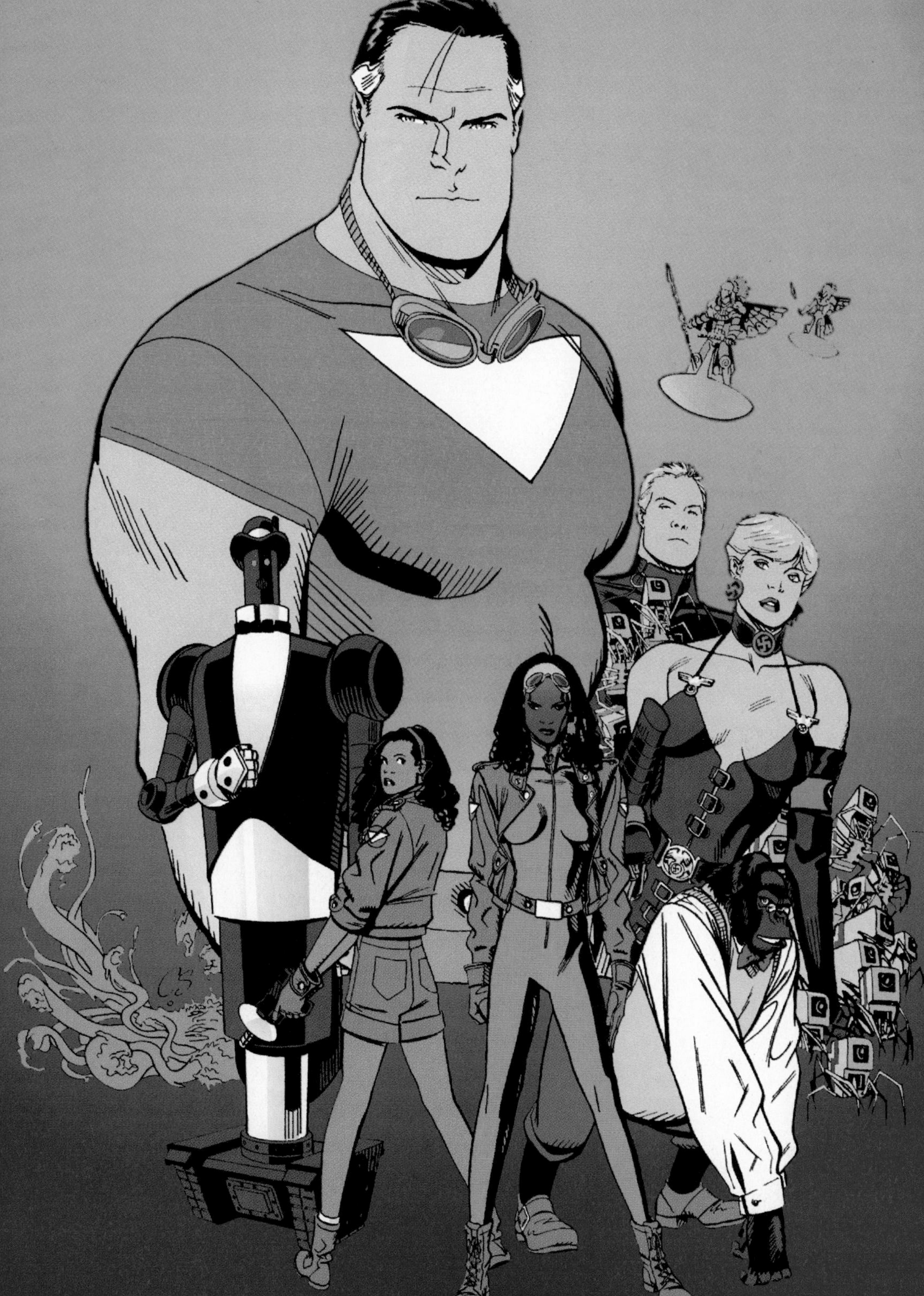

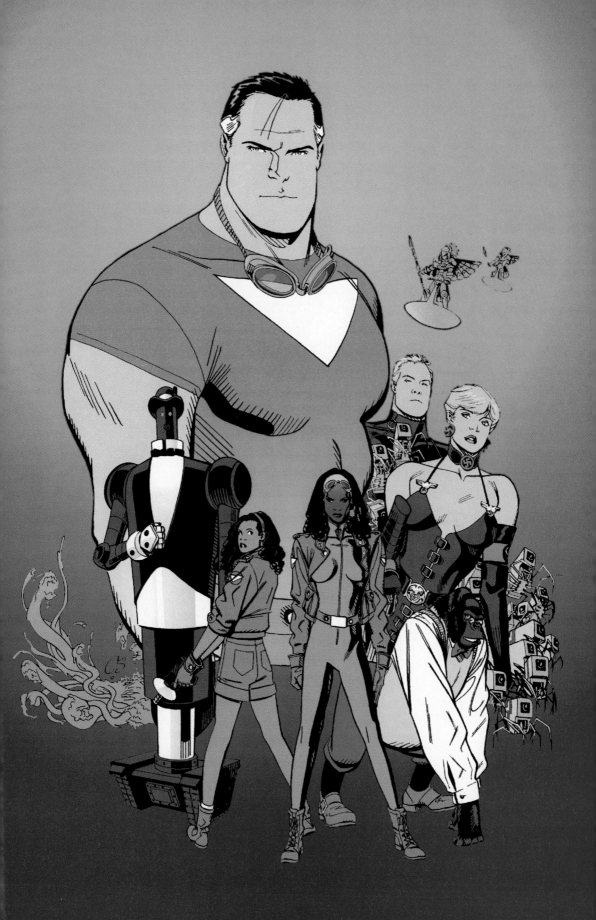

TOM STRONG GALLERY

Designs by CHRIS SPROUSE based on concepts by ALAN MOORE

Before beginning to draw the finished pages of TOM STRONG, Chris develops the characters and costumes in a series of design/model drawings, such as those included here and on the following pages.

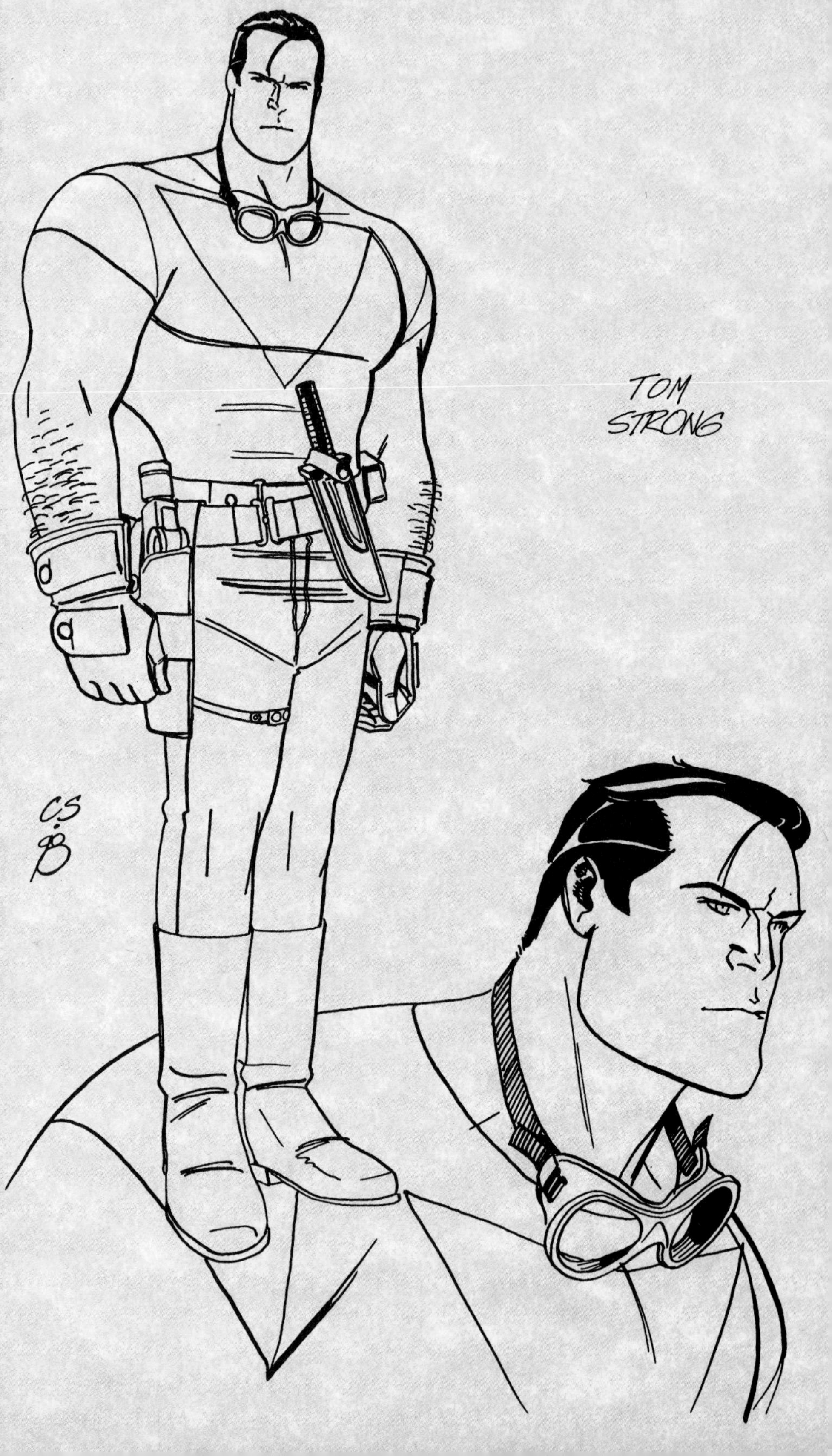
TOM STRONG

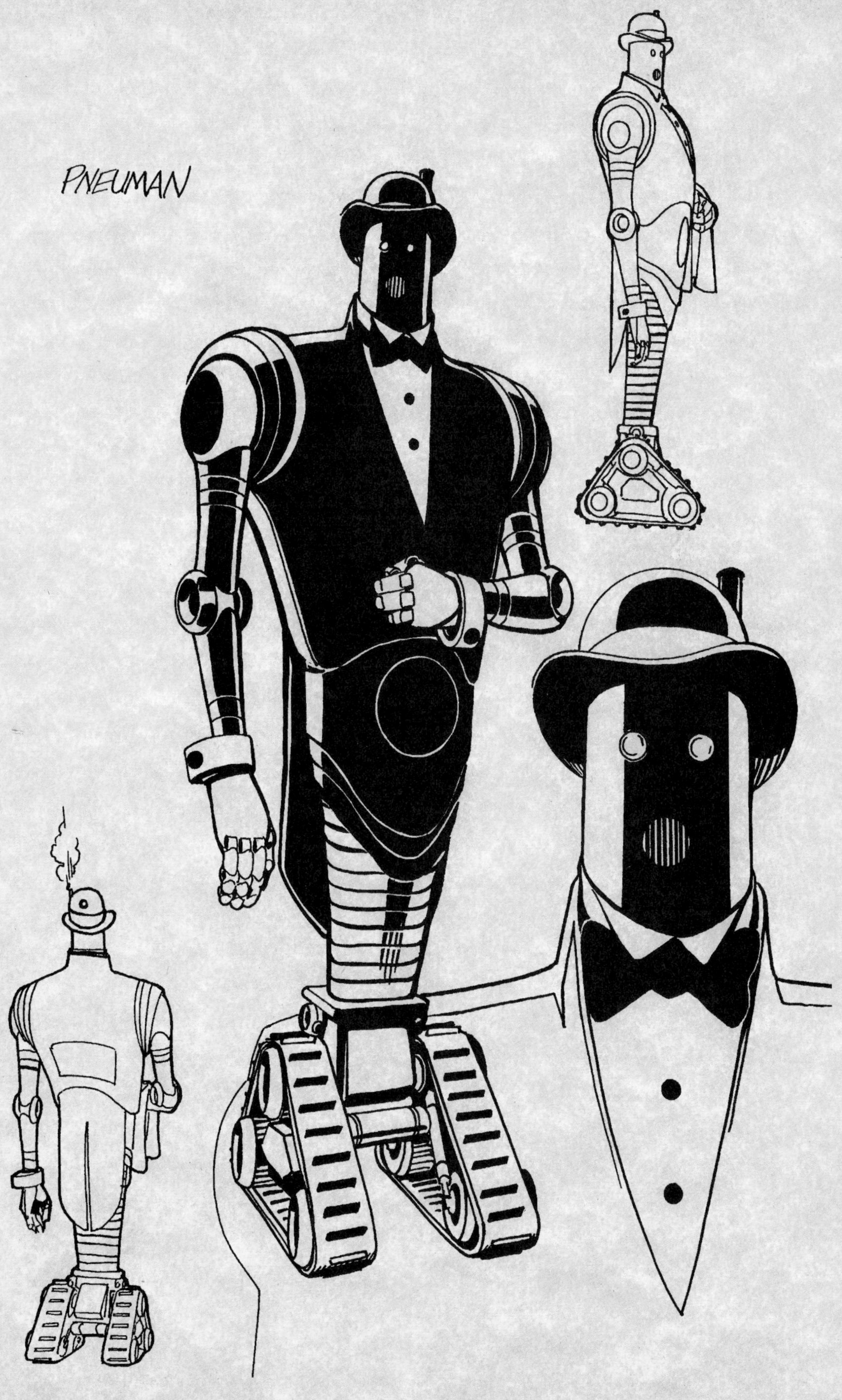
PNEUMAN

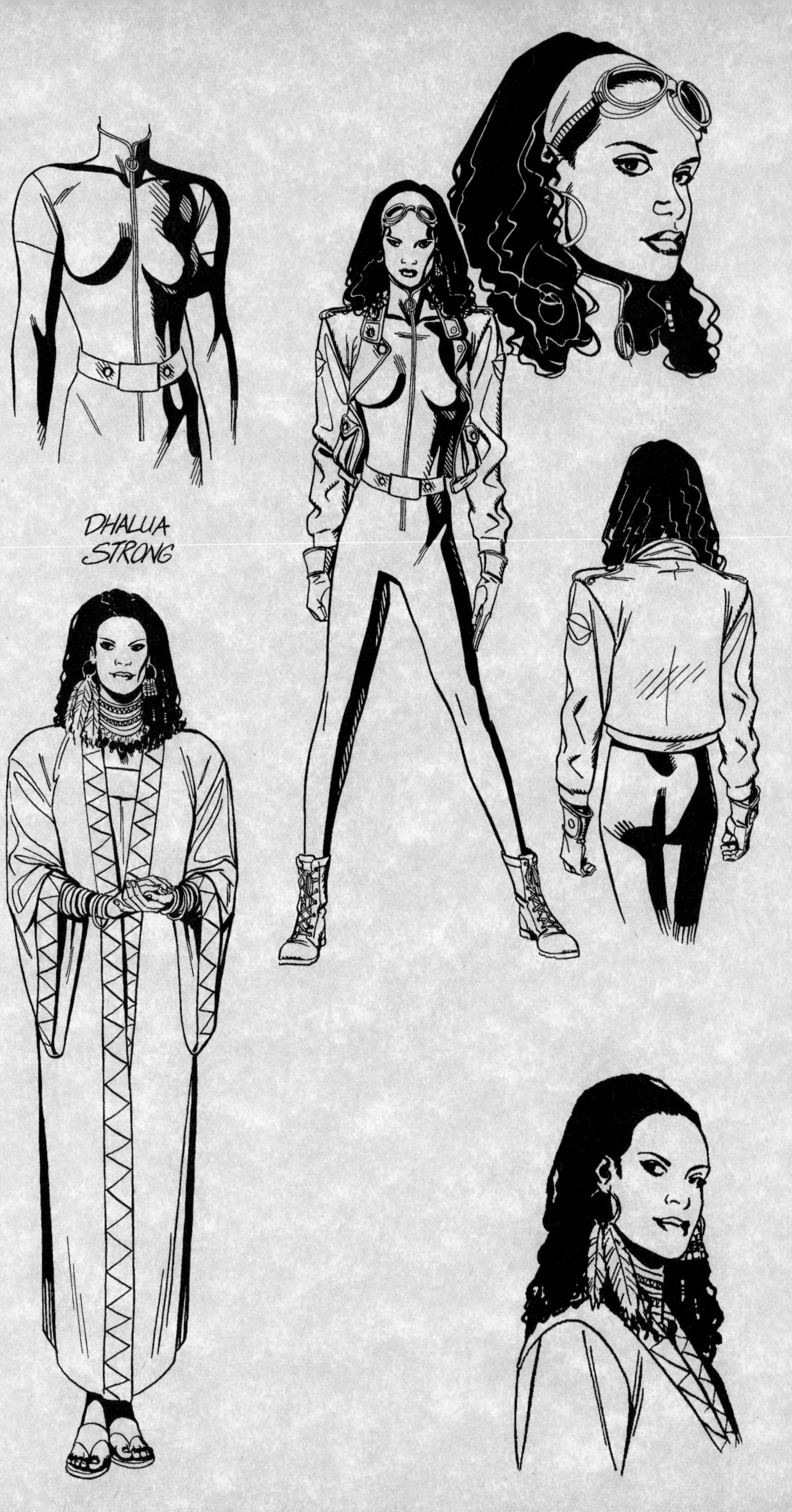
DHALUA
STRONG

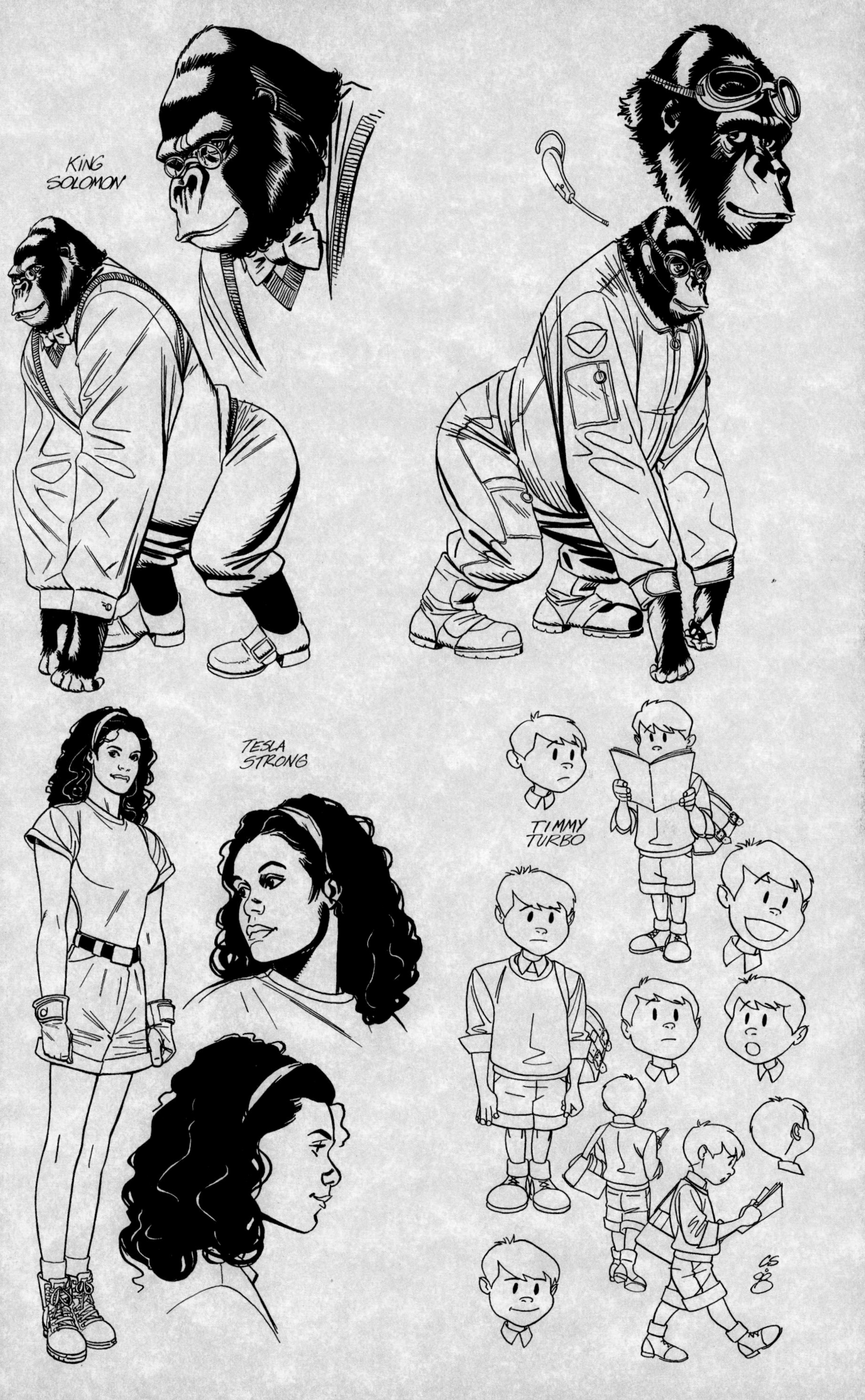
KING SOLOMON
TESLA STRONG
TIMMY TURBO
CS 98

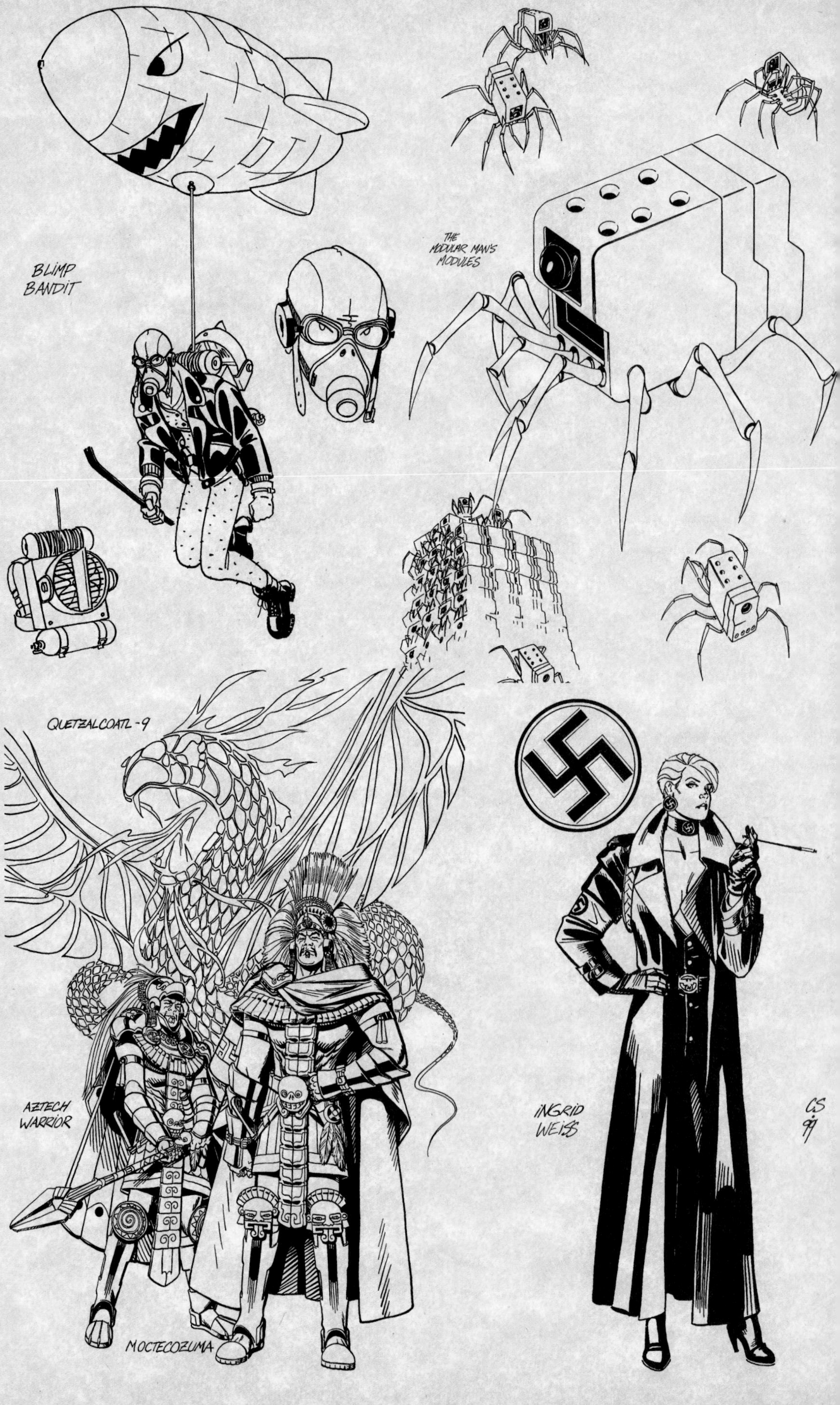
BLIMP BANDIT
THE MODULAR MAN'S MODULES
QUETZALCOATL-9
AZTECH WARRIOR
MOCTECOZUMA
INGRID WEISS
CS 99

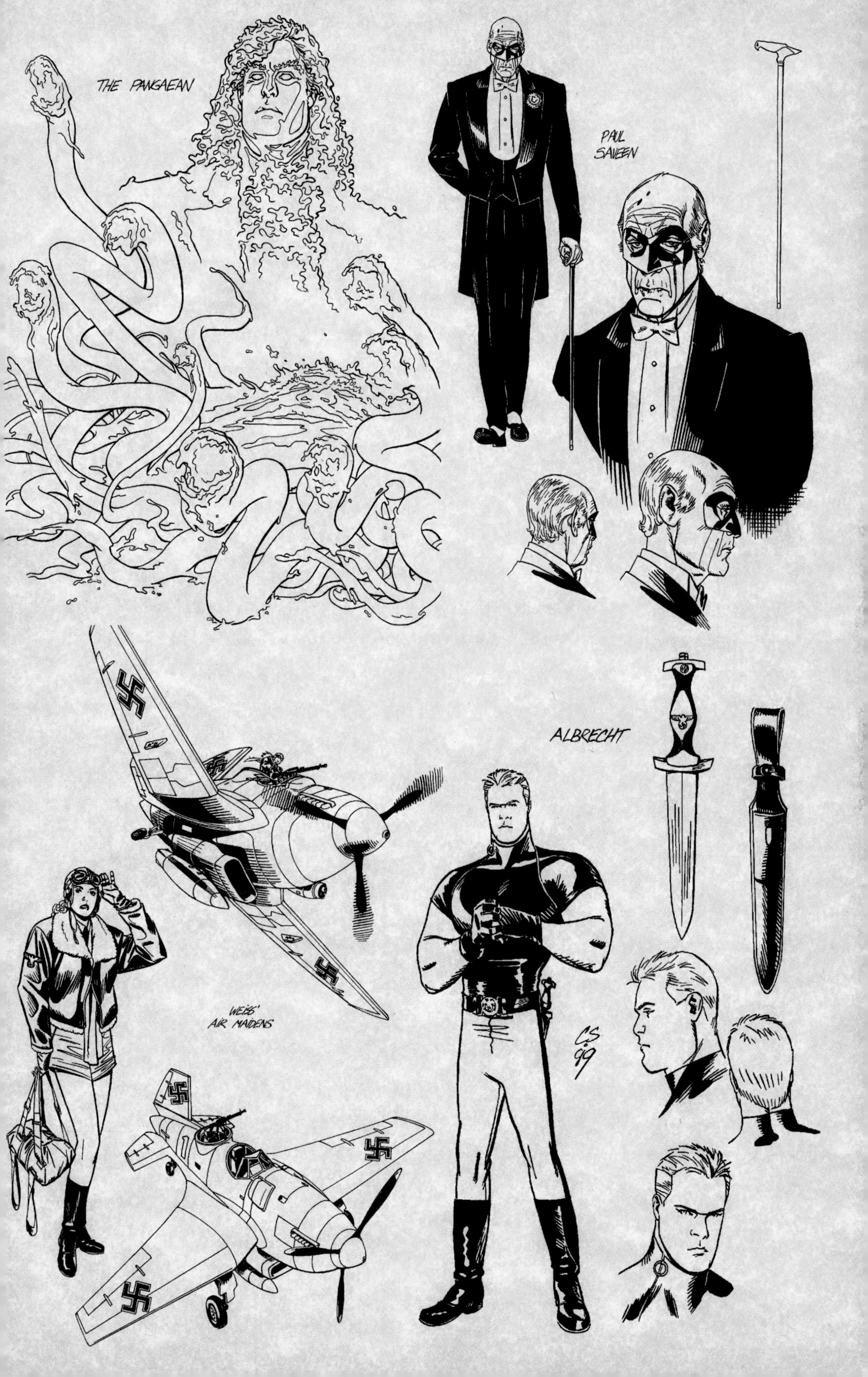
THE PANGAEAN
PAUL SAVEEN
ALBRECHT
WEISS' AIR MAIDENS
C.S. 99

Here are three more unpublished pieces by Chris for your enjoyment, including a variant on the Strongmen of America button art.

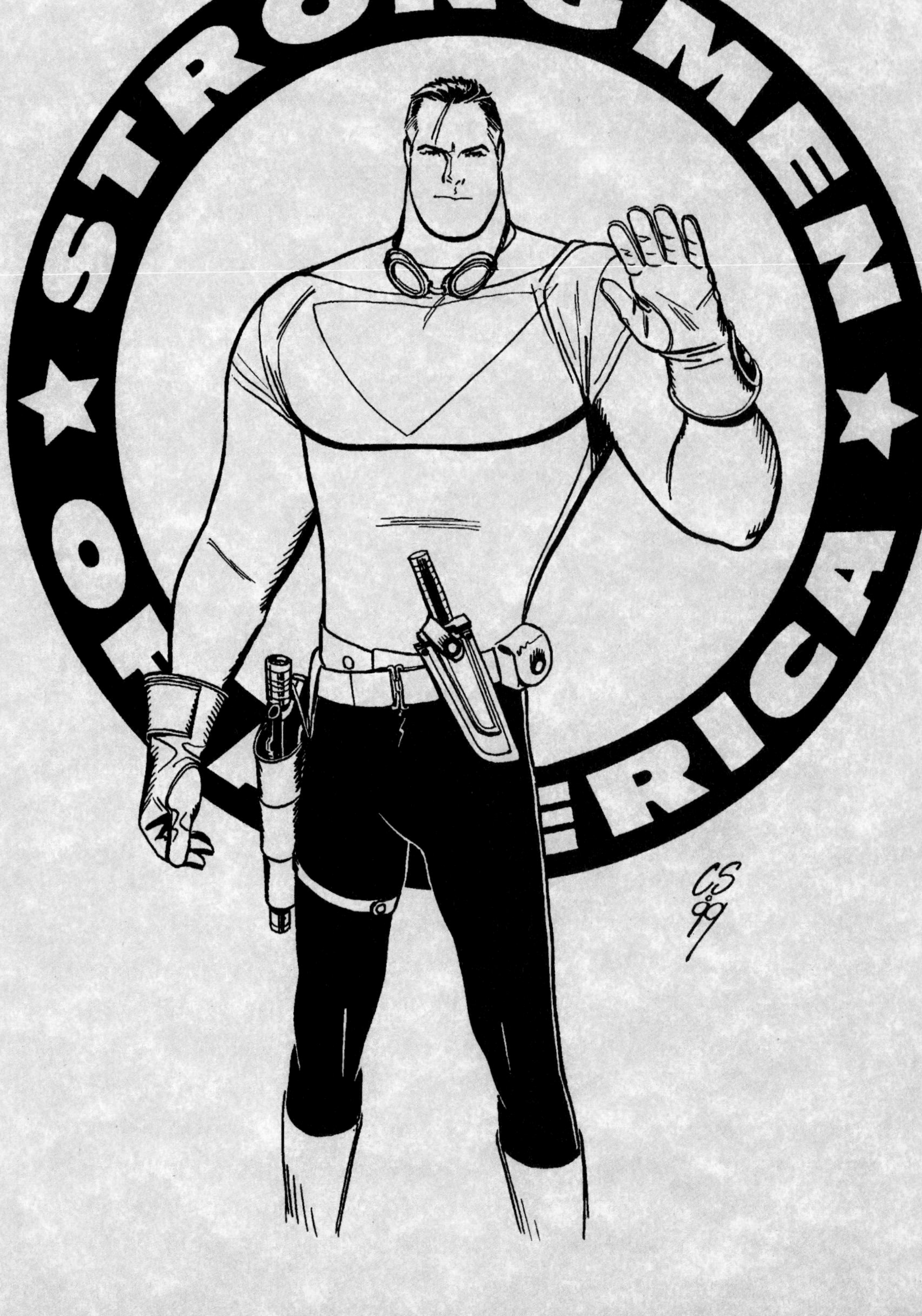
STRONGMEN
OF AMERICA
CS 99

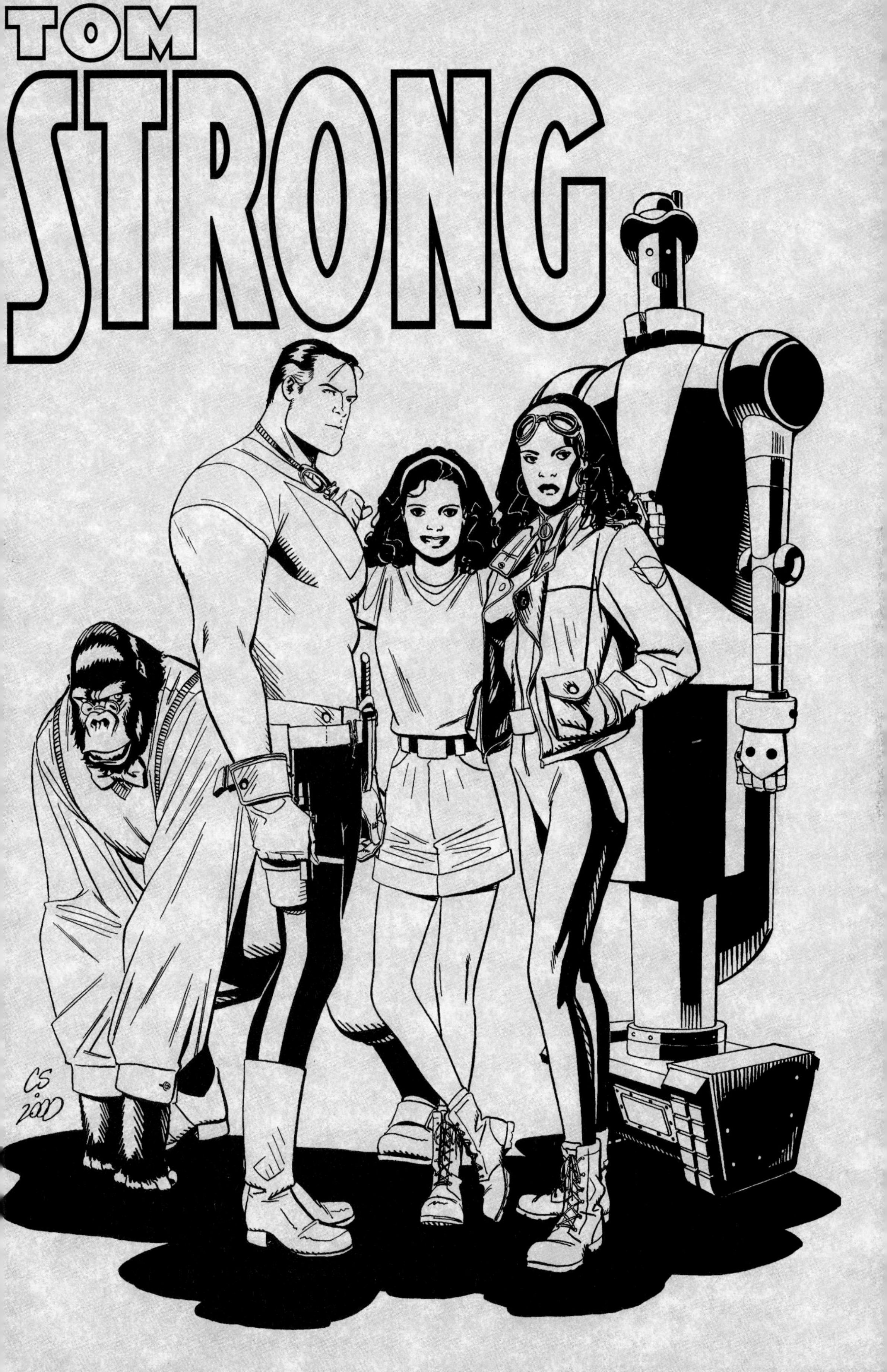
TOM
STRONG
CS
2000

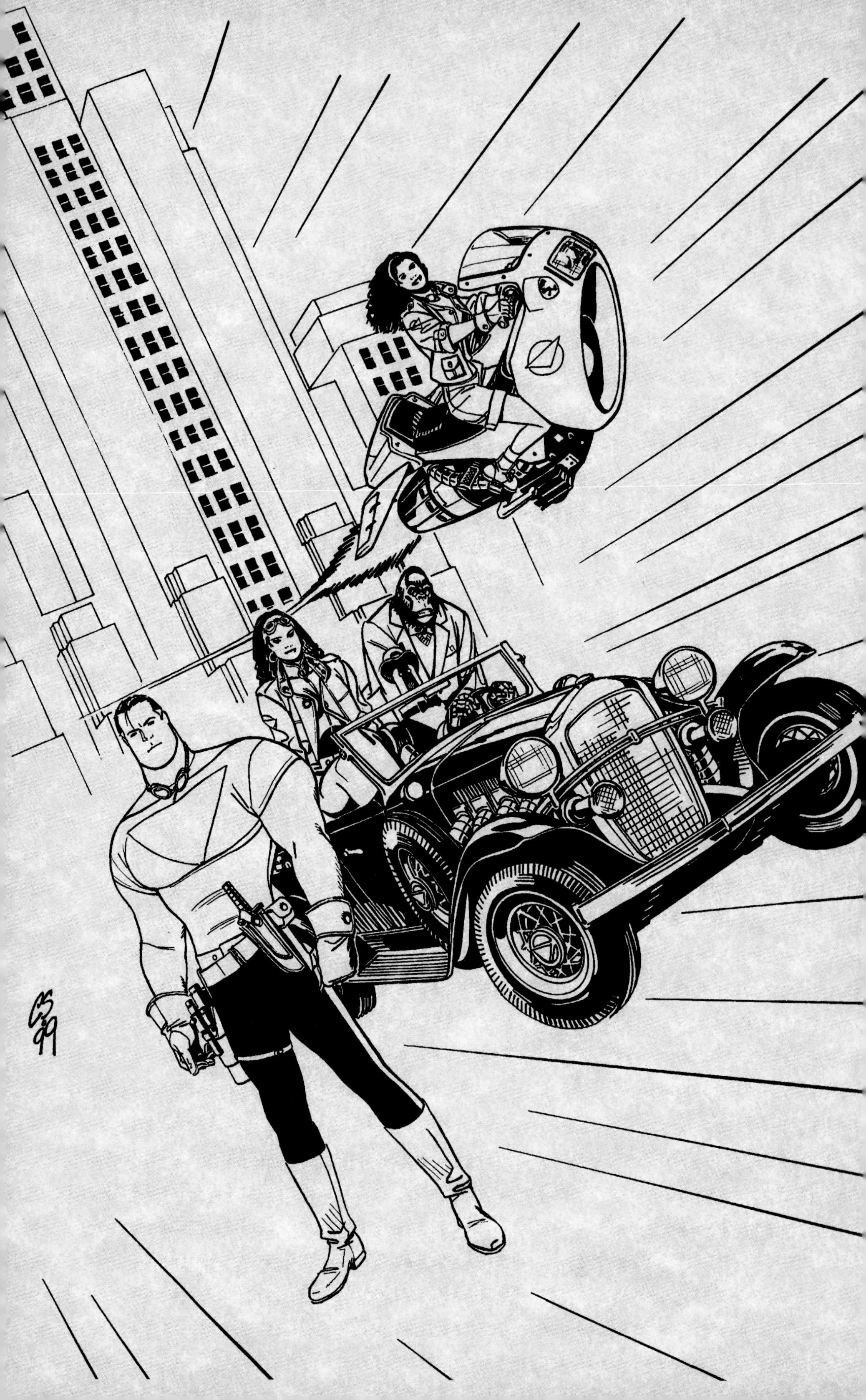
CS
99

DEDICATIONS

To Leah, Amber, and Melinda;
To all my family, all my friends.

Thanks to Alan for giving me the
chance to do this; to Mike, Gary,
Robert and Hiroshi for their
friendship and support; and
especially to Patty for being
there through it all.

ALAN MOORE is perhaps the most acclaimed
writer in the graphic story medium, having
garnered many awards for such works as
**WATCHMEN, FROM HELL, MIRACLEMAN, SWAMP
THING** and **SUPREME,** among others, along
with the many fine artists he has collaborated
with on those works. He is currently master-
minding the entire America's Best Comics line,
writing **PROMETHEA, TOP 10** and **TOMORROW
STORIES** in addition to **TOM STRONG,** with
more in the planning stages. He resides in
central England.

CHRIS SPROUSE, the penciller and co-creator
of **TOM STRONG,** began working in comics in
1989, gathering approval for his work on
such books as **LEGIONNAIRES.** He previously
worked with Alan Moore on **SUPREME.** Chris
currently lives in Ohio.

Tom Strong is about a lot of things. If
you were to judge from his name, you'd
assume it's about strength...though, I
think, not the physical kind.
To my mom and my brother, who
taught me about strength.

ALAN GORDON, teamed as inker with Chris
on **TOM STRONG,** is a veteran of the comics
business, having worked on many projects.
His favorites include **WILDSTAR** and **JUSTICE
LEAGUE.** He began partnering with Chris on
LEGION OF SUPER-HEROES, and joined Alan
and Chris on **SUPREME.**
Al lives in California.

AMERICA'S BEST COMICS COLLECTED EDITIONS

TOM STRONG BOOK 1
Alan Moore, Chris Sprouse & Alan Gordon

Forthcoming:

PROMETHEA BOOK 1
Alan Moore, J. H. Williams III & Mick Gray

TOP 10 BOOK 1
Alan Moore, Gene Ha & Zander Cannon

Look for our magazines each month
at fine comics retailers everywhere.

To locate a comics retailer near you,
call 1-888-COMIC BOOK

AMERICA'S
BEST COMICS